Microsoft®
Office XP BASICS

Second Edition

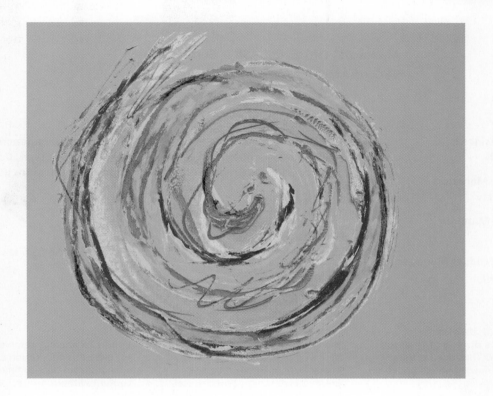

Connie Morrison, M.A.
Instructional Technology Consultant

**COURSE
TECHNOLOGY**

THOMSON LEARNING

Australia • Canada • Mexico • Singapore • Spain • United Kingdom • United States

**COURSE
TECHNOLOGY**

THOMSON LEARNING

Microsoft® Office XP BASICS, Second Edition

by Connie Morrison, M.A.

Sr. Vice President:
Chris Elkhill

Sr. Product Manager:
Dave Lafferty

Marketing Manager:
Kim Wood

Associate Product Manager:
Jodi Dreissig

Development Editor:
Rose Marie Kuebbing,
Custom Editorial Productions Inc.

Print Buyer:
Denise Sandler

Production:
Christine Spillett

Production Management:
Megan Smith-Creed, Custom
Editorial Productions Inc.

Design:
Abby Scholz

Compositor:
Gex Publishing Services

Printer:
Banta

Get Back to the Basics...
With these exciting
new products!

Our exciting new series of short, application suite books will provide everything needed to learn this software. Other books include:

How to Use this Book

What makes a good computer instructional text? Sound pedagogy and the most current, complete materials. That is what you will find in *Microsoft® Office XP BASICS*. Not only will you find an inviting layout, but you will also find many features to enhance learning.

Objectives— Objectives are listed at the beginning of each lesson, along with a suggested time for completion of the lesson. This allows you to look ahead to what you will be learning and to pace your work.

SCANS (Secretary's Commission on Achieving Necessary Skills)—The U.S. Department of Labor has identified the school-to-careers competencies. The eight workplace competencies and foundation skills are identified in exercises where they apply. More information on SCANS can be found on the *Instructor Resource Kit* CD-ROM.

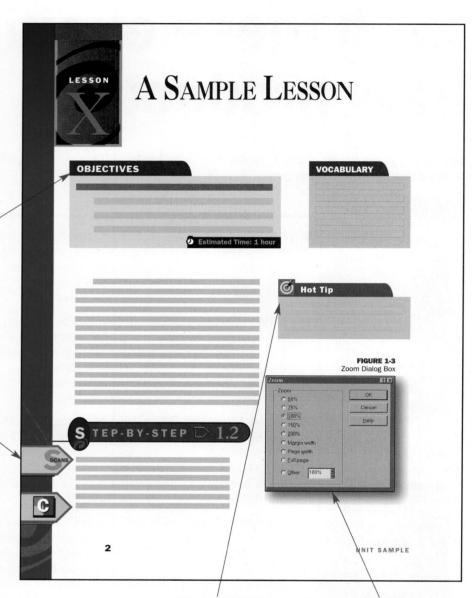

Marginal Boxes— These boxes provide additional information for Hot Tips, fun facts (Did You Know?), and Concept Builders as well as special features for historical facts (Historically Speaking) and computer ethics.

Enhanced Screen Shots—Screen shots now come to life on each page with color and depth.

How to Use this Book

Summary—At the end of each lesson you will find a summary to prepare you to complete the end-of-lesson activities.

Review Questions—Review material at the end of each lesson and each unit enables you to prepare for assessment of the content presented.

Lesson Projects—End-of-lesson hands-on application of what has been learned in the lesson allows you to actually apply the techniques covered.

Web Projects—Each project requires you to use the Web for research or activities related to the information covered in the lesson.

Critical Thinking Activities—Each lesson gives you an opportunity to apply creative analysis and use the Help system to solve problems.

Command Summary—At the end of each unit, a command summary is provided for quick reference.

Projects—End-of-unit hands-on application of concepts learned in the unit provides opportunity for a comprehensive review.

Cross-Curricular Projects—These projects at the end of each unit provide the opportunity to apply skills learned in the unit to the areas of Math, Social Studies, Science, and Language Arts.

Simulation—A realistic simulation runs throughout the text at the end of each unit, reinforcing the material covered in the unit.

Portfolio Checklist—Checklist contains a list of assignments from various lessons and the Unit Review that may be appropriate for a portfolio.

Appendices—Appendices include Working with Windows 2000, Working with New Features in Office XP, and Developing Keyboarding Skills.

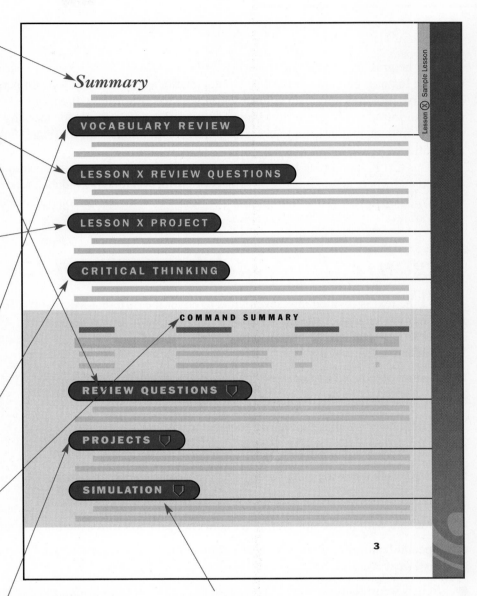

Summary

Lesson X Sample Lesson

VOCABULARY REVIEW

LESSON X REVIEW QUESTIONS

LESSON X PROJECT

CRITICAL THINKING

COMMAND SUMMARY

REVIEW QUESTIONS

PROJECTS

SIMULATION

3

PREFACE

The primary purpose of *Microsoft® Office XP BASICS* is to provide instruction for learning to use the basic features of Microsoft Office XP applications effectively as tools in personal and business lives. The course provides introductory instruction with easy-to-follow directions and activities. Though written for an introductory level, the course is comprehensive enough for learning the essential features to perform fundamental tasks in Internet Explorer, Word, Publisher, FrontPage, PowerPoint, Excel, Access, and Outlook.

This text is appropriate for any course where basic, introductory instruction in Microsoft Office XP is required and where approximately 35+ hours of instruction time is available. *Microsoft® Office XP BASICS* is structured in independent units and thus provides a flexible instruction package that is adaptable to a wide variety of needs and class-time schedules.

Organization and Features of the Text

The text is divided into seven units to cover the different Microsoft Office XP applications. The units are independent of each other and can be completed in any sequence.

Lessons within each unit introduce new concepts in a logical progression to build on previously learned features within the unit. Each lesson includes the following features:

- Lesson objectives that specify goals for the learner.

- Estimated time for completion of the lesson.

- Vocabulary lists that summarize the new terms introduced in the lesson.

- Step-by-step exercises that provide guidance for using the features.

- Exercises that provide guidance in using the Help feature to find information and to answer questions.

- Screen illustrations that provide visual reinforcement of the features.

- Sidebars with notes, tips, computer concepts, and other information related to the lesson topics.

- Special features that provide information about communication skills, computer ethics, and historical issues.

- SCANS correlations provided throughout the lessons and summarized in the IRK.

- NETS correlations provided in the IRK.

The end-of-lesson features focus on review and reinforcement of the skills and concepts presented in the lesson. They provide a comprehensive review of the lesson and a variety of ways to apply the newly learned skills. The end-of-lesson features include the following:

- A lesson summary.

- A vocabulary review summarizing the new terms presented in the lesson.

- Review questions to assess the comprehension of the material presented in the lesson.

- Lesson projects for applying the concepts and features presented in the lesson.

- Web projects to encourage Internet access and Web research.

- Teamwork projects that suggest activities in which class members work together to complete an assignment.

- Critical thinking activities which require learners to analyze and process information or to do research.

   Each unit is summarized in a unit review designed to check understanding. Each unit review includes the following:

- A command summary that reviews the menu commands, toolbar buttons, and keyboard shortcuts introduced in the unit.

- A portfolio checklist that guides learners in selecting documents appropriate for a student portfolio.

- Review questions covering material from all lessons in the unit.

- Projects that provide integration of the skills and functions presented within the unit.

- Cross-curricular projects for math, science, social studies, and language arts.

- Simulation jobs that propose real-world tasks in an ongoing simulated activity that builds upon itself from unit to unit. These capstone activities provide reinforcement of the basic skills through realistic projects using a combination of Microsoft Office XP applications.

Integrated Exercises

The integrated exercises help you learn how to use more than one Office application in a document. These exercises represent a few of the ways Office applications can be used together.

Appendices

The appendices include an introduction to Windows 2000, an introduction to the new features in Office XP, and keyboarding drills for developing speed and accuracy.

Activities Workbook

The *Activities Workbook* offers paper-and-pencil exercises for each lesson in the course. The paper-and-pencil exercises include, among other activities, true/false, fill in the blank, multiple choice, and written questions, as well as exercises in which students must identify items in a figure and provide the proper sequence for steps to complete a task. Hands-on exercises are also supplied, so that students can gain further practice in applying the concepts learned in the lesson.

Acknowledgments

Thanks to Rose Marie Kuebbing and her colleagues at Custom Editorial Productions for their fine work and valuable support throughout the writing and publishing of this book. I also want to thank my family, Gene, Al, Amy, and Chris for their support in all that I do.

Author's Commitment

In writing *Microsoft® Office XP BASICS*, the author was committed to creating an instructional package that would make teaching and learning the basic features of Office XP easy, comprehensive, and interesting. With these instructional materials, learners can successfully master concepts, knowledge, and skills that will help them use the Office applications now and in the future.

About the Author

Connie Morrison has over 25 years of combined experience in education and educational publishing. She has taught students at all levels from elementary through college levels, and has also provided training in industry. She currently works as a consultant with school districts and provides staff training and development.

WHAT'S NEW

Microsoft® Office XP has many features that help you to be more productive and to enjoy using your computer.

■ Software is easier to install, use, and manage.

■ Office XP identifies and corrects installation and operating errors.

■ The task pane, which opens automatically in all of the Office applications, contains commonly used commands that can help a user work more efficiently.

■ Speech Recognition is integrated in all applications. This new feature enables the user to dictate text and select menu, toolbar, and dialog box items through voice commands.

■ In Word, the Mail Merge Wizard is simplified and easier to use.

■ It is even easier for Word users to share and collaborate on documents. Tracked changes are illustrated in easy-to-read markup balloons. Distributing documents is a complete, integrated process.

■ Word recognizes handwriting that you enter using a handwriting input device such as a graphics table or using your mouse. You can choose to leave the text in handwritten form or to convert the handwriting to typed characters.

■ Text formats and styles are easier to create and apply in Word. The Reveal Formatting task pane enables users to display text formatting attributes.

■ In Outlook, a user can choose to see a single reminder window for all appointment or task reminders.

■ In PowerPoint, a user can send a presentation to someone else for review. After viewing any changes made to the presentation, the user can choose to merge the changes back into the original document.

■ Sharing data on the Web is possible using XML.

START-UP CHECKLIST

HARDWARE

Minimum Configuration

✓ PC with Pentium 133 MHz or higher processor

✓ RAM requirements

  ✓ Windows 98 and Windows 98 Second Edition: 24 MB of RAM plus 8 MB for each application running simultaneously

  ✓ Windows Me, Windows NT Workstation 4.0, or Windows NT Server 4.0: 32 MB of RAM plus 8 MB for each application running simultaneously

  ✓ Windows 2000 Professional: 64 MB of RAM (128 MB RAM recommended) plus 8 MB for each application running simultaneously

✓ Hard disk with 245 MB free for typical installation

✓ CD-ROM drive

✓ Super VGA monitor with video adaptor. 800 x 600 or higher resolution. 256 colors or more required

✓ Microsoft Mouse, IntelliMouse, or compatible pointing device

✓ 14,000 or higher baud modem

✓ Printer

Recommended Configuration

✓ Pentium III PC with 128 MB RAM or higher

✓ 56,000 baud modem

✓ Multimedia capability

  ✓ Accelerated video card

  ✓ Audio output device

✓ For e-mail, Microsoft Mail, Internet, SMTP/POP3, or other MAPI-compliant messaging software

SOFTWARE

✓ Windows 95, 98, Me, or NT Workstation 4.0 with Service Pack 6.0 installed, or Windows 2000

✓ For Web collaboration and Help files, Internet Explorer 5 browser or Windows 98

GUIDE FOR USING THIS BOOK

Please read this *Guide* before starting work. The time you spend now will save you much more time later and will make your learning faster, easier, and more pleasant.

Terminology

This text uses the term *keying* to mean entering text into a computer using the keyboard. Keying is the same as "keyboarding" or "typing." *Text* means words, numbers, and symbols that are printed.

Conventions

The different type styles used in this book have special meanings. They will save you time because you will soon automatically recognize from the type style the nature of the text you are reading and what you will do.

WHAT YOU WILL DO	TYPE STYLE	EXAMPLE
Text you will key	**Bold**	Key the text **Don't litter.**
Individual keys you will press	**Bold**	Press **Enter** to insert a blank line.
WHAT YOU WILL SEE	**TYPE STYLE**	**EXAMPLE**
Filenames in book	**Bold upper and lowercase**	Open **Step2-1** from the data files.
Glossary terms in book	***Bold and Italics***	The ***menu bar*** contains menu titles.
Words on screen	*Italics*	Highlight the word *pencil* on the screen.
Menus and commands	**Bold**	Open the **File** menu and choose **Open**.
Options and areas dialog boxes	*Italics*	Key a new name in the *File name* box.

Review Pack CD-ROM

All data files necessary for the Step-by-Step exercises, end-of-lesson Projects, end-of-unit Projects and simulations, and Integrated Exercises for this book are located on the *Review Pack* CD-ROM supplied with this text. Data files for the *Activities Workbook* are also stored on the *Review Pack* CD-ROM.

Data files are stored in folders according to the unit in which they first appear. These files are named according to the first exercise in which they are used. A data file for a Step-by-Step exercise in the Word unit would be stored in the Unit 2 (Word) folder and would have a filename such as **Step2-1**. This particular filename identifies a data file used in the first Step-by-Step exercise in Lesson 2. Other data files have the following formats:

- End-of-lesson projects: **Project1-1**.

- End-of-unit projects: **Project2**.

- Simulation jobs: **Job3**.

Instructor Resource Kit CD-ROM

The *Instructor Resource Kit* CD-ROM contains a wealth of instructional material you can use to prepare for teaching Office XP. The CD-ROM stores the following information:

- Both the data and solution files for this course.

- ExamView® tests for each lesson. ExamView® is a powerful objective-based test generator that enables you to create paper, LAN or Web-based tests from test banks designed specifically for your Course Technology text. Utilize the ultra-efficient QuickTest Wizard to create tests in less than five minutes by taking advantage of Course Technology's question banks, or customize your own exams from scratch.

- Electronic *Instructor's Manual* that includes lecture notes for each lesson, answers to the lesson and unit review questions, and references to the solutions for Step-by-Step exercises, end-of-lesson activities, and Unit Review projects.

- Instructor lesson plans as well as learner study guides that can help to guide students through the lesson text and exercises.

- Copies of the figures that appear in the student text, which can be used to prepare transparencies.

- Grids that show the SCANS workplace competencies and skills.

- Suggested schedules for teaching the lessons in this course.

- Additional instructional information about individual learning strategies, portfolios, and career planning, and a sample Internet contract.

- Answers to the *Activities Workbook* exercises.

- PowerPoint presentations showing Office XP features for each unit in the text.

Additional Activities and Questions

An *Activities Workbook* is available to supply additional paper-and-pencil exercises and hands-on computer applications for each unit of this book. In addition, testing software is available separately with a customizable test bank specific for this text.

SCANS

The Secretary's Commission on Achieving Necessary Skills (SCANS) from the U.S. Department of Labor was asked to examine the demands of the workplace and whether new learners are capable of meeting those demands. Specifically, the Commission was directed to advise the Secretary on the level of skills required to enter employment.

SCANS workplace competencies and foundation skills have been integrated into *Microsoft Office XP BASICS*. The workplace competencies are identified as 1) ability to use resources, 2) interpersonal skills, 3) ability to work with information, 4) understanding of systems, and 5) knowledge and understanding of technology. The foundation skills are identified as 1) basic communication skills, 2) thinking skills, and 3) personal qualities.

Exercises in which learners must use a number of these SCANS competencies and foundation skills are marked in the text with the SCANS icon.

NETS

The National Education Technology Standards (NETS) Project is an ongoing initiative of the International Society for Technology in Education (ISTE). The primary goal of NETS is to develop national standards for educational uses of technology that facilitate school improvement in the United States. The NETS Project defines standards for students by integrating curriculum technology, technology support, and standards for student assessment and evaluation.

A list of the NETS computer workplace competencies is provided in the IRK. In addition, a correlation of these competencies is provided to show how the lessons in this book help to teach those competencies and facilitate each student gaining knowledge and skills for practical applications in a computer-oriented society and workforce.

SAM

Skills Assessment Manager for Microsoft Office XP (SAM) is the pioneer of IT assessment. SAM is the most powerful Office XP assessment and reporting tool that will help you gain a true understanding of your students' proficiency in Microsoft Word, Excel, Access, and PowerPoint 2002.

TOM

Training Online Manager (TOM) for Microsoft Office XP is efficient, individualized learning when, where, and how you need it. TOM is Course Technology's MOUS-approved training tool for Microsoft Office XP. Available via the World Wide Web and CD-ROM, TOM allows students to actively learn Office XP concepts and skills by delivering realistic practice through both guided and self-directed simulated instruction.

TABLE OF CONTENTS

UNIT 1 INTRODUCTION TO OFFICE XP AND INTERNET EXPLORER

UNIT 2 WORD

UNIT 3   POWERPOINT

UNIT 4   EXCEL

INTRODUCTION TO OFFICE XP AND INTERNET EXPLORER

UNIT 1

lesson 1

1.5 hrs.

Introduction to Office XP
Applications and
Internet Explorer

Estimated Time for Unit 1: 1.5 hours

INTRODUCTION TO OFFICE XP APPLICATIONS AND INTERNET EXPLORER

OBJECTIVES

Upon completion of this lesson, you should be able to:

- Start Office XP applications.
- Open, save, and print documents.
- Close documents and applications.
- Use onscreen help.
- Use speech and handwriting recognition.
- Launch Microsoft Internet Explorer.
- Access and browse the Internet.

Estimated Time: 1.5 hours

VOCABULARY

Client

Hypertext transfer protocol (HTTP)

Internet

Internet Service Provider (ISP)

Links

Path

Server

Uniform Resource Locator (URL)

Web browser

World Wide Web (WWW)

Microsoft Office XP is an integrated software package that enables you to share information between several applications. The applications available to you are dependent upon the Office XP suite that is installed and the selections made during the installation. Microsoft offers several different Office XP suites, each with a different combination of applications. Among the Office XP applications are Word, Publisher, FrontPage, PowerPoint, Excel, Access, Outlook, and Designer. Each application performs specific tasks. Table 1-1 provides a brief description of the uses for the Office applications you will learn about in this text.

TABLE 1-1
Office applications you will learn about in this text

APPLICATION	DESCRIPTION
Word	A word processing application that enables you to create documents such as letters, memos, and reports.
Publisher	A desktop publishing application that enables you to design professional-looking documents such as brochures, calendars, signs, and posters.
FrontPage	A Web page application that enables you to create and maintain your own Web site.
PowerPoint	A presentation application that enables you to create multimedia slide shows, transparencies, outlines, and organizational charts.
Excel	A spreadsheet application that enables you to work with text and numbers to create tables, worksheets, and financial documents involving calculations.
Access	A database application that enables you to organize and manipulate information such as addresses and inventory data.
Outlook	A schedule/organization application that enables you to efficiently keep track of e-mail, appointments, tasks, contacts, and events.

Start an Office XP Application

Depending on your computer setup, you can start Office XP applications by double-clicking the application icon on the desktop or by using the Start menu. When you launch most Office applications, a new Office document (word processing document, spreadsheet, database, etc.) is displayed. You can have multiple applications open at the same time. Each open application will display in the taskbar at the bottom of the screen. To switch from one application to another, click on the application button in the taskbar. The taskbar, with three open applications, is illustrated in Figure 1-1.

FIGURE 1-1
The taskbar

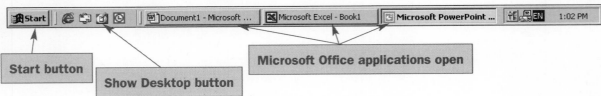

3

1. Do one of the following:

   a. Click the **Start** button on the taskbar and point to the **Programs** folder. When the submenu appears, click **Microsoft Word**.

OR

   b. Double-click the **Microsoft Word** icon on the desktop.

2. Do one of the following:

   a. Click the **Start** button, point to **Programs**, and click **Microsoft Excel**.

OR

   b. Click the **Show Desktop** button on the taskbar to display the desktop, and then double-click the **Microsoft Excel** icon on the desktop.

3. Microsoft Excel is now the active application, although Microsoft Word is still open and running. Do one of the following:

   a. Click the **Start** button, point to **Programs**, and click **Microsoft PowerPoint**. The PowerPoint application opens with a dialog box presenting options for opening a presentation or creating a new presentation.

OR

   b. Click the **Show Desktop** button on the taskbar, and then double-click the **Microsoft PowerPoint** icon on the desktop.

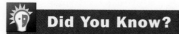

4. Microsoft PowerPoint is now the active application, although Microsoft Word and Microsoft Excel are both still open and running. The taskbar should show buttons for Word, Excel, and PowerPoint. Click the **Document1 - Microsoft Word** button in the taskbar to switch to that application. See Figure 1-1.

5. Leave the Word, Excel, and PowerPoint applications open for the next Step-by-Step.

Did You Know?

If the Microsoft Office Shortcut Bar is installed, you can use it to open an Office application. The Shortcut Bar floats on the screen and often appears in the top right corner of the screen.

Open, Save, and Print Documents

You use the same procedures to open and save documents in all Office applications. Opening a document means to load a file from a disk into the open application. A file is a collection of information saved on a disk. The terms "document" and "file" are used interchangeably. Each file is identified by a filename.

To save a document means to store it on a disk. A file extension is automatically added to the filename when the document is saved. A period separates the filename and the extension. The extension is three characters and varies depending on the application used to create the document. For example, Word automatically assigns the extension *doc*, PowerPoint assigns *ppt*, Excel assigns *xls*, and Access assigns *mdb*.

Folders can be used to organize the documents within a disk. The ***path*** is the route the operating system uses to locate a document. The path identifies the disk and any folders relative to the location of the document. Figure 1-2 illustrates a typical path and identifies the items in the path.

FIGURE 1-2
A typical path

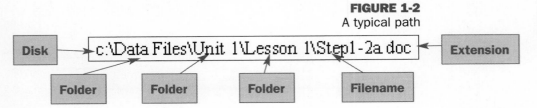

Figure 1-2 illustrates that the Word document called Step1-2a.doc is saved in a folder called Lesson 1. The Lesson 1 folder is, in turn, stored in a folder called Unit 1 which can be found in the Data Files folder on the local (this computer's) hard drive—drive C.

Open a Document

You have several choices for the way in which you open a file. You can choose Open Office Document on the Start menu; you can choose Open in the File menu of the Office application; or you can simply click the Open button on the Office application's toolbar. All of these procedures display the Open dialog box which enables you to open a file from any available disk and folder. By using the Open dialog box, you can work with multiple files at the same time—in either the same Office program or different programs.

Computer Concepts

To display file extensions in Windows 2000, click the Start button, choose Programs, choose Accessories, and then choose Windows Explorer. Open the Tools menu and choose Folder Options. Select the View tab and turn off the option *Hide file extensions for known file types*. The option is turned off when the checkmark is removed.

To locate a specific drive or folder, you select from the options available in the *Look in* box. You can use the *Up one level* button to return to the next highest level in the path. Clicking the *Back* button will return you to the previous drive, folder, or Internet location.

STEP-BY-STEP 1.2

1. Word should be displayed in the active window. Click **File** in the Menu bar, then click **Open** in the drop-down menu. (To see the Open command in the menu, you may need to click on the double arrow at the bottom of the menu for the full menu to display.) An

Open dialog box similar to the one shown in Figure 1-3 will display. Use the Places Bar on the left side of the Open dialog box to go to the folders and locations you use the most.

FIGURE 1-3
The Open dialog box

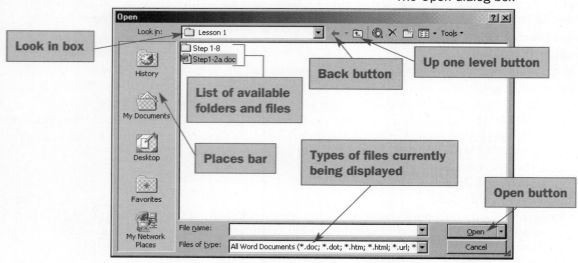

Look in box

Back button

Up one level button

List of available folders and files

Places bar

Types of files currently being displayed

Open button

Hot Tip

Word remembers the last file you opened and automatically takes you to the drive and folder where the last file came from, so your Open dialog box may look very different from the one shown.

2. Click the down arrow to the right of the **Look in** box to see the available disk drives. Select the drive that contains your data files.

3. Double-click the **Data Files** folder. Double-click the **Unit 1 – Intro to Office** folder. There is only one lesson folder in Unit 1. Double-click the **Lesson 1** folder. There is one folder (*Step 1-8*) and one Word file (*Step1-2a*) in the Lesson 1 folder.

4. Click the down arrow at the right of the *Files of type* box at the bottom of the dialog box and select **All Files (*.*)**. The names of all files in the **Lesson 1** folder are displayed, including those created in applications other than Word.

5. Click the filename **Step1-2a** once to select it, then click **Open** in the dialog box.

6. Click the **Microsoft Excel** button in the taskbar to switch to that application.

7. Click the **Open** button on the Standard toolbar.

8. Find the data files again and open the **Unit 1 – Intro to Office** folder. Select the **Lesson 1** folder, and click **Open**.

9. Click the **Up One Level** button in the Open dialog box toolbar to return to the list of folders/files in the Unit 1 folder. Click the **Up One Level** button again to return to the list of Unit folders.

10. Click the **Back** button in the Open dialog box toolbar to return to the list of folders/ files in the Unit 1 folder. Click the **Back** button again to see the contents of the Lesson 1 folder.

11. Double-click the filename **Step1-2b** to open it.

12. Leave the applications and files open for the next Step-by-Step.

Computer Concepts

When you click the **History** button in the Places Bar, you will see the last 20 to 50 documents and folders that you have accessed.

Save a Document

The quickest and easiest way to save a document is to click the Save button on the Standard toolbar. The document is saved with the same filename and in the same location. To save a file with a new filename or a new location, open the File menu and choose the Save As command. If the file does not already have a name, the application prompts you to name the file upon saving.

To make it easier to find documents, choose filenames with words that help describe the document. The complete path to the file can include up to 255 characters. Filenames cannot include any of the following characters: /, \, >, <, *, ?, ", |, :, ;.

S TEP-BY-STEP ➡ 1.3

1. Click the Word **Step1-2a** button in the taskbar to switch to that document.

2. Open the **File** menu and choose **Save As.** The Save As dialog box shown in Figure 1-4 is displayed.

FIGURE 1-4
The Save As dialog box

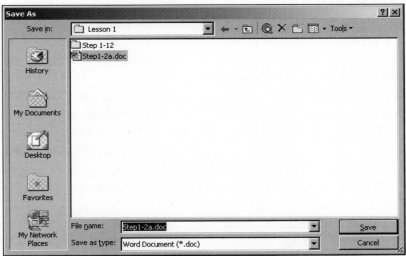

3. In the *File name* box, with Step1-2a.doc already selected, key **Vehicle Recycling**. (If the text in the *File name* box is not high-lighted, click in the box and select or delete that text and then key the new filename.)

4. Click the **Save** button in the dialog box. The document is saved to the same folder where you opened it, but with a different name. (The original document, with the original name, remains also.)

5. Click the Excel **Step1-2b** button in the taskbar to switch to that document.

6. Open the **File** menu and choose **Save As**. Name this document **Travel Expenses** and click **Save** in the dialog box.

7. Keep the documents and applications open for the next Step-by-Step.

Print a Document

The quickest and easiest way to print a document is to click the Print button on the Standard toolbar when the document is active. The document is sent to the printer using all the default print settings (such as paper size, paper orientation, number of copies, etc.). If your computer accesses more than one printer, however, you will probably want to print from the File menu. This option displays the Print dialog box. Here you can view the selected printer and change it, or the printer settings, if necessary.

Check with your instructor about the policy for printing documents in this course.

STEP-BY-STEP ⟩ 1.4

1. Click the Word **Vehicle Recycling** button in the taskbar to switch to that document.

2. Open the **File** menu and choose **Print**. The Print dialog box shown in Figure 1-5 is dis-played. The Print dialog box looks different for each Office application, but most of the print options are similar for all applications.

3. Click the down arrow in the **Name** box. If your computer is connected to more than one printer, the other printers will be listed in this drop-down box. Click to select the printer from which you would like to print this file.

4. Click to select **Current Page** under *Page Range*. When this option is selected, only the page where you last left the insertion point will print.

5. Click the option for **Pages**. When this option is selected, you can enter a specific page number in the text box (for example, 2). Use hyphens for a page range (for example, 1-3), and use commas to separate pages or page ranges (for example, 1, 3-5).

6. Click **Cancel** to close the dialog box without printing. (To print, you would click OK.)

FIGURE 1-5
The Print dialog box

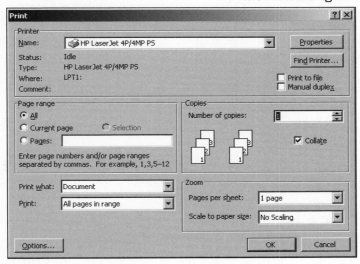

Close Documents and Applications

You use the same procedures to close documents and applications in all Office applications. To close a document, you can open the File menu and choose the Close command or you can use the Close button on the document window. To close an application, you can open the File menu and choose the Exit command or you can use the Close button on the application window. When you close a document, the application remains open and so do any other files you have open. If you have no other files open, the application shows a blank screen, and is ready for you to open or create another document. When you close an application, you will also close any open files.

STEP-BY-STEP 1.5

1. Click the Excel **Travel Expenses** button in the taskbar to switch to that document.

2. Click the **Close** button on the right side of the **Travel Expenses** document window. Be sure

to click the document window **Close** button. See Figure 1-6.

FIGURE 1-6
The Close buttons for the document window and the application window

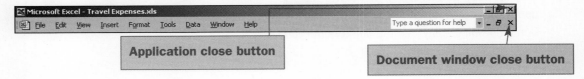

3. Open the **File** menu and choose **Exit** to close the Excel application.

4. Click the **PowerPoint** button in the taskbar to switch to that application. Click the **Close** button on the right side of the application window. Be sure to click the application window **Close** button.

5. Keep the Word document **Vehicle Recycling** open for the next Step-by-Step.

Use Onscreen Help

The Microsoft Office XP applications have some very powerful Help features that will assist you as you work. The biggest advantage is that you can get help without interrupting your work by using onscreen Help.

Use ToolTips and ScreenTips

If you do not know the function of a toolbar button, rest the mouse pointer on the button, but do not click it. After a few seconds, the name of the function appears in a ToolTip. If you want more information about an option in a dialog box, click the Help button in the title bar of the dialog box, then click the option for which you want to display a ScreenTip. You can also right-click the option in the dialog box. A pop-up dialog box will appear displaying *What's This?*. Click *What's This?*, and the ScreenTip will appear.

1. Position the pointer over the **Print** button on the Standard toolbar. (If the name doesn't display at first, you may need to move the pointer slightly so that it rests fully on the button.) The name of the button (**Print**), as well as the name of the printer currently selected, will appear in the ToolTip.

2. Point to other buttons on the toolbar to see the name of each button.

3. Open the **File** menu and choose **Print**.

4. Click the Question Mark icon (the **Help** button) at the top, right-hand corner of the dialog box. The question mark will display with the pointer until you click an area to display a Screen Tip.

5. Click the **Properties** button in the dialog box. You should see a ScreenTip  that explains the option in the dialog box.

6. Click anywhere and the ScreenTip and dialog box will disappear.

7. Click the **Cancel** button in the Print dialog box.

Hot Tip

Office displays ScreenTips for all toolbar buttons. However, ScreenTips do not display for all options or items in a dialog box.

Use the Office Assistant

As you worked through the first three Step-by-Steps in this lesson, you may have seen the Office Assistant displayed on your screen. The Office Assistant is an animated Help character that offers tips and messages to help you work more efficiently. For example, if you close a document without saving it, the Office Assistant will ask you if you want to save the changes before closing. If you have a specific question, the Office Assistant will help you search for the answer. To access the Office Assistant, you must have an application open. You can then ask the Office Assistant for help with information about the active Office application.

Did You Know?

You can change the way the Office Assistant provides help by right-clicking the Office Assistant, selecting **Choose Assistant**, and then making selections. You can also use this shortcut menu to hide the Office Assistant if it gets in the way!

STEP-BY-STEP ▷ 1.7

1. If the Office Assistant is not displayed on the screen, open the Help menu and choose **Show the Office Assistant**.

2. Click the **Office Assistant**. An Office Assistant dialog box similar to Figure 1-7 appears. Your dialog box will look different depending on what application you are using and what information was last requested of the Office Assistant.

FIGURE 1-7
The Office Assistant
dialog box

3. The existing search text is already selected. Key the following request to replace the existing search text: **How do I use the Office Assistant?**

4. Click **Search** (or press **Enter**). A list of topics that may provide an answer is displayed.

5. Click the topic **Display tips and messages through the Office Assistant**.

6. Click the topic **View a tip** and read the information about the light bulb that appears next to the Office Assistant.

7. Click the **Close** button to close the Help dialog box.

8. Close the Word document window and the Word application window. (This can be done in one step by using the **Close** button for the application window.)

Hot Tip

Sometimes the Office Assistant gets in the way. To move the Office Assistant, simply point to it, hold down the left mouse button, and drag it to a new location on the screen.

Use Speech and Handwriting Recognition

You've probably seen people talk to computers in movies or television programs. Have you ever wished that you could talk to your computer? Imagine what it would be like to sit back and dictate your reports instead of keyboarding pages of text. Or, imagine writing your name and phone number on a graphics tablet and having your computer automatically recognize and store the data for future use. Well, you no longer have to imagine. You have access to the technology in Office XP applications. Office XP offers two new and exciting methods of input: handwriting and speech recognition.

The handwriting feature allows you to input information, either by controlling a mouse or an input device such as a graphics tablet, computer aided drafting (CAD) software, or a tablet-PC. You can choose to leave the text in handwritten form, or you can convert the handwriting to typed characters and insert the characters in a line with existing text. The handwriting feature is easy to learn, but it requires a custom installation. Check with your instructor to see if handwriting features are installed on your computer. If you'd like to explore the features, go to Appendix B of this text. There you will find some steps to get you started.

The speech feature enables you to speak to your computer via a microphone. You can dictate commands (such as to save or print a document), and you can dictate text (such as the paragraphs of a report). The speech recognition feature also requires some special installation, and you will need to spend some time learning how to use the feature successfully. If your computer has speech recognition capability, you can explore the technology in Appendix C of this text. Step-by-step instructions will get you started and guide you through

Computer Concepts

Over time, as you become proficient in using the features, the speech and handwriting features can save you considerable time entering text and controlling menus. However, neither feature is intended to replace the need for using the keyboard for input. Instead, the features are designed to help you become more productive and to make your experience with Office applications more enjoyable.

the necessary training for interacting with your computer. In each lesson throughout this text you will see speech recognition tips describing how you can use the speech recognition technology to complete tasks. Moreover, the tips will illustrate how the technology is integrated into each of the applications.

Use Internet Explorer to Access the Internet

The **Internet** is a network of computers that makes the exchange of information possible. To connect to the Internet, you need special hardware and software, and you also need an **Internet Service Provider (ISP)**. It is the ISP that directs the flow of information.

Although the term "Web" is often used interchangeably with the term "Internet," they are actually two different things. The **World Wide Web (WWW)** is a system of interlinked documents that work together using **HTTP**. HTTP stands for "*hypertext transfer protocol.*" It is a set of rules that enables computers to "talk" with each other. All of these documents reside at different locations (i.e., different computers). The Web uses a **Uniform Resource Locator (URL)** to locate documents on the Internet. The following are examples of URLs:

http://www.nps.gov
http://www.microsoft.com

To access the Web, you need a particular type of software known as a ***Web browser***. Microsoft Internet Explorer is an example of a Web browser. The browser is known as a ***client***, and it accesses data from a remote computer called a ***server***. The server can be located across town or it may be located on another continent. The amount of time it takes for a browser to access data depends on the size of the files, the modem speed, the ISP's modem speed, how busy the server is, and the "traffic" (flow of data) on the Internet.

Navigate Web Pages

When you first open Internet Explorer, your home page will appear. Your home page is the page that is displayed every time you open Internet Explorer. When the Internet Explorer image in the top right corner of your screen is animated, it means that Internet Explorer is accessing data from a remote computer.

The buttons on the Internet Explorer Standard Buttons toolbar will help you browse the Web faster and easier. ***Links*** are connections to specific locations on the Web. They make it easy to navigate Web sites because they enable you to quickly jump from one site to another.

You can open Web pages using the Open command if you know where they are located on your system or the Internet.

Sometimes you may get a message that a Web page cannot be displayed; or sometimes when a file transfer is interrupted, not all of the elements of a Web page are loaded. In either case, click the Refresh button.

Did You Know?

The World Wide Web was originally developed in 1990 at CERN, the European Laboratory for Particle Physics. The WWW is managed by The World Wide Web Consortium, also known as the World Wide Web Initiative.

Computer Concepts

There are two basic types of Internet connections: dial-up access and direct access. Dial-up access uses a modem and a telephone line. Direct access uses a special high-speed connection that is faster.

S TEP-BY-STEP ▷ 1.8

1. If necessary, connect to your ISP and then launch the Internet Explorer application by double-clicking the **Internet Explorer** button on your desktop. Your screen should look similar to Figure 1-8. However, your home page will likely be a different site. Even if your default setting is the Microsoft Web site, your screen will look different because the site is updated daily.

2. Click any link in your home page. You will know that an item is a link when you point to the item and the mouse pointer changes to a hand.

3. Click in the Address bar on the Standard Buttons toolbar to select the current URL. With the text selected, key **www.msn.com** and then click **Go** (or press **Enter**). The MSN home page is displayed.

Hot Tip

If a page you are trying to view takes too long to open, you can stop the process by clicking the **Stop** button on the Standard Buttons toolbar.

FIGURE 1-8
The Microsoft home page

Standard Buttons toolbar

Address bar

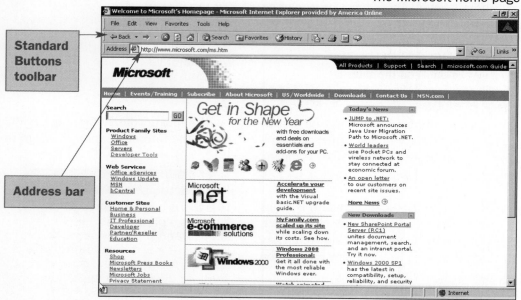

4. Open the **File** menu and choose **Open**. The Open dialog box appears.

5. Click **Browse** to open the Microsoft Internet Explorer dialog box. Locate your **Data Files** folder, open the **Unit 1 – Intro to Office** folder, open the **Lesson 1** folder, and then open the **Step 1-8** folder.

6. Select the **index.htm** document and then click **Open**. Click **OK** in the Open dialog box. Internet Explorer displays the home page of a Web site created in Microsoft FrontPage. Notice the three links to other pages in the last paragraph of the home page.

7. Click the **Flowering Trees** link to open a new page. You will see the series of links below the heading that can take you to other pages or back to the home page.

8. Click the **Deciduous Trees** link, and then click the **Evergreen Trees** link.

9. Click the **Back** button to return to the previous link, Deciduous Trees.

10. Click the list arrow next to the Back button on the Standard Buttons toolbar to see a list of the pages you have viewed. Select **Flowering Trees** in the list to return to the Flowering Trees page.

11. Click the **Forward** button to go to the next page, Deciduous Trees. On the Deciduous Trees page, click the **Home** link to return to the Greenwood Arboretum home page.

12. Click **History** on the Standard buttons toolbar to display the History bar. Click the link that will take you back to the MSN home page (the link might read *Welcome to MSN.com.*) Click the **Close** button at the top right of the History bar.

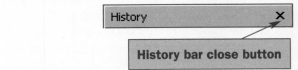

History bar close button

13. Leave Internet Explorer open for the next Step-by-Step.

Search the Web

You can search for Web sites, e-mail addresses, businesses, previous searches, and maps. With hundreds of millions of Web pages online, finding specific information can be very time consuming. You can narrow down the search results by using several search words. After you go to a Web page, you can search for specific text within that Web site.

Another way to search the Web using Internet Explorer is to key the search words directly into Internet Explorer's Address bar. Internet Explorer performs an AutoSearch to try to locate your key words in Web page URLs.

Computer Concepts

When you locate Web pages that you like, you can save them in a list—often called Favorites or Bookmarks—so you can return to the pages quickly. The bookmarks are saved in a folder for quick reference. The process for creating the bookmark depends on your Internet browser. For example, in Internet Explorer, you simply open the Favorites menu, choose Add to Favorites, and then identify the folder where you want the bookmark to be saved.

1. In the *Search the Web* text box on the MSN home page, key **flowering trees** and click **Go**.

2. The search results in a number of links. The first fifteen matches are displayed.

3. In the Address bar on the Standard Buttons toolbar, key **Microsoft** and then click **Go**. Even though you did not enter the URL for the Microsoft Web site, the Microsoft home page opens.

4. The search box provided on this home page enables you to search for words witnin the Microsoft site. In the Search box for this page, key **Office XP** and click **Go**. The search results display links related to the search text.

5. Explore the site and click on any of the links that interest you.

6. Close the Internet Explorer application window and, if necessary, disconnect from your ISP.

Hot Tip

Most search engines provide tips for refining searches. Read these tips so you know how to make your searches more effective and productive.

In the 1840s, George Boole, a self-educated mathematician from England, developed ways of expressing logical processes using algebraic symbols. The Boolean logic uses words called operators to determine whether a statement is true or false. This Boolean logic has become the basis for computer database searches. The most common operators used are AND, OR, and NOT. These three simple words can be extremely helpful when searching for data online. For example, if you search for "railroad AND models," the results will include documents with both words. If you search for "railroad OR models," the results will include the greatest amount of matches listing documents with either word. A good way to limit the search is to search for "railroad NOT models." The results will then include all documents about railroads but not documents about models.

Summary

In this lesson, you learned:

■ You can start Office applications by clicking the Start button on the taskbar and selecting the application from the Programs folder, or you can double-click the application icon on the Desktop.

■ The Open dialog box enables you to open a file from any available disk and folder.

■ To save a document using a new filename, open the File menu and choose the Save As command.

■ To print a document, you can use either the Print button on the application's toolbar or you can open the File menu and choose Print.

■ To close document windows and application windows, you click the Close button or open the File menu and choose Close or Exit.

■ ToolTips and ScreenTips provide immediate Help without interrupting your work. The Office Assistant offers tips and will help you search for answers to specific questions.

■ You can input information using your own handwriting. The handwriting feature enables the computer to recognize your handwriting. You can also convert your handwriting to typed characters and insert them in a line of existing text.

■ If your computer has speech recognition capability, you can use the speech feature to dictate commands and text.

■ To access the Web, you need browser software such as Microsoft Internet Explorer.

■ Internet Explorer provides many tools to help you navigate Web pages and search for information.

VOCABULARY REVIEW

Define the following terms:

Client
Hypertext Transfer
    Protocol (HTTP)
Internet

Internet Service Provider (ISP)
Links
Path
Server

Uniform Resource Locator
    (URL)
Web browser
World Wide Web (WWW)

LESSON 1 REVIEW QUESTIONS

TRUE/FALSE

Circle T if the statement is true or F if the statement is false.

T F 1. You use the same procedures to open and save documents in all Office applications.

T F 2. To save a file with a new filename or to a new location, open the File menu and choose the Save command.

T F 3. The Office Partner is an animated Help character that offers tips and messages to help you work more efficiently.

T F 4. To access the World Wide Web, you need a Web browser.

T F 5. One way to find information on the Internet is to perform a search using several search words.

FILL IN THE BLANK

Complete the following sentences by writing the correct word or words in the blanks provided.

1. The Office application you would use to organize and manipulate information such as addresses and inventory data is _____.

2. _____ are used to organize the documents within a disk.

3. Rest the mouse pointer on a toolbar button to see the name of the button appear in a(n) _____.

4. When viewing a Web page, you can click a(n) _____ to jump quickly to another page or location on the Web.

5. Click the _____ button on the Standard Buttons toolbar to return to a page you have already visited.

LESSON 1 PROJECTS

In the following projects, you will become familiar with other Office applications.

PROJECT 1-1

If you do not have Microsoft Publisher installed, go to Project 1-2.

1. Using a desktop shortcut or the **Start** menu, launch Microsoft Publisher. The Microsoft Publisher Quick Publications dialog box appears on your screen. You can use the Catalog to choose the type of publication you want to create.

2. At the left of the Quick Publications is a list of new publications in the pane on the left. Click the **Flyers** option in the **New Publications** pane. Notice that a list of types of different flyers appears below the Flyers heading and sample flyers display in the window at the right.

3. Click **Event** in the list of flyers at the left to see the different event flyers available.

4. Select other publication types in the **New Publications** list to see what kinds of publications you can create using Publisher.

5. Close Publisher by clicking the application **Close** button.

PROJECT 1-2

1. Using a desktop shortcut or the **Start** menu, launch Microsoft Outlook.

2. Using a desktop shortcut or the **Start** menu, launch Microsoft PowerPoint.

3. Click **More presentations** in the task pane (or just **Presentations**) to display the Open dialog box.

4. Open **Project1-2** from the data files. The PowerPoint window displays a slide, an outline of the current presentation, and an area where you can make notes.

5. Move the mouse pointer over some of the toolbar buttons to display ToolTip for each button.

6. To learn more about the different views you can use in PowerPoint, click the Office Assistant, key **PowerPoint views**, and then click **Search**. In the list of topics that displays, choose **About PowerPoint views**.

7. Read about the different views available in PowerPoint, then close the Help window.

8. Save the PowerPoint presentation as **Three Rs**.

9. Click the **Outlook** button on the taskbar to return to Outlook. Notice the vertical bar at the left of the Outlook window named *Outlook Shortcuts*.

10. Click the **Calendar** shortcut. The calendar for the current date opens in the Outlook window. If you wanted to schedule a time to present your Three Rs slide show, you could do so using this Outlook tool.

11. Close Outlook by clicking its application **Close** button.

12. Close PowerPoint by clicking its application **Close** button.

PROJECT 1-3

1. If necessary, connect to your ISP and then launch Internet Explorer.

2. If the MSN home page does not appear when you launch Internet Explorer, click in the Address bar to select the current URL and key **www.msn.com**.

3. Explore the site and click on some of the links that interest you.

4. Click the **Search** button on the Standard Buttons toolbar. The default search engine for your connection will appear.

5. In the *Search* box, key **nasa** and then click **Search**. How many matches were found for your search word?

6. Click any of the links that look interesting to you to display the page.

7. If you are going to complete the Web project next, keep Internet Explorer open and do not disconnect. Otherwise, close the Search bar and then close Internet Explorer. If necessary, disconnect from your ISP.

WEB PROJECT

1. If necessary, connect to your ISP and open Internet Explorer. In Internet Explorer, click in the Address bar to select the current URL and then key **national park service** and click **Go**.

2. Internet Explorer should correctly locate the home page for the National Park Service. Explore this site briefly by clicking on any links that interest you.

3. Use the **Back** button to return to the National Park Service home page.

4. Select the current URL in the Address bar and key **smithsonian** and click **Go**. Internet Explorer should locate the Smithsonian Institution home page. (Notice the URL in the Address bar does not contain the word "smithsonian," but Internet Explorer was able to find the home page anyway.)

5. Follow links to find out how much it costs to visit the Smithsonian museums and what days during the year they are closed.

6. Close Internet Explorer and, if necessary, disconnect from your ISP.

TEAMWORK PROJECT

Using Internet Explorer to search the Web can help you find a lot of information. To make your searches more specific, however, you should use a search engine. A search engine is software that creates indexes of Internet sites. You enter text describing what you're looking for, and the search engine presents results of the Internet sites that match your search. There are many search engines available on the Web, with new ones appearing all the time. Team up with a classmate to learn about and test some of the most popular search engines.

1. Frequently used search engines include AltaVista, Excite, Lycos, Hotbot, MSN, Google, Ixquick, and Yahoo. Evenly divide this list of search engines with your teammate so that each of you has a list to check.

2. Locate each search engine on the Web by keying its name in the Internet Explorer Address bar.

3. Search engines usually display a Help link that gives you specific information on how to perform a search. Read the tips and suggestions on searching using each search engine.

4. With your teammate, select a search topic that can be used to compare search results for all the search engines on your lists. This search topic can either be a single keyword (such as "grape-fruit"), a phrase (such as "ruby red grapefruit"), or a proper name. If you decide to search for a phrase, follow any special instructions given by the search engine so that you find only instances of the entire phrase, not each word in the phrase. For example, some search engines suggest enclosing the phrase in quotation marks.

5. Run your search in each of the search engines on your list. Write down the links to the first three matches and then compare them with those your teammate received.

6. If time allows, try to refine your search using more keywords as well as AND, OR, or NOT.

7. Compare notes with your teammate on speed, ease of use, and useful results provided by each search engine.

CRITICAL THINKING

ACTIVITY 1-1

In exchange for riding privileges, you have agreed to help the owner of a local riding stable with a number of computer-related tasks. The owner has created the following list of jobs she needs to have done:

- Write letters to people who board their horses at the stable to tell them feed bills will go up at the beginning of the year.

- Store information on owners, frequent riders, equipment, and employees.

- Schedule regular visits by the vet, keep track of regular chores, and plan activities in coming months.

- Create flyers to place at local clubs with information about riding clinics and other special activities.

- Create a Web site to provide information on classes, boarding fees, and facilities at the stable.

- Calculate expenses for running the stable as well as income from riders and boarders.

- Come up with a presentation that can be used to train new employees and new riders.

What Office applications can you use to complete each of these jobs? Make a table that lists each job and the Office application you would use to complete the task. Are there other jobs you could do for the stable owner using Office applications?

ACTIVITY 1-2

As you have visited various Web pages in this lesson, you might have wondered what all those letters in the pages' URLs really mean. You might be able to guess that www stands for World Wide Web. But what are the letters after www for? And if a URL ends with the suffix .edu and not .com, what does that mean?

Use Internet Explorer's Help files to locate information on Internet addresses. Read the explanation of each part of an Internet address and how it directs the browser to a specific location on the Web. Then explain each part of the following URL:

http://www.msn.com

WORD

UNIT 2

Estimated Time for Unit 2: 10 hours

INTRODUCTION TO WORD

OBJECTIVES

Upon completion of this lesson, you should be able to:

- Create a new document.
- Switch between document windows.
- Enter text in a document.
- Navigate through a document.
- Use Click and Type.

🕐 **Estimated Time: 1 hour**

VOCABULARY

Default

I-beam

Normal view

Print Layout view

Scroll

Word wrap

Word is a powerful, full-featured word processor. You can use Word to create reports, tables, letters, memos, Web pages, and much more. The Word lessons in this course will introduce you to features that enable you to prepare documents efficiently. You will also learn how to edit documents and enhance their appearance.

Create a New Document

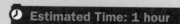

When you first open the Word application, a new blank document is displayed. The document is currently titled Document1. This filename will remain until you open the File menu and choose Save As and assign the document a new filename.

The New Document task pane is also displayed. This task pane enables you to quickly open documents that you have recently accessed or to create a new document. You can open additional documents on top of the blank Document1. Thus, you can have multiple Word documents open at the same time.

When you open a new document using the *Blank Document* option in the task pane, the document contains *default* settings to create a traditional printed document. Default settings are preset options or variables. You can change the default settings as you work with the document.

After you open an existing document or create a new document, the task pane will disappear. You can open additional documents by using the New Blank Document button or the Open button on the Standard toolbar.

S TEP-BY-STEP ▷ 1.1

1. Launch the Word application. Your screen will look similar to Figure 1-1. Do not be concerned if your screen does not match the figure exactly.

2. If necessary, click the **Normal View** button in the lower left corner of the screen, just above the status bar, to switch to Normal view.

3. Take some time to review Figure 1-1 to become familiar with the various parts of the Word application window. As you work through these Word lessons, refer to the figure if you need help remembering the names of parts of the Word window.

4. In the New Document task pane, under *New*, click the **Blank Document** option to open a second blank document. Notice that the document title bar displays **Document 2**.

Hot Tip

If the New Document task pane is not displayed, open the **View** menu and choose **Task Pane**. If a task pane other than New Document displays, click the down arrow on the task pane title bar and select **New Document**.

Hot Tip

To display or hide toolbars, open the View menu and select the desired toolbar to turn the option on or off. A checkmark in front of the toolbar name indicates that the toolbar is displayed.

FIGURE 1-1
Document in Normal view

Title bar · Formatting toolbar · Standard toolbar · Insertion point · Menu bar · End-of-file marker · Ruler · Task pane · Scroll box · Vertical scroll bar · Office Assistant · View buttons · Horizontal scroll bar · Task bar · Status bar

5. Click the **New Blank Document** button on the Standard toolbar to open a third document.

6. Leave all three documents open for the next Step-by-Step.

Switch between Document Windows

You can have several Word documents open at the same time. However, regardless of how many documents you have open, you can only work in one document at a time. The document you are working in is called the active document. To switch between documents and make a different document the active document, click the document name in the taskbar.

 STEP-BY-STEP ⇒ 1.2

1. Click the **Document1** button in the taskbar to switch to that document.

2. Click the **Close** button for that document window to close the document.

3. Click the **Document2** button in the taskbar to switch to that document.

4. Click the **Close** button for that document window to close the document.

5. The **Document3** window should still be open. Leave the document open for the next Step-by-Step.

Enter Text in a Document

As you enter text in a Word document, the insertion point will move to the right and the status bar will change to reflect the position of the insertion point. As you key, you may see a red or green wavy line under some of the words. Word automatically checks the spelling and grammar in a document as you enter the text. The red wavy line identifies a word that may be misspelled. The green wavy line identifies a possible grammatical error. If you make any errors while keying, press Backspace to remove the errors, then rekey your text correctly.

If the text you are keying extends beyond the right margin, Word will automatically wrap the text to the next line. This feature is called *word wrap*. Press Enter only to start a new paragraph. To insert a blank line between paragraphs, press Enter twice.

STEP-BY-STEP ▷ 1.3

1. Key the sentences illustrated in Figure 1-2 into **Document3**. Notice as you enter the text that the insertion point moves and the status bar reflects the position of the insertion point. Remember: do not press **Enter** until you reach the end of the paragraph, then press **Enter** twice to create a blank line between paragraphs.

Speech Recognition
If your computer has speech recognition capability, enable the Dictation mode and dictate the two paragraphs.

2. Open the **File** menu and choose **Save As** to display the Save As dialog box.

Hot Tip
F12 is a shortcut to open the Save As dialog box.

3. Click the down arrow in the *Save in* box and locate the folder where you are to save your work.

4. In the *File name* box, key **Greenways** followed by your initials, then click **Save** in the dialog box.

Speech Recognition
If your computer has speech recognition capability, enable the Command mode and say the commands to open the Save As dialog box, locate the folder, name the file, and save the document.

5. Leave the document open for the next Step-by-Step.

Computer Concepts
By default, the AutoRecover feature automatically saves a temporary copy of your document every 10 minutes. The temporary copy will open automatically when you start Word after a power failure or similar problem.

FIGURE 1-2
Text for Step-by-Step 1.3

Today the majority of the American population lives in cities and suburbs. The people who live in metropolitan areas depend on parks and recreational paths close to their homes for both recreation and contact with nature.

To preserve acres of green open space, greenways are interconnected open spaces surrounding and running through metropolitan areas. Sometimes these greenways even link cities together.

Navigate through a Document

To insert new text or change existing text, you must know how to *scroll* and how to reposition the insertion point. Scrolling enables you to move through the document on the screen without repositioning the insertion point. You can use either the mouse or the keyboard to move the insertion point and scroll.

Use the Mouse

When you use the mouse to scroll, you use the horizontal or vertical scroll bars. When you use the mouse to reposition the insertion point, you simply move the mouse pointer to the desired location within the document. The pointer changes to an *I-beam*, indicating you can now key text. Position the I-beam where you want the insertion point to be, and then click the mouse button. Figure 1-3 shows an I-beam and some quick ways to scroll using the mouse.

FIGURE 1-3
Ways to scroll with the mouse

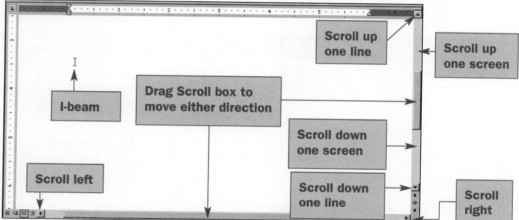

STEP-BY-STEP ▷ 1.4

1. Move the I-beam to the end of the first paragraph and click once. The insertion point is positioned at the end of the paragraph.

2. Click below the scroll box in the vertical scroll bar. The view of the document moves down one screen and the text disappears.

3. Click the scroll up arrow until you can see the first line of text in the document.

4. Drag the scroll box to the bottom of the vertical scroll bar to view the end of the document.

5. Drag the scroll box to the top of the vertical scroll bar to view the beginning of the document.

6. Click the right scroll arrow twice to display the right edge of the document.

7. Drag the scroll box to the left side of the horizontal scroll bar to display the left edge of the document.

8. Find the insertion point. Notice that even though you scrolled to several different parts of the document, the insertion point never moved.

9. Leave the document open for the next Step-by-Step.

Use the Keyboard

You can use the arrow keys on the keyboard to move the insertion point one character at a time or one line at a time. If you need to move across several characters or lines, however, the keyboard shortcuts shown in Table 1-1 will make the task easier and quicker.

TABLE 1-1
Keyboard shortcuts for moving the Insertion point

To move the insertion point	Press
Right one character	right arrow
Left one character	left arrow
To the next line	down arrow
To the previous line	up arrow
To the end of a line	End
To the beginning of a line	Home
To the next screen	Page Down
To the previous screen	Page Up
To the next word	Ctrl+right arrow
To the previous word	Ctrl+left arrow
To the end of the document	Ctrl+End
To the beginning of the document	Ctrl+Home

 Did You Know?

If you have good keyboarding skills, learning keyboard shortcuts to move the insertion point can speed your work. Using the keyboard shortcuts eliminates the need to take your hands from the keyboard to navigate through the document. Table 1-1 provides a list of shortcuts for common commands to move the insertion point. You can find a comprehensive list of keyboard shortcuts in online Help by searching for the keywords *keyboard shortcuts*.

1. Press **Home** to move the insertion point to the beginning of the line.

2. Press the **down arrow** twice to move the insertion point down two lines.

3. Press the **right arrow** three times to move the insertion point three characters to the right.

4. Hold down **Ctrl** and then press the **left arrow** to move the insertion point to the previous word.

5. Press **End** to move the insertion point to the end of the line.

6. Hold down **Ctrl** and then press **End** to move the insertion point to the end of the document.

7. Hold down **Ctrl** and then press **Home** to move the insertion point to the beginning of the document.

8. Hold down **Ctrl** and then press the **right arrow** to move the insertion point to the next word.

9. Leave the document open for the next Step-by-Step.

Speech Recognition

If your computer has speech recognition capability, enable the Command mode and say the commands to move the insertion point.

Use Help to Find More Ways to Scroll and Move the Insertion Point

Figure 1-3 and Table 1-1 described some of the ways to scroll and position the insertion point. In the following Step-by-Step you will use the Help feature to find a more comprehensive list of ways to scroll through a document and move the insertion point.

Word proposes a list of topics that will link you to information related to the key words. A link is represented by colored, underlined text. When you click the link, you will "jump" to a different Help screen. There you may see even more links. Using these links will help you locate information that explains the features of Word. Once you have clicked a link, the text color of the link will change to show that you have used that link.

STEP-BY-STEP ▷ 1.6

1. Click the **Office Assistant**, or open the **Help** menu and choose **Microsoft Word Help**.

2. In the *What would you like to do?* text box, key **viewing and navigating documents** and then click **Search**.

3. The Assistant displays a list of topics. Point to the topic *Move around in a document*. Your mouse pointer changes to a hand, indicating a link to information about the topic. Click the link **Move around in a document**.

4. The Microsoft Word Help dialog box opens and the topic *Move around in a document* is displayed at the right. Click the link **Scroll through a document** to display information about using the scroll bar features.

5. Use the vertical scroll bar to view the information above and below the current topic.

6. If necessary, drag the scroll box in the vertical scroll bar until you see the link *Tips*. Click the link **Tips** to display more information about scrolling more slowly and using built-in scrolling and zooming capabilities.

7. Click the **Close** box on the Help window to close the Help screens.

8. Leave the document open for the next Step-by-Step.

Use Click and Type

Click and Type is a feature that enables you to quickly position the insertion point within a blank area of a document. Most likely the documents you have been working with have been displayed in *Normal view* or in *Print Layout view*. Normal view shows a simplified layout of the page. Print Layout view shows how a document will look when it is printed. To use the Click and Type feature, the document must be displayed in Print Layout view. To switch between these views, open the View menu or click one of the buttons at the bottom left of the document window.

1. Make sure that the Click and Type feature is turned on. Open the **Tools** menu and choose **Options**. Click the **Edit** tab to display the dialog box shown in Figure 1-4.

2. If necessary, select the *Enable click and type* check box to toggle the option on. The option is turned on when there is a checkmark in the box as shown in Figure 1-4.

3. Click **OK** to apply the option and close the dialog box.

4. Click the **Print Layout View** button at the bottom left corner of the screen to switch to Print Layout view.

5. Point to the middle of the screen just above the status bar and double-click. The insertion point is now positioned in the center of the document at the bottom of the screen.

6. Key your name.

7. Click the **Save** button on the Standard toolbar to save the changes. Click the **Close** box on the title bar to close the Greenways document window and the Word application simultaneously.

FIGURE 1-4
Edit tab in the Options dialog box

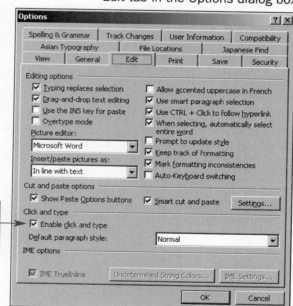

Make sure this box has a checkmark.

Summary

In this lesson, you learned:

- You can open multiple Word documents, but you can only work in one document at a time. The document you are working in is called the active document.

- If you have multiple documents open, you can quickly switch to a different document by clicking the document button in the status bar.

- Word automatically wraps text to the next line when the line of text extends beyond the right margin.

- When you scroll through the document, the insertion point does not move. To reposition the insertion point, you can use either the mouse or the keyboard.

- The Click and Type feature enables you to quickly position the insertion point in a blank area of the document.

VOCABULARY REVIEW

Define the following terms:

Default
I-beam

Normal view
Print Layout view

Scroll
Word wrap

LESSON 1 REVIEW QUESTIONS

TRUE/FALSE

Circle T if the statement is true or F if the statement is false.

T   F   1. The task pane provides an easy and quick way to open a recently accessed document or create a new document.

T   F   2. To switch from one document to another, click the document name in the status bar.

T   F   3. As you key a paragraph of text, you should press Enter to stop each line at the right margin.

T   F   4. Clicking the mouse pointer below the scroll box on the vertical scroll bar lets you scroll down one screen.

T   F   5. To move quickly to the beginning of a document, click the Home key.

FILL IN THE BLANK

Complete the following sentences by writing the correct word or words in the blanks provided.

1. Preset options already in place in a new document are called _____ settings.

2. The _____ feature automatically moves text to the next line when you reach the end of the current line.

3. To relocate the insertion point in a document, point the _____ at the proper location and then click the left mouse button.

4. To move to the next word in a document, press _____ and then the right arrow key.

5. To use Click and Type, you must be in _____ view.

LESSON 1 PROJECTS

PROJECT 1-1

1. Open a new Word document.

2. Open **Project1-1** from the data files. Save the document as **Tiger**, followed by your initials.

3. Click the document button in the taskbar to return to the new blank document you created when you started Word.

4. Key the following text:

   Someone Else's Fault

   Almost everyone knows about the San Andreas Fault in California. Shifting along this fault line resulted in numerous damaging earthquakes throughout the twentieth century.

   Relatively unknown by comparison, the New Madrid Fault in the central United States caused three of the most powerful earthquakes in U.S. history in the nineteenth century. One earthquake along this fault line was so powerful it caused the Mississippi River to run backward for a brief stretch. Damage from the earthquake was reported as far away as Charleston, South Carolina, and Washington, DC.

5. Save the document as **New Madrid**. Print the document and then close it.

6. Leave the **Tiger** document open for the next Project.

PROJECT 1-2

1. The document **Tiger** should still be open. Position the insertion point following the period after the number *1,000* in the second paragraph of the document.

2. Press the spacebar once and key the following sentences:
    `The South China tiger is dangerously close to extinction. Only 20 to 30`
    `tigers are thought to be alive in a few isolated areas. Because there have`
    `been no recent sightings of this tiger, some people believe it might`
    `already be extinct.`

3. Use **Ctrl + End** to move to the end of the document. Key the following sentence:
    `They state that only an immediate, widespread effort by concerned individu-`
    `als and support from governments of countries where tigers still exist will`
    `keep tigers alive in the wild.`

4. Navigate to the top of the document. If you are not already in Print Layout view, change to this view.

5. Position the I-beam pointer so that it is in the white space immediately above the first paragraph and in the center of the document. Double-click to insert the insertion point, and then key **Tiger, Tiger** to create a title for the document. After you key the title, press **Enter** to insert a blank line between the title and the first paragraph of text.

6. Save your changes and close the document.

WEB PROJECT

In Project 1-1, you keyed information about the New Madrid Fault. Using Web resources such as an encyclopedia or a search engine, find out where the New Madrid Fault is located. Use Word to write a brief report describing the location. Print a page from the Web site that shows a map of the area. Try to find out what area of the United States would be affected by a major earthquake along this fault. Would your home or school be affected?

TEAMWORK PROJECT

As you worked through this lesson, you may have noticed that Word offers a total of four views to help you work with specific types of documents. Learn more about the different Word views in this project.

1. Divide the class into four groups. Each group should be assigned a different Word view: Normal, Web Layout, Print Layout, or Outline.

2. Each group should use observation and the Word Help system to learn as much as possible about its assigned view. Be sure to answer these questions as you gather information:
    A. How can you tell where the top and bottom of the page are in this view?
    B. This view is designed for working with what kinds of documents?

C. What happens to the document window when you change to this view?

D. Are there any objects that will not display in this view?

E. How many ways can you find to switch to this view?

3. Each group should write a short report on the information it has gathered on its view. One member of the group should summarize the group's findings in a brief presentation to the class.

CRITICAL THINKING

Use the Word Help system to find information on Word's personalized menus and toolbars. Write a brief summary of this feature and state whether you feel this feature will be useful to you in this course.

EDITING DOCUMENTS

OBJECTIVES

Upon completion of this lesson, you should be able to:

- Display nonprinting characters.
- Use the Backspace and Delete keys.
- Use the Overtype mode.
- Use the undo, redo, and repeat features.
- Select text.
- Use drag-and-drop editing.
- Use cut, copy, and paste commands.
- Highlight text.
- Insert a file.

⏱ **Estimated Time: 1 hour**

VOCABULARY

Clipboard
Drag-and-drop
Insert mode
Overtype mode
Select
Toggle

Editing involves adding, deleting, changing, or moving text in a document. Editing enables you to correct errors and refine the appearance of the document.

Display Nonprinting Characters

Word considers characters to be letters, numbers, and graphics. All of these elements are visible on your screen just as they will look when printed. To simplify editing, you can also display some special characters. These characters are known as nonprinting characters because, although you can display these symbols on the screen, they do not print.

The Show/Hide ¶ button on the Standard toolbar enables you to *toggle* the display of these nonprinting characters. Toggling is the process of turning an option on or off using the same procedure, such as clicking a button.

Nonprinting characters include hard returns, blank spaces, and tabs. Initially, you may not like displaying nonprinting characters while you work with a document, but give it a try. Once you get used to seeing the nonprinting characters on the screen, you will find them very useful as you create and edit the document.

1. Open **Step2-1** from the data files.

2. Save the document as **Carbohydrates** followed by your initials.

3. Compare your document to Figure 2-1. The nonprinting symbols are identified in the figure. If you do not see the nonprinting characters on your screen, click the **Show/Hide ¶** button on the Standard toolbar.

4. Leave the document open for the next Step-by-Step.

Computer Concepts

Descriptive filenames help you locate files on your computer.

FIGURE 2-1
Document with nonprinting characters displayed

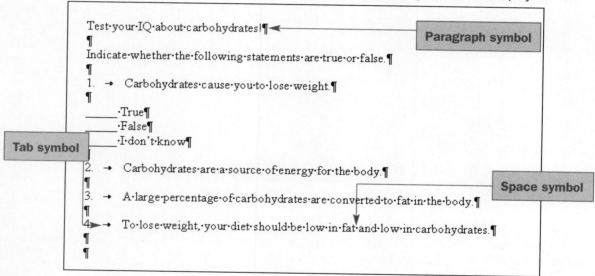

Delete and Replace Characters

When you edit documents, you often need to delete and replace existing text. This is very easy to do in Word.

Use the Backspace and Delete Keys to Delete Characters

You can quickly delete characters one at a time by using either the Backspace or the Delete keys. The Backspace key deletes the character to the left of the insertion point. The Delete key removes the character to the right of the insertion point. If you hold down either of these keys, the characters will continue to delete until you release the key.

STEP-BY-STEP ▷ 2.2

1. Position the insertion point at the end of the first sentence in your document.

2. Press **Backspace** several times to erase the last two words in the sentence (*about carbohydrates!*).

3. Move the insertion point to the beginning of the first sentence.

4. Press **Delete** several times to erase the remaining words in the sentence. Leave at least one paragraph symbol above the line that begins, *Indicate whether...*

5. Save the changes and leave the document open for the next Step-by-Step.

Use Overtype Mode to Replace Characters

By default, Word enters text in a document using the *Insert mode*. In this mode, when you type new text in front of existing text, the existing text shifts to the right to make room for the new text. When the Insert mode is turned off, the *Overtype mode* is activated. In the Overtype mode, new text you key replaces the existing text. You can toggle between the Insert mode and the Overtype mode by double-clicking OVR in the status bar or by pressing the Insert key (on the keyboard). Regardless of how you toggle, when OVR is dimmed, Insert mode is on; when OVR is dark or bold, Overtype mode is on.

STEP-BY-STEP ▷ 2.3

1. Make sure *OVR* in the status bar is dimmed. If the option is bold in the status bar, double-click it to toggle off the Overtype mode.

2. Position the insertion point to the right of the letter "C" in the word *Carbohydrates* in Question 1. See Figure 2-2.

FIGURE 2-2
Position the insertion point in the word Carbohydrates

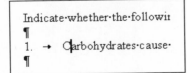

3. Key **omplex c**. In Insert mode, Word inserts the text between the existing characters.

4. Position the insertion point in front of the word *source* in Question 2. Key **primary** and press the **Spacebar**.

5. Double-click **OVR** in the status bar to toggle on the Overtype mode.

6. Position the insertion point in front of the word *lose* in Question 1.

7. Key **gain**. Word replaces the word *lose* with the new text.

8. Double-click **OVR** in the status bar to switch back to the Insert mode.

9. Save the changes and leave the document open for the next Step-by-Step.

Use Undo, Redo, and Repeat

Sometimes you may delete or replace text unintentionally. Whenever you perform an edit that you want to change back, you can use the Undo command. If you undo an edit and then change your mind, you can reverse the undo action by using the Redo command. You can undo and redo multiple actions at one time by choosing from the Undo or Redo drop-down list on the Standard toolbar. When you undo or redo an action from the drop-down list, Word will also undo or redo all the actions listed above it on the list.

There may be times when you want to repeat your last action. For example, you may enter your name in a document and then want to add your name in other locations in the document. You can use the Repeat command to repeat your last action. You can access the Repeat command in the Edit menu, or you can use the shortcut key combination Ctrl + Y to execute the command. If you can't repeat the last action, the Repeat command in the Edit menu will change to *Can't Repeat*.

STEP-BY-STEP ▷ 2.4

1. Position the insertion point at the end of the document and press **Enter** three times.

2. Key your name.

3. Position the insertion point at the beginning of the document.

4. Open the **Edit** menu and choose **Repeat Typing**. The three blank lines and your name are inserted in the document.

5. You change your mind. Click the **Undo** button on the Standard toolbar. The blank lines and your name disappear from the top of the document.

> **Hot Tip**
>
> The shortcut key combination for the Undo command is **Ctrl + Z**.

> **Speech Recognition**
>
> If your computer has speech recognition capability, enable the Command mode and say the commands to undo and redo edits.

6. Click the down arrow next to the **Undo** button and select *Typing "primary"*.

(You may have to scroll down.) All the previous actions will remain highlighted. See Figure 2-3. The last six actions are reversed.

FIGURE 2-3
Select multiple actions in the Undo list box

7. Click the **Redo** button on the Standard toolbar to undo only the last undo. The word *primary* is reinserted in Question 2.

> **Hot Tip**
>
> If the **Redo** button is not visible on the Standard toolbar, you can display it by clicking More Buttons on the toolbar and then choosing it from the list of buttons.

8. Click the down arrow next to the **Redo** button and select *Typing n*. The word *lose* is replaced with the word *gain*.

9. Save the changes and keep the document open for the next Step-by-Step.

Select Text

When you *select* text, you identify blocks of text you want to edit. The text can be a single character, several characters, a word, a phrase, a sentence, one or more paragraphs, or even the entire document. Once you select text, you can edit it by deleting it, replacing it, changing its appearance, moving it, copying it, and so on.

You can use the mouse or the keyboard to select text. The quickest way to select text using the mouse is to drag the mouse pointer over the desired text. Sometimes it is difficult to select precisely when you are dragging the mouse. The click-Shift-click method makes it easy to select the right text on the first try. Click where you want the selection to begin, hold down Shift, then click where you want the selection to end. Table 2-1 lists several options for selecting text using the mouse and the keyboard. To deselect the text (remove the selection), click an insertion point anywhere in the document or press an arrow key. If you accidentally delete or replace selected text, or if you just change your mind, click the Undo button.

Computer Concepts

To make many editing changes, you must first select text. Become familiar with the different ways to select text.

Computer Concepts

Be cautious when working with selected text. If you press keys on the keyboard when text is selected, the new keystrokes will replace the selected text. Pages of text could accidentally be replaced with a single character.

TABLE 2-1
Ways to select text

TO SELECT TEXT USING THE MOUSE	DO THIS
Any amount of text	Drag over the text.
A word	Double-click the word.
A sentence	Hold down the Ctrl key, then click anywhere in the sentence.
A paragraph	Triple-click anywhere in the paragraph, or double-click in the left margin.
An entire document	Move the pointer to the left of any text. When the pointer changes to a right-pointing arrow, triple-click, or open the Edit menu and choose Select All.
A line	Click in the left margin.
Multiple lines	Drag in the left margin.

TABLE 2-1 (continued)

TO SELECT TEXT USING THE MOUSE	DO THIS
Any amount of text	Drag over the text.
A word	Double-click the word.
A sentence	Hold down the Ctrl key, then click anywhere in the sentence.
A paragraph	Triple-click anywhere in the paragraph, or double-click in the left margin.
An entire document	Move the pointer to the left of any text. When the pointer changes to a right-pointing arrow, triple-click, or open the Edit menu and choose Select All.
A line	Click in the left margin.
Multiple lines	Drag in the left margin.

STEP-BY-STEP ▷ 2.5

1. Move the I-beam mouse pointer until it is at the beginning of the first line of text.

2. Hold down the mouse button and drag through the entire line of text including the paragraph mark. When all the text is selected, release the mouse button. The sentence is now selected as shown in Figure 2-4.

FIGURE 2-4
Selected text

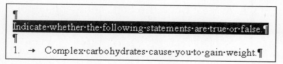

3. Double-click on the second occurrence of the word low in Question 4.

4. Key **high**. The selected text is replaced with the new text.

5. Press **Ctrl + A** to select the entire document.

6. Cllick at the beginning of Question 1 to position the insertion point there. Hold down **Shift**, then click at the end of Question 4. All the questions are selected.

7. Click at the end of Question 3 to position the insertion point there. Hold down **Ctrl + Shift** and then press **Home**. All the text from the insertion point to the beginning of the document is selected.

8. Practice other methods of selecting text following the instructions in Table 2-1.

9. Click anywhere in the document window to deselect the text. Then save the changes and leave the document open for the next Step-by-Step.

Copy and Move Text

Selected text can be copied or moved from one location in a Word document to a new location in the same document, to a different Word document, or even to a different document in another application program. There are several ways to copy and move text. You can use the mouse to drag selected text from the existing location and then drop the selected text in its new location. This is called *drag-and-drop* editing. You can also use the Cut and Paste commands to relocate selected text.

Use Drag-and-Drop Editing

Drag-and-drop editing makes moving text quick and easy, especially when you are moving the text short distances. You simply drag selected text to the next location and then release the mouse button.

You can also copy text using drag-and-drop editing. Hold down Ctrl as you drag, and the selected text will be copied instead of moved.

Hot Tip

If the selected text is not replaced with the new text, click **Undo**, then open the **Tools** menu and choose **Options**. Make sure *Typing replaces selection* is turned on in the Edit sheet.

STEP-BY-STEP ▷ 2.6

1. Select all of the text in Question 3 including the number 3 at the beginning of the line and the blank paragraph after the question.

2. Point to the selection and hold down the left mouse button. An arrowhead, a small dotted box, and a dotted insertion point will be displayed. See Figure 2-5.

FIGURE 2-5

Selected paragraph before dragging to a new location

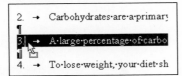

3. Drag the dotted insertion point in front of the number 2 at the beginning of Question 2, then release. See Figure 2-6.

FIGURE 2-6

Position of pointer after dragging selected paragraph to a new location

4. With Question 3 still selected, hold down **Ctrl** and use the left mouse button to drag the text to the end of the document. The text is copied to the new location.

5. Click **Undo**.

6. Click to deselect the text, then renumber the questions in the new order.

7. Save the changes and leave the document open for the next Step-by-Step.

Did You Know?

To drag text beyond the current screen of text, drag the pointer toward the top or bottom of the screen. As you hold the pointer at the edge, the document will automatically scroll in that direction.

Use the Cut, Copy, and Paste Commands

    You can access the Cut, Copy, and Paste commands by clicking the appropriate buttons on the Standard toolbar. You can also access the commands by right-clicking the selected text. Then choose the desired command from the shortcut menu that is displayed.

    When you use the Cut, Copy, and Paste commands, Word stores the selected text in the *Clipboard*. The Clipboard is a temporary storage place in your computer's memory. The Clipboard is a shared item between all the Office applications. It can store data of all Office types and that data can be pasted from the Clipboard to other office programs. You send selected contents of your document to the Clipboard by using the Cut or Copy commands. Then you can retrieve those contents by using the Paste command.

    The Clipboard will store up to 24 items. If you display the Clipboard task pane, you can see the items that are stored in the Clipboard. To display the Clipboard task pane manually, open the View menu and choose Task Pane. If necessary, click the down arrow in the title bar of the task pane and select Clipboard. A shortcut to open the Clipboard task pane is to press Ctrl + C twice. See Figure 2-7. Make sure that nothing is selected when you press Ctrl + C. If text is selected, the shortcut will copy the selected text to the Clipboard instead of opening the Clipboard task pane.

Hot Tip

The shortcut keys for Cut are **Ctrl + X**; for Copy, **Ctrl + C**; and for Paste, **Ctrl + V**. Cut, Copy, and Paste can also be found on the **Edit** menu.

Computer Concepts

It is not necessary to display the Clipboard task pane when you are cutting or copying text. The Clipboard still functions even if the task pane is not displayed.

FIGURE 2-7
Clipboard task pane

    You can select any one of the items in the task pane and paste it, or you can choose the Paste All button to paste all the Clipboard items at once. If you choose the Clear All button, all the contents are removed from the Clipboard. The items are inserted at the location of the insertion point. Pasting the contents of the Clipboard does not delete the contents from the Clipboard. Therefore, you can paste Clipboard items as many times as you want. When you turn off the computer, the Clipboard contents are lost.

Did You Know?

If you cut or copy text and fail to leave a blank space between sentences, Word will automatically adjust the spacing by adding a blank space.

STEP-BY-STEP ▷ 2.7

1. Press **Ctrl + C** twice to display the Clipboard task pane. If any items are displayed in the task pane, click the **Clear All** button in the task pane.

2. Select the blank paragraph and the three lines of text under Question 1. Be sure to include the paragraph mark at the end of the third line of text. See Figure 2-8.

FIGURE 2-8
Selected lines of text

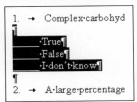

3. Click the **Copy** button on the Standard toolbar. Word copies the selected text to the Clipboard and displays the item in the task pane. See Figure 2-7 on page 44.

4. Position the insertion point in the blank paragraph below Question 2.

5. Click the **Paste** button on the Standard toolbar. Word pastes the contents of the Clipboard at the location of the insertion point. Notice that the item is still displayed in the Clipboard task pane.

Did You Know?

If the Office Clipboard icon is displayed on the right side of the taskbar, the Clipboard is already displayed in at least one active Office application. Double-click the Office Clipboard icon to open the Clipboard task pane in the active application.

6. Position the insertion point in the blank paragraph below Question 3, then click the item in the task pane.

7. Select the entire line of text for Question 4, then click the **Copy** button.

8. Select the entire line of text for Question 3, then click the **Copy** button again.

Speech Recognition

If your computer has speech recognition capability, enable the Command mode. Then select the text and say the commands to copy and paste the text.

9. You should see three items in the Clipboard task pane. Position the insertion point in the blank paragraph below Question 4. Click on the last item in the Clipboard task pane with the____*True*____*False* contents.

10. Click the **Clear All** button to remove the items from the Clipboard.

11. Save the changes and leave the document open for the next Step-by-Step.

Hot Tip

To cut text, select the text and click the **Cut** button on the Standard toolbar.

Computer Concepts

Cutting removes text from the document and stores it in the Clipboard. Copying also stores the text on the Clipboard, but it leaves the text in the document.

Use Help to Learn More about Clipboard Options

Word offers many options for using the Office Clipboard. Word's Online Help is a good resource for reviewing the features and determining which option will best meet your needs. One way to access Help is to enter keywords and begin a search for that text. Often times when you access Help, you will see words in the topics that are formatted as hyperlinks. These hyperlinks will either link you to demonstrations on how to do something or the links may define words and provide additional details. When you see *Show All* above the topic information, details regarding the topic have been collapsed. You can click on each of the hyperlinks to toggle the display of the details on and off. Or, you can click on *Show All* to display all the details at once.

STEP-BY-STEP ▷ 2.8

1. If the Office Assistant is not displayed, Open the Help menu and choose Show the Office Assistant. Click the **Office Assistant**, enter the keywords **Clipboard options** in the text box, and then click the **Search** button.

2. When the Office Assistant suggests some topics, select *Turn Office Clipboard command options on or off*.

3. When the topic is displayed, click the first link **task pane**. The definition of *task pane* is displayed. Click the *task pane* link again to hide the definition.

4. Click the link **How?** to display the linked information. Click the link again to hide the information.

5. Click the **Show All** link at the top of the Help screen. All the information for each of the links related to the current topic is displayed.

6. Scroll down through the list and read the descriptions of the four options available for the Clipboard.

7. Click the **Hide All** link at the top of the Help screen. Click the **Close** box in the Help window to exit Help.

8. If necessary display the Clipboard task pane. Then, click the **Options** button at the bottom of the task pane and turn on the option for *Show Office Clipboard Automatically*. The option is turned on when there is a checkmark next to it.

9. Click outside the options list to close it and leave the document open for the next Step-by-Step.

Highlight Text

To emphasize important text within a document, you can use Word's highlight feature. Color highlights are most effective when the recipient of the document is going to be viewing the document online or on a color printout. If the document is to be printed in black and white, light highlight colors work best.

To remove the highlight from text, select None for the highlight color.

S TEP-BY-STEP ▷ 2.9

1. If necessary, scroll to display the first line of text.

2. If necessary, click the down arrow to the right of the **Highlight** button on the Formatting toolbar and select **Yellow**. The I-beam pointer changes to a highlighter.

 Speech Recognition

If your computer has speech recognition capability, enable the Command mode and then say the commands to open the Insert menu and choose the File command.

3. Highlight the first line of text. You can drag the highlighter pointer across the text and release at the end, or click in the left margin alongside the line of text. The selected text is highlighted in yellow.

Insert a File

You can quickly insert all of the contents of one file into an open document without even opening the file. Simply position the insertion point where the file contents should be inserted, and then open the Insert menu and choose the File command.

4. Click the down arrow to the right of **Highlight**, select a new color, and highlight Question 1.

5. Highlight questions 2, 3, and 4 in different colors.

6. Select **None** for the highlight color.

7. Drag across the highlighted text for the first line of text.

8. Click the **Highlight** button to turn off the highlight option.

9. Save the changes and leave the document open for the next Step-by-Step.

 Hot Tip

When you position the pointer on one of the highlight colors, a ScreenTip will display with the color name.

 Hot Tip

Before you insert files, be sure the insertion point is positioned correctly. Files are inserted at the insertion point.

S TEP-BY-STEP ▷ 2.10

1. Position the insertion point at the end of the document.

2. Open the **Insert** menu and choose **File**.

3. Select **Step2-10** from the data files and click **Insert** in the dialog box. The entire file is inserted at the insertion point.

4. Save the changes and close the document.

4 7

Summary

In this lesson, you learned:

- The Show/Hide ¶ button on the Standard toolbar toggles the display of nonprinting characters such as tab symbols, blank spaces, and paragraph marks.

- The Delete key and the Backspace key can be used to delete characters.

- When you add new text in Insert mode, the new characters are inserted between existing text. When text is entered in Overtype mode, the new text replaces existing text.

- The Undo and Redo commands make editing easy when you make mistakes or change your mind.

- The Repeat command lets you repeat your most recent action.

- Text must be selected before you can move, copy, or delete it. Text can be selected using the mouse or the keyboard.

- Selected text can be copied or moved from one location in a Word document to a new location in the same document, to a different Word document, or to another application. Drag-and-drop editing is especially helpful when you are moving or copying text short distances.

- When you use the Cut, Copy, and Paste commands, Word stores the selected text in the Clipboard. The Clipboard stores up to 24 items.

- The highlight feature emphasizes important text and is most effective when the recipient views the document online or from a color printer.

- The File command on the Insert menu quickly inserts all of the contents of one file into an open document.

VOCABULARY REVIEW

Define the following terms:

Clipboard	Insert mode	Select
Drag-and-drop	Overtype mode	Toggle

LESSON 2 REVIEW QUESTIONS

TRUE/FALSE

Circle T if the statement is true or F if the statement is false.

T F   1. Characters can be letters, numbers, or graphics.

T F   2. In Overtype mode, new text is inserted between existing text.

T F   3. To repeat your last action, you can use the Redo command.

T F 4. To copy text using drag-and-drop, hold down the Ctrl key as you drag.

T F 5. The Clipboard stores up to 10 items.

FILL IN THE BLANK

Complete the following sentences by writing the correct word or words in the blanks provided.

1. Use the _____ key to remove characters to the left of the insertion point.

2. Before you can copy or move text, you must first _____ it.

3. You can find the Cut, Copy, and Paste buttons on the _____ toolbar.

4. Use the _____ feature to emphasize text in a document that will be viewed online or printed in color.

5. Use the _____ command on the _____ menu to add the entire contents of one document to another.

LESSON 2 PROJECTS

PROJECT 2-1

1. Open **Project2-1a** from the data files.

2. Save the document as **Walking Weather**, followed by your initials. If nonprinting characters are displayed, turn them off.

3. Turn on Overtype mode and replace the word *dangerous* in the first sentence with **hazardous**. Turn Overtype mode off.

4. Position the insertion point at the end of the second sentence in the second paragraph of the document. Backspace to remove the words *or lightheaded*. If necessary, replace the period at the end of the sentence.

5. Turn on the display of nonprinting characters. Select the heading *Walking in Hot Weather* (including the paragraph symbol at the end of the heading) and copy it.

6. Position the insertion point to the left of the tab symbol at the beginning of the first paragraph on walking in cold weather.

7. Paste the heading at the location of the insertion point. Delete the word *Hot* in the pasted heading and key **Cold** in its place.

8. Position the insertion point to the left of the tab symbol at the beginning of the last paragraph that begins *On a cold,…*. Insert the **Project2-1b** file at the location of the insertion point.

9. Highlight the second sentence under the *Walking in Hot Weather* heading using the **Yellow** color. Highlight the second sentence under the *Walking in Cold Weather* heading using the **Turquoise** color.

10. Save your changes. Print and close the document.

PROJECT 2-2

You've been helping out at your local community center. Today, the director of programs gave you a file containing a description of some of the courses offered at the center. She admitted she created the document in a hurry and asked you to edit the document for her using her file and her notes.

1. Open **Project2-2** from the data files. Save the document as **Languages**, followed by your initials.

2. Display the Clipboard task pane, and clear all items from the Clipboard.

3. Scroll down the page and notice that there is a course title separated from its description. Cut the *Japanese for Beginners* title from its current location and paste it above the course description that begins *Build a solid foundation for communicating in Japanese…*

4. Remove the blank line below the *Japanese for Beginners* heading. (Display nonprinting characters, if necessary, to see the paragraph symbol for the blank line.)

5. According to the director's notes, Spanish for Beginners and Japanese for Beginners are offered on the same day and time and for the same number of weeks. You need to add information to both class descriptions.
   A. First, copy the class dates (*September 25–November 13*) that appear below the Japanese instructor's name. Do not include the paragraph symbol at the end of the dates in the selection.
   B. Then, position the insertion point below the Spanish instructor's name and paste the dates. Press **Enter** to insert a blank line below the dates.
   C. Next, position the insertion point after the Spanish instructor's name (*Ken Grazzi*) and press **Enter** to insert a new line. Key **Tuesday, 6–8 p.m.**
   D. Position the insertion point after the Japanese instructor's name (*Hiroki Sasaki*) and use the Repeat command. Word should move to a new line and insert the same day and time you keyed for the Spanish class.

6. Clear all the items from the Clipboard. Copy to the clipboard the name of the German for Beginners instructor and the fee for the German for Beginners class.

7. Paste the German instructor's name after the course number for *Continuing German for Beginners*.

8. All classes have the same fee, so you can paste the class fee after the dates for each class.

9. The director's notes indicate that Ken Grazzi may not be able to teach the Spanish class. Delete his name.

10. After checking with the director, you learn that Mr. Grazzi will be able to teach the class after all. Use Undo to restore his name.

11. Using cut and paste and/or drag-and-drop, reorganize all information for the classes to be in alphabetical order by the class title.

12. Save your changes. Print and close the document.

WEB PROJECT

In this lesson, you learned some facts about carbohydrates and weight control. Proper weight control is important for good health. One way to measure how fit a person is, is to find out their body mass using the body mass index. Use a Web search tool to find information on the body mass index. How is it calculated? Find a Web site that contains a table of values or a body mass index calculator and check the body mass for a 5' 2", 20-year old female weighing 122 pounds. Then check the body mass for a 5' 11", 20-year old male weighing 160 pounds. Using Word, write a brief report that states what you have learned about the body mass index.

TEAMWORK PROJECT

If you completed Project 2-1, you learned a bit about exercising in both hot and cold weather. Many people have preferences for warm or cool weather for a variety of reasons. Team up with a partner to explore these reasons.

1. With your partner, decide who will take the warm weather topic and who will take the cool weather topic. If both of you prefer the same season, flip a coin to decide who will take which season.

2. Using Word, create lists of advantages and disadvantages of your "temperature." If you live in a climate that is more or less warm all year round, use your imagination to list the advantages and disadvantages of cold weather.

3. Use the editing skills you have learned in this lesson to organize your advantages and disadvantages in order of importance. Use your own personal opinion to determine the importance.

4. Compare your lists with your partner and discuss whose arguments are more persuasive.

5. Take a poll in the whole class to determine how many prefer warm weather and how many prefer cool weather.

You have been copying multiple items to the Clipboard. You learned in this lesson that the Clipboard will hold up to 24 items. What do you think will happen when you copy the 25th item? Use the Help feature to see if your answer was correct.

FORMATTING DOCUMENTS

OBJECTIVES

Upon completion of this lesson, you should be able to:

■ Change fonts and point sizes.

■ Change line spacing and align text.

■ Change margins and page orientation.

■ Use Print Preview and zoom in or out of a document.

■ Format tabs.

■ Format indents.

■ Format bullets and numbering.

■ Insert page numbers and create a header and footer.

🕐 Estimated Time: 1.5 hours

VOCABULARY

First-line indent

Font

Footer

Hanging indent

Hard page break

Header

Landscape orientation

Points

Portrait orientation

Soft page break

Format features enable you to change the appearance of a document so you can make it more attractive and easier to read. Word offers a number of formats. Character formats and paragraph formats can be applied to specific portions of text. Character formats can be applied to as much text as desired, from a single character to the entire document. Text color and underline are examples of character formats. You can apply more than one character format at a time. For example, you can format characters in both bold and italic formats.

A paragraph format is applied to an entire paragraph and cannot be applied to only a portion of a paragraph. For example, you cannot single-space part of a paragraph and double-space the rest. Word defines a paragraph as any amount of text that ends with a paragraph mark—which is caused by a *hard return* (pressing the Enter key).

Another format Word offers is document formats. Document formats apply to an entire document. For example, margins and paper size are document formats. You can position the insertion point anywhere in a document to change the entire document format. Document formats can be applied either before or after you key text in your document.

Computer Concepts

If you change the format *before* you enter text, all the text you enter will be formatted with the new format until you change the format again. If you have already entered the text, you can change the paragraph formats by clicking in the paragraph and then applying the new format. To change a paragraph format in more than one paragraph or for more than one character, select all the text before applying the format.

Format Fonts and Point Sizes

A *font* is the design of the typeface in your document. Fonts are available in a variety of styles and sizes, and you can use multiple fonts in one document. The size of the font is measured in *points*. The higher the points, the larger the font size.

You can quickly change font style and point size by using the Formatting toolbar. However, when you open the Font dialog box from the Format menu to change the font, you can also apply other font options such as color, outline, superscript, and shadow. The Font dialog box can be very useful when you want to make several font changes at one time or if you want to explore what options are available and what they would make the text look like.

S TEP-BY-STEP ▷ 3.1

1. Open **Step3-1** from the data files and save the document as **Wild Things** followed by your initials.

2. Select the first line of text, then open the **Format** menu and choose **Font**. If necessary, click the **Font** tab to display the Font sheet. See Figure 3-1. Do not be concerned if your dialog box does not exactly match the dialog box illustrated in the figure.

3. In *Font* list box, (or in the *Latin text font* box) scroll up and select **Arial**. In the *Font style* list box, scroll down if necessary and select **Bold Italic**. Notice the text in the *Preview* box changes as you select different character formats.

4. In the *Size* list box, scroll down and select **48**. Click **OK**.

FIGURE 3-1
The Font tab in the Font dialog box

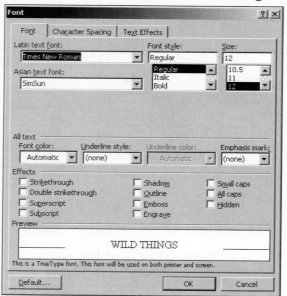

5. Select the second line of text, then click the down arrow at the right of the *Font* box in the Formatting toolbar. A list of fonts appears. The fonts you used most recently are shown at the top of the list, and separated by a double line from the rest of the font list.

6. Select any font style. The text in the document changes, and the name of the selected font displays in the *Font* box.

7. Click in the *Font Size* box and key **32**, then press **Enter**. The text in the document is enlarged, and the size of the font displays in the *Font Size* box. Do not be concerned if the text wraps to the next line.

8. With the text still selected, click the **Bold**, **Italic**, and **Underline** buttons on the Formatting toolbar.

9. Click anywhere in the document to deselect the text so you can see all the font changes. Click **Undo** once to remove the underline format.

10. Select each of the remaining paragraphs, and format each paragraph with a different font and point size. Also practice applying bold, italic, and underline formats.

11. Save the changes and leave the document open for the next Step-by-Step.

Hot Tip

When you apply multiple character formats to text, you can use the **Format Painter** button to quickly copy the formatting to other text. Select the text with the formatting you want to copy. Double-click the **Format Painter** button on the Standard toolbar. When the pointer changes to a paintbrush, click on the word to which you want to apply the formatting. If you want to apply the formatting to a group of words, drag the pointer across the words to select them. To turn off the feature, click the **Format Painter** button again or press **ESC**.

Change Line Spacing and Align Paragraphs

The default line spacing in Word is single spacing. When text is double-spaced, there is a blank line between each line of text. The blank line between each line of text is half the space for 1½ line spacing. You can choose from several line spacing options by using the Line Spacing button on the Formatting toolbar or by opening the Format menu, choosing Paragraph, and selecting from the line spacing options in the Paragraph dialog box.

Alignment refers to how text is positioned between the left and right margins. Text can be aligned in four different ways: left, center, right, or justified. The default setting is left alignment. Center alignment is often used for titles, headings, and invitations. Right alignment is often used for page numbers and dates. You can quickly apply any of these alignments using the buttons on the Formatting toolbar. See Figure 3-2.

Hot Tip

The shortcut key combination for single spacing is Ctrl + 1. For 1½ spacing the shortcut key combination is Ctrl + 5; and for double spacing it is Ctrl + 2.

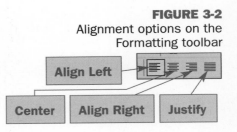

FIGURE 3-2
Alignment options on the Formatting toolbar

1. Select the entire document, then click the down arrow on the Line Spacing button on the Formatting toolbar. Select **2.0**. The lines are now double-spaced.

2. With the entire document still selected, click the down arrow on the Line Spacing button and select **1.5**. The spacing between lines is reduced to 1 ½ line spacing.

3. Click in the first line of the document, then click the **Center** button on the Formatting toolbar.

4. Select all the remaining lines in the document, then click **Center**. All the lines are centered on the page.

5. Position the insertion point in the paragraph of the document that begins, *Join us in...* Click **Justify**.

6. Position the insertion point in the last line of text in the document and click the **Align Right** button to align the text at the right margin.

7. Save the changes and leave the document open for the next Step-by-Step.

Speech Recognition

If your computer has speech recognition capability, enable the Command mode. Position the insertion point (or select the designated paragraphs) and say the toolbar button name to align the current or selected paragraph.

Hot Tip

Click the **Align Left** button on the Formatting toolbar to align all the lines in a paragraph at the left.

Change Page Orientation and Margins

Portrait orientation formats the content of the document with the short edge of the page at the top. This is the default setting, and most printed documents are formatted this way. You can change to landscape orientation in the Page Setup dialog box. *Landscape orientation* formats the content of the document sideways with the long edge of the page at the top. Figure 3-3 illustrates the two options for page orientation. Your onscreen document will accurately reflect the page orientation you choose.

FIGURE 3-3
Portrait and landscape orientations

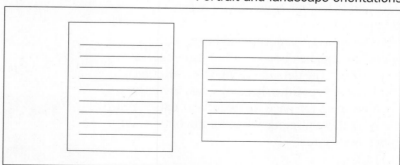

Margins are the blank space around the edges of the page. In general, text only appears in the printable area inside the margins. The default settings are 1 inch for top and bottom margins, and 1.25 inches for left and right margins.

Computer Concepts

You can also change margins by dragging the margin markers on the Ruler.

STEP-BY-STEP ▷ 3.3

1. Open the **File** menu and choose **Page Setup**. If necessary, click the **Margins** tab to display the Page Setup dialog box illustrated in Figure 3-4.

Speech Recognition

If your computer has speech recognition capability, in Command mode you can say the commands to open the Margins tab in the Page Setup dialog box. Then continue to dictate the commands to change the selected options in the dialog box.

2. Notice that the top and bottom margins are 1" and the left and right margins are 1.25".

3. Select the **Landscape** option under Orientation. When you select landscape orientation, Word automatically reverses the default margins settings. The top and bottom margins are now 1.25".

4. Select the text in the *Top* box, then key or select **1**. It is not necessary to key the inch symbol. Then, change the value in the Bottom text box to **1** and click **OK**.

5. Save the changes and leave the document open for the next Step-by-Step.

FIGURE 3-4

Margins sheet in the Page Setup dialog box

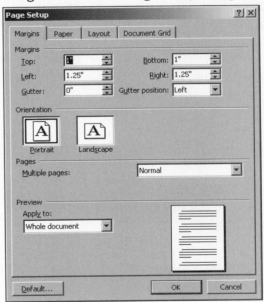

View a Document before Printing

To avoid wasteful printing, it is a good idea to preview your document and make adjustments before you print it.

Use Print Preview to Display a Document

Print Preview is an on-screen, reduced view of the layout of a completed page or pages. In Print Preview, you can see such things as page orientation, margins, and page breaks. If you find errors or necessary changes, you can edit the document in print preview or you can change back to Normal view.

STEP-BY-STEP ▷ 3.4

1. Click the **Print Preview** button on the Standard toolbar. The Print Preview toolbar similar to the one shown in Figure 3-5 is displayed.

2. If necessary, click the **One Page** button on the Print Preview toolbar to display the entire page in Normal view.

3. Click the **Close** button on the Print Preview toolbar to return to the document window.

4. Leave the document open for the next Step-by-Step.

Speech Recognition

If your computer has speech recognition capability, enable the Command mode. Say the toolbar button name to display the document in Print Preview. Then say the commands to view one page and to close Print Preview.

FIGURE 3-5
Print Preview toolbar

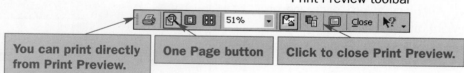

You can print directly from Print Preview.

One Page button

Click to close Print Preview.

Use Help to Learn How to Edit a Document in Print Preview

In Lesson 2, you learned that the Office Assistant can help you with many Word features and problems you may have. Some people prefer not to have the Office Assistant displayed. If you choose not to use the Office Assistant, you can still access the Help screens using the Microsoft Word Help command. To get help without the Office Assistant, the Assistant must be turned off. With the Assistant turned off, you can access the Help screens using the Contents tab, the Answer Wizard, or the Index tab.

STEP-BY-STEP ▷ 3.5

1. If the Office Assistant is not displayed, open the **Help** menu and choose **Show the Office Assistant**. Then point to the Office Assistant and right-click. Then, choose **Options** in the shortcut menu. Uncheck the box for *Use the Office Assistant* and click **OK**.

2. Open the **Help** menu and choose **Microsoft Word Help**. If necessary, click the **Show** button on the toolbar to display the *Contents, Answer Wizard,* and *Index* tabs.

3. If necessary, click on the **Index** tab to display the dialog box shown in Figure 3-6.

4. Click in the text box below *1. Type keywords*, and key **print**. As you enter the text, the list in the section below (*2. Or choose keywords*) will scroll to display the keywords beginning with those characters.

5. Double-click **print preview** (in the *2. Or choose keywords* section) to open a list of applicable topics. Under *3. Choose a topic*, click the topic **Edit text in print preview**. Information related to that topic will display in a separate popup box at the right. Read this information.

6. Under *3. Choose a topic*, click on the topic **Change page margins**. Read the topic, then close the Help window.

7. To turn the Office Assistant back on, open the **Help** menu and choose **Show the Office Assistant**.

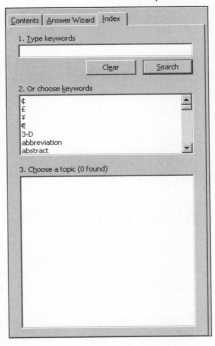

FIGURE 3-6
Index sheet in Microsoft Word Help window

8. If you noticed when you viewed the document in Print Preview (in the previous Step-by-Step) that your document was more than one page long, change the point sizes so that the entire document fits on one page.

9. If you made any changes, save your work and leave the document open for the next Step-by-Step.

Use Zoom to View How a Document Will Print

An alternative to viewing a document in Print Preview is to zoom in or out of a document. You can "zoom in" to get a close-up view of your document or "zoom out" to see more of the page at a reduced size.

STEP-BY-STEP ▷ 3.6

1. Click the down arrow in the **Zoom** box on the Standard toolbar to display the zoom options.

3. Experiment with different view percentages, then return the zoom to **100%**.

4. Close the document.

> **Did You Know?**
>
> If you're using the Microsoft IntelliMouse, you can use it to zoom in or out. Hold down **Ctrl** as you rotate the wheel forward or backward.

2. Select **50%**. Word provides a reduced view of the document.

> **Did You Know?**
>
> Instead of selecting the zoom percentage in the *Zoom* drop down box, you can select the current zoom percentage and key the new percentage.

Format Tabs

Tabs are useful for indenting paragraphs and lining up columns of text. Word's default tabs are set at every half inch. You can, however, set custom tabs at other locations. When you set new tabs, the default tab(s) to the left of the new tab stop are automatically removed. The default tab style is left-aligned. When you begin to enter text at the tab, the text lines up at the left and extends to the right. With a center-aligned tab, the text is aligned evenly on either side of the tab position. With a right-aligned tab, the text lines up at the right and extends to the left. A decimal tab can be used to align numbers or text. Numbers with decimals are all aligned at the decimal point; text aligns on either side of the tab.

To set custom tabs, position the insertion point in the paragraph where you want to set a tab stop. Then choose the alignment by clicking the tab alignment symbol at the left edge of the Ruler. Next, click the Ruler where you want to set the tab. A tab marker appears on the Ruler to show the tab setting. Figure 3-7 shows the Ruler with some tab markers and what each of the tab markers looks like for different alignment settings. Dragging any tab marker to a new position on the Ruler changes the location of the tab. To remove the tab setting, drag and drop the marker off the Ruler. If you want to set precise measurements for tabs, open the Format menu and choose Tabs.

FIGURE 3-7
Tab symbols on the Ruler

Change tab symbols here.   Left Tab   Center Tab   Right Tab   Decimal Tab

S TEP-BY-STEP ▷ 3.7

1. Open **Step3-7** from the data files and save the document as **Parks** followed by your initials. If necessary, open the **View** menu and choose **Ruler** to display the Ruler.

2. Position the insertion point anywhere in the line that begins *Mount Rushmore...*

3. Click the tab symbols at the left end of the Ruler until the **Right Tab** symbol is displayed.

4. Click near the 5-inch mark on the Ruler (just to the left of the Right Margin marker). Then, drag the **Right Tab** marker on the Ruler and position it exactly at the right indent marker.

5. Position the insertion point in front of *April 11* and press the **Tab** key. The date is now aligned at the right margin.

6. Position the insertion point in the paragraph beginning *Yellowstone....* Notice that there are no tab markers displayed on the Ruler. The tab you set in the *Mount Rushmore* paragraph was applied to that paragraph only.

7. Format a right tab at the right margin, then insert a tab character in front of the date in the *Yellowstone...* paragraph to align the date at the right margin.

8. Format a right tab at the right margin for the paragraph beginning *Glacier....*Then insert a tab character in front of the date in that paragraph.

9. Save the changes and leave the document open for the next Step-by-Step.

Format Indents

An indent is a space insert between the margin and where the line of text appears. You can indent text from the left margin, from the right margin, or from both the left and right margins. For example, to draw attention to specific paragraphs in a document, you can indent all the lines of the paragraph from the left and right margins. If you are creating a long document and you want the first line of all the paragraphs to be indented, you can format a *first line indent*. A first line indent can make a document easy to read, because a person can easily tell where a new paragraph begins. If you are creating a bibliography for a report, you can format a *hanging indent*. A hanging indent is when the first line of text begins at the left margin, and all other lines of the paragraph "hang," or are indented, to the right of the first line. To quickly format an indent, position the insertion point in the paragraph to be formatted and then drag the indent markers on the Ruler. See Figure 3-8.

FIGURE 3-8
Indent markers on the Ruler

First Line Indent marker

Left Indent marker

Hanging Indent marker

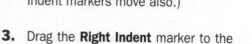

1. Position the insertion point in the paragraph that begins *This national memorial....*

2. Drag the **Left Indent** marker to the ½" mark on the Ruler. (Notice that the First Line Indent and Hanging Indent markers move also.)

3. Drag the **Right Indent** marker to the 5" mark on the Ruler.

4. Click in the paragraph that begins *The park was established....* Notice that the Left Indent marker is positioned at the 0" mark on the Ruler. When you moved the Left Indent marker in Step 2, the indent format was applied only to that paragraph.

5. Drag the **Left Indent** marker to the ½" mark on the Ruler. Then, drag the **Right Indent** marker to the 5" mark on the Ruler.

6. Format similar left and right indents for the paragraph beginning *This national park....*

7. Position the insertion point in the paragraph that begins *Each documentary....* Drag the **First Line Indent** marker to the ½" mark on the Ruler.  Notice that just the first line of the paragraph is indented from the left ½".

8. Position the insertion point in the last paragraph in the document.  Point to the **Hanging Indent** marker and drag the marker to the ½" mark on the Ruler. All lines but the first line are indented from the left ½".

9. Save the changes and close the document.

▪ Computer Concepts

If you drag the bottom half of the **Hanging Indent** marker, the **First-line Indent** marker will also move. If you point to the middle of these markers, a two-headed arrow will display and you can drag to change the left margin.

Format Bullets and Numbering

Bullets and numbers are easy to add using the Bullets and Numbering buttons on the Formatting toolbar.

Bulleted and numbered lists are automatically formatted with a hanging indent. Word automatically calculates the best distance for the hanging indent. You can change the bullet symbol, the number style, or the distance for the hanging indent in the Bullets and Numbering dialog box.

▪ Computer Concepts

If you apply the bullet or number format before you enter text, each new paragraph will be formatted with the bullet or number. To end the format, press **Enter** a second time and backspace over the unwanted bullet or number, or click the button on the toolbar to toggle the option off.

STEP-BY-STEP ▷ 3.9

1. Open **Step3-9** from the data files and save the document as **Expo** followed by your initials.

2. Select all the lines (paragraphs) in the list below the first heading that begins *Displays and Demonstrations....*

3. Click the **Bullets** button on the Formatting toolbar. Each paragraph in the selection is formatted with a bullet symbol. The symbol will vary depending on the symbol last used for bullets.

4. Select the list below the second heading that begins *A Look at....* Open the **Format** menu

and choose **Bullets and Numbering**. If necessary, click the **Bulleted** tab to display the bullet options.

5. Select one of the bullet symbols, then click **OK**.

6. Select the list below the third heading *Seminars and Films.* Click the **Numbering** button on the Formatting toolbar.

7. Save the changes and leave the document open for the next Step-by-Step.

Format Page Numbers and Headers and Footers

Word begins new pages when needed by inserting *soft page breaks*. A soft page break is automatically inserted for you when you fill a page with text or graphics. You can also break pages manually by inserting *hard page breaks*. A hard page break forces a page break at a specific location, regardless of how full the page of text is. The location of a soft page break will change if you add or delete text so that each page remains completely filled with text. A hard page break will remain where you insert it until it is deleted.

When your document has multiple pages, you may want to insert page numbers. The Page Numbers command on the Insert menu is a quick way to add page numbers that do not need accompanying text. (What this actually does is create a *header* or *footer* with a page number as the only text.)

Headers and footers are information and/or graphics that print in the top and bottom margins of each page. Your document can have a header, a footer, or both. Headers and footers can be a single paragraph or multiple paragraphs. Creating a header or footer is another way to add page numbers to a document. The advantages of formatting a header or footer rather than just using the Insert Page Numbers command is that you can include text with the page number. (Note that you can always edit the header or footer—and hence the page number—if you change your mind about how you want them to appear.)

STEP-BY-STEP ▷ 3.10

1. Select the entire document and change to double-spacing.

2. Position the insertion point in front of the second heading that begins *A Look at....* Open

the **Insert** menu and choose **Break**. **Page break** should already be selected in the dialog box. Click **OK**.

Hot Tip

The shortcut for inserting a hard page break is **Ctrl + Enter**.

3. Open the **Insert** menu and choose **Page Numbers**. The dialog box shown in Figure 3-9 is displayed.

FIGURE 3-9
Page Numbers dialog box

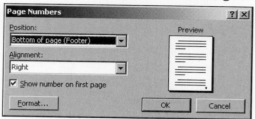

4. In the *Position* box, verify that **Bottom of page (Footer)** is selected. In the *Alignment* box, select **Center**. Click **OK**. If your document is displayed in Print Layout View, you can scroll to the bottom of the first or second page to see the page number. These are dimmed because they are part of the footer and you must open the header or footer pane to edit them.

5. Open the **View** menu and choose **Header and Footer**. The Header and Footer toolbar and a blank header pane appear. The document pane is dimmed as shown in Figure 3-10. This indicates that you can now edit the header (and footer) but not the document.

6. Key **Environmental Expo** and then press **Tab** twice. (Notice that, by default, the headers and footers have a left align tab, a center tab, and a right align tab.) The insertion point is now positioned at the right margin in the header pane.

7. Click the **Insert Date** button on the Header and Footer toolbar. The current date is inserted in the header pane. This will automatically be updated each time the document is opened.

8. Click the **Switch Between Header and Footer** button. The footer pane is displayed and you can see the page number that you inserted in the last Step-by-Step.

9. Click **Close** in the Header and Footer toolbar to close it and to return to working in the document.

10. View the document in Print Preview or change the zoom to view the document in a reduced image.

11. Save the changes and close the document.

FIGURE 3-10
Header and Footer toolbar and header pane

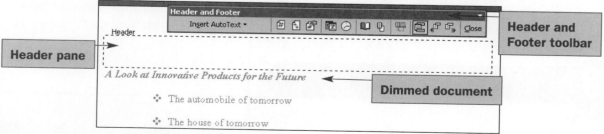

Summary

In this lesson, you learned:

- Fonts are available in a variety of styles and point sizes.

- You can adjust the line spacing in a paragraph to create more or less white space between the lines of text. Formatting the paragraph alignment for left, center, right, or justified positions the text appropriately between the left and right margins.

- The page orientation determines how the document will print on the page. Adjusting the margins affects the white space around the edges of the page.

- Print Preview shows a reduced view of the layout of a document. You can also reduce the view of a document by changing the zoom. Print Preview can help eliminate wasteful printing.

- Custom tabs can be set by clicking on the Ruler.

- Options for indenting text include left indents, right indents, first-line indents, and hanging indents.

- The Bullets and Numbering feature automatically adds and formats bullets and numbers in lists.

- The Insert Page Number command automatically numbers all the pages in a document. You can include text with the page number byformating a header or footer.

VOCABULARY REVIEW

Define the following terms:

First Line Indent	Hard page break	Points
Font	Headers	Portrait orientation
Footers	Landscape orientation	Soft page break
Hanging Indent		

LESSON 3 REVIEW QUESTIONS

TRUE/FALSE

Circle T if the statement is true or F if the statement is false.

T F   1. It is best to use only one font in a document.

T F   2. Landscape orientation prints sideways with the long edge of the page at the top.

T F   3. You can edit a document while in print preview.

T F   4. When you set a tab, you position the tab marker on the Formatting toolbar.

T F   5. Bulleted and numbered lists are automatically formatted using a first-line indent.

MATCHING

Match the correct term in Column 1 to its description in Column 2.

Column 1	**Column 2**

____ 1. font

____ 2. indent

____ 3. margin

____ 4. alignment

____ 5. hard page break

A. Space you insert between the margin and the line of text

B. How text is positioned between the left and right margins

C. Break you insert manually to end a page

D. Break Word automatically inserts when a page is full

E. Design of a typeface

F. Blank space around the edges of a page

LESSON 3 PROJECTS

PROJECT 3-1

Your good work at the community center has convinced the director to give you another assignment. Help her create the title and contents pages for the Recreation Commission's fall program guide.

1. Open **Project3-1** from the data files. Save the document as **Contents** followed by your initials.

2. Change the page orientation to landscape. Change the top and bottom margins to 1 inch, and change the left and right margins to 2 inches.

3. Center the first eight lines of text, beginning with *Oak Creek Recreation Commission* and ending with *Mt. Washington Recreation Center*.

4. Format the centered text as follows:
   A. Change the font style of the first line (*Oak Creek Recreation Center*) to bold and the font size to 28 point.
   B. Change the size of the next two lines (*Community Center* and *Program Guide*) to 20 point.
   C. Change the size of the next line (*Fall*) to 20 point and apply bold style.
   D. Change the size of the last four centered lines to 20 point.

5. Position the insertion point in front of the word *Contents* and insert a page break. On the new page, format the word *Contents* as 20 point bold.

6. Select all the text below the *Contents* heading and then set a right tab at the 6.5-inch mark on the ruler. Format the program listings as follows:
   A. Apply bold and italic formatting to the first three lines below the *Contents* heading (*Registration*, *Memberships*, and *Hours*) and the last two lines (*Special Events* and *Community Meetings*). Change the size of these lines to 12 point and the font to Arial.
   B. Apply bold and underline formatting to the headings (including the page number) for each age group (*ELEMENTARY PROGRAMS*, *TEEN PROGRAMS*, and *ADULT PROGRAMS*). Change the size of these headings to 11 point and the font to Arial.
   C. Apply a 0.25-inch left indent to the lists of programs under each age group heading and change their point size to 12.

7. View the document in Print Preview. You decide that the first page could be "spread out" a little to fill up more of the page. Close Print Preview and display the first page. Add blank lines as desired to improve the look of the first page. Check your adjustments using Print Preview.

8. Save your changes and close the document.

PROJECT 3-2

1. Open **Project3-2** from the data files. Save the document as **Hummingbirds** followed by your initials.

2. Format the document as described in Figure 3-11.

3. For every paragraph except the bulleted paragraphs and the numbered list, change the line spacing to 1 ½ lines.

4. For every paragraph except the headings, the bulleted paragraphs, and the numbered list, create a first-line indent of 0.5 inches.

5. Use the Zoom feature to view your document at the Two Pages setting.

6. Save your changes and close the document.

FIGURE 3-11
Document with formatting notes

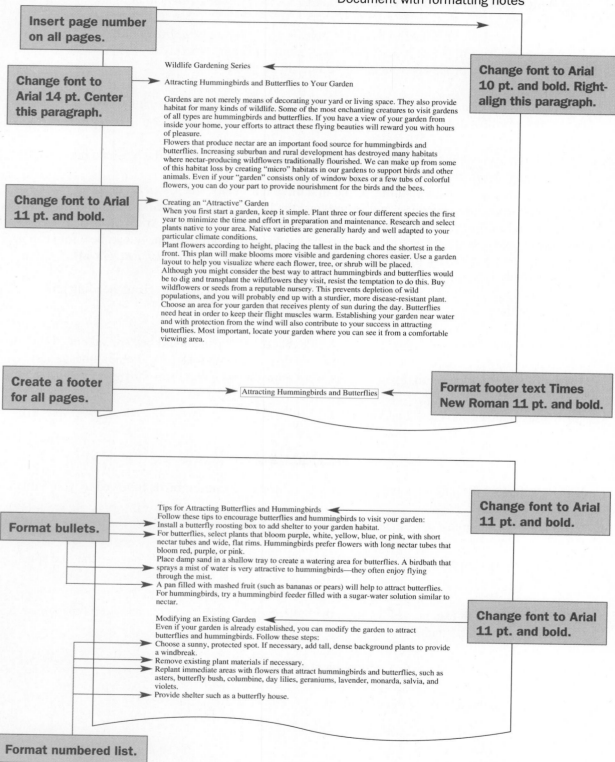

Insert page number on all pages.

Change font to Arial 14 pt. Center this paragraph.

Change font to Arial 11 pt. and bold.

Create a footer for all pages.

Change font to Arial 10 pt. and bold. Right-align this paragraph.

Format footer text Times New Roman 11 pt. and bold.

Format bullets.

Change font to Arial 11 pt. and bold.

Change font to Arial 11 pt. and bold.

Format numbered list.

Wildlife Gardening Series

Attracting Hummingbirds and Butterflies to Your Garden

Gardens are not merely means of decorating your yard or living space. They also provide habitat for many kinds of wildlife. Some of the most enchanting creatures to visit gardens of all types are hummingbirds and butterflies. If you have a view of your garden from inside your home, your efforts to attract these flying beauties will reward you with hours of pleasure.

Flowers that produce nectar are an important food source for hummingbirds and butterflies. Increasing suburban and rural development has destroyed many habitats where nectar-producing wildflowers traditionally flourished. We can make up from some of this habitat loss by creating "micro" habitats in our gardens to support birds and other animals. Even if your "garden" consists only of window boxes or a few tubs of colorful flowers, you can do your part to provide nourishment for the birds and the bees.

Creating an "Attractive" Garden

When you first start a garden, keep it simple. Plant three or four different species the first year to minimize the time and effort in preparation and maintenance. Research and select plants native to your area. Native varieties are generally hardy and well adapted to your particular climate conditions.

Plant flowers according to height, placing the tallest in the back and the shortest in the front. This plan will make blooms more visible and gardening chores easier. Use a garden layout to help you visualize where each flower, tree, or shrub will be placed.

Although you might consider the best way to attract hummingbirds and butterflies would be to dig and transplant the wildflowers they visit, resist the temptation to do this. Buy wildflowers or seeds from a reputable nursery. This prevents depletion of wild populations, and you will probably end up with a sturdier, more disease-resistant plant. Choose an area for your garden that receives plenty of sun during the day. Butterflies need heat in order to keep their flight muscles warm. Establishing your garden near water and with protection from the wind will also contribute to your success in attracting butterflies. Most important, locate your garden where you can see it from a comfortable viewing area.

Attracting Hummingbirds and Butterflies

Tips for Attracting Butterflies and Hummingbirds
Follow these tips to encourage butterflies and hummingbirds to visit your garden:
Install a butterfly roosting box to add shelter to your garden habitat.
For butterflies, select plants that bloom purple, white, yellow, blue, or pink, with short nectar tubes and wide, flat rims. Hummingbirds prefer flowers with long nectar tubes that bloom red, purple, or pink.
Place damp sand in a shallow tray to create a watering area for butterflies. A birdbath that sprays a mist of water is very attractive to hummingbirds—they often enjoy flying through the mist.
A pan filled with mashed fruit (such as bananas or pears) will help to attract butterflies. For hummingbirds, try a hummingbird feeder filled with a sugar-water solution similar to nectar.

Modifying an Existing Garden
Even if your garden is already established, you can modify the garden to attract butterflies and hummingbirds. Follow these steps:
Choose a sunny, protected spot. If necessary, add tall, dense background plants to provide a windbreak.
Remove existing plant materials if necessary.
Replant immediate areas with flowers that attract hummingbirds and butterflies, such as asters, butterfly bush, columbine, day lilies, geraniums, lavender, monarda, salvia, and violets.
Provide shelter such as a butterfly house.

WEB PROJECT

If you have ever seen a hummingbird up close, you are aware of how rapidly they beat their wings to stay in flight. Use a Web search tool to locate sites relating to hummingbirds on the Web. Find out some basic facts about hummingbirds, such as how fast they flap their wings and how often and how much they eat. Use Word to write a brief report on what you have learned. Be sure to cite your Web sources!

TEAMWORK PROJECT

The fonts you use to format a document can be divided into two types: serif and sans serif. Serif faces are often used for the main body of a document, while sans serif faces are used for headings and other display items. Learn more about the differences between these two types of typefaces with a partner.

1. With your partner, decide who will research serif typefaces and who will research sans serif typefaces.

2. Use the Web, an online encyclopedia, or other reference to read about typography, the art of designing typefaces. Concentrate on your chosen type, either serif or sans serif.

3. You and your partner should be able to answer these questions after your research:
   A. What is a serif?
   B. What is the main difference between a serif typeface and a sans serif typeface?

4. Select a paragraph of text and a heading from any source and key the material using the type of typeface you have been studying (you key in serif, for example, and your partner in sans serif). Copy the text several times and apply different fonts of either serif or sans serif to each copy.

5. With your partner, decide which of the fonts is most readable and appropriate for each type of text.

CRITICAL THINKING

If you completed Project 3-1, you had to add blank lines to center the text vertically on the first page of the document. There is another way to center text vertically. Use Word's Help feature to find out how to do this. Using Word, write a brief explanation of the steps you need to take. What would happen to the second page of the Contents document if you follow these steps? Describe at least two other documents in which you could use this feature.

USING AUTO FEATURES IN WORD

OBJECTIVES

Upon completion of this lesson, you should be able to:

■ Check and correct spelling.

■ Check and correct grammar.

■ Check for formatting inconsistencies.

■ Use AutoCorrect.

■ Use the Thesaurus.

■ Use AutoComplete.

■ Count words in a document.

■ Insert the date, time, and filename.

■ Find and replace text and formats.

■ E-mail a document.

⏱ **Estimated time: 1 hour**

VOCABULARY

Antonym

AutoComplete

AutoCorrect

Field

Synonym

By now you have probably seen some messages from the Office Assistant offering to help you format a document. Sometimes, however, Word goes ahead and helps you without even asking. For example, you may have noticed that Word has automatically corrected some of your keyboarding errors. Word offers many automatic features to help you create professional documents.

Check Spelling, Grammar, and Formatting

Spell checking a document can significantly reduce the amount of time you spend proofreading and editing. Word can help you with both spell checking and proofreading. Word has a standard dictionary that you can use to check your spelling. You can check the spelling of one word, a selected group of words, or the entire document.

Computer Concepts

Although the spell checker is very helpful for identifying spelling errors, you still need to proofread. The spell checker simply verifies that the word is spelled correctly. It does not, however, confirm that you have used the correct word. For example, if you use the word *their* instead of *there*, the spell checker will not identify the error.

Good proofreading skills also include checking grammar. When you check for the grammar in a document, you read for content and make sure each sentence makes sense. Word can also help you find grammatical errors such as incomplete sentences, the wrong use of words, and capitalization and punctuation errors.

Check Spelling, Grammar, and Formatting as You Enter Text

As you enter text in a document, Word automatically checks the spelling of each word against its standard dictionary. If Word cannot find the word in its dictionary, it will underline the word with a wavy red line. This does not always mean the word is misspelled. It simply means the word is not listed in Word's dictionary. To view suggestions for alternative spellings of the word, you can right-click the underlined word to display a shortcut menu. You can select an alternative spelling from the shortcut menu, or you can choose to ignore the misspelling. In any case, once you have indicated your preference, the red wavy line disappears until you close and reopen the document.

Word also automatically checks for grammar errors as you enter text. When it finds a possible error, Word underlines the word, phrase, or sentence with a wavy green line. You can then access a shortcut menu to view suggestions for changes.

Formatting gives documents a professional look, but only if the formatting is applied consistently throughout the document. Word has a feature that will alert you of formatting inconsistencies in a document. For example, if most of your paragraphs of text are formatted in 12 point, but you change the font size for the text in one of the paragraphs to 11 point. Word will identify the inconsistency as you enter the text or enter the new format. The text is marked with a blue wavy line.

Computer Concepts

Although the grammar checker is a helpful tool, you still need to have a good working knowledge of English grammar. The grammar checker can identify a possible problem, but it's up to you to decide if the change should be made depending on the context of the sentence.

Hot Tip

To check for formatting inconsistencies, two options must be turned on. Open the **Tools** menu, choose **Options**, and click the **Edit** tab. If necessary, turn on Keep track of formatting and Mark formatting inconsistencies.

Computer Concepts

The red, green, or blue underlines are only visible when you display your document. They will not appear when you print the document.

STEP-BY-STEP ▷ 4.1

1. Launch Word. Open a new document. Open the **Tools** menu, choose **Options**, and click the **Spelling & Grammar** tab. Make sure the selected options match those shown in Figure 4.1 and then click **OK**.

2. Key the following text: **In the erly 1800s,**. Notice that as you press the spacebar after *erly*, Word underlines the word with a red wavy line.

71

FIGURE 4-1

Spelling & Grammar Options dialog box

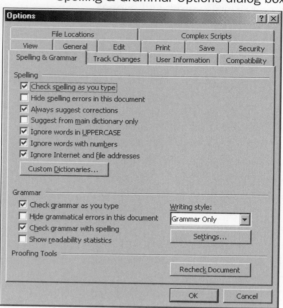

3. Point to the word *erly* and right-click. A shortcut menu is displayed as shown in Figure 4-2 and several word choices are displayed at the top of the menu.

FIGURE 4-2

Spelling shortcut menu

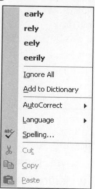

4. Select **early** in the shortcut menu. The correct spelling replaces the original spelling in the document.

5. Position the insertion point after the comma you keyed and press **Spacebar**. Then key **Potawatomi Indians**. Notice that as you press the spacebar after *Potawatomi*, Word underlines the word with a red wavy line.

6. Right-click on the word *Potawatomi*. The proposed spelling *Pottawatomie* in the shortcut menu is an alternative way to spell the name of the Indian tribe. However, the spelling you entered is also correct. Click **Ignore All** in the shortcut menu. The red wavy line is removed, and the word *Potawatomi* will not be flagged as misspelled again in this document until you check the Recheck Document (or Check Document) button in the Spelling and Grammar dialog box.

7. Position the insertion point after the word *Indians*. Key a period and then press **Enter**. The entire sentence is underlined with a green wavy line.

8. Point to any part of green underlined portion of the sentence and right-click. A shortcut menu is displayed, and the words *Fragment (consider revising)* appear at the top of the menu. See Figure 4-3.

FIGURE 4-3
Grammar shortcut menu

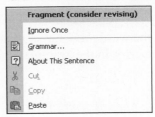

9. Click outside the shortcut menu to close it. Then edit the sentence to read *In the early 1800s,* **the** *Potawatomi Indians* **made the path.** Then, press **Enter** twice.

10. Select the entire sentence and copy it to the Clipboard.

11. Position the insertion point at the end of the document and paste the contents from the Clipboard.

Speech Recognition

If your computer has speech recognition capability, make sure you are in Command mode and say the appropriate command to position the insertion point at the end of the document.

12. Select the copied sentence and change the font size to 11 point.

13. Click outside the copied sentence to deselect the text. A blue wavy line appears below the copied sentence.

14. Point to the text with the blue underline and right-click. The shortcut menu shown in Figure 4-4 is displayed.

FIGURE 4-4
Inconsistent Formatting shortcut menu

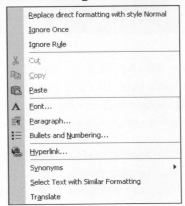

15. Select the first suggestion **Replace direct formatting with style Normal**. The Normal style is the font size that was applied when you began entering text in the document. The font size for the copied sentence is restored to the Normal point size.

16. Close the document without saving the changes.

Correct Spelling and Grammar Errors All at Once

Instead of checking the spelling and grammar as you enter text, you can correct the spelling and grammar errors all at once after all the text is entered in the document. When you check the entire document at once, the unknown words and possible grammar errors are displayed in the Spelling and Grammar dialog box.

It is common for proofreaders to check a document only for misspelled words. Good proofreading skills, however, include reading for content. That means checking to be sure each sentence makes sense. For example, you may have used the word *there* rather than *their*. Word will not identify this as a misspelled word, and it may not catch the error in the grammar check.

Computer Concepts

Word allows you to add words to its standard dictionary or to custom dictionaries that you create. You can have several different custom dictionaries. You can add words to the dictionaries while the Spelling and Grammar dialog box is open during a spell check.

STEP-BY-STEP ▷ 4.2

1. Open **Step4-2** from the data files and save the document as **Path** followed by your initials. Notice that several words in the document are underlined with wavy, colored lines.

2. Click the **Spelling and Grammar** button on the Standard toolbar. The Spelling and Grammar dialog box is opened on top of the document window. See Figure 4-5.

FIGURE 4-5
The Spelling and Grammar dialog box

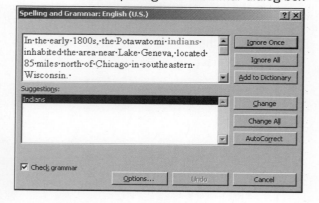

3. The word *indians* is displayed in red type. The correct spelling with a capital *I* is proposed in the *Suggestions* box. Click **Change**. Word replaces the misspelled word in the document and continues checking for the next spelling or grammar issue.

4. The letters *Kee* are selected in the document and are displayed in red type in the dialog box. Click **Ignore Once** to skip this occurrence of the letters.

5. The words *Chicago Fire* are displayed in green. There are two spaces between the words. The suggestion corrects the extra space between the words. Click **Change**.

6. The word *the* is now displayed in red. The suggestion to delete the repeated word is correct. Click **Delete**.

7. The word *remin* is now displayed in red. Click on the correct spelling *remain* in the Suggestions box, then click **Change**.

8. When the dialog box is displayed indicating the spelling and grammar check is complete, click **OK**.

9. Proofread the document. There is an error in the third sentence in the first paragraph. Can you find it? Make the necessary correction.

10. Save the changes and leave the document open for the next Step-by-Step.

Use Help to Turn Off Wavy Lines

Most users think the wavy lines are helpful in identifying typos and in detecting grammatical errors and inconsistent formatting. However, some people do not like the wavy lines to display on the screen. If you like the wavy lines, and they are not appearing on your screen, what would you do? Or, if you don't like the wavy lines, how would you get rid of them? In the next Step-by-Step you will use Help to learn how to show or hide the wavy lines.

You've already learned to access Help using the Office Assistant and by selecting the Help command in the Help menu. New in Office XP is the *Ask a Question* box, positioned on the right side of the menu bar. See Figure 4-6. You can enter your questions in this box to quickly access the Help topics.

Did You Know?

The Ask a Question box keeps a list of all your questions during your Word session. If you want to access help information for a question you already asked, click the down arrow in the Ask a Question box and select your question.

FIGURE 4-6
Ask a Question box in the menu bar

STEP-BY-STEP ➡ 4.3

1. Click in the *Ask a Question* box and key **spell check** and then press **Enter**.

Speech Recognition

If your computer has speech recognition capability, switch to the Dictation mode. Then, position the insertion point in the Ask a Question box and then dictate your question.

2. A list of topics is displayed. Select **Show or hide wavy underlines**. The Microsoft Word Help window opens and the topic is expanded to show a paragraph of text and two more expandable hyperlinks. Read the paragraph.

3. Click the hyperlink **Formatting consistency** to expand the subtopic. Read the steps that describe how to turn off the display of wavy lines for formatting consistency.

4. Click the hyperlink **Formatting consistency** to collapse the subtopic.

5. Click the hyperlink **Spelling and grammar**. Read the information, then collapse the subtopic.

6. Close the Help window and leave the document open for the next Step-by-Step.

Correct Spelling Errors Automatically

It is common for us to make the same spelling error over and over. For example, you may often key *teh* instead of *the*. The **AutoCorrect** feature automatically corrects errors as you enter text in a document. Therefore, AutoCorrect can save editing time. You can set the options for the AutoCorrect feature in the AutoCorrect dialog box.

S TEP-BY-STEP ▷ 4.4

Hot Tip

You can add words to the AutoCorrect list during a spellcheck by clicking the AutoCorrect option in the Spelling and Grammar dialog box.

1. Position the insertion point at the top of the document (above the first paragraph).

2. Open the **Tools** menu and choose **AutoCorrect Options**. The dialog box shown in Figure 4-7 will display.

FIGURE 4-7
AutoCorrect dialog box

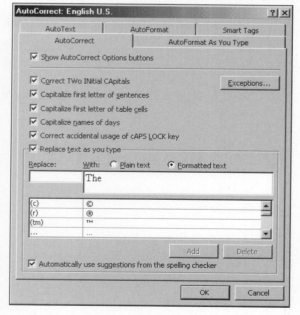

3. Make sure all the options in the dialog box are turned on. If any options are not checked, turn them on and then click **OK**.

4. Key the following text: **teh**.

5. Watch as you press **Spacebar**. Word automatically corrects the spelling and capitalizes the first letter of the word.

6. Point to the word *The*. Notice there is a small, blue box under the letter *T*. Point to the blue box and the AutoCorrect Options button displays. See Figure 4-8.

FIGURE 4-8
AutoCorrect Options button

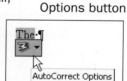

7. Click the **AutoCorrect Options** button to display a menu of the undo options. Click outside the submenu to close it without making any changes.

8. If necessary, position the insertion point after the word *The* and key **Potawatomi Path**.

9. Center the heading, then save the changes and leave the document open for the next Step-by-Step.

Use the Thesaurus

A good writer must be able to keep the attention of the reader. This means knowing who will be the intended audience and using language that is appropriate for that audience. Using the Word Thesaurus, you can replace a word or group of words in your document with a *synonym*, which is a word that has the same or nearly the same meaning. You may want to use a synonym of a word because it is more appropriate, easier to understand, or simply different (to avoid overusing a word). You can also replace a word or group of words with an *antonym*, which is a word that has an opposite meaning.

S TEP-BY-STEP ▷ 4.5

1. Point to the word *grand* in the second line of the second paragraph, then right-click to display the shortcut menu illustrated in Figure 4-9.

FIGURE 4-9
Shortcut menu

2. Point to **Synonyms** near the bottom of the shortcut menu to display a submenu with a list of synonyms.

3. In the list of synonyms, select **magnificent**. Word replaces the original word with the synonym.

4. Point to the word *ritziest* in the last paragraph and right-click. Then, click **Synonyms**. This time Word does not propose any synonyms.

5. Select **Thesaurus**. The Thesaurus dialog box opens. See Figure 4-10.

FIGURE 4-10
The Thesaurus dialog box

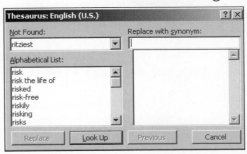

6. The word *ritziest* is not found. Scroll down in the Alphabetical list to find and select **ritzy**.

7. Click the **Look Up** button. A list of synonyms is displayed at the right. Select **classy** and click **Replace**.

Hot Tip

When you can't find a word (like ritziest), you can often look for the root word in the Thesaurus. Then if you locate a synonym, you can edit the synonym for the correct grammar.

8. The word *classy* is now displayed in the document. Edit the word to read **classiest**.

9. Save the changes and leave the document open for the next Step-by-Step.

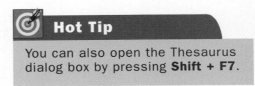
Hot Tip

You can also open the Thesaurus dialog box by pressing **Shift + F7**.

Use AutoComplete

The **AutoComplete** feature suggests the spelling for frequently used words and phrases. AutoComplete will fill in days of the week, months, salutations, and complimentary closings commonly used in letters. As you begin to key the first few characters of these frequently used words, Word suggests the entire spelling in a box on the screen (often referred to as a ScreenTip). You can accept the suggested spelling by pressing Enter. If you do not wish to accept the suggested spelling, continue keying and the ScreenTip will disappear.

STEP-BY-STEP ▷ 4.6

1. Position the insertion point at the end of the document (below the last paragraph) and press **Enter**.

2. Key **Refe**. A ScreenTip will display suggesting *Reference*. See Figure 4-11.

FIGURE 4-11
AutoComplete ScreenTip

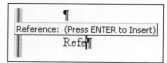

3. Press **Enter** to accept the suggested text.

4. Press **Spacebar** and then key **Lake Tours, Lake Geneva, Wisconsin**.

5. Press **Enter** and begin to key the day of the week. For example: **Wedn**. When the ScreenTip with the suggested spelling appears, press **Enter** to accept the suggested spelling.

6. Save the changes and leave the document open for the next Step-by-Step.

Count Words in a Document

How many times have you counted the words in a report you prepared for a class assignment to see if you met the instructor's minimum requirement for total words? Word has a feature that will automatically count the words for you. Furthermore, if you are editing the document, you can update the count any time you want.

 Did You Know?

You can also view the document statistics (number of pages, words, characters, paragraphs, and lines) by opening the File menu, choosing Properties, and clicking on the Statistics tab.

STEP-BY-STEP ▷ 4.7

1. Open the **Tools** menu and choose **Word Count**. The dialog box shown in Figure 4-12 is displayed.

FIGURE 4-12
Word Count dialog box

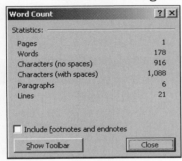

2. Click **Show Toolbar**, then click **Close**. The Word Count toolbar is displayed, indicating that the document contains 178 words. See Figure 4-13.

FIGURE 4-13
Word Count toolbar

3. Leave the document and toolbar open for the next Step-by-Step. If necessary, move the Word Count toolbar out of the way by pointing to the title bar and dragging the toolbar to the side of the screen.

Insert the Current Date and the Document Filename

You can easily insert the current date into a document by using the Insert Date and Time command. Once inserted, you can choose whether or not the date will be updated automatically each time you open and/or print the document. For example, when creating a letter or memo, you would want the date to remain fixed for record keeping purposes. However, if you were inserting the date in a report that you will be working on for several days, you will want the date of the final draft to appear in the document. In that case, you would want the current date displayed each time you open the document.

Adding the filename to your document can also be helpful. If you need to revise or reuse the document at a later time, you will know which file to open. When you insert the date or a filename in your document, Word enters the data as a field. A *field* is a special instruction which tells Word to automatically insert variable data. The date is an example of variable data, because it changes every day. Many fields are updated automatically when you print a document. To update fields manually, select the field and press F9.

Hot Tip

To automatically insert the current date using AutoComplete, begin keying the name of the month. When a ScreenTip pops up giving the full month name, press Enter to insert the month. Key a space and when the ScreenTip pops up with the current date, press Enter to insert both the day and the year in the document.

1. Press **Enter** to begin a new paragraph.

2. Open the **Insert** menu and choose **Date and Time**. A dialog box similar to Figure 4-14 is displayed. Your dialog box will show the current system date.

FIGURE 4-14
The Date and Time dialog box

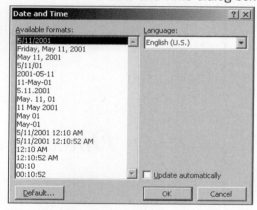

3. Select the option that looks like December 13, XXXX.

4. If necessary, click in the box next to *Update automatically* to turn the option on. Then click **OK**. The current date is inserted in the document. Click the date that was inserted. The shading that displays when you click on the date indicates that this is a field. The shading will not print.

Hot Tip

If a type of code displays instead of the field results (in this case, the current date), open the **Tools** menu, choose **Options**, click the **Print** tab, and then clear the Field codes check box.

5. Place the insertion point after the date if it is not already there and press **Enter** twice.

6. Open the **Insert** menu and choose **Field**. The Field dialog box shown in Figure 4-15 is displayed.

FIGURE 4-15
The Field dialog box

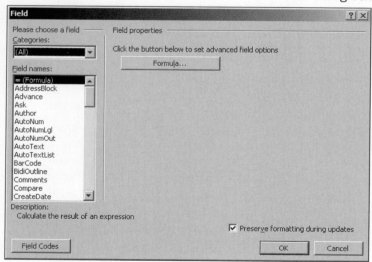

7. Under *Categories*, select **Document Information** from the drop down list. Notice the options available under *Field names* change.

8. Under *Field names*, select **FileName** and click **OK**. The filename is inserted in the document.

9. Notice that the Word Count on the Word Count toolbar is no longer displayed. This is because the content of the document has changed. Click **Recount** to update the count.

10. Close the Word Count toolbar. Then save the changes and close the document.

 Computer Concepts

To remove a filename or date field that has been inserted in the document, double-click on the field to select it. The entire filename will be selected. Then, press **Delete**.

Find and Replace Text and Formats

Scrolling through a long document to locate a specific section of text is time-consuming and not very efficient. The Find feature in Word makes searching for text and/or formats much easier. When you need to replace or reformat multiple occurrences of the same text, you can use the Replace feature to replace each occurrence automatically.

Find Text

You use the Find command to search a document for every time specific word or phrase occurs. The search will begin at the location of the insertion point. If you want to search only a specific portion of a document, you can select the desired text before beginning the search.

STEP-BY-STEP ➩ 4.9

1. Open **Step4-9** from the data files. Save the document as **Treadwall** followed by your initials.

2. If necessary, move the insertion point to the top of the document.

3. Open the **Edit** menu and choose **Find**. The Find sheet in the Find and Replace dialog box is displayed. See Figure 4-16.

FIGURE 4-16
The Find sheet in the Find and Replace dialog box

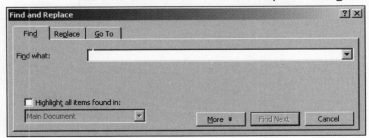

Hot Tip

The shortcut keys to execute the Find command are **Ctrl + F**.

4. In the *Find what* box, key **workout**, then click **Find Next**. Word locates the first occurrence of the word, and the word is selected in the document window. The dialog box remains open.

5. Click **Find Next** again. Word finds the next occurrence of the word in the open document.

6. Click **Cancel** to close the dialog box.

7. Leave the document open for the next Step-by-Step.

Find and Replace Text

If you want to replace the search text with new words, you choose the Replace command. The replacements can be made individually, or all occurrences can be replaced at once.

STEP-BY-STEP ➡ 4.10

1. Move the insertion point to the beginning of the document. (*Hint*: Hold down **Ctrl** and press **Home**.)

2. Open the **Edit** menu and choose **Replace**. The Replace sheet in the Find and Replace dialog box is displayed. See Figure 4-17. Notice the

word workout from your last search is still displayed in the *Find what* box.

3. Key **tread wall** in the *Find what* box.

4. Click in the *Replace with* box and key **Treadwall**.

FIGURE 4-17
The Replace sheet in the Find and Replace dialog box

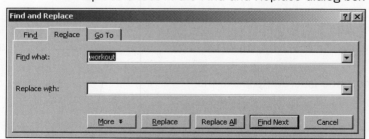

5. Click **Find Next**. Word locates and selects the first occurrence of the words *tread wall*. (Notice that the Find function ignores case.)

6. Click **Replace**. Word changes the selected text to *Treadwall* and then locates the next occurrence of the search text. The dialog box remains open.

7. Click **Replace All**. Word replaces all occurrences of the search text with the replace text. The Assistant balloon (or a message

box) is displayed indicating that three replacements were made. Click **OK**.

8. Click **Close** in the Find and Replace dialog box.

9. Save the changes and leave the document open for the next Step-by-Step.

Hot Tip

The shortcut keys to execute the Replace command are Ctrl + H.

Find and Replace Formats

You can also use the Find command to search for character and paragraph formats. You can search for combined formats such as bold and italic. When you need to replace multiple occurrences of the same format, you can use the Replace command to reformat each occurrence automatically.

STEP-BY-STEP ➡ 4.11

1. Position the insertion point at the beginning of the document. Then open the **Edit** menu and choose **Replace**.

2. Delete the text in the *Find what* and *Replace with* boxes.

3. Click **More** in the Find and Replace dialog box. The expanded dialog box shown in Figure 4-18 is displayed.

4. Position the insertion point in the *Find what* box.

5. Click **Format**. A shortcut menu is displayed.

FIGURE 4-18
The Replace sheet with More

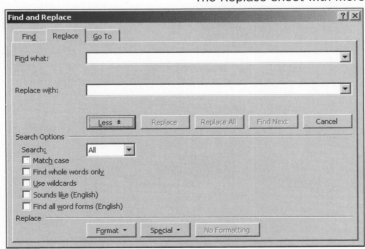

6. Click **Font** to display the Find Font dialog box. Under *Font style*, select **Bold** and then click **OK**. Notice that the words *Font: Bold* are displayed below the *Find what* box.

7. Click in the *Replace with* box. Click on **Format**, then select **Font** in the shortcut menu.

8. Under *Font style*, select **Italic** and click **OK**.

9. Click **Replace All**. A balloon (or message box) is displayed indicating that four occurrences of bold text are changed to bold and italic. Click outside the balloon to close it (or click **OK**).

10. Click in the *Find what* box and then click **No Formatting**. This removes the format from the search box. Click in the *Replace with* box and then click **No Formatting** to remove the format.

11. Click **Less** to return the dialog box to the condensed view, then click **Close** in the Find and Replace dialog box.

12. Save the changes and leave the document open for the next Step-by-Step.

E-mail a Document

Sending a Word document via e-mail is quick and easy. Click the E-mail button on the Standard toolbar. An e-mail header form is displayed. Fill it in and then send the document.

STEP-BY-STEP ⟹ 4.12

1. The Treadwall document should already be the current active document. Click the **E-mail** button on the Standard toolbar. The e-mail header form shown in Figure 4-19 will display.

Speech Recognition

If your computer has speech recognition capability, make sure you are in Command mode and say **"e-mail"** to access the e-mail button on the Standard toolbar.

2. Click in the *To* box and key **Conrad908ad@ud.edu**.

3. Click in the *Introduction* box and key **This is my report on treadwalls**.

4. The document is ready to send. In this case, however, you will not send the e-mail. Click

the e-mail button to remove the e-mail header.

5. Save the changes (Word will store the information you entered into the e-mail header with the document). Close the document and Word.

FIGURE 4-19
E-mail header form

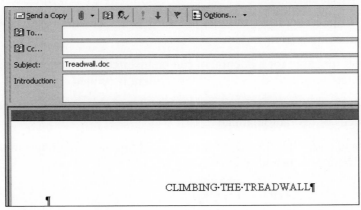

Summary

In this lesson, you learned:

- Word checks spelling, grammar, and formatting as you enter text. Misspelled words are marked with red wavy lines; possible grammar errors are marked with green wavy underlines; and formatting inconsistencies are marked with blue wavy underlines.

- Spelling and grammar errors can be corrected as you enter text using a shortcut menu. To check all spelling and grammar at once, use the Spelling and Grammar dialog box.

- The AutoCorrect feature corrects errors as you enter text.

- The Thesaurus suggests synonyms (and sometimes antonyms) for words and phrases.

- The AutoComplete feature suggests spellings for commonly used words and phrases.

- The Word Count feature counts the number of words in a document. You can update the word count as you edit the document.

- The date, time, and filename for a document can be inserted in the document as a field. These fields can be updated automatically when the document is printed.

- The Find command makes searching for text and/or formats easy. The Replace command replaces multiple occurrences of text automatically.

- You can quickly and easily e-mail a document by clicking the E-mail button on the Standard toolbar and filling in the e-mail header form.

VOCABULARY REVIEW

Define the following terms:

Antonym   AutoCorrect   Synonym
AutoComplete   Field

LESSON 4 REVIEW QUESTIONS

TRUE/FALSE

Circle T if the statement is true or F if the statement is false.

T   F   1. You can trust Word's grammar checker to always provide the correct solution to a grammar problem.

T   F   2. Word's AutoCorrect feature completes common words and phrases as you key them.

T   F   3.   To find a word opposite in meaning to a word in your document, you can use the Thesaurus in Word.

T   F   4.   When creating a letter that you want to keep as a permanent record, it is best not to insert a date that will update automatically.

T   F   5.   To replace one format with another in a document, you must first click the Display button to display the expanded Find and Replace dialog box.

FILL IN THE BLANK

Complete the following sentences by writing the correct word or words in the blanks provided.

1.   Possible spelling errors are underlined with a wavy _____ line, while possible grammar errors are underlined with a wavy _____ line.

2.   If you want Word to skip all instances of a particular word as you check spelling, click the _____ button in the Spelling and Grammar dialog box.

3.   If you accidentally key **teh** instead of *the*, the _____ feature in Word will automatically correct the error for you.

4.   If you begin keying the day of the week and Word displays a ScreenTip with the day, you can press _____ to insert the suggested word in your document.

5.   When you insert a date, time, or filename in your document, Word can actually insert a(n) _____ that stands for variable data.

LESSON 4 PROJECTS

PROJECT 4-1

1.   Open **Project4-1** from the data files. Save the document as **Influenza** followed by your initials.

2.   Several errors, including spelling, grammar, and formatting are marked with wavy lines. Fix them as follows:
   A.   Right-click anywhere in the first formatting problem (several words in the first paragraph). Click on the suggested fix: **Make this text consistent with formatting 12 pt**.
   B.   Using the shortcut spelling menu, fix the misspelling of *runnny* in the first paragraph.
   C.   Accept the suggestion to capitalize the first word in the sentence (*For*) in the second paragraph.
   D.   Accept the suggestion to capitalize *spanish*.

3.   The italicized terms in the document don't show up very well. Use the Replace command to replace the italic formatting with bold italic formatting.

4. The first sentence in the second paragraph uses the word *dangerous* twice. Use the Thesaurus to find a replacement word for the first *dangerous* in the sentence.

5. You intend to add more to this document and want to indicate the time and date of your latest update. Click in the first right-aligned blank line at the top of the document and key **Last updated** and a space. Insert the date and time as a field that will automatically update. Then press **OK**.

6. To remind yourself of what you named the document, click in the second right-aligned blank line and insert the FileName field.

7. You found some of the information in this document on a Web site hosted by a federal government agency, the Centers for Disease Control and Prevention. Not only do you need to make clear for others where you got your information, you might want to return to the site to gather more information. Position the insertion point at the end of the document and insert the following Web address after the word *Source*: **www.cdc.gov**. Press **Enter**. Word automatically formats the address with an underline and a different font color (indicating that it is a hyperlink to that Web site).

8. Save your changes. Close the document.

PROJECT 4-2

1. Open **Project4-2** from data files. Save the document as **Fitness** followed by your initials. Be sure the nonprinting characters are displayed.

2. Insert the date in the first blank line in the document. Make sure the date will not update automatically.

3. Check the document's spelling and grammar as follows, using the Spelling and Grammar dialog box:
   A. When Word identifies a sentence fragment, insert the word **are** following the word *classes* in the top half of the Spelling and Grammar dialog box and then click **Change**.
   B. The word *Hatha* is spelled correctly.
   C. Accept all other grammar and spelling suggestions.

4. Position the insertion point at the end of the second paragraph (*There's a fitness class...*) of text and key the following sentence just as shown: **For more infomation abbout these classes, call 555-3345.** Word automatically corrects the spelling errors as you key them.

5. Position the insertion point to the left of the first tab symbol in the list of courses. Key **Mond** and then press **Enter** to accept the AutoComplete entry. Position the insertion point to the left of the third tab symbol and key **Tues** and then accept the AutoComplete entry. Insert **Wednesday**, **Thursday**, and **Friday** next to each group of classes in the same way.

6. Your document mentions cardio fitness several times. Use the Replace command to replace *cardio* with **cardiovascular**. (*Hint*: Make sure the format criteria is removed from the *Find what* and *Replace with* boxes by clicking the No Formatting button).

7. Save your changes. Close the document and exit Word.

WEB PROJECT

CANS

If you completed Project 4-1, you read some facts about influenza. The influenza document mentions the worldwide outbreak of flu from 1918 to 1919 called the Spanish flu. Use any Web search or reference tool to learn more about the Spanish flu. Try to find the answers to these questions and use them to write a brief report:

1. How did this type of flu enter the United States?

2. About how many people in this country died from the Spanish flu?

3. Could the Spanish flu ever return?

TEAMWORK PROJECT

CANS

In this lesson, you have worked with several of the automatic features of Word. As you have learned, Word's automatic features can help you create and customize many types of documents. Many AutoComplete entries are specifically designed for business documents such as letters and memos. With a partner, explore how automatic features can speed the process of creating business letters.

1. With your partner, make a list of elements that commonly appear in business letters, such as the date, the inside address, a salutation, and a complimentary close. Use a writer's style guide if one is available.

2. You and your partner should then key some of the elements you have identified in a new document. What happens when you begin keying Dear Sir, for example, or Sincerely?

3. Work with your partner to create a list of AutoComplete entries that can be used when writing a business letter. What other automatic tools have you learned about in this lesson that can help you prepare a good letter?

CRITICAL THINKING

SCANS

ACTIVITY 4-1

In Project 4-1, you used the Replace command to change italic terms to bold italic. Suppose you needed to change all the terms in a very long document from italic to just bold—not bold italic. Experiment with the Replace command to find out how you could make this formatting change. Write a brief report in Word that describes your findings.

ACTIVITY 4-2

In Project 4-1, you inserted a Web address and Word automatically formatted it as a hyperlink. Use the Help feature to find out what kind of automatic feature this is. Word will make other similar changes for you automatically. Write a brief report in Word that describes some of the other changes this automatic feature will make.

WORKING WITH TABLES

OBJECTIVES

Upon completion of this lesson, you should be able to:

- Create a table.

- Insert and delete rows and columns.

- Adjust column width and center a table.

- Edit table text.

- Use the Draw Table and Eraser tools to create a table grid.

- Format text alignment and direction within a table cell.

- Format borders and shading.

- Convert text to a table and AutoFormat the table.

⏱ **Estimated Time: 1.5 hours**

VOCABULARY

Cell

Gridlines

Merging cells

Splitting cells

Suppose you need to arrange several lines of information in two or three columns. How could you create the columns? If your answer is "Set tab stops," you're correct. However, there's also an easier and faster way. The table features in Word make the task of arranging text and numbers in columns both quick and easy.

Create a Table

A table consists of cells (boxes) to which you add text or graphics. A *cell* represents one intersection of a row and a column in a table. In a table, rows go across and columns go down.

By default, Word formats a border around all the cells in a table. If you don't want this border to print, you can remove the border. However, the boundary lines for each of the cells still remain. These boundary lines in a table are called *gridlines*. Gridlines are used for layout purposes; they do not print.

Insert a Table

To create a table, you must first decide how many columns and rows you want in the table. Then you create a table grid and enter the data.

S·TEP-BY-STEP ▷ 5.1

1. Launch Word and open a blank document. Click the **Insert Table** button on the Standard toolbar. A grid of table cells appears.

 Computer Concepts

The Insert Table button appears on the Standard toolbar and on the Tables and Borders toolbar. However, the button on the Tables and Borders toolbar will not display a grid. Instead, it will open the Insert Table dialog box. Or, if you click the down arrow next to the button it will display the options available in the Insert Table command.

2. Click in the first cell in the grid and drag down the grid until seven rows of cells are displayed; then drag across until the bottom of the grid reads *7 x 3 Table*. See Figure 5-1. The table appears in the document.

 Did You Know?

You can also manually enter the table size (number of columns and rows) through the Insert Table dialog box. To open the dialog box, click the **Insert Table** button on the Tables and Borders toolbar or open the **Table** menu, choose **Insert**, and then select **Table** in the submenu.

3. Leave the document open for the next Step-by-Step.

FIGURE 5-1
Table grid

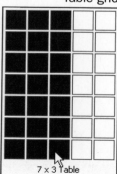

7 x 3 Table

Enter Text in the Table

To move the insertion point from one cell to another, you can press the arrow keys or Tab. If the text that you enter is wider than the column, Word automatically wraps the text to a new line within the cell. When you reach the end of a row and press Tab, the insertion point moves to the first cell in the next row.

STEP-BY-STEP ▷ 5.2

1. The insertion point should be positioned in the first cell. Key **Activity**.

2. Press **Tab** to move the insertion point to the next cell to the right in the same row. Key **20 Minutes**. Press **Tab** and then key **40 Minutes**.

Hot Tip

To move the insertion point to the cell that is to the left of the current cell, press **Shift + Tab**.

3. Press **Tab** to move the insertion point to the first cell in the next row.

4. Press the down arrow to move the insertion point down to the third row.

5. Key the rest of the table as illustrated in Figure 5-2. Use **Tab** or the arrow keys to move from one cell to another.

6. Save the document as **Calories** followed by your initials. Leave the document open for the next Step-by-Step.

FIGURE 5-2
Completed table for Step-by-Step 5.2

Activity	20 Minutes	40 Minutes
Cross-country skiing	192	384
Downhill skiing	144	288
Golf: carrying clubs	132	264
Mountain biking	204	408
Running: 9 min/mile	264	528

Did You Know?

If you have access to the Internet, you can click the Search on Web button and access technical resources from the Microsoft Office as well as other Microsoft Web sites. If a topic begins with "Web:," the Office Web article is available when you are connected to the Internet.

Use Help to Learn about Table Gridlines and Borders

As you worked with the table you created, you probably thought you were looking at the gridlines for your table. But the lines you saw on the screen are actually borders. You can go to the Help screen to find out more about borders.

You can use the Answer Wizard in Help to ask a question or key search words. A list of topics related to your question is displayed, and when you click on one of the proposed topics, details about the topic are provided in the same dialog box at the right.

STEP-BY-STEP ▷ 5.3

1. If necessary, display the Office Assistant by opening the **Help** menu and choosing **Show the Office Assistant**.

2. Click the Office Assistant and key **table gridlines** and press **Enter**. In the list of topics, click on **Display or hide gridlines in a table**. Read the information about the gridlines.

3. You decide you want to remove the default border but you don't know how. If necessary, click the **Show** button on the Help toolbar to display the

   Contents, Answer Wizard, and *Index* tabs. (If you do see the *Contents, Answer Wizard,* and *Index* tabs, the Hide button will be displayed in the toolbar.)

4. If necessary, click the **Answer Wizard** tab to display the dialog box shown in Figure 5-3.

5. Click in the *What would you like to do?* text box, key **remove a border**, then click **Search**. Notice the list of topics that display in the **Answer Wizard** folder under *Select topic to display*.

FIGURE 5-3
Answer Wizard sheet of the Help dialog box

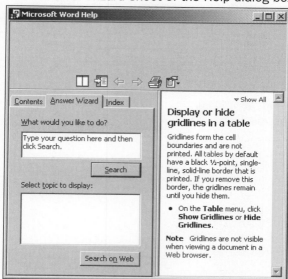

6. At the right, click on the link **Remove a border from a picture, a table, or text**.

7. Study the directions in Steps 1–3. Click the hyperlinks for *table* and *cells*. The first time you click on the hyperlink, a definition will display. When you click on the hyperlink again, the definition will be hidden.

8. Change the text in the *What would you like to do?* box to **select cells** and click **Search**. Then click the link **Select items in a table with the mouse**. Study the examples. Be sure to read the section *Multiple cells, rows, or columns*.

9. Leave the Help screen open. Click the **Calories** document button in the taskbar.

10. Experiment with selecting cells, rows, and columns. If you need to refresh your memory,

refer back to the Microsoft Help screen to reread the directions.

11. Switch back to Help, then close the Help screen. Leave the document open for the next Step-by-Step.

Hot Tip

You can click on the Help button in the task bar to display the Help window on top of the Calories document. You can click the Hide button in the Help window to reduce its size, and you can also resize the window so it doesn't take up as much space on the screen. Drag the title bar of the Help window to move it out of the way.

Remove Table Borders

Now that you have read about how to remove borders from a table, give it a try. In the following Step-by-Step, you will practice one of the Tips provided in the Help screen. However, you can explore the other methods of removing table borders on your own.

STEP-BY-STEP 5.4

1. Position the insertion point anywhere inside the table.

2. Open the **Format** menu and choose **Borders and Shading**. If necessary, select the **Borders** tab to display the dialog box shown in Figure 5-4.

FIGURE 5-4
Borders and Shading dialog box

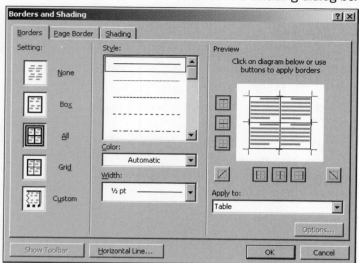

Speech Recognition

If your computer has speech recognition capability, enable the Command mode and say the commands to open the Borders and Shading dialog box and select the options.

3. Under *Setting*, select **None** and then click **OK**.

4. Your document should now display lines that indicate the cell boundaries. If you don't see any lines in your document, open the **Table** menu and choose **Show Gridlines**. The gridlines are similar to the borders you removed, but they are much lighter in color. (If you do see gridlines, the menu item on the Table menu would read **Hide Gridlines**.) Leave the document open for the next Step-by-Step.

Insert and Delete Rows and Columns

After you create a table, you may decide to change it. For example, you may need to add more rows or delete a column. Word has many features that make these changes easy.

Change the Number of Rows and Columns

If you want to insert a new row at the end of the table, you can position the insertion point in the last table cell and press Tab. To insert a new row anywhere else in the table, use the Insert command in the Table menu.

If you select the content in a cell or group of cells and press Delete, the text is deleted but the cells are still there. To remove rows or columns, you must choose the Delete command in the Table menu. When you delete a row or column, the text is also deleted.

S TEP-BY-STEP ▷ 5.5

1. Position the insertion point in the last cell in the table (the cell contains the text *528*). Press **Tab** to create a new row.

2. Key the following information in the new row:
Walking: 15 min/mile   108   216

3. Press **Tab** and key the following information in the new row:
Weight lifting   72   140

4. Move the insertion point to the cell containing the text *Golf: carrying clubs*. Open the **Table** menu and choose **Insert**, then select **Rows Below** in the submenu.

5. Key the following information in the new row:
Golf: using a cart   84   168

6. Position the insertion point in the blank row (the second row). Open the **Table** menu and choose **Delete**, then select **Rows** in the submenu.

7. Position the insertion point in any cell in the *40 Minutes* column. Open the **Table** menu and choose **Delete**, then select **Columns** in the submenu.

Hot Tip

To insert or delete multiple rows and columns at one time, first select the desired number of rows or columns. For example, if you want to insert or delete three rows, select three rows in the table. Then choose the Table Insert or Table Delete command.

8. Click **Undo** to restore the column you deleted.

9. Move the insertion point to the second cell in the third column (the cell contains the text 384). Open the **Table** menu and choose **Insert**, then select **Columns to the Left** in the submenu.

10. Click in the first cell of the new column and key **30 Minutes**. Press the down arrow to move down one cell below the current cell and key **288**. Key the following numbers to complete the column:
216
198
126
306
396
162
108

Speech Recognition

If your computer has speech recognition capability, enable the Dictation mode and dictate the cell contents. (*Hint:* Say "Tab" to move to the next cell.)

11. Save the changes and leave the document open for the next Step-by-Step.

Did You Know?

You can use the number pad on your keyboard to enter numbers. Make sure that NUMLOCK is turned on.

Merge and Split Table Cells

When you remove the boundary between two cells, it is called *merging cells*. You can merge cells horizontally or vertically. You can merge cells when you want to create a heading to span across two or more columns. To merge cells, the cells must be selected.

When you convert a cell into multiple cells, it is called *splitting cells*. You can split a cell into two or more rows and/or two or more columns. To split a cell, the insertion point must be positioned in the cell.

STEP-BY-STEP 5.6

1. Position the insertion point in the first cell in the table (*Activity*).

2. Open the **Table** menu and choose **Insert**, then select **Rows Above**. A new row is added and the four cells in the new row are selected.

3. With the new row still selected, open the Table menu and choose **Merge Cells**. (*Hint:* You may need to expand the menu to see the *Merge Cells* command.)

4. Click anywhere in the window to deselect the row. The four cells have been converted into a single long cell.

5. Position the insertion point in the new blank row and then open the **Table** menu and choose **Split Cells**. (*Hint:* You may need to expand the menu to see the **Split Cells** command.) The dialog box shown in Figure 5-5 is displayed.

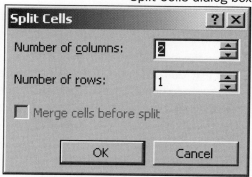

FIGURE 5-5
Split Cells dialog box

6. Change the number in the *Number of columns* box to **1**. Change the number in the *Number of rows* box to **2**. Click **OK**. Click anywhere in the window to deselect the row. You will see that the row is split into two rows.

7. Position the insertion point in the top blank row and key the following title for the table: **NUMBER OF CALORIES BURNED.** Press **Enter**, and then key **Body weight: 150 lbs.** The height of the cell is automatically adjusted to accommodate the two lines of text.

8. Save the changes and leave the document open for the next Step-by-Step.

Adjust Column Width and Center the Table

When you create a table grid, Word makes all the columns the same width. You can adjust the width of each column automatically using the AutoFit feature. Word offers five AutoFit options. In this lesson, you will learn and practice AutoFit to Contents. With AutoFit to Contents, Word automatically adjusts all column widths as needed to accommodate the contents within the cells.

To align a table on the page horizontally, you must first select the entire table. Then you format the alignment in the same way you align text paragraphs.

Computer Concepts

If a table cell is formatted for AutoFit, Word will automatically adjust the cell width each time the cell contents change.

STEP-BY-STEP ▷ 5.7

1. Position the insertion point anywhere within the table. Open the **Table** menu and choose **AutoFit**. In the submenu, choose **AutoFit to Contents**. The text in the first column no longer wraps within the cell, and the extra white space in the other three columns is eliminated.

2. With the insertion point still positioned in the table, open the **Table** menu and choose **Select**. Then select **Table** in the submenu. All the cells in the table are selected.

3. Click the **Center** button on the Formatting toolbar.

4. Click anywhere in the window to deselect the table rows. The table is now positioned in the middle between the left and right margins.

5. Save the changes and leave the document open for the next Step-by-Step.

Hot Tip

If you want rows or columns to be spaced evenly throughout the table, select the particular rows or columns and then click the **Distribute Rows Evenly** or **Distribute Columns Evenly** button on the Tables and Borders toolbar.

Edit Text in a Table

Editing table text is similar to editing other document text. You can insert, delete, copy, or move text within the table cells. You can apply several formats to change the font and alignment of the text within a cell.

Computer Concepts

If you have the **Show/Hide ¶** button on the Standard toolbar toggled on, small squares will display in the left corner of each table cell. These squares are called end-of-cell markers. They will move to the right as you enter text in the cell. End-of-cell markers do not print.

1. Click in the last cell in the table (*140*). Change the number to **144**.

2. Click in the first cell to the right of Cross-country skiing (*192*).

3. Click the **Align Right** button on the Formatting toolbar. The number shifts to the right edge of the cell.

4. With the insertion point still in the *192* cell, hold down **Shift** and then click in the last cell of the table (*144*). All of the cells containing numbers are selected.

5. Click the **Align Right** button.

6. Position the pointer to the left of the first row. When the pointer changes to a right-pointing arrow, click to select the entire row.

7. Click the **Center** and **Bold** buttons on the Formatting toolbar.

8. Select the row beginning with *Activity* and apply the center and bold formats.

9. Save the changes and close the document.

Use the Draw Table and Eraser Tools

There may be occasions when you need to create and customize a more complex table. For example, the table may require cells of different heights or a varying number of columns per row. The Draw Table tool is very useful for creating complex tables. You use the Draw Table tool much the same way you use a pen to draw a table on a sheet of paper. When you use the Draw Table tool you draw the table using the mouse. The document must be displayed in Print Layout view when you use the Draw Table tool.

The Eraser tool enables you to remove cell boundaries. Click on the Eraser button, and the pointer changes to an eraser. When you point and click on a cell gridline, the line will be selected. When you release, the gridline is deleted. The Eraser tool is especially useful if you want to delete a gridline or if you want to change the layout by moving a gridline.

1. Open a new blank document. If necessary, open the **View** menu and choose **Ruler** to display the Ruler at the top of the document. The Ruler is displayed when there is a checkmark to the left of the command in the menu.

2. If necessary, display the Tables and Borders toolbar. Open the **View** menu and choose **Toolbars** and turn on the **Tables and Borders** toolbar shown in Figure 5-6.

FIGURE 5-6
Tables and Borders toolbar

Tables and Borders

Computer Concepts

Sometimes when you display a toolbar, it is floating on the screen. You can move a floating toolbar anywhere on the screen by dragging the title bar. If you drag the toolbar to the edge of the program window or to a location beside another docked toolbar, it becomes a docked toolbar. To move a docked toolbar, drag the move handle at the left side of the toolbar.

3. Click the **Draw Table** button on the Tables and Borders toolbar. The pointer changes to a pencil and Word automatically changes to Print Layout View.

4. To draw the outside boundary of the table grid, position the pointer at the left margin. Then click and drag down and to the right to create a table boundary. Release when the table (box) is approximately 6 inches wide by 2 ½ inches high.

5. Create the vertical and horizontal lines inside the table. Position the point of the pencil where you want the line to begin. Then click and drag to the point where you want the line to end. A broken line will display as you drag the mouse. Repeat to draw all of the lines illustrated in Figure 5-7. Note that there are four horizontal lines at ½ inch apart, and three vertical lines at 1 inch, 4 ½ inches and 5 ½ inches on the ruler.

FIGURE 5-7
Table grid for Step-by-Step 5.9

6. Click the **Draw Table** button to deselect it.

7. Click the **Eraser** button. The pointer changes to an eraser.

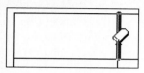

8. Point the eraser on the first vertical line in the first row. When the bottom corner of the eraser is positioned over the line, click to select the line and delete it. If you click and the line is not selected, reposition the eraser and try again. The line will only be deleted if it is selected when you click. See Figure 5-8.

FIGURE 5-8
Eraser tool with selected line

9. Erase two more lines in the first column so your table grid matches the grid illustrated in Figure 5-9.

FIGURE 5-9
Layout for grid for Step-by-Step 5.9

10. Click the Eraser button to deselect it.

11. Enter the table text illustrated in Figure 5-10.

12. Save the document as **Recycling Rate** followed by your initials and leave it open for the next Step-by-Step.

FIGURE 5-10
Text for Step-by-Step 5.9

Recycling Rate		2000	2002
PET	Soft drink bottles	48%	52%
	Vegetable oil bottles	12%	18%
HDPE	Milk jugs	29%	33%
	Bleach and laundry detergent bottles	14%	19%

Align Text within Table Cells

The Tables and Borders toolbar displays several buttons you can use to align text within the cells. You can align text at the top, center, or bottom of a cell, as well as left or right. You can quickly change the direction of text in a table cell by clicking the Change Text Direction button. The direction of the text toggles between three text positions: top to bottom, bottom to top, and horizontal (the default position with which you began).

1. Select the entire table. (*Hint:* Place the insertion point somewhere within the table, then open the **Table** menu, choose **Select**, and then choose **Table** in the submenu).

2. Click the down arrow next to the **Align Top Left** button on the Tables and Borders toolbar. A box with nine alignment options is displayed. See Figure 5-11.

FIGURE 5-11
Cell Alignment options

3. Select the **Align Center Left** option in the second row of options. (*Hint:* Point to the option and wait for the ScreenTip to display so you know you have the correct option.) The text in each cell is centered between the top and bottom boundaries of the cell.

4. Point to the cell *PET* and drag down to select it and the cell *HDPE*.

5. With both cells selected, click the **Change Text Direction** button on the Tables and Borders toolbar. The text rotates to the right and is displayed from top to bottom.

6. Click the **Change Text Direction** button again. The text rotates to the right and is now displayed from bottom to top.

7. Notice that several of the buttons on the Formatting toolbar are altered to reflect the new text direction. Click the **Center** button on the Formatting toolbar. The text is centered between the top and bottom boundaries of the cells. Your document should now look like Figure 5-12.

8. Save the changes and leave the document open for the next Step-by-Step.

Computer Concepts

You can also use the Draw Table tool to add rows or columns to an existing table and to split table cells.

FIGURE 5-12
Document with text rotated and aligned

Recycling Rate			2000	2002
PET		Soft drink bottles	48%	52%
		Vegetable oil bottles	12%	18%
HDPE		Milk jugs	29%	33%
		Bleach and laundry detergent bottles	14%	19%

Format Borders and Shading in a Table

Borders and shading can greatly enhance the appearance of a table, and even help to make the table easier to read. The default setting for tables is to print with a ½-point single-line border around all cells. Generally this border will be appropriate for the tables you create. However, there may be occasions when you want to customize the border and add shading to some of the table cells. You may even want to remove the border completely. Word makes it easy to format borders and change the shading of cells in your table.

STEP-BY-STEP ▷5.11

1. Select the top row of cells. (*Hint:* Point to the left side of the first row. When the pointer changes to a right-pointing arrow, click.)

2. Click the down arrow next to the *Line Weight* button on the Tables and Borders toolbar. In the submenu, select **1 ½ pt**.

3. Click the **Outside Border** button on the Tables and Borders toolbar. The border line becomes heavier.

4. With the row still selected, click the down arrow next to the **Shading Color** button on the Tables and Borders toolbar. If you have a color

printer available, choose a light color. Select **Gray-10**% if you have a black and white printer. (*Hint:* Point to one of the shading options and wait for the ScreenTip to display so you know you have the correct option.)

5. Select the two cells at the left edge of the table (*PET* and *HDPE*). Repeat the shading color format. (*Hint:* Press **F4**.)

6. Click in the first cell *Recycling Rate* and center the text horizontally.

7. Select the last two columns (including the headings) and align the numbers at the right.

8. Save the changes and close the document.

Convert Text to a Table and AutoFormat

Assume that you've already created a multicolumn list using tab settings. You decide that you want to organize the data in a table because it will be easier to format. Do you have to key all the data again? The answer is no. Word can quickly convert text separated by paragraph marks, commas, tabs, or other characters into a table with cells.

When converting text to a table, Word determines the number of columns needed based on paragraphs, tabs, or commas in the text. When converting a table to text, Word inserts tabs to show where the column breaks are.

The AutoFormat feature provides several built-in table styles that include borders, background shading, and character formats. You can apply a table style by opening the Table menu and choosing Table AutoFormat. When you select a style in the dialog box, a preview area shows the effect of the style you select.

1. Open **Step5-12** from the data files. Save the document as **Scores** followed by your initials.

2. Select the entire document. (*Hint:* Press **Ctrl + A.**)

3. Open the **Table** menu and choose **Convert**. In the submenu, select **Text to Table**. The dialog box shown in Figure 5-13 is displayed.

FIGURE 5-13
Convert Text to Table dialog box

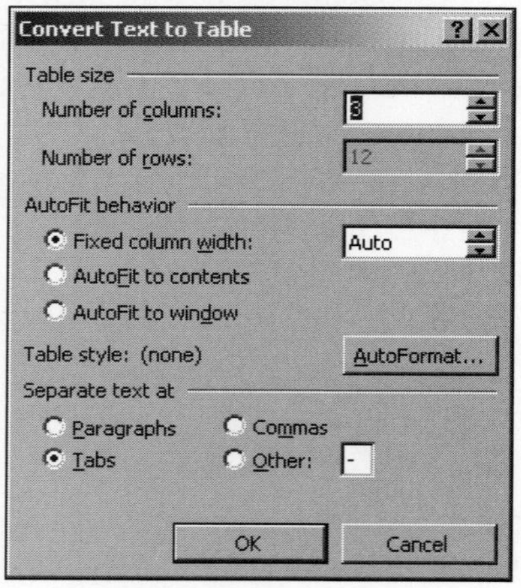

4. Under *Table size*, the number of columns should already be set to **3**. Under *AutoFit behavior*, select **AutoFit to contents**. Under *Separate text at*, make sure *Tabs* is selected. Click **OK**. Click anywhere in the window to deselect so you can see the revised table.

5. Position the insertion point in the table, then open the **Table** menu and click **Table AutoFormat**. The dialog box shown in Figure 5-14 is displayed.

FIGURE 5-14
Table AutoFormat dialog box

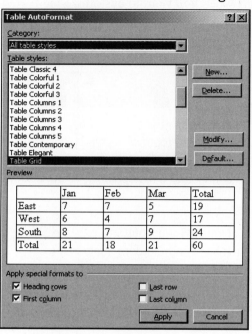

Speech Recognition

If your computer has speech recognition capability, enable the Command mode. With the insertion point positioned within the table, say the commands to autoformat the table and position the table horizontally.

6. Select **Table Colorful 2** in the *Table styles* list. Notice the *Preview* box shows approximately how your table will be formatted. Click **Apply**.

7. With the insertion point still positioned in the table, center the table horizontally on the page by selecting the entire table and clicking the **Center** button on the Standard toolbar.

8. Save the changes and close the document.

Summary

In this lesson, you learned:

- The table feature in Word enables you to organize and arrange text and numbers easily.

- If you need to change the organization of information after you create a table and enter data, you can remove rows and columns.

- The AutoFit feature automatically adjusts the width of a column based on the contents of the cells in a column.

- Format fonts and text alignment in table cells the same way you apply those formats in other Word documents.

- The Draw Table tool and the Eraser tool are especially useful when you need to create a complex table. You can draw the table boundaries with the Draw Table tool much like you would draw a table on a sheet of paper. You can use the Eraser tool to remove cell boundaries.

- Borders and shading greatly enhance the appearance of a table and often make the table easier to read.

- Word will convert text to a table or a table to text.

- The AutoFormat feature automatically adds borders and shading to your table.

VOCABULARY REVIEW

Define the following terms:

Cell
Gridlines

Merging cells

Splitting cells

LESSON 5 REVIEW QUESTIONS

TRUE/FALSE

Circle T if the statement is true or F if the statement is false.

T F 1. Table rows go across a page, and columns go down a page.

T F 2. You can choose to hide or display a table's gridlines.

T F 3. When you remove the boundary between two cells, you are splitting the cells.

T F 4. The AutoAdjust command automatically adjusts all column widths in a table.

T F 5. Word can create a table from text in which data is separated by paragraph marks, tabs, or commas.

FILL IN THE BLANK

Complete the following sentences by writing the correct word or words in the blanks provided.

1. A table consists of rows and columns of _____ to which you add text or graphics.

2. If you wanted to add a new row in the middle of a table beneath the row in which your insertion point is located, you would choose the _____ menu, click Insert, and then select Row Below.

3. Converting one cell into multiple cells is called _____ cells.

4. To create a complex table, use the _____ tool to position gridlines just where you want them.

5. The _____ feature automatically adds borders and shading to a table.

LESSON 5 PROJECTS

PROJECT 5-1

1. Open **Project5-1** from the data files. Save the document as **Population** followed by your initials.

2. Position the insertion point in the last blank line of the document and use the **Insert Table** button to create a grid for a 6 row by 3 column table.

3. Complete the table by entering the data shown in Figure 5-15:

FIGURE 5-15
Data for Project 5-1 table

	1990	2000
18 – 24	30,388	28,513
25 – 34	52,697	44,248
45 – 54	27,157	40,347
55 – 64	23,864	25,890
65+	33,640	39,048

4. You realize you left out the data for the 35–44 age group. Insert a row in the proper location and key the following data: **35–44   42,802   50,938**

5. It would be helpful to see the percent change in population. Add a column to the right of the *2000* column and key the column heading **% Change** in the first row. Insert the following information in the cells of the new column:

   –6.2
   –16.0
   19.0
   48.6
   8.5
   16.0

6. Insert a new row above the first row of the table and merge all cells in it. Key the table title **Population by Age**. Center and boldface the first two rows of the table.

7. Use AutoFit to adjust column widths, then center the table in the page.

8. The data in the *% Change* column would look better if the decimal points were aligned. Right-align the numbers (but not the column head) in this column.

9. Remove all the borders in the table, then shade alternate rows of the data beginning with the *18–24* row.

10. Save your changes and close the document.

PROJECT 5-2

1. Open **Project5-2** from the data files. Save the document as **Orders** followed by your initials.

2. Use the Draw Table tool to edit the table as shown in Figure 5-16.

FIGURE 5-16
Revisions for table in Project 5-2

Customer							
		Item	Color	Size	Qty	Price	Total
Clothing		Lakeside Hat					
		Lakeside T-Shirt					
		Lakeside Sweatshirt					
Goodies		Red Hot Jam					
		Navel Oranges					
		Lakeside Crunch					
						Total	

3. Follow the steps below to edit the new table cells so they will look like the cells illustrated in Figure 5-17:
   A. Position the insertion point in the large empty cell just to the right of the Customer cell. Split this cell, using settings of 1 column and 4 rows.
   B. In the four new rows, key **Name**, **Address**, **City**, and **Phone**.
   C. Split the next large empty cell into 4 rows (and 1 column). Customers will write their names and addresses in these rows.

FIGURE 5-17
Revisions for new table cells in Project 5-2

Create four new rows and add the text shown here

Customer¤	Name¤	¤	¤
	Address¤	¤	¤
	City¤	¤	¤
	Phone¤	¤	¤

4. Center all text vertically in the table cells using the Align Center Left option.

5. Format the table using features you have learned in this lesson. You can remove or modify borders, add shading to emphasize portions of the form, and use other text formatting features such as bold, italic, and alignment to make the form easier to read.

6. Save your changes and close the document.

PROJECT 5-3

1. Open **Project5-3** from the data files. Save the document as **Hurricanes** followed by your initials. You have compiled the information in this document while doing research on hurricanes, and you decide you could format the information more clearly and attractively if you converted it to a table.

2. Select only the tabbed data (not the blank line or the source line) and convert the text to a table. Accept the suggested number of columns, select AutoFit to contents, and separate the text at tabs.

3. AutoFormat the table using the **Table Web3** format.

4. Insert a new row at the top of the table and merge all cells in it. Key the title **Costliest U.S. Hurricanes of the 20th Century**, and then press **Enter** and key **(In Billions)**. Center and boldface the first two rows of the table.

5. Center the data in the *Category* column, and right-align the data in the *Damage* column.

6. You keyed the wrong year for Hurricane Andrew. Change the year for Andrew to **1992**.

7. You decide the first ten entries in the table give enough information about the destructive power of hurricanes. Delete the last two rows in the table.

8. Center the table horizontally.

9. Save your changes. Print and close the document.

WEB PROJECT

CANS

If you completed Project 5-1, you read a brief description of a change in demographics. What are demographics, exactly? Using a Web search tool such as Ask Jeeves, find a definition of demographics and key it in Word. Then follow one or more links to find demographic data about your county or city. (The City and County Data Book at the University of Virginia is especially easy to use.) See if you can find out what percent of the population in your city is your age. You may also explore other interesting facts about your city or county such as number of births, how many children are in school, and so on. Below your definition of demographics, summarize in a table the demographic facts you have obtained about your city or county.

TEAMWORK PROJECT

SCANS

If you completed Project 5-3, you learned how costly hurricanes can be in terms of property damage. The data shown in the Hurricanes table was compiled by the National Oceanic and Atmospheric Administration and, at the time of this writing, is current only through 1996. With a partner, see if you can update the table with more recent data.

1. Write down the years from 1997 to the last complete hurricane season (hurricane season begins in June and ends in November, so if you are working on this project before the end of November, do not include the current year in your list).

2. Split the years with your partner so that you each have half of them to research.

3. Using Web search tools or other research tools, try to locate a summary of hurricane damage for each year.

4. If any of the years you research total more dollar damage than the hurricanes shown in the Hurricanes table, insert new rows to add the data you have found.

CRITICAL THINKING

SCANS

The owner of the stable where you ride horses has been complaining about the comings and goings of her part-time staff and unpaid helpers (of whom you are one). She'd like a way to keep track of names, phone numbers, what days and hours each worker is scheduled, and hourly salary (if any). Use what you have learned in this lesson to create a table that will help the stable owner organize the information about her staff. Key several fictitious entries in the table (including yourself) to test your solution.

DESKTOP PUBLISHING

OBJECTIVES

Upon completion of this lesson, you should be able to:

- Format text in columns.
- Insert clip art and other graphics.
- Resize and position graphics.
- Format borders and shading.
- Create WordArt Objects.
- Use drawing tools.
- Insert and format text boxes.
- Use AutoShapes to Create Objects.

⏱ **Estimated Time: 1 hour**

VOCABULARY

Banner

Clip art

Crop

Desktop publishing

Drawing canvas

Drawing objects

Graphics

Hard column break

Sizing handles

Text box

Thumbnails

Publishing a professional-looking newsletter or report could only be accomplished with the combined efforts of several people. Artists created the graphics and artwork, typesetters created the text, and designers completed the page layouts and prepared the pages of type for the printer. The process was often quite expensive. Today, with personal computers and inexpensive software, you can prepare attractive, professional-looking documents on your desktop computer. *Desktop publishing* is the process of using a computer to combine text and graphics to create an attractive document.

Word provides a number of features to make documents more attractive. You can format text in columns, import pictures, draw your own pictures, add borders and shading, and use WordArt to shape and rotate text.

Format Text in Columns

One common application for desktop publishing is newsletters. Newsletter text is often formatted in multiple columns. The text flows down one column and begins again in the next column if necessary. Usually, the heading (or title of the newsletter) is formatted as a single-column *banner* where the heading spreads the full width across the multiple newsletter-style columns.

It is easy to apply columns in Word, and there are a few different ways to do so. When you apply the column format, the columns are usually balanced so that the column lengths are approximately equal. There may be occasions, however, when you want to control where columns break. To adjust where a column ends, you can insert a *hard column break*.

1. If necessary launch Word. Open **Step6-1** from the data files and save the document as **Newsletter** followed by your initials. If necessary, click **Show/Hide ¶** to display nonprinting characters.

2. Select the paragraph of text under the heading *PROTECTION FROM THE SUN*. Do not include the blank paragraph marks above or below the text in the selection.

3. Click the **Columns** button on the Standard toolbar. A grid displaying four columns appears.

4. Drag across the grid to select two columns. See Figure 6-1. When you release the mouse button, the selected text is formatted in two columns of equal width.

FIGURE 6-1
Columns grid

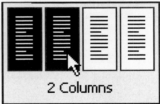

5. Select the three paragraphs of text under the heading *THE HEALTH RISKS OF LIVING ALONE*. Click the **Columns** button and select three columns in the grid, then release. The selected text is formatted in three columns of equal width.

6. Select the paragraph of text below the heading *HIKING AND BIKING ADVENTURES*.

7. Open the **Format** menu and choose **Columns**. The dialog box shown in Figure 6-2 is displayed.

FIGURE 6-2
Columns dialog box

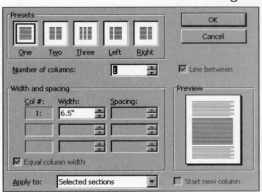

8. Select **Right** under *Presets* and turn on the option **Line between**. Word automatically adjusts the column widths under *Width and spacing* and updates the *Preview*.

9. Click **OK**. The text is formatted in two columns of unequal width, with a vertical line between the columns.

10. Position the insertion point in front of the third paragraph in *THE HEALTH RISKS OF LIVING ALONE*. The paragraph begins *Ironically,...* Open the **Insert** menu, choose **Break**, and then select **Column break** and click **OK**.

11. Position the insertion point in front of the second paragraph in the same article that begins *Studies show that...* Insert a column break.

12. Save the changes and leave the document open for the next Step-by-Step.

Insert a Graphic

You can use graphics to illustrate an idea presented in the document, to enhance the appearance of the document, or to make the document more functional. *Graphics* are items other than text and can include photos, borders, clip art, and drawing objects. *Clip art* is artwork that is ready to insert in a document. *Drawing objects* are Word tools that enable you to create your own artwork.

Speech Recognition

If your computer has speech recognition capability, enable the Command mode. With the text selected, say the commands to open the Format Columns dialog box and apply the column formats.

Insert Clip Art

Word has numerous clip art images and photos that are stored in the Office Collections folder. You can also access clip art that you have saved (in My Collections folder). If you have an Internet connection open, you can search for clip art at the Microsoft Web site. Search results are displayed as *thumbnails*, which are miniature representations of a picture, in the task pane.

STEP-BY-STEP 6.2

1. Position the insertion point in front of the paragraph in the second article that begins *Doctors now believe....*

2. Open the **Insert** menu, choose **Picture**, and then select **Clip Art** from the submenu. The Insert Clip Art task pane is displayed. Compare your screen to Figure 6-3. Do not be concerned if your screen does not match exactly.

3. Select the text in the *Search text* text box and key **doctor**. If there is no text to be selected, just position the insertion point within the box.

Computer Concepts

You may find it easier to work with the graphics in a document by reducing the view of the document. For example, you can change the zoom of the document view to 75%.

FIGURE 6-3
Insert Clip Art task pane

4. Specify where Word should search for clip art. Under *Other Search Options*, click the down arrow in the *Search in* list box. Double-click the option **Everywhere**. This toggles the selection of the option on or off. The option is selected when a checkmark is displayed in the box to the left of the option name. See Figure 6-4.

FIGURE 6-4
Options for specifying where to search for clip art

Computer Concepts

If there is a plus sign in front of the Everywhere option, click the plus sign to expand the list and display the option where clip art can be found. If there is a minus sign in front of the Everywhere option, as shown in Figure 6-4, the list of options is already expanded.

5. Click the Search button in the task pane. The results should display at least one clip art image as a thumbnail. See Figure 6-5.

FIGURE 6-5
Clip Art matching the search word *doctor*

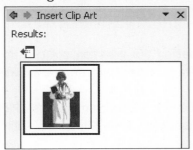

6. Click the clip shown in Figure 6-5 (or any clip of a doctor) to insert the image in the document at the location of the insertion point.

Computer Concepts

If you click the down arrow on the right side of the clipart thumbnail, a shortcut menu will display and provide options for copying and pasting, deleting the clip from the Clip Organizer, copying the clip to a Collection folder, and so on.

Did You Know?

You can leave the Insert Clip Art task pane open as you work so you can quickly access additional Clip Art images.

7. Close the task pane.

Hot Tip

To restore the settings from the previous search, click Restore.

8. Save the changes and leave the document open for the next Step-by-Step.

Insert a Picture from a File

You can also insert photos and clip art that are stored in other folders. This is called importing a picture. To insert a picture from a graphics file, position the insertion point where you want the picture inserted, open the Insert menu, choose Picture, select From File in the submenu. When the Insert Picture dialog box opens, browse to locate and select the graphics file.

STEP-BY-STEP ▷ 6.3

1. Position the insertion point in front of the paragraph beginning *Are you looking....*

2. Open the **Insert** menu, choose **Picture**, and then select **From File** in the submenu. The Insert Picture dialog box is displayed.

3. Locate the Lesson 6 data files in the *Look in* box. Select the file **Biking** and click **Insert**. The picture is inserted at the location of the insertion point, and the document wraps to a second page.

4. Save the changes and leave the document open for the next Step-by-Step.

Speech Recognition

If your computer has speech recognition capability, enable the Command mode and say the commands to insert the picture from a file. You can dictate all the commands necessary to open the dialog box, locate the file, and insert the file in the document.

Resize and Position Graphics

Once you have inserted a graphic or picture in a document, there are many ways to manipulate the picture. To work with a graphic, you must click on it to select it. You will know it is selected when you see eight small squares on the border of the graphic. These squares are called *sizing handles*. When a graphic is selected, you can cut, copy, paste, delete, and move it just as you would text.

Change the Size of a Graphic

The easiest way to change the size of a graphic is to drag one of the sizing handles. As you drag the sizing handle, you can see the effects of the change on your screen. If you want to change the size to exact measurements, you need to use the Format Picture command.

When you scale a graphic proportionally, you change all dimensions of the graphic (height and width) approximately equally. You can also scale a graphic just vertically or just horizontally, which distorts the image.

A text wrapping format must be applied to the graphic before you can reposition it in your document. You can then move the graphic by dragging it to a new location.

STEP-BY-STEP ▷ 6.4

1. If necessary, turn on the display of the Ruler. (*Hint:* Open the **View** menu, and choose **Ruler**.)

2. Click on the clip art image of the doctor. When the picture is selected, the Picture toolbar shown in Figure 6-6 is displayed. Eight sizing handles appear on the outside border of the image. See Figure 6-7.

FIGURE 6-6
Picture toolbar

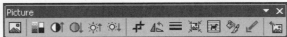

FIGURE 6-7
Picture with sizing handles

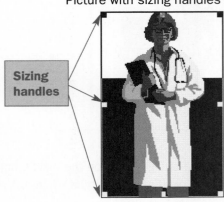

3. Point to the lower right corner of the image. When the pointer changes to a two-headed arrow, drag the corner sizing handle toward the center of the picture. When the picture is approximately 1 ¼ inches high and 1 ¼ inches wide, release the mouse. Use the rulers at the top and left edges of the document to judge the picture size.

4. Save the changes and leave the document open for the next Step-by-Step.

Crop a Graphic

When you **crop** a graphic, you cut off portions of the graphic that you do not want to show. You might want to crop extra white space around an image or actually remove part of the image altogether.

STEP-BY-STEP ▷ 6.5

1. Click the biking clip art picture. The nonprinting border around the picture is displayed. Notice that there is excess white space on the right side and bottom of the picture.

2. Click the **Crop** button on the Picture toolbar. The pointer changes to a cropping box.

Hot Tip

If the Picture toolbar is not displayed, open the **View** menu and choose **Toolbars**, then select **Picture**.

3. Position the cropping box on the sizing handle on the middle right of the picture. Then drag the sizing handle to the left to trim the white space. See Figure 6-8. When you release the mouse button, the portion of the picture you cropped is now gone.

FIGURE 6-8
Cropping a picture

5. Click the **Crop** button to turn off the cropping feature.

6. Resize the picture so it is approximately 1 inch high and 1 inch wide. (*Hint:* Be sure to drag a corner handle so you will resize the image proportionately.)

7. Save the changes and leave the document open for the next Step-by-Step.

4. Point to the sizing handle on the middle bottom of the picture and crop the white space at the bottom of the picture.

Wrap Text Around a Graphic

By default, Word inserts graphics in the line of text. This means that the graphic is positioned directly in the text at the insertion point. Instead of being in the line of text, however, you can format the text in the document to wrap around the graphic. By changing the wrapping style, you can drag and drop the graphic anywhere within the printable area of the page.

To create a tighter wrap around the graphic, you can edit the wrap points for the graphic. The wrap points identify the edge of the graphic. You can drag these wrap points to reposition them.

STEP-BY-STEP ⟹ 6.6

1. If necessary, click on the biking picture to select it.

2. Click the **Text Wrapping** button on the Picture toolbar. A drop-down list of wrapping options appears. Figure 6-9 provides a description of each of the options displayed in the drop-down list.

FIGURE 6-9
Text wrapping options

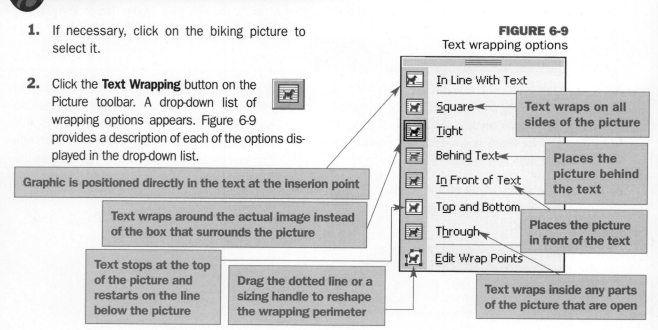

3. Select the **Square** option. The text now wraps along the right side and bottom of the picture.

 Computer Concepts

If the Picture toolbar is not displayed, make sure the picture is selected.

4. With the biking picture still selected, click the **Text Wrapping** button and then click **Edit Wrap Points**.

5. Point to the sizing handle on the bottom right of the picture and drag the handle to the left to create a diagonal line as shown in Figure 6-10. When you release the mouse button, the text shifts to the left along the diagonal line.

FIGURE 6-10
Editing the Wrap point
of a picture

6. Point to the center of the picture. When the pointer changes to a four-headed arrow, drag the picture to the left so it aligns with the left margin.

 Computer Concepts

You cannot drag and drop a picture until after you have applied a text wrapping style.

7. Select the doctor picture, click the Text Wrapping button, and select the Tight option. The text wraps tightly around the actual image instead of the rectangle boundary of the image. The way the text wraps will depend on the clip art image you selected.

8. Drag the picture to the right side of the article.

9. Save the changes and leave the document open for the next Step-by-Step.

Format Borders and Shading

Borders and shading can help enhance the appearance of a document. Word offers many options for line styles, line weights, colors, and shading effects. To access these borders and shading features, you can open the Format menu and choose Borders and Shading to display the Borders and Shading dialog box. Or, you can quickly access most of the features by displaying the Borders and Shading toolbar. To display the toolbar, right click on any toolbar on your screen and choose Tables and Borders in the shortcut menu. A checkmark before the toolbar name indicates that the toolbar is already displayed. Clicking on the toolbar name will then turn off the shortcut menu and display or remove the toolbar you selected.

1. Position the insertion point in the blank para-graph above the first line of text *PROTECTION FROM THE SUN.*

2. Right-click on any toolbar and choose **Tables and Borders** in the shortcut menu to display the Tables and Borders toolbar. Click the down arrow on the **Line Weight** button on the Tables and Borders toolbar and select **3 pt**.

3. Click the down arrow on the Border but-ton (the ScreenTip for this button proba-bly says Outside Border) just to the left of the Shading Color button. Select **Top Border**.

4. Position the insertion point in the blank paragraph at the end of the document. Click the down arrow alongside the **Border** button and select **Bottom Border**.

5. Position the insertion point in the first heading *PROTECTION FROM THE SUN.*

6. Click the down arrow next to the **Shading Color** button on the Table and Borders toolbar and select the color **Tan**. (*Hint:* Point to a color in the color pallette and wait for the ScreenTip to display the name of the color.) A tan shade format is applied to the entire paragraph.

Speech Recognition

If your computer has speech recognition capability, enable the Command mode. With the inser-tion point positioned correctly, say the commands to access the toolbar buttons and select the shading color.

7. Position the insertion point in the second heading *THE HEALTH RISKS OF LIVING ALONE,* then click the **Shading Color** button. (Note that the color Tan is already selected and is showing on the **Shading Color** button.)

8. Repeat the format for the third heading *HIK-ING AND BIKING ADVENTURES.*

9. Close the Table and Borders toolbar by click-ing the **Close** button in the top right corner.

10. Save the changes and leave the document open for the next Step-by-Step.

Create WordArt Objects

WordArt is a feature that enables you transform text into a graphic. You can create your own styles or you can choose from several predefined styles in the WordArt Gallery. When you create a WordArt object, the WordArt toolbar is displayed.

STEP-BY-STEP ▷ 6.8

1. Position the insertion point at the beginning of the document—at the first paragraph mark.

2. Click the **Drawing** button on the Standard toolbar to display the Drawing toolbar. The Drawing toolbar is automatically docked at the bottom of your Word document window—above the Status bar.

3. Click the **Insert WordArt** button on the Drawing toolbar. The dialog box shown in Figure 6-11 is displayed.

4. Select the fourth style in the second row, then click **OK**. The Edit WordArt Text dialog box shown in Figure 6-12 is opened.

FIGURE 6-11
WordArt Gallery dialog box

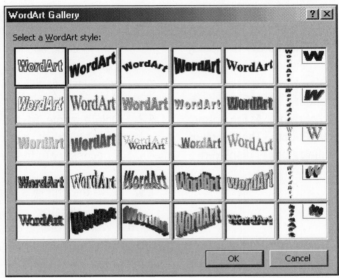

FIGURE 6-12
Edit WordArt Text dialog box

5. Key **Health News** and click **OK**. Word formats the text as a WordArt object and positions the object in your document.

6. Click on the object to select it. Then, point to the sizing handle in the lower right corner and drag it to the right edge of the document. The WordArt object will expand to the width of the document, leaving a one inch margin on the right.

7. With the object still selected, point to the object and right-click. Choose **Format WordArt** from the shortcut menu. If necessary, click the **Color and Lines** tab to display the dialog box shown in Figure 6-13.

8. In the *Color* list box under *Fill*, click the down arrow to display a grid of colors. At the bottom of the grid, select **Fill Effects**. The **Gradient** tab in the Fill Effects dialog box is displayed.

9. For *Color 1*, select **Orange**. For *Color 2*, select **Tan**. Under *Shading styles*, select **Diagonal up**. Click **OK**. The Fill Effects dialog box closes, and the Format WordArt dialog box is still open.

10. In the *Color* list box under *Line*, select **Orange**. Click **OK**. The border lines and the fill colors for the WordArt object are formatted with the new colors.

11. With the WordArt object selected, click the WordArt Shape button on the WordArt toolbar. Choose a different shape. Notice that the shape changes but the text, fill color, and line colors remain unchanged. Explore other shapes and choose one that is appropriate for this newsletter.

12. Delete some of the blank lines under the WordArt object, and make other adjustments if necessary to fit the document on one page.

13. Save the changes and close the document.

FIGURE 6-13
Format WordArt dialog box

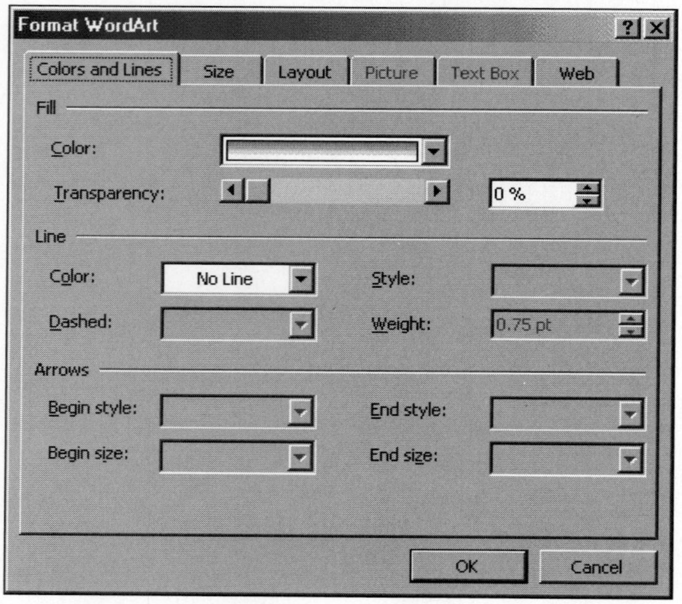

Use Drawing Tools

Sometimes you may need to create your own artwork. For example, you may need to illustrate a map with directions. You can use the Drawing toolbar in Word to create drawing objects. When you insert a drawing object in Word, a ***drawing canvas*** displays. The drawing canvas helps you arrange your drawing and keep parts of your drawing together, while also providing a frame-like boundary between your drawing and the rest of the document.

Hot Tip

If you don't want the drawing canvas to display, press Esc after you select a drawing tool but before you begin drawing.

Did You Know?

You can format a background or border for the drawing canvas. You can also add a picture by choosing the floating wrapping style and then dragging the picture onto the drawing canvas.

STEP-BY-STEP ▷ 6.9

1. Open a new document and, if necessary, display the Drawing toolbar.

2. Click the **Line** button on the Drawing toolbar. The pointer changes to a crosshair and the drawing canvas is displayed. Notice, too, that the Drawing Canvas toolbar is displayed. These toolbar buttons enable you to adjust the canvas size and fit the drawing within the drawing canvas. See Figure 6-14.

FIGURE 6-14
Drawing Canvas and Drawing Canvas toolbar

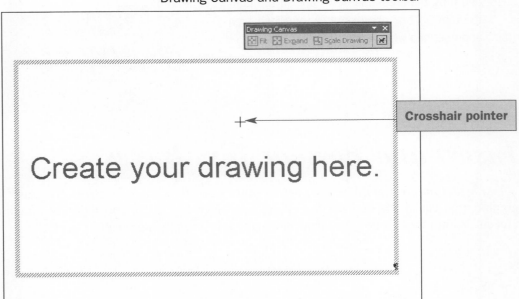

3. Point to the top left corner of the drawing canvas and drag the crosshair across the width of the canvas. Do not release the mouse button until the line is straight and even and the length you want.

4. Click the **Line** button again and draw a second line below the first one.

5. With the second line still selected, (*Hint:* The sizing handles on each end of the line indicate that the line is selected.) click the **Line Style** button on the Drawing toolbar and select **3 pt** (the 3 pt single line, not the double line). The weight of the selected line is now heavier.

6. With the line still selected, click the down arrow next to the **Line Color** button on the Drawing toolbar. Select **Green**. The color of the selected line changes.

7. Click the **Rectangle** button on the Drawing toolbar. Position the crosshair in the middle of the screen and drag the crosshair down and to the right to create a box approximately one inch high and one inch wide.

8. With the rectangle object still selected, click the down arrow to the right of the **Fill Color** button on the Drawing toolbar and select **Blue**. The rectangle is filled with the blue color. You do not need to save this document, but leave it open for the next Step-by-Step.

Hot Tip

If the drawing canvas does not display, open the **Tools** menu, choose **Options**, select the **General** tab, and make sure there is a checkmark for the option **Automatically create drawing canvas when inserting AutoShapes**.

Computer Concepts

An object must be selected before you can choose an option from the Drawing toolbar. If the format you want to apply is dimmed, make sure the object you want to format is selected.

Hot Tip

To create a perfect square, hold down Shift as you drag the crosshair, or just click once in the document without dragging.

Insert and Format Text Boxes

A ***text box*** is a graphic that enables you to add text to your artwork. Because the text box is a graphic, you can resize and position it the same way you resize and reposition pictures and drawing objects. Within the text box, you can change the font and the alignment of the text.

STEP-BY-STEP 6.10

1. If necessary, display the Ruler. Click the **Text Box** button on the Drawing toolbar.

2. Point anywhere on the screen and drag the crosshair to create a box approximately 1 inch wide and 1 inch high. When you release the mouse button, the insertion point will be inside the text box and the Text Box floating toolbar will appear. See Figure 6-15.

FIGURE 6-15
Text Box toolbar

 Did You Know?

After you have clicked the Text Box button, if you just point to a single spot in your document and click, a text box will appear—the default size is 1 inch wide and 1 inch high. This is also true for inserting rectangles and circles, but remember that you cannot insert text in these objects without adding a text box inside of them.

3. Key your name inside the box. Select your name and change the font size and color (in the same manner that you would change any other text within the document).

4. If the box is too small to display all the text, drag a sizing handle on either the corner or side to make the box bigger. If the box is too high or too wide, drag a sizing handle to eliminate the excess white space.

5. Click inside the text box. Click the **Center** button on the Formatting toolbar to center the text.

6. If necessary, click on the text box to select it. Then point to a border (not the sizing handle) of the text box. When you see a four-headed arrow, drag the text box to position it under the second line you drew.

 Computer Concepts

When you click inside a text box, the text box displays a cross-hatched border. If you click directly on the text box border, the cross-hatched design will change to dots indicating that the text box is selected.

7. With the text box selected, click the down arrow next to the **Line Color** button on the Drawing toolbar. Select **No Line** in the submenu. Click outside the text box. The border is no longer visible.

8. Draw a tall, narrow text box (approximately 2 inches high and ½ inch wide).

9. Click the **Change Text Direction** button on the Text Box toolbar two times.

10. Key today's date.

11. You do not need to save the document, but leave it open for the next Step-by-Step.

 Hot Tip

To delete a text box, click the hatched border until it turns into a border of small dots. Then press **Delete**.

Use AutoShapes to Create Objects

The AutoShape feature in Word enables you to create a variety of predesigned drawing objects. Stars, arrows, shapes, and callouts are among the AutoShape designs from which you can choose.

Create an AutoShape

You create an AutoShape the same way you create other drawing objects. Select the AutoShape that you want to draw. The pointer changes to a crosshair which you drag to the desired size of the AutoShape. When you create a callout, the AutoShape is automatically formatted as a text box so you can add text inside the object. You can resize and reposition AutoShapes in the same way you change the size and position of pictures and drawing objects.

STEP-BY-STEP ⬠ 6.11

1. Click the **AutoShapes** button on the Drawing toolbar. Select **Block Arrows** in the submenu, then select the first arrow option (*Right Arrow*).

   AutoShapes ▾

2. Position the crosshair anywhere on the screen and drag it up and to the right to create the AutoShape object.

3. Point to the **AutoShape** arrow and right-click. Select **Add text** in the shortcut menu. An insertion point displays inside the AutoShape object.

4. Key the name of your school. Click the **Center** button on the Formatting toolbar to center the text.

5. If the *AutoShape* arrow is too small to display all of the text, drag a sizing handle on the corner or side of the AutoShape to make the arrow bigger. If the *AutoShape* arrow is too big, drag a sizing handle to eliminate the excess white space.

6. With the *AutoShape* arrow still selected, fill the object with any color you choose.

7. With the arrow still selected, position it in a different location in the document.

8. Click on the **AutoShapes** button and select **Callouts** in the submenu. Select the second option in the second row (Line Callout 2).

9. Position the crosshair anywhere in the document where there is space to create the callout. Drag to create the desired size for your callout object.

10. Key your address inside the callout box.

11. If the callout box is too small to display all of the text, drag a sizing handle to make the box bigger. If the callout box is too high or too wide, drag a sizing handle to eliminate the excess white space. You do not need to save this document, but leave it open for the next Step-by-Step.

Use Help to Learn How to Change an AutoShape

You decide you want the AutoShape arrow you drew to point in the opposite direction. Word makes it easy to change the AutoShape without creating a new AutoShape.

126

S TEP-BY-STEP ▷ 6.12

1. If necessary, display the Office Assistant by opening the Help menu and choose **Show the Office Assistant**.

2. Click on the Office Assistant, key **autoshape**, and press **Enter**.

3. Click on **Change a shape to another shape**.

4. Read the information at the right. Leave the Help screen open so you can refer to it if needed as you work.

5. Change the **AutoShape** arrow to a left-pointing arrow. Close the Help screen when you are done changing the AutoShape.

6. You do not need to save this document, but leave it open for the next Step-by-Step.

Resize the Drawing Canvas

The drawing canvas is especially helpful if your drawing contains several shapes because it keeps your shapes together as one object. Now you will practice resizing the drawing canvas and using the drawing canvas to scale your drawing.

S TEP-BY-STEP ▷ 6.13

1. If necessary, click in the center of the Drawing Canvas to display the toolbar shown in Figure 6-16. (*Hint:* If the toolbar does not display, right-click in the center of the Drawing Canvas and choose Show Drawing Canvas Toolbar in the shortcut menu.)

FIGURE 6-16
Drawing Canvas toolbar

2. Drag one of the sizing handles to resize the drawing canvas. For example, drag a marker inward to eliminate excess white space around the drawing objects.

3. Click the **Fit** button on the Drawing Canvas toolbar. The boundary area of the drawing canvas automatically adjusts to fit the drawing objects and all excess space is eliminated.

4. Click the **Expand** button. The drawing canvas is enlarged in increments each time you click the expand button.

5. Click the **Scale Drawing** button. The boundary of the drawing canvas changes to display eight sizing handles. Drag a corner handle to resize the drawing canvas just as you would resize a drawing object or a picture. The drawing objects are resized as a unit.

6. Click the **Text Wrapping** button on the Drawing Canvas toolbar and select the **Square** option. The text wrapping format is applied to the canvas just as it is applied to any drawing object. You can reposition the drawing canvas, and all the objects will move as a unit.

7. Close the document without saving the changes.

Summary

In this lesson, you learned:

- Text can be arranged in a variety of multicolumn formats, all within the same document.

- Clip art and other pictures help to enhance the appearance and effectiveness of a document.

- When you format a picture for text wrapping, you can position the graphic anywhere on the page by dragging it to a new position.

- Borders and shading are also important tools for desktop publishing. You can choose from a variety of options for line styles, colors, and shading effects.

- WordArt enables you to convert text to a graphic. WordArt objects can be positioned and resized the same as pictures.

- You can create your own artwork using the drawing tools.

- Text boxes enable you to add text to your artwork. The text box can be resized and positioned the same as drawing objects. You can also format the text within the box.

- AutoShapes and callout designs help you make a professional-looking document.

- The drawing canvas helps you arrange, position, and resize your drawing objects. You can format and move the drawing canvas just as you format other objects.

VOCABULARY REVIEW

Define the following terms:

Banner	Drawing canvas	Sizing handles
Clip art	Drawing objects	Text box
Crop	Graphics	Thumbnails
Desktop publishing	Hard column break	

LESSON 6 REVIEW QUESTIONS

TRUE/FALSE

Circle T if the statement is true or F if the statement is false.

T F 1. When you create a document with columns, you can format the document's heading text in a single-column banner.

T F 2. Drawing objects are predrawn artwork ready to insert in a document.

T F 3. When you size a graphic proportionally, you change all the dimensions approximately equally.

T F 4. You will find drawing tools on the Formatting toolbar.

T F 5. To insert an AutoShape, select AutoShape on the Tools menu.

FILL IN THE BLANK

Complete the following sentences by writing the correct word or words in the blanks provided.

1. The process of using a computer to combine text and graphics is called _____ .

2. _____ are small squares on the border of a graphic that let you know it is selected.

3. When you _____ a graphic, you remove a part of the graphic that you don't want to show.

4. You can select a text wrapping option from the _____ toolbar.

5. The _____ helps you arrange and size your drawing objects.

LESSON 6 PROJECTS

PROJECT 6-1

1. Open **Project6-1** from the data files. Save the document as **Garden News** followed by your initials.

2. Select the first two lines in the document. Apply a green shading to the selected headings. If necessary, select the text and change the font color to white. Note that if you choose a dark color, Word will automatically change the font color so it will display against the dark shading.

3. Position the insertion point in the *Fall Gardening* heading. Insert a 2 ¼-point border below the heading. Use the **Repeat** command to insert borders below the other two headings.

4. Position the insertion point at the beginning of the second paragraph below the *Fall Gardening* heading. Insert a clip art picture that relates to autumn. Resize the picture proportionately so it is about 1.5 inches tall. Choose an appropriate text wrapping option. Adjust the position of the picture so that the top of the picture lines up with the first line of the second paragraph.

5. Select the text (but not the blank line above the text) that describes the Annual Tree Sale. Apply a yellow shading to the selected text.

6. Position the insertion point at the beginning of the second paragraph under the *Gardening Today Spotlight* heading and insert the picture file **flower** from your data files. Crop the white space on the right side of the picture. Resize the picture to approximately 1 ½ inches high and 1 inch wide.

7. Apply a square text wrapping option to the new picture. Move the picture to the right side of the page and position it so the top of the picture lines up with the first line of the second paragraph under the *Gardening Today Spotlight* heading.

8. Select the last paragraph in the document and apply the same green shading you used for the two headings at the top of the document. If necessary, change the font color to white.

9. Save your changes and close the document.

PROJECT 6-2

1. Open **Project6-2** from the Data Files. Save the document as **Creamery** followed by your initials.

2. Click to the left of the first word in the document. Then use the scroll bar to scroll down to locate the *2.00* price below the description of the *Mocha Delight* coffee. Hold down the **Shift** key and click to the right of the price to select everything in the document **except** the last paragraph and the blank line above it.

3. Format the selected text in two columns of equal width.

4. If the *THICK LIQUIDS* heading is at the bottom of the first column of text, insert a column break to move it (and any other text below it) to the next column.

5. The first column is now shorter than the second column. To fill up the empty space at the bottom of the first column, insert clip art relating to ice cream or create an appropriate drawing object in this space. Resize and position the graphic as necessary so it attractively fits in the space.

6. Create a WordArt title for the page using the words *The Creamery*. Position the WordArt graphic at the top of the page and center it horizontally. Apply the **Top and Bottom** text wrap option to force the column text to move below the graphic. Modify the WordArt graphic as desired to change color or other formatting.

7. Save your changes and close the document.

PROJECT 6-3

1. Open a new document. Save it as **Map** followed by your initials.

2. Use the **Line**, **Rectangle**, and **Fill Color** drawing tools to create the lines and box illustrated in Figure 6-17. The Rulers on the edges of the screen are displayed in the figure to help you judge the size and position of the objects.

FIGURE 6-17
Drawing objects for Project 6-3

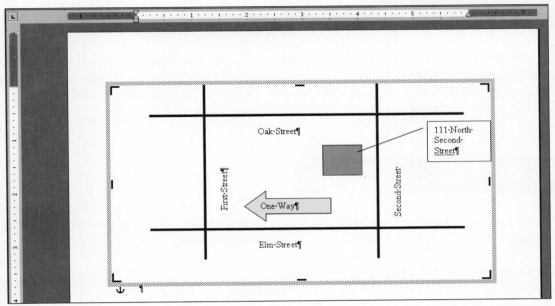

3. Fill the rectangle with the bright red color.

4. Create four text boxes for the street names:
   A. To create the First Street and Second Street text boxes, draw tall, narrow boxes. Then use the Text Direction button on the Text Box toolbar to change the direction of text in the text box.
   B. Remove the borders from the text boxes.

5. Use an AutoShape to create the **One Way** arrow in the map. Fill the AutoShape with the bright yellow color.

6. Create the callout that points out the exact address of the red rectangle.

7. Rescale the drawing object by resizing the drawing canvas so that the map fills the width of the page. Then apply the Square text wrapping format and position the map in the center of the page horizontally.

8. Save your changes and close the document.

WEB PROJECT

Your aunt is a keen gardener who has mentioned more than once a fascination with "black" tulips. Use an Internet search tool to locate retail gardening sites on the Web that specialize in tulip bulbs. Gather information about the very dark tulip bulbs they call black tulips. Using the tools you learned about in this lesson (such as columns, banner headings, WordArt, and graphic images), create a flyer to promote this unique tulip bulb.

TEAMWORK PROJECT

In this lesson, you have learned some desktop publishing basics. Put your knowledge into practice by designing a newsletter for your class or school. Follow these steps:

1. The class should divide into three or four groups.

2. Each group should brainstorm ideas for the layout of the newsletter, appropriate graphics, and what kinds of stories to use in the newsletter. Use features you have learned about in this lesson, such as borders, shading, columns, and WordArt, to make your newsletter design visually interesting and easy to read.

3. Each group should create a sample newsletter using its design. You need not write a number of real stories to fill up the spaces. Instead, write one paragraph of sample text and copy it as many times as necessary to show how text will appear in the newsletter.

4. As a class, compare the designs and discuss the strengths and weaknesses of each.

CRITICAL THINKING

You have created a drawing that contains a number of drawing objects. Although you have worked as carefully as you can, you cannot place some of the objects as precisely as you would like. Is there any way to move the objects in small increments without dragging them using the mouse? Is there any way to specify that your drawing object be positioned in a specific location? You would also like to align some of the objects precisely with one another. Is there any way to specify this kind of alignment for drawing objects?

Use the Help system in Word to find answers to these questions. Write a brief summary of what you learn.

CREATING WEB PAGES AND WEB DOCUMENTS

OBJECTIVES

Upon completion of this lesson, you should be able to:

- Use Web page templates.
- Edit and create hyperlinks.
- Change formats on a Web page.
- Preview a Web page.
- Work with frames pages.
- Use the Web Page Wizard.

🕑 **Estimated Time: 1.5 hours**

VOCABULARY

Frames page

HTML

Hyperlink

Template

Web site

Wizard

Using the Web features in Word, you can create Web pages that range from simple to sophisticated. A Web page should contain a good mix of text and graphics. The text should be brief and to the point. The graphics should communicate the Web page topic and grab the viewer's attention. Word makes it easy to format a document that will look just the way you want it to in a Web browser.

Use a Template to Create a Web Page

A *template* is a file that contains document, paragraph, and character formats for documents that you create frequently. The template saves all standard text and formatting choices so all you need to do is enter the variable text.

When you open a Web page template, you will discover that the template is really a Word table. The columns and rows help you organize the text and graphics on your Web page. You can then replace the sample text with your own text.

Although the Web page document looks like any other Word document, it is very different. When the document is saved, it will be saved in a format called *HTML*. HTML (an acronym that stands for Hypertext Markup Language) is a system for marking text so that it can be displayed on the World Wide Web.

Computer Concepts

Every Word document is based on a template. The default settings for the "blank" or new document margins and fonts are stored in this template. Depending on your Word installation, many types of document templates may be available to you.

1. If necessary, open the New Document task pane and choose **General Templates**. The Templates dialog box opens. Click the **Web Pages** tab and choose the **Column with Contents** template. Click **OK**. Word automatically changes to Web Layout View. Your screen should look like Figure 7-1. The text and graphics appear the way they would in a Web browser.

Computer Concepts

If column/table dividers show on your screen, they will not display in the Web browser. If you have the Show/Hide ¶ button toggled on, nonprinting characters will appear on your screen but they will not print, and they will not display in a Web browser.

FIGURE 7-1
The Column with Contents Web page template

·Main·Heading·Goes·Here¤

ʼSection·1¶
Part·1¶
Part·2¶
Part·3¶
Part·4¶

Section·2¶
Part·1¶
Part·2¶
Part·3¶

Section·3¶
Part·1¶
Part·2¶
Part·3¶
Part·4¶
¶

Section·1·Heading·Goes·Here¶
Select·text·you·would·like·to·replace·and·type·over·it.·Use·styles·such·as·Heading·1-3·and·Normal·in·the·Style·control·on·the·Formatting·toolbar.¶
¶
The·quick·brown·fox·jumps·over·the·lazy·dog.··The·quick·brown·fox·jumps·over·the·lazy·dog.··The·quick·brown·fox·jumps·over·the·lazy·dog.··The·quick·brown·fox·jumps·over·the·lazy·dog.··The·quick·brown·fox·jumps·over·the·lazy·dog.¶

Section·2·Heading·Goes·Here¶
The·quick·brown·fox·jumps·over·the·lazy·dog.··The·quick·brown·fox·jumps·over·the·lazy·dog.··The·quick·brown·fox·jumps·over·the·lazy·dog.··The·quick·brown·fox·jumps·over·the·lazy·dog.··The·quick·brown·fox·jumps·over·the·lazy·dog.¶
¶
The·quick·brown·fox·jumps·over·the·lazy·dog.··The·quick·brown·fox·jumps·over·the·lazy·dog.··The·quick·brown·fox·jumps·over·the·lazy·dog.··The·quick·brown·fox·jumps·over·the·lazy·dog.··The·quick·brown·fox·jumps·over·the·lazy·dog.¶

Section·3·Heading·Goes·Here¶
The·quick·brown·fox·jumps·over·the·lazy·dog.··The·quick·brown·fox·jumps·over·the·lazy·dog.··The·quick·brown·fox·jumps·over·the·lazy·dog.··The·quick·brown·fox·jumps·over·the·lazy·dog.··The·quick·brown·fox·jumps·over·the·lazy·dog.¶
¤

2. Save the new Web page as **Resort Home Page** followed by your initials.

3. Select the heading *Main Heading Goes Here* and replace it with **Winter Sports Resort**.

4. Select the heading *Section 1 Heading Goes Here* in the text column (not Section 1 in the contents column at the left) and replace it with **Welcome**.

Computer Concepts

You may have noticed in the Save As dialog box that Word automatically assigned the extension *htm*. Word saves a Web document in HTML format so it can be viewed in a Web browser.

5. Select both paragraphs of text under the *Welcome* heading, including the last paragraph mark, and delete the text. Insert the data file **Step7-1a**.

6. Change the heading *Section 2 Heading Goes Here* in the text section to **Skiing**. Delete all the text under the heading, including the last paragraph mark. Then insert the data file **Step7-1b**.

7. Change the heading *Section 3 Heading Goes Here* in the text section to **Snowmobile Adventures**. Delete all the text under the heading, including the last paragraph mark. Then insert the data file **Step7-1c**.

Speech Recognition

If your computer has speech recognition capability, enable the Command mode and say the commands to locate and insert the data files in the Web page.

8. Replace the graphic with clip art or an image relating to snow. Resize as necessary. Change the caption below the graphic to read **Winter Fun** and then center the caption. Your Web page should look similar to the one shown in Figure 7-2.

Hot Tip

If a dialog box displays asking you to catalog all media files, choose Later.

Did You Know?

The Clip Organizer allows you to browse through clip collections, add clips, or catalog clips in folders you specify. For example, you can create a collection to group the clips you use most frequently, or you can let the Clip Organizer automatically add and catalog media files on your hard disk.

FIGURE 7-2
Web page with new contents

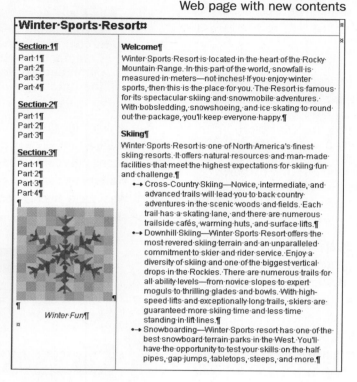

9. Save the changes and leave the document open for the next Step-by-Step.

Edit and Create Hyperlinks

You already know that when you click on a link in the Help screens, it takes you to a new location in the Help screens. A link (also called a *hyperlink*), enables users to go to a file, a location in a file, or to an HTML page on the World Wide Web or on an intranet. You can use a link on a Web page to move quickly to a different location in the same Web page, to a different Web page, to a URL, to an E-mail address, or to information saved in another application such as a Word or Excel document. When several Web pages are linked together, it is called a **Web site**. The template file you opened already had some hyperlinks formatted in the left column of the table. A well-designed Web page will also contain hyperlinks to take viewers back to the home page or to the top of the current page. These hyperlinks are formatted in a different color so you can easily identify them.

To test the hyperlinks in Word, you can hold down Ctrl and click the hyperlink.

Did You Know?

You can create hyperlinks in all Word documents to go to another location in the same document, to another location in another Word document, to a document in another application, or to a Web page.

STEP-BY-STEP ▷ 7.2

1. Scroll to the top of the page. Point to the *Section 1* hyperlink in the left column and right-click. Choose **Edit Hyperlink** in the submenu. The Edit Hyperlink dialog box opens.

2. In the *Text to display* box, change the text to **Welcome**.

3. Under *Link to*, click **Place in This Document**.

4. Under *Select a place in this document*, the list of headings should already be expanded. Click the *Welcome* heading to select it. When the dialog box looks like Figure 7-3, click **OK**.

> ### Computer Concepts
>
> The plus sign to the left of a heading indicates that there are subheadings. Click on the plus sign to expand the list. A minus sign indicates that the list is expanded. Click on the minus sign to collapse the list.

FIGURE 7-3
Edit Hyperlink dialog box

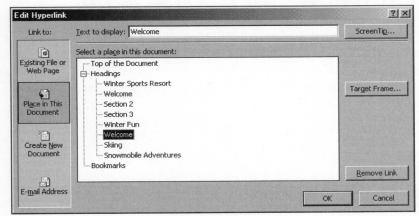

5. Notice that the hyperlink now displays Welcome.

6. Delete the part titles and numbers (*Part 1, Part 2,* etc.) under the *Welcome, Section 2,* and *Section 3* hyperlinks.

7. Point to the *Section 2* hyperlink and right-click. Choose **Edit Hyperlink** in the submenu.

Edit the text to display **Skiing**. Click **Place in This Document** and under *Select a place in this document*, select **Skiing**. Click **OK**.

8. Point to the Section 3 hyperlink and right-click. Choose **Edit Hyperlink** in the submenu. Edit the text to display **Snowmobile Adventures**. Set the link to the heading **Snowmobile Adventures**. Click **OK**.

137

9. Position the insertion point at the end of the document and press **Enter**. Key **Back to the Top**. Center the paragraph.

10. Select the text and click the **Insert Hyperlink** button on the Standard toolbar. The Insert Hyperlink dialog box is displayed.

11. Under *Select a place in this document*, select **Top of the Document** and click **OK**.

12. Test the hyperlinks: hold down **Ctrl** and click a link. The document should scroll to display that portion of the Web page and the insertion point should move to the beginning of that section.

Hot Tip

If a hyperlink does not work, select the linked text, right-click on the hyperlink and choose **Edit Hyperlink**. Then check to make sure the correct options are selected as described in Steps 2-11.

13. Save the changes and leave the document open for the next Step-by-Step.

Change Formats on a Web Page

The Web page template in Word provides a standard layout and formats for text. You can change the layout and text formats at any time. You can also change the look of your Web page by applying a theme or a background to the Word template. To separate sections of text, you can insert graphic horizontal lines. You can also jazz up bulleted lists by choosing picture bullets.

HISTORICALLY SPEAKING

In the 1960s, the Department of Defense developed the computer network ARPANET to link U.S. researchers and universities. Initially the network was used for e-mail, online discussion groups, and access to distant databases. The users of the network found that it provided a very convenient way to communicate. During the early 1980s, the National Science Foundation created NSFNET, a service that enabled all the networks connected to ARPANET to send data back and forth. Corporations such as MCI and Sprint began to build their own networks and link them to NSFNET. The Internet was born! In 1990, HTML was introduced. With HTML, individuals could display text and become part of a huge network called the World Wide Web.

1. Open the **Format** menu and choose **Background**, then select **Fill Effects** in the submenu. Click the **Texture** tab to display the dialog box shown in Figure 7-4.

FIGURE 7-4
Texture tab in the Fill Effects dialog box

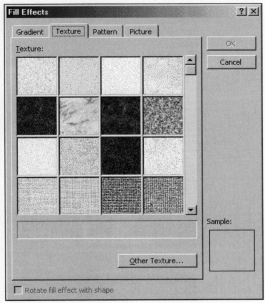

2. Select the first option in the third row (Blue tissue paper). Click **OK**.

Speech Recognition

If your computer has speech recognition capability, enable the Command mode and say the commands to open the Fill Effects dialog box, switch to the Texture tab, and select the options.

3. Position the insertion point in front of the heading *Welcome*. Open the **Format** menu and choose **Borders and Shading**. Then click the **Horizontal Line** button at the bottom of the Borders and Shading dialog box. The Horizontal Line dialog box shown in Figure 7-5 is displayed.

Horizontal Line...

FIGURE 7-5
Horizontal Line dialog box

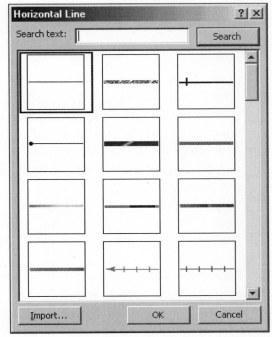

4. Select the first line option that is available on your computer and click **OK**. The line appears above the heading.

5. Click on the line to select it. Click the **Copy** button on the Standard toolbar. Position the insertion point at the end of the paragraph of text below the heading *Welcome*. Click the **Paste** button on the Standard toolbar.

139

6. Select the three paragraphs in the bulleted list under the heading *Skiing*. Open the **Format** menu and choose **Bullets and Numbering**. Click the **Customize** button at the bottom of the dialog box to display the Customize Bulleted List dialog box.

7. Click the **Picture** button in the dialog box. The Picture Bullet dialog box opens.

8. Select any available bullet that complements your Web page design. Click **OK**. The Customize Bulleted List dialog box shown in Figure 7-6 is displayed.

9. Under *Bullet position*, set the *Indent at* to 0.**25"**. Under *Text position*, set the *Tab space after* to 0.**5"** and the *Indent at* to 0.**5"**. When your settings match those shown in Figure 7-6, click **OK**. The bullets are replaced with the picture bullet you selected.

10. Select the main heading *Winter Sports Resort* and change the font point size to **26**.

11. Save the changes and leave the document open for the next Step-by-Step.

FIGURE 7-6
Customize Bulleted List dialog box

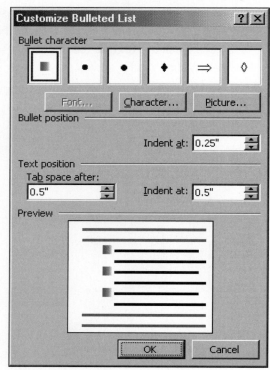

Computer Concepts

The backgrounds and themes that you add to a Web page can be viewed only in Web layout view. These backgrounds do not print.

Preview a Web Page

Y̶ou can preview a Web page at any time while you are creating it. Your browser will open to display the Web page as it will look when viewed on the Web.

STEP-BY-STEP ▷ 7.4

1. Open the **File** menu and choose **Web Page Preview**. Your browser will open, and then the Web page should display. If necessary, maximize the window.

2. Click on each of the hyperlinks to test them.

3. Close your browser and then close the document.

Hot Tip

To see your Web page full-size in Internet Explorer, press the **F11** key. Press **F11** again to return the view to the previous window size.

Work with Frames Pages

You can also create a Web page using a *frames page*. A frames page uses separate panes called frames to organize files and graphics on a Web page. Think of a frame in terms of a picture or window frame. Frames pages are helpful in creating your own layout. You can then insert and create a number of different document files or graphics in the layout.

Use Help to Learn About Frames

In the next section's Step-by-Step, you will create a frames page. Before you begin, though, you can go to the Help screens to learn more about frames. You will often see Help screen links that begin with the word *About*. These links will display information that introduces you to the topic and provides conceptual information that helps you understand the purpose of the feature.

Computer Concepts

When you work with frames pages, a folder is created for each frame. The folder contains all the text and graphic files and formatting information for the contents of that frame. The contents are all linked to that folder, and if you move the files or folder or change the filenames or folder name, the links can be broken.

STEP-BY-STEP ▷ 7.5

1. Open a new document window. If the Office Assistant is displayed, click it. If it is not displayed, open the **Help** menu and choose **Show Office Assistant**. Click the Assistant to "activate" it.

2. Key **frames**, and then click **Search**.

3. Select **About Web frames**. Read the information that appears at the right. Click each hyperlink to read the definition of the term, then click the hyperlink again to hide the definition.

4. After reading the information, you should be able to answer the following questions. If you do not know all the answers, reread the information to find the answer.
   a. What is a frame?
   b. How do frames help you design a Web page?
   c. What do you call the container that hosts a group of frames?
   d. Can a frame have its own scrollbar?

5. Close the Help screen.

Create a Frames Page

A frames page is a collection of files. When you key information in a frame, Word saves that text in a separate file. If you try to print a frames page in Word, Word will print only the text in the currently active frame (the one in which the insertion point is positioned). To print the entire frames page as it appears on your screen, you need to print from your Web browser.

STEP-BY-STEP ▷ 7.6

1. Open **Step7-6** from the data files and save it as **Packages** followed by your initials. Note that the text has already been formatted and a background has been applied. The document was originally saved as a Web page, so when you save the document again it will automatically be saved in HTML format.

Did You Know?

You can save any Word document as an HTML file so it can be viewed using a Web browser. To save a file in HTML format, open the **File** menu. In the *Save as type* list box, select **Web Page (*.htm; *.html)**.

2. Close the Web page.

3. Open a new Web page by displaying the New Document task pane and clicking **Blank Web Page**.

4. Open the **Format** menu and choose **Frames**, then select **New Frames Page** in the submenu. The Frames toolbar is displayed. Save the document as **Package Information** followed by your initials.

5. Open the **View** menu and choose **Ruler** to display the Ruler. The Ruler will display when there is a checkmark in front of it.

6. Click the **New Frame Right** button on the Frames toolbar. A frame border displays in the

middle of the page. Drag the frame border to the left to the 2 inch mark on the Ruler.

7. Click in the frame on the left. Change the font point size to **26 point** and key **Interested in Winter Sports Resort packages?**

Hot Tip

If the floating Frames toolbar is in the way, drag it to the side or dock it at the top with the other toolbars or at the bottom or side of the document window.

8. Click in the frame on the right, then click the **New Frame Below** button on the Frames toolbar. A frame border displays about halfway down the wider column.

Hot Tip

To remove a frame, click inside the frame on the frames page. Then click the Delete Frame button on the Frames toolbar.

9. Insert the clip art image you used for the Resort home page into the lower frame. Resize the image so it is no more than one inch high and one inch wide. Position the insertion point to the right of the clip art image and key **WinterSportsResort@wsr.com**.

10. Drag the horizontal frame border down toward the bottom of the screen, but make sure you can still read the e-mail address next to the clip art image. Your screen should look similar to Figure 7-7. Drag the frame borders to make any required adjustments.

11. Position the insertion point in the frame at the top right. Click the Frame Properties button on the Frames toolbar. If necessary, click the **Frame** tab to display the **Frame Properties** dialog box shown in Figure 7-8.

FIGURE 7-7
Web page with three frames

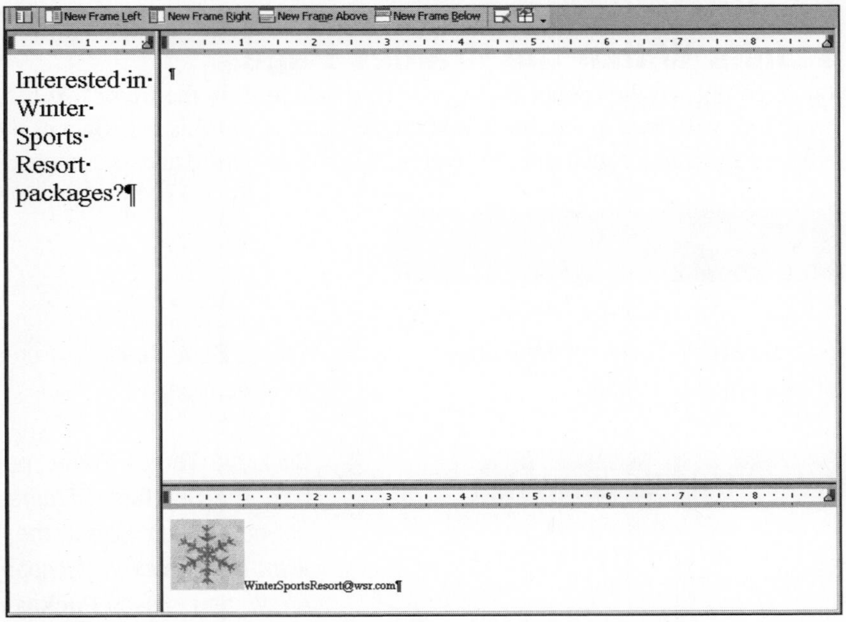

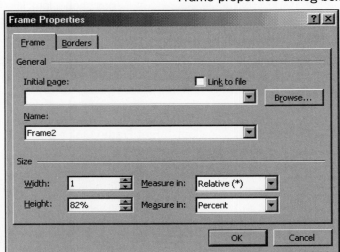

FIGURE 7-8
Frame properties dialog box

12. Click **Browse** and locate the **Packages.htm** Web page you just saved. (Locate the file, not the folder.) Select it and click **Open**. In the *Name* box of the Frame Properties dialog box, replace *Frame2* with **Packages** to name the frame. Click **OK**. The file is inserted in the frame.

13. Format the other two frames with the Blue tissue paper background.

14. Click the **Frame Properties** button. Click the **Borders** tab and select the **No borders** option. Click **OK**.

15. Save the document and leave it open for the next Step-by-Step.

Setting Up Links Within the Frames Page

Now that you've completed the frames page, you can create links in the frames. You can specify that the contents to which you link will open in another frame on the same page. This is known as the target frame. By specifying a target frame, the frame containing the hyperlink is still displayed and its contents are still accessible.

STEP-BY-STEP ⟹ 7.7

1. Open the data file **Step7-7** and save the page as **Deals** followed by your initials.

Computer Concepts

You should save all files for a frames page (or any Web site, for that matter) in the same folder. This makes it possible for the links to always work correctly, even if that folder is moved to another location.

2. Open the **Window** menu and switch to the **Package Information** page. Click at the end of the text in the left frame. Press **Enter** twice and key **Best Deals**.

3. Select **Best Deals** and create a hyperlink to the Deals page

4. Click the **Target Frame** button in the dialog box. The Set Target Frame dialog box is displayed. Under *Select the frame where you want the document to appear*, click the down arrow and select **Packages**. This specifies that when the file is opened the window will be opened in the Packages frame. Your dialog box should look like Figure 7-9. Click **OK** twice to close both dialog boxes.

FIGURE 7-9
Set Target Frame dialog box

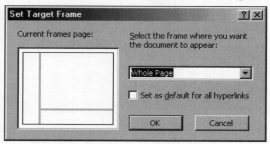

5. Click at the end of the text in the center of the top right frame, press **Enter** twice, and key and center **Resort Home Page**. Select the new text and create a hyperlink to **Resort Home Page**. Click **Target Frame** and then select **Whole Page** in the drop-down list box. Click **OK** twice.

6. Save the changes and close the documents.

7. Open the **Resort Home Page** Web page. Position the insertion point below the *Snowmobile Adventures* hyperlink in the contents area of the Web page and press **Enter**.

8. Click the **Insert Hyperlink** button on the Standard toolbar. The Insert Hyperlink dialog box is displayed.

9. If necessary, click the **Existing File or Web Page** button. In the *Text to display* box, key **Package Information**. Select **Package Information.htm** in the list below. Click **Target Frame** and then select **Whole Page** in the drop-down list box. Click **OK** twice.

10. Select the new hyperlink. Then click the **Bold** button on the Formatting toolbar. Deselect the text.

Did You Know?

You can print the Web page as it is laid out on the screen. In the browser, open the Print dialog box. To print the entire page as you see it, choose the *As laid out on screen* option. To print each frame separately, choose the *All frames individually* option.

11. Save the changes. View the pages in your browser and test the links. Then close the browser and the document.

Hot Tip

If a hyperlink does not work, select the linked text, right-click on the hyperlink and choose Edit Hyperlink. Then check to make sure the correct options are selected as described in Steps 3-10.

Use the Web Page Wizard

Word has a special feature called a wizard. A *wizard* asks you a series of questions about a particular kind of document and then creates the document based on your answers. The Web page wizard in Word asks questions about what kind of pages you want to include in a Web site and then creates the Web site for you according to your specifications.

Run the Web Page Wizard

Using the Web Page Wizard to create a Web page saves you time in setting up the document. When you use the Wizard, Word sets up all the files and hyperlinks for a Web site at once, making this task easier for you.

1. Open the New Document task pane, choose **General Templates**, click on the **Web Pages** tab, and then select **Web Page Wizard** and click **OK**. The Wizard dialog box shown in Figure 7-10 is displayed.

Hot Tip

If you have previously used the Web Page Wizard, the link to it will be displayed in the task pane.

FIGURE 7-10
Web Page Wizard dialog box

2. Click **Next** to begin the Wizard.

3. In the text box under *Web site title*, key **The Critter Sitter** followed by your initials. This will be the name for your new Web site.

4. If necessary, use the **Browse** button to locate the folder where your other Lesson 7 solution files are stored. Click **Next**.

Computer Concepts

You may be prompted to enable macros when you start the Web Page Wizard. This is a security dialog box to warn you about computer viruses. It is okay to enable the macro to run the Web Page Wizard.

5. If necessary, choose the **Vertical frame** option for navigation. Click **Next**.

6. Specify pages for your Web site as follows:
   a. Click the **Remove Page** button three times to remove all three pages in the *Current pages in Web site box*.
   b. Click the **Add Template Page** button and select the **Simple Layout** template. Click **OK**.
   c. Click the **Add Template Page** button again and add the **Right-aligned Column** template. Click **OK**.
   d. Click the **Add Template Page** button again and add the **Left-aligned Column** template. Click **OK**, then click **Next**.

7. Rearrange the order of the Web pages. Click on **Simple Layout** in the list of pages, then click the **Move Down** button twice to move the Simple Layout page to the end of the list.

Speech Recognition

If your computer has speech recognition capability, enable the Command mode and say the commands to launch the Web Page wizard. Then respond to the prompts.

8. With Simple Layout still selected, click the **Rename** button in the Web Page Wizard dialog box. The Rename Hyperlink box displays. Key **Affordable Rates**, then click **OK**.

9. Select the **Left-aligned Column** hyperlink, click **Rename**, key **Paws-itively Purr-fect Care**, and click **OK**.

10. Select the **Right-aligned Column** hyperlink, click **Rename**, key **Specialized Care**, and click **OK**. Click **Next**.

11. Click the **Browse Themes** button and select the **Sandstone** theme (or another appropriate theme if Sandstone is not available). Click **OK**, then click **Next**. Click **Finish** to create the Web pages and all other files that accompany them.

Hot Tip

To browse the themes quickly and easily, select the first theme. Then press the down arrow key to move down to the next theme. Installed themes will display as you highlight the name.

12. Word displays the default.htm Web page on your screen, along with the Frames toolbar.

13. Save the document and leave it open for the next Step-by-Step.

Complete the Web Site

After creating a Web site using the Web Page Wizard, you open each of the pages and add your own content. You can then format the content and adjust the layout using the features you have already learned in this lesson.

1. Hold down **Ctrl** and click the *Specialized Care* hyperlink to go to that page. Change the main heading to read **The Critter Sitter**. Change the first section heading to read **Specialized Care for Your Special Pet**.

2. Delete all the remaining text and section headings on this page. Insert the data file **Step7-9a**.

3. Delete the graphic and replace it with an image of a dog or dog bone. Resize the graphic if necessary. Change the caption under the graphic to read **Bone Voyage!** Save the changes.

4. Click in the left frame, hold down **Ctrl**, and click the *Paws-itively Purr-fect Care* hyperlink to go to that page. Delete the main heading. Change the first section heading to read **Paws-itively Purr-fect Care**.

5. Delete all the remaining text and section headings on this page. Insert the data file **Step7-9b**.

6. Delete the graphic and replace it with an image of a cat. Resize the graphic if necessary. Change the caption under the graphic to read **Purrrrrrrrr** and center the caption. Save the changes.

7. Click in the left frame. Then, hold down **Ctrl** and click the *Affordable Rates* hyperlink to go to that page. Delete the main heading. Change the first section heading to read **Affordable Rates**.

8. Delete all the remaining text and section headings on this page. Insert the data file **Step7-9c**.

9. Save the changes and test all the hyperlinks. Then close the document.

Summary

In this lesson, you learned:

- Web page templates help you organize text and graphics for Web pages. The pages are already formatted; you simply replace the existing contents.

- You can edit existing hyperlinks by changing the text that displays and/or the location for the link.

- The layout and formats of a Web page can be changed at any time. Themes and backgrounds can be added to customize the page.

- You can preview the Web page at any time to see how it will look when viewed on the Web.

- The frame pages in Word make it easy to plan the layout and organize the text and graphics of your Web page.

- The Web Page Wizard saves you time in setting up all the pages for a Web site.

VOCABULARY REVIEW

Define the following terms:

Frames page   Hyperlink   Web site
HTML   Template   Wizard

LESSON 7 REVIEW QUESTIONS

TRUE/FALSE

Circle T if the statement is true or F if the statement is false.

T F 1. A Word Web page template is really an outline, and all you have to do is fill in your own text.

T F 2. When you save a Word Web page, Word automatically supplies the .htm extension.

T F 3. It is helpful to have a hyperlink at the bottom of a long Web page that will take you back to the top of the page.

T F 4. A frames page is actually a collection of files that display together each time you open the page.

T F 5. Using the Web Page Wizard is the fastest way to set up a Web site that contains a number of pages.

FILL IN THE BLANK

Complete the following sentences by writing the correct word or words in the blanks provided.

1. A(n) _____ is a file that contains document, paragraph, and character formats for a specific type of document.

2. A(n) _____ lets you jump from one Web page to another, or from one location in a page to another location.

3. To insert a decorative line in a Web page, click the _____ button in the _____ dialog box.

4. To print an entire frames page, you must print from your _____.

5. A(n) _____ asks you a series of questions about a document and then creates it for you.

LESSON 7 PROJECTS

PROJECT 7-1

1. Open a new Web page that uses the Column with Contents Web page template. Save the Web page as **Suspense** followed by your initials.

2. Replace the main heading with **Oak Creek Film Society**. Replace the Section 1 heading with **Film Society News**.

3. Replace the paragraphs below the **Film Society News** heading with the text contained in the **Project7-1a** data file.

4. Replace the Section 2 heading with **Hitchcock: A Capsule Biography**, and then replace the paragraphs below the heading with the text contained in the **Project7-1b** data file.

5. Replace the Section 3 heading with **Selected Hitchcock Filmography**, and then replace the paragraph below the heading with the text contained in the **Project7-1c** data file.

6. Delete the part titles and numbers under the hyperlinks. Then edit the hyperlinks in the left column to match the heads in the right column. Insert a hyperlink at the bottom of each section to take users back to the top of the page.

7. Replace the sample graphic with clip art that relates to movies or suspense. Resize the clip art as needed. Delete the sample caption.

8. Apply the **Blends** theme to the Web page.

9. In the last section of the Web page, format the list of movies for each decade with decorative bullets of your choice.

10. Save your work and then preview the Web page in your browser. Test your hyperlinks. Then close your browser and Web page.

PROJECT 7-2

1. Open a new blank Web page and save it as **Title** followed by your initials.

2. Change the font size to **24 point** and then key **Lakeside Little Symphony**.

3. Apply the **Parchment** background texture (third option in the first row on the Texture tab) to the page, then save and close the page.

4. Open the data file **Project7-2a** and save the page as **Winter** followed by your initials in the same folder where you saved **Title**. Close the document.

5. Open the data file **Project7-2b** and save the page as **December** followed by your initials in the same folder where you saved the other two pages. Insert any decorative horizontal line you like below the heading December. If the horizontal line is centered, click on it to select it and then click the **Align Left** button on the Formatting toolbar. Save the changes and close the document.

6. Open the data file **Project7-2c** and save the page as **January** (with the other pages) followed by your initials. Insert and format the same horizontal line you used in Step 5 below the January heading. Save the changes and close the document.

7. Open the data file **Project7-2d** and save the page as **February** followed by your initials. Insert and format the same horizontal line you used in Step 5 below the February heading. Save the changes and close the document.

8. Create a new Web frames page and save it as **Symphony** followed by your initials. Insert frames and files as follows:
    A. Create a top frame about 1.5 inches tall and specify that the **Title** document open in this frame. Name the frame **Title**.
    B. In the larger bottom frame, create a frame at the left about 2 inches wide and specify that the Winter document open in this frame. Name the frame **Winter**.
    C. In the larger right-hand frame, specify that the **December** document open initially. Name the frame **Month**.
    D. Create hyperlinks from the months in the Winter frame to the **December, January**, and **February** documents. To make the month documents appear in the proper frame, click the **Target Frame** button and select **Month**.

9. If desired, insert clip art or a graphic in the Title or Winter frame that relates to music.

10. Adjust frame sizes if necessary to display all text. Then, in the Frame Properties dialog box, specify no borders for any of the frames.

11. Preview your Web page and test the hyperlinks to make sure they work correctly. Print the frames page from your browser.

12. Save your changes and close the page.

PROJECT 7-3

In this project, use the Web Page Wizard to create a Web site for a business or organization you know well.

1. First decide on the subject of your Web site. You can create a Web site for a club, an organization, a business, a restaurant, or any other operation for which you know enough details to create two or three pages of information. You can research information for your pages on the Web if necessary.

2. Plan what kinds of pages you want in the Web site and what kind of content each page should have. If desired, create the Web pages in advance using Web page templates or blank Web pages.

3. Run the Web Page Wizard and choose a layout for the Web site. Then select the pages to be in your Web site.

4. Rename the pages with appropriate names, and then choose a theme for the Web site.

5. If you have not already created the pages, add content to them. Don't forget what you have learned in this lesson about balancing text with graphics and graphic elements such as lines and bullets. Your pages should be not only readable but also interesting to look at.

6. Preview your Web site in your browser and then make any necessary adjustments. Print the first page of the Web site from your browser.

7. Save and close the Web site.

WEB PROJECT

If you completed Project 7-1, you learned something about Alfred Hitchcock's life and films. Search the Web for information on an artist or performer of your choice (musician, writer, director, actor, or other performer). Try to locate biographical information as well as information on the performer's work. Create a Web page to display the results of your research. You should have several sections of information and create hyperlinks to jump directly to each section. If possible, locate pictures on the Web to illustrate your Web page.

TEAMWORK PROJECT

If you completed Project 7-3, you discovered that creating an entire Web site can result in a lot of work. The author of a Web site has to design each page in the site, write content for the pages, and select appropriate illustrations, besides making sure that all the pages are properly linked. For this reason, companies that create and maintain Web sites often take a team approach to the process, with each team member responsible for specific pages of the site. Try this approach with your classmates to create a Web site.

1. With three or four other classmates, decide on a subject for your Web site. Limit your choices to subjects you know well, such as a particular sport or recreation. With the group, decide on several pages that should be included in the Web site.

2. Each team member should take one of these pages and complete all work on it, from design to content to illustrations. Use a Web page template to help design the page, or use a blank Web page and create the design yourselves.

3. Each page should be saved and then transferred to a folder on one computer so that all files can stay together. Then use the Web Page Wizard to create the site, specifying the saved pages in the step where you are asked what pages to include in the site.

4. Preview the completed site and decide if any adjustments are necessary. Make your corrections and then, if possible, publish the Web site to your local network so others can view it.

CRITICAL THINKING

If you completed the projects for this lesson, you might have had difficulty selecting certain horizontal lines or picture bullets. You might have received a message saying the bullet or line couldn't be found. Picture bullets and horizontal lines are related to themes. Why do you think you might not have had access to some lines and bullets?

Use the Help system in Word to try to find the answer to this question. Then write a brief description of your findings.

Word

COMMAND SUMMARY

FEATURE	MENU COMMAND	KEYSTROKE	TOOLBAR BUTTON	LESSON
1.5 line spacing	Format, Paragraph	Ctrl + 5		3
AutoShape, insert	Insert, Picture, AutoShape		AutoShapes ▾	6
Background, insert	Format, Background			7
Bold, apply	Format, Font	Ctrl + B	**B**	3
Borders	Format, Borders and Shading		▣ ▾	5
Bullets	Format, Bullets and Numbering		☰	3
Center alignment	Format, Paragraph	Ctrl + E	☰	3
Clipboard, clear all				2
Clipboard, open task pane		Ctrl + C two times		2
Close document	File, Close	Ctrl + F4	✕	1
Column break, insert	Insert, Break			6
Column format	Format, Columns		▤	6
Copy text	Edit, Copy	Ctrl + C	▤	2
Crop picture			⌗	6
Cut text	Edit, Cut	Ctrl + X		2
Date and time, insert	Insert, Date and Time			4
Double line spacing	Format, Paragraph	Ctrl + 2		3
Filename, insert	Insert, Field			4
Find text	Edit, Find	Ctrl + F		4
FONT SIZE, CHANGE FORMAT, FONT				3
Font, change	Format, Font			3
Footer, insert	View, Header and Footer			3
Frame properties, change			▥	7

FEATURE	MENU COMMAND	KEYSTROKE	TOOLBAR BUTTON	LESSON
Grammar, check	Tools, Spelling and Grammar	F7		4
Header, insert	View, Header and Footer			3
Help	Help, Microsoft Word Help	F1	🔲	3
Highlight text			🔲	2
Horizontal line, insert	Format, Borders and Shading			7
Hyperlink, insert	Insert, Hyperlink	Ctrl + K	🔲	7
Indent, apply	Format, Paragraph			3
Insert clip art	Insert, Picture, Clip Art		🔲	6
Insert file	Insert, File			2
Insert mode		Insert (toggle on)		2
Italic, apply	Format, Font	Ctrl + I	𝐼	3
Justify alignment	Format, Paragraph	Ctrl + J	▤	3
Landscape orientation	File, Page Setup			3
Left alignment	Format, Paragraph	Ctrl + L	▤	3
Line color	Format, AutoShape, Color and Lines		🔲	3
Line weight, change	Format, Borders and Shading		½ ▾	5
Line, draw			◻	6
Margins, change	File, Page Setup			3
New document	File, New, Blank Document	Ctrl + N	◻	1
Nonprinting characters			¶	2
Normal view	View, Normal	Alt + Ctrl + N	▤	1
Numbering	Format, Bullets and Numbering		▤	3
Overtype mode		Insert (toggle off)		2
Page break	Insert, Break	Ctrl + Enter		3
Page numbers	Insert, Page Numbers			3
Paste text	Edit, Paste	Ctrl + V	🔲	2

FEATURE	MENU COMMAND	KEYSTROKE	TOOLBAR BUTTON	LESSON
Picture bullets, insert	Format, Bullets and Numbering			7
Picture, insert from file	Insert, Picture, From File			6
Portrait orientation	File, Page Setup			3
Print Layout view	View, Print Layout	Alt + Ctrl + P	▤	1
Print Preview	File, Print Preview		▣	3
Rectangle, draw			▢	6
Redo	Edit, Redo	Ctrl + Y	↻ ▾	2
Repeat	Edit, Repeat	Ctrl + Y		2
Replace text	Edit, Replace	Ctrl + H		4
Right alignment	Format, Paragraph	Ctrl + R	▤	3
Ruler, display	View, Ruler			3
Save file	File, Save	Ctrl + S	▯	1
Save file as	File, Save As	F12		1
Select block of text		click, Shift, click		2
Select entire document	Edit, Select All	Ctrl + A		2
Shading, apply	Format, Borders and Shading		▨ ▾	5
Single line spacing	Format, Paragraph	Ctrl + 1		3
Spelling, check	Tools, Spelling and Grammar	F7	▧	4
Table AutoFormat	Table, Table AutoFormat		▤	5
Table cells, merge	Table, Merge Cells		▤	5
Table cells, split	Table, Split Cells		▦	5
Table column, delete	Table, Delete, Columns			5
Table column, insert	Table, Insert, Columns to the Left or Columns to the Right			5
Table column width, adjust	Table, AutoFit			5
Table, draw	Table, Draw Table		✎	5
Table, insert	Table, Insert, Table		▥ ▾	5
Table, select	Table, Select, Table			5
Table gridlines, display or hide	Table, Show or Hide Gridlines			5

FEATURE	MENU COMMAND	KEYSTROKE	TOOLBAR BUTTON	LESSON
Table row, delete	Table, Delete, Rows			5
Table row, insert	Table, Insert, Rows Above or Rows Below			5
Tabs, set	Format, Tabs			3
Text box, insert	Insert, Text Box		▣	6
Text, convert to table	Table, Convert, Text to Table			5
Theme, apply	Format, Theme			7
Thesaurus	Tools, Language, Thesaurus	Shift + F7		4
Toolbars, display	View, Toolbars			2
Underline, apply	Format, Font	Ctrl + U	U	3
Undo	Edit, Undo	Ctrl + Z	↺ ▾	2
Web page, preview	File, Web Page Preview			7
Web page template	File, New	Ctrl + N		7
Web Page Wizard	File, New	Ctrl + N		7
WordArt, create	Insert, Picture, WordArt		𝐀	6
Wrap text	Format, Picture		▣	6
Zoom	View, Zoom		100% ▾	3

TRUE/FALSE

Circle T if the statement is true or F if the statement is false.

T F 1. To use Click and Type, you must be in Normal view.

T F 2. Use the Delete key to remove characters to the right of the insertion point.

T F 3. If you forget to turn off Overtype mode, you might key over characters you didn't want to replace.

T F 4. To manually move text to a new page, you can insert a hard page break.

T F 5. Alignment refers to the white space between the edge of the paper and the text.

T F 6. Possible spelling errors in text are underlined with a wavy red line.

T F 7. You should always insert dates that automatically update in all of your documents.

T F 8. If you need to create a complex table, you should use the Draw Table tool.

T F 9. You can crop a graphic using the Crop tool on the Formatting toolbar.

T F 10. To insert picture bullets in a Web page, choose the Picture Bullets icon on the Web toolbar.

MATCHING

Match the correct term in Column 1 to its description in Column 2.

Column 1	Column 2
____ 1. Default	**A.** A temporary storage place in your computer's memory
____ 2. Points	**B.** Word suggests the spelling of frequently used words
____ 3. Portrait orientation	**C.** The document content is formatted with the long edge of the page at the top
____ 4. Merge	**D.** Small squares surrounding a graphic or object, indicting that it is selected
____ 5. Clipboard	
____ 6. Sizing handles	**E.** A full-width headline that spans across multiple newsletter-style columns such as the title for a newsletter or report
____ 7. AutoCorrect	**F.** A unit of measurement for fonts
____ 8. AutoComplete	**G.** Converting two or more cells into a single cell
____ 9. Template	**H.** A setting that is automatically used unless another option is chosen
____ 10. Banner	**I.** Word automatically corrects errors as you enter text
	J. The document content is formatted with the short edge of the page at the top
	K. A file that contains formatting and text that you can customize to create a new document similar to, but slightly different from, the original

MATH

Use the drawing tools in Word to draw a square that is 2 inches on each side, a rectangle that is 2 inches by 5 inches, and a circle that is about 2 inches across. Calculate the area of each object. (If necessary, refer to a textbook to find out how to calculate the area.) Create a text box below each object and enter the area measurement for that object in the text box.

SOCIAL STUDIES

Use a Web search tool or other reference to find the names of the U.S. congressional representatives for your region (for both the Senate and the House of Representatives). Use Word to key each name. Press Tab and then key that person's party affiliation. Adjust tabs for the list so that the party affiliations align at the left. Then italicize the party affiliations.

SCIENCE

Use a Web search tool or other reference to find information on the solar system. Create a table that organizes names, orbit time, distance from the sun, number of moons, and names of moons for all nine planets.

LANGUAGE ARTS

Use Word to create a numbered list of the books and magazine articles you read in a specific period of time, such as a couple of weeks or a month. Format the book titles in italics. The magazine articles should be in quotes, with the names of the magazine in which they appear in italics. Make sure you also include the authors of both books and magazines. Below each book or article, insert a bulleted list of the main events or key points in each book or article.

PROJECTS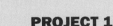

PROJECT 1

1. Open **Project1** from the data files. Save the document as **Invitation** followed by your initials.

2. Change the document margins to 2 inches on all sides.

3. Select the last five lines of the document (beginning with *Special Thanks to:...*) and right align them. Center align the rest of the text.

4. Change the line spacing of the centered text to 1.5. Notice that this causes the invitation text to run to two pages. Undo the line spacing change.

5. Select only the first two lines of the invitation and change the line spacing to 1.5 line spacing. Then select the three lines relating to the guest speaker (*special guest speaker…*, *John Hanley…*, and *Historial Researcher…*) and use the Repeat command to apply 1.5 line spacing.

6. Format the invitation as follows:
   A. Select the first line of text (Travelers Aid International) and change its font to a script font such as Brush Script and its size to 18 (or a size large enough to display well).
   B. Use the Format Painter to apply the same formats to the lines *80th Annual Meeting* and *John Hanley*.
   C. Format the remaining centered text in 11-point italic text.
   D. Format the line that begins *Special Thanks to:…* in bold italic.

7. You now have confirmation on the date of the event. Position the insertion point to the left of the time 6:30 p.m. and press **Enter**. Move the insertion point up into the new line. Key **Nove** and then accept the AutoComplete suggestion for the month. Press the **Spacebar** and key **6**, 2004.

8. Position the insertion point at the end of the line *Please reply by…* and press **Enter**. In the new line, key **Mond** and accept the AutoComplete suggestion for the day. Key , **Octo** and accept the AutoComplete suggestion for the month. Press the **Spacebar** and key **25**, 2004.

9. Preview the invitation, then close the preview.

10. Save your changes and close the document.

PROJECT 2

1. Open **Project2** from the data files. Save the document as **Refuge** followed by your initials.

2. Change the page orientation to landscape. Then position the insertion point in the blank line at the top of the document and specify three columns.

3. Position the insertion point in the second blank line below the heading *National Wildlife Refuge* and insert an appropriate clip art image for the topic. Resize the picture to be about 2 inches high. Center the picture, but do not wrap text around it.

4. Insert a 3-point blue-gray border below the *National Wildlife Refuge* heading. Use Repeat to insert the same border for the first blank paragraph beneath the clip art picture.

5. Create a WordArt heading for the first column of text using the word **Massassoit**. Size the graphic so it is as wide as the column. Move the WordArt graphic to the top of the first column and wrap text above and below it. Adjust the graphic if necessary so that it is at the top of the column, with the blank line and the words *National Wildlife Refuge* below it. Change the color of the graphic if desired to coordinate with the clip art picture.

6. Use drag-and-drop to move the first paragraph of text (the description of the National Wildlife Refuge System) to the last blank line in the document.

7. Use bullets to format the entries beneath the *Wildlife and Ecosystem*, *Public Use*, and *Safety Information* headings. (*Hint:* Align the bullet with the left edge of the column, if necessary, by opening the Bullets and Numbering dialog box and clicking the **Customize** button. Then change the Bullet position indent to 0 and the Text position indent to 0.25.)

8. Under the *Wildlife and Ecosystem* heading, delete the bullet that reads **Do not remove any plant life from the Refuge**. Then, in the bullet that reads *Do not remove any animals from the Refuge*, use Overtype to replace the word *animals* with **species**.

9. You're pretty sure you misspelled Lyme when keying information about ticks and Lyme disease. Find the word *Lime* and replace it with **Lyme**.

10. Find the list of unusual bird visitors to the Refuge in column 3. Select these bird names and insert a left-aligned tab at approximately 1 ½" on the Ruler above the column. This tab should line up the second column of names.

11. Use Find to locate the phrase *Enjoy all wildlife from a distance...* and then use a light shade of blue to emphasize the entire sentence.

12. Insert another appropriate picture that fits the content. Resize the picture to be about 1 inch square. Wrap text around the picture and move it to the end of the document, so that the last paragraph of text wraps around it. Make sure the picture aligns at the bottom with the last line of text and with the right edge of the column.

13. Create a footer with the current date left aligned (make sure the date will update automatically).

14. Preview the document to see if any changes need to be made in the layout. If necessary, resize pictures and the WordArt graphic to fit all text on one page. Insert column breaks if any headings fall at the bottoms of columns.

15. Save your changes and close the document.

PROJECT 3

1. Open **Project3a** from the data files. Save the document as **Caffeine** followed by your initials.

2. Position the insertion point in the last line of the document and insert the file **Project3b**.

3. Select the three lines of text below the first paragraph and format them as a numbered list. Format all the other paragraphs in the document (except for the tabular material) with a 0.5-inch first-line indent and justified alignment.

4. Check the grammar and the spelling in the document. *Coffea arabica*, *Thea sinensis*, and *theobromine* are spelled correctly and should not be changed. Use your judgment in correcting the grammar errors.

5. Position the insertion point at the end of the *Drinking* heading, press the **Spacebar**, and key **Caffeine**. Copy the space and the word *Caffeine* and then paste them after the single-word heading *Eating* to change the heading to **Eating Caffeine**.

6. In the second sentence below the heading *Drinking Caffeine*, use the Thesaurus to find a replacement for the word *strong*.

7. Convert the tabular material to a table with three columns. Edit and format the table as follows:
    A. AutoFit the table to its contents.
    B. You forgot to include the data for decaffeinated coffee. Insert a row below the instant coffee row and insert this information: **Decaffeinated   2 – 5**
    C. It would be helpful to know what quantities are being measured for each beverage. Insert a new column to the right of the *Type* column and key **Quantity** as the column heading. Key **5 oz.** as the quantity in the first coffee row and the first tea row. Key **12 oz.** as the quantity for Iced tea and in the first soft drink row.
    D. Use an AutoFormat to format the table, and then center the numbers in the Caffeine (mg) column. Center the table in the page.

8. Create a header that contains the filename left-aligned and a footer that contains the page number right-aligned.

9. Save your changes and close the document.

PROJECT 4

1. Open a new blank web page document. Change the alignment to center and key **Lakeside Bargain Days**. Press **Enter** twice and key the following line of text just as shown:

    [About Bargain Days] [Items for Sale] [Map]

2. Format *Lakeside Bargain Days* in Comic Sans, bold, 24 point. Format the other line of text in Comic Sans 14 point.

3. Apply the Blue tissue paper background to the page and then save it as **Heading** followed by your initials. Close the page.

4. Open **Project4a** from the data files and save it as **About** followed by your initials. Insert a horizontal line below the heading. Save and close the page.

5. Open **Project4b** and save it as **Items** followed by your initials. Insert the same horizontal line as in step 4 below the heading. Replace the sample graphic with a clip-art picture that relates to one of the items for sale. Delete the caption. Format the list of book types with picture bullets. Save and close the page.

6. Open **Project4c** and save it as **Map** followed by your initials. Insert the same horizontal line as in step 4 below the heading. Below the existing text, create the simple map shown in Figure UR-1. Then highlight the third sentence of the paragraph with the turquoise color. Save and close the page.

Madison

Lakeside

Bargain Days

Lake Nesbitt

7. Create a new web frames page and name it **Bargain**. Divide the page into two horizontal frames. The top frame should be about 2 inches tall.

8. Insert the **Heading** page in the top frame. Insert the **About** page as the initial page in the lower frame. Name that frame **Main**. Apply the Blue tissue paper background to the Main page.

9. Use the *About Bargain Days*, *Items for Sale*, and *Map* text in the top frame to create hyperlinks to the **About**, **Items**, and **Map** pages. The *About, Items,* and *Map* pages should all be targeted to display in the *Main* frame.

10. Remove the frame border. Save your changes and preview the page in your browser. Test your hyperlinks. Make any necessary adjustments and then view the page again.

11. Save and close the page.

SIMULATION

You volunteer at the local Rails-to-Trails organization which converts old railroad beds into trails for public use. These trails can be used for a variety of activities including: walking, biking, running, and in-line skating. You have been asked to complete several jobs for the organization that will help distribute information about rail-trails in your area.

JOB 1

A new section of a popular rail-trail is about to open for use. In this Job, you will create a press release giving general information about rail-trails.

1. Open **Job1a** from the data files folder. Save the document as **Press Release** followed by your initials.

2. Check spelling and grammar in the document and make all changes. You would like to use the phrase "rail-trail" rather than "rail trail" throughout. Use Replace to locate any instances of rail trail and change them to rail-trail.

3. Apply Arial bold 11-point font to all the following text: *Press Release*, *For Immediate Release*, *Contact*, *Date*, *Headline*, and *Body*.

4. Apply 10% gray shading to the *Press Release*, *For Immediate Release*, and *Date* paragraphs. Position the insertion point following *Contact:*, press the **Spacebar**, and key **Diane Twining**. Insert a left tab at the 4.25-inch mark so that Diane Twining is close to the right margin.

5. Insert the current date (it should not update automatically) after the tab symbol following *Date*.

6. Select the *Headline* paragraph and the first line of the Body and set a left tab at 0.75 inches. Position the insertion point following the tab symbol in the Headline paragraph and key the headline **Little Miami Scenic Trail Open to Springfield**.

7. In the first Body paragraph, set a hanging indent at 0.75 inches so all text aligns with the first word of the body text. Apply a left indent of 0.75 inches to the remaining body paragraphs.

8. Open **Job1b** and select the map graphic by clicking on any of the lines in the map. When white handles appear around the graphic, copy it to the Clipboard. Return to the **Press Release** document and paste the map in the document. Move it to the right side of the second paragraph of body text.

9. Insert a centered page number at the bottom of each page. Preview the document.

10. Save your changes and close the document. Close the **Job1b** document.

JOB 2

Someone has requested a list of the ten longest rail-trails in Ohio. You began this list in Word using tabs to organize the information, but some of the trail names are very long, so a table would make more sense. In this Job, you will create and format the table.

1. Open **Job2** from the data files. Save the document as **Ohio Trails** followed by your initials.

2. Convert the tabular text to a table with 5 columns.

3. Add the remaining table information shown below:

Oberlin Bike Path	25.0	Kipton	Elyria	Asphalt
Richland B & O Trail	18.4	Butler	Mansfield	Asphalt
Olentangy-Scioto Bike Path	17.0	Columbus	Worthington	Asphalt/concrete
Hockhocking-Adena	16.4	Athens	Nelsonville	Asphalt
Thomas J. Evans Trail	14.5	Newark	Johnstown	Asphalt
Kokosing Gap	14.0	Mt. Vernon	Danville	Asphalt

4. You left out one trail. Insert the following information in the proper location (based on trail length):

Ohio & Erie Canal	27.5	N. Akron	Valley View	Crushed stone

5. You made a mistake in determining one of the trail lengths. The Little Miami Scenic Trail is actually 68.0 miles long. Make this correction.

6. Center the numbers in the Length (miles) column. Apply the **Table List 2** AutoFormat.

7. Save your changes and close the document.

JOB 3

Your organization wants to get the word out to cyclists about the new section of trail opening soon. In this Job, you will create a DTP document that can be posted in cycling, running, and other sporting goods stores around the area.

1. Open **Job3** from the data files. Save the document as **Now Open** followed by your initials.

2. Using features you have learned about in this unit, format the document as you wish. You can change orientation, margins, fonts, font sizes, font styles, alignments, tabs, and line spacing to create a document with visual impact. Don't forget graphic elements such as shading and borders.

3. Somewhere in the document, insert a clip art picture that relates to bicycles, running, walking, or other type of exercise that can be done on a rail-trail.

4. Preview your document. Then make any necessary adjustments to present your information attractively.

5. Save your changes and close the document.

PORTFOLIO CHECKLIST

Include the following files from this unit in your portfolio.

_____ Carbohydrates	_____ Orders
_____ Languages	_____ Newsletter
_____ Expo	_____ Creamery
_____ Hummingbirds	_____ Resort Home Page
_____ Fitness	_____ Symphony
_____ Recycling Rate	

POWERPOINT

UNIT 3

🕐 **Estimated Time for Unit 3: 4.5 hours**

WORKING WITH PRESENTATIONS

OBJECTIVES

Upon completion of this lesson, you should be able to:

- Open and save an existing presentation.
- Identify the parts of the PowerPoint screen.
- Navigate through a presentation.
- Apply a design template.
- Add slides.
- Add and edit text.
- Delete, copy, and rearrange slides.
- Use Help to get assistance.
- View the presentation in full-screen view.

🕐 **Estimated Time: 1 hour**

VOCABULARY

Clipboard

Normal view

Placeholders

Slide design

Slide layout

Slide Show view

Slide Sorter view

PowerPoint helps you create, edit, and manipulate professional-looking slides, transparencies, or on-screen presentations. You can also use PowerPoint to create speaker's notes and audience handouts. The presentations you create can include text, drawing objects, clip art, pictures, tables, charts, sound, and video clips.

Creating a presentation may seem like an overwhelming task, but PowerPoint provides many features that make that task easy and fun.

Open and Save an Existing Presentation

When you first start PowerPoint, the New Presentation task pane is displayed at the right. This task pane provides several options for opening an existing presentation or for creating a new presentation. The most recently opened presentations are displayed at the top of the task pane, but you can also search for additional files by using the open command.

S TEP-BY-STEP 1.1

1. Start PowerPoint. A blank slide will open and a task pane similar to the one shown in Figure 1-1 is displayed.

2. Under *Open a presentation* in the task pane, click the option **More presentations** to display the Open dialog box shown in Figure 1-2. Do not be concerned that your screen does not match the figure exactly.

FIGURE 1-1
New Presentation task pane

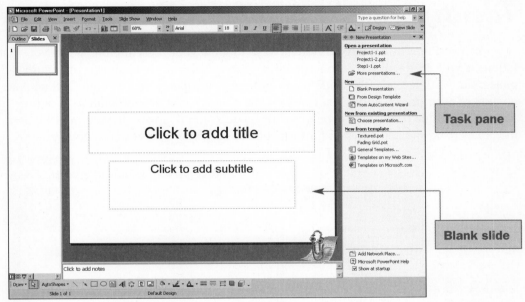

FIGURE 1-2
Open dialog box

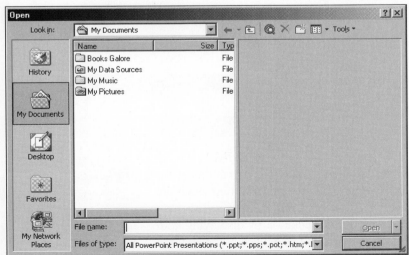

3. Locate and select the file **Step1-1** from the data files. Click **Open**.

4. Save the presentation as **The 3Rs** followed by your initials. Leave the presentation open for the next Step-by-Step.

Did You Know?

You can save a presentation so it can be viewed using a web browser. To save the presentation in HTML format, open the **File** menu and choose **Save as Web Page**.

Identify the Parts of the PowerPoint Screen

PowerPoint offers three different ways to view your presentation. When you first open a presentation, it will be displayed in one of three views. *Normal view*, shown in Figure 1-3, displays three panes: the Outline pane, the Slide pane, and the Notes pane. You use the Outline pane to organize the content of your presentation. You can view the content of your presentation in outline format or in slide format. The Slide pane allows you to see the slide as it will appear in your presentation. You can click in the Notes pane and add notes and information to help you with your presentation.

FIGURE 1-3
Presentation displayed in Normal view

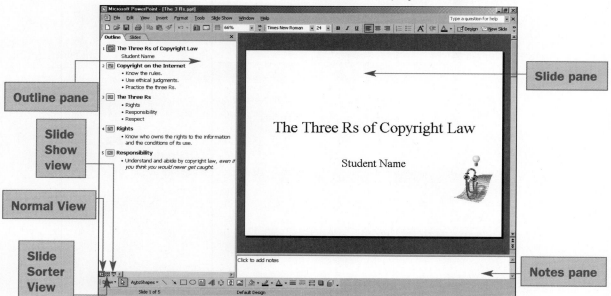

You can change the view by clicking the buttons at the lower left of the PowerPoint window. The other two views are *Slide Sorter view* and *Slide Show view*. Slide Sorter view gives you an overall picture of your presentation by displaying your slides as thumbnails (miniature versions of each of the slides in the presentation). Slide Sorter view makes it easy to add and

Hot Tip

To adjust the size of the panes in Normal view, point to the pane borders and when the pointer changes to a double-headed arrow, drag the pane border.

delete slides and change the order of the slides. In Slide Show view, the current slide fills the whole computer screen. You use this view when you present the show to your audience.

STEP-BY-STEP ▷ 1.2

1. Compare your screen to Figure 1-3 and take time to identify the three panes on the screen. Notice that the current slide displayed in the slide pane is the first of five slides.

2. Look at the contents in the outline pane. If necessary, click the Outline tab to display all of the text contained on each of the five slides in the presentation.

3. In the outline pane, click the **Slides** tab. The display changes to show thumbnail images of the slides.

4. In the Outline pane at the left, click anywhere on the thumbnail for the number 4 slide (*Rights*). The display in the Slide pane changes to show the fourth slide.

5. Click the **Slide Sorter View** button at the bottom of the screen. The display changes to show all the slides in the presentation as shown in Figure 1-4. Notice that the fourth slide has a blue border around it, indicating it is selected.

6. Click the Normal View button at the bottom of the screen to return to Normal view. You do not need to save the changes, but do leave the presentation open for the next Step-by-Step.

FIGURE 1-4
Presentation displayed in Slide Sorter view

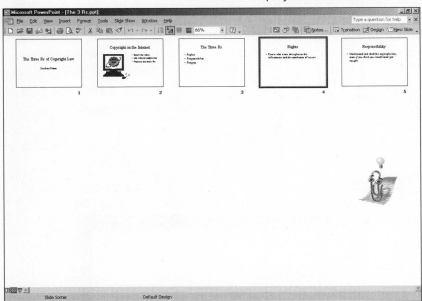

Navigate through a Presentation

Y̲ou already know that you can move to a different slide by clicking on the slide text in the Outline pane. You can also use the scroll bar or shortcut keys to navigate through a presentation in Normal view.

S TEP-BY-STEP ▷ 1.3

1. Click the **Next Slide** button at the bottom of the vertical scroll bar on the right. Each time you click the Next Slide button, the next slide in the presentation is displayed.

2. Click the **Previous Slide** button at the bottom of the vertical scroll bar. Each time you click the **Previous Slide** button, the previous slide in the presentation is displayed.

3. Press **Ctrl + End** to move to the last slide in the presentation. Notice that each time you move to a different slide, the thumbnail of that slide is selected in the Outline pane.

> **Computer Concepts**
>
> If the Outline tab is selected in the Outline pane, the slide icon next to the slide number in the Outline pane changes to gray to indicate the current slide.

4. Press **PageUp** to move to the previous slide.

5. Press **PageDown** to move to the next slide.

6. Press **Ctrl + Home** to move to the first slide in the presentation.

> **Speech Recognition**
>
> If your computer has speech recognition capability, enable the Command mode and say the commands to navigate through the presentation.

7. Drag the scroll box down the vertical scroll bar. As you drag the box, a label to the left of the scroll bar shows the title and number of the slide. When you see *Slide: 3 of 5 The Three Rs*, as shown in Figure 1-5, release the mouse button. The third slide of the presentation is displayed.

8. Leave the presentation open for the next Step-by-Step.

FIGURE 1-5
Slide label on scroll bar

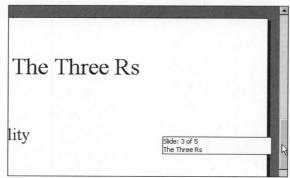

Apply a Design Template

You can easily give your presentation a professional look by applying a slide design. A ***slide design*** specifies a color scheme, text format, backgrounds, bullet styles, and graphics for all the slides in the presentation. PowerPoint provides several professionally-designed templates from which you can choose. Each design template has a specific look and feel. When you apply a design template, each slide in the presentation has a consistent look. However, the content of your slides does not change.

To apply a slide design template, open the Format menu and choose Slide Design. The Slide Design task pane will display, showing the template currently used in this presentation, recently used designs, and designs that are available for use.

If you like a slide design but you don't like the colors used in the design, you can easily change the color scheme of the design. PowerPoint offers several standard color schemes for each slide design. You can apply a new color scheme to all the slides or just to selected slides.

Computer Concepts

The design template you choose for your presentation, if possible, should reflect the theme of the presentation topic. Moreover, the design should not detract from the message you want to deliver.

STEP-BY-STEP ▷ 1.4

1. Open the **Format** menu and choose **Slide Design**. The Slide Design task pane shown in Figure 1-6 is displayed at the right of your screen.

Speech Recognition

If your computer has speech recognition capability, enable the Command mode and say the commands to open the Slide Design task pane.

2. Under *Available For Use*, scroll down to view all the thumbnails for the available designs. Then, locate and click the design titled **Balance**. (*Hint:* The design has a brown background. When you point to the thumbnail of the slide design, a ScreenTip will display with the design name. The designs are organized alphabetically.) The slide design is applied to all slides and the new design appears in the Slide pane.

FIGURE 1-6
Slide Design task pane

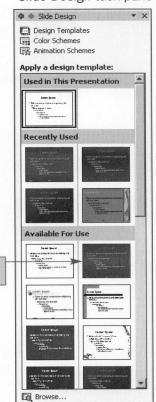

Balance slide design

Hot Tip

You can apply a different slide design at any time to change the look of your presentation.

3. At the top of the task pane, click the link **Color Schemes**. Several color schemes are displayed in the task pane as shown in Figure 1-7.

FIGURE 1-7
Task pane with color scheme options

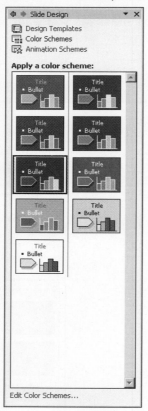

4. Click the down arrow on the right side of the first option. A drop-down menu with three options displays. Select **Show Large Previews**.

5. Use the scroll bar to view the color scheme options. Click some of the options to view the different color schemes. The new colors are applied to all the slides in the presentation, and the new colors appear in the Slide pane and in the Outline pane. Notice that not only does the background color change, but the text color also changes.

6. Select a color scheme that you prefer. Click the down arrow to display the drop-down menu, then select **Apply to All Slides**.

Extra Challenge

If you'd like to create your own color scheme, click the **Edit Color Schemes** link at the bottom of the Slide Design task pane. The Edit Color Scheme dialog box will display. If necessary, click the **Custom** tab, select the item you want to edit (such as Title text or Fills) and then click the **Change Color** button, select the new colors, and click **OK**. When you're done selecting the new colors, click **Apply** in the Edit Color Scheme dialog box.

7. Save the changes. Leave the presentation open for the next Step-by-Step.

Add Slides

You can add new slides in Normal view or Slide Sorter view. In the next Step-by-Step, you will learn to add slides in both views.

To add a new slide, open the Insert menu and choose New Slide, or click the New Slide button on the Formatting toolbar.

When you add a slide, the design that you have already applied to the presentation is automatically applied to the new slide. The *slide layout* used in the previous slide is also applied. The slide layout refers to the way things are arranged on the slide. All but one of the layout options provide placeholders. The *placeholders* provide placement guides for adding text, pictures, tables, or charts. The placeholder will not print or display in the actual presentation.

You can resize and move the placeholders on the slide. You can even format the placeholders with fill colors and borders. And, if you do not use a placeholder, you can delete it.

Computer Concepts

PowerPoint automatically adjusts the layout if you insert items that don't fit the original layout. For example, if you fill a text box with several lines of text and keep entering text, PowerPoint will reduce the font size as needed so all the text will fit inside the text box.

STEP-BY-STEP ▷ 1.5

1. Go to the fourth slide in the presentation. (*Hint*: Use the scroll bar or click the #4 slide text in the Outline pane.)

2. Click the **New Slide** button on the Formatting toolbar. A new blank slide is created and placed after slide number 4. Notice that the Outline pane is updated to show that the new slide has been added.

3. Notice that the Slide Layout task pane shown in Figure 1-8 is now displayed at the right of your screen. The new blank slide is formatted with the same layout that was used for the number 4 slide. This layout is also selected under *Text Layouts* in the task pane. The ScreenTip in the task pane describes this layout as *Title and Text*.

FIGURE 1-8
Slide Layout task pane

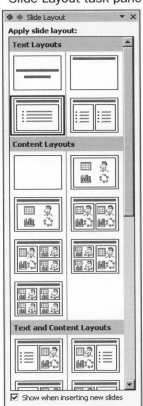

175

4. Select the *Title and 2 Column Text* option in the task pane. (*Hint:* it is directly to the right of the currently selected layout. When you point to the option, the ScreenTip will show the option name.) The slide layout for the new slide will change to display a text box for a title with two columns for text below.

Computer Concepts

Some placeholders for text automatically format a bullet at the beginning of each paragraph. The bullet color and symbol are formatted based on the design template. To remove the bullet, position the insertion point in the paragraph containing the bullet, and then click the Bullet button on the Formatting toolbar.

5. Switch to Slide Sorter view. (*Hint:* Click the **Slide Sorter View** button at the bottom left corner of the screen.) Notice the new blank number 5 slide.

6. Click between slides number 3 and number 4 to position the insertion point between the two slides. The insertion point will be displayed as a long vertical line between the two slides.

7. Click the **New Slide** button on the toolbar. A new slide is created. You now have a total of seven slides in your presentation.

8. Save the changes and leave the presentation open for the next Step-by-Step.

Add and Edit Text

To add text to a slide or to edit a slide, you must display the slide in Normal view. If the slide contains a placeholder for text, you simply click inside the placeholder and enter the text. If the slide does not have a placeholder for text, you can easily change the slide layout to accommodate text. When you add and edit text, the contents in the Outline pane are automatically updated.

S TEP-BY-STEP ▷ 1.6

1. Double-click slide number 4 to open it in Normal view so you can add text. Notice that in the Outline pane, the #4 slide is selected. However, there is no text displayed for slide #4 or #6.

2. Click in the placeholder at the top of the slide that says *Click to add title*. Key **Respect**.

3. Click in the next placeholder that *says Click to add text* and key **Respect the people who invested the time and energy to develop and report the information.**

Speech Recognition

If your computer has speech recognition capability, click in the placeholder, enable Dictation mode, and dictate the text for the slides.

4. Click outside the placeholder to deselect it. Then press **Ctrl + Home** to move to the first slide.

5. Position the insertion point in front of the word *of* in the title. Press **Enter** to move the text to the next line.

6. Click *Student Name* to move to that placeholder. Select the words *Student Name* and replace the words with your first and last names.

7. Save the changes and leave the presentation open for the next Step-by-Step.

Computer Concepts

To remove a slide in Normal view, you must open the **Edit** menu and choose **Delete Slide**. To delete a slide in the Outline pane, click the slide icon to the right of the slide number to select the slide number and its contents, then press **Delete**.

Delete, Copy, and Rearrange Slides

You can delete slides in Normal view or Slide Sorter view. It is easy to delete multiple slides in Slide Sorter view, and this view also makes it easy to copy slides and rearrange the order of slides. You can use the Cut, Copy, and Paste commands to copy or move slides, or you can also use drag-and-drop editing.

When you use the Cut, Copy, and Paste commands, PowerPoint stores the slide content and design in the Clipboard. The *Clipboard* is a temporary storage place in your computer's memory. You send selected slides to the Clipboard by using the Cut or Copy commands. Then you can retrieve those contents by using the Paste command. The contents remain in the Clipboard until you copy or paste something new, or when you turn off your computer. You can paste Clipboard items as many times as you want.

Instead of using the Cut and Paste commands, you can rearrange one or more slides by using drag-and-drop editing. Select the slide(s) to be moved, then drag the slide(s) to the new location. When you release the mouse button, the slide(s) will be repositioned at the new location of the insertion point.

Hot Tip

The shortcut keys for the Cut command are **Ctrl + X**. The shortcut keys for the Copy command are **Ctrl + C**. The shortcut keys for the Paste command are **Ctrl + V**. These are the same shortcut keys for performing these functions in other Microsoft Office applications.

1. Switch to Slide Sorter view.

2. Click slide number 6 to select it. Then press **Delete**. The slide is removed and the next slide numbers are revised to reflect the change.

Hot Tip

You can select multiple slides before you move, copy, or delete. To select multiple slides in Slide Sorter view, click the first slide, hold down the **Ctrl** key, and click each additional slide to be included in the selection. Or, you can select a series of slides by clicking the first slide in the series and then holding down the **Shift** key while clicking the last slide in the series. All slides between and including the two slides you clicked will be selected.

3. Click slide number 3 to select it. Click the **Copy** button on the Standard toolbar. The slide content and design are copied to the Office Clipboard.

Computer Concepts

If you do not know the function of a toolbar button, rest the mouse pointer on the button, but do not click it. After a few seconds, the name of the function appears in a ScreenTip. If you want more information about an option in a dialog box, click the Help button in the title bar of the dialog box, then click the option about which you want to display a ScreenTip.

4. Position the insertion point after slide #6. Click the **Paste** button on the Standard toolbar.

5. The slides are out of order. The #4 slide should follow slide #6. Select the #4 slide and click the **Cut** button on the Standard toolbar. The #4 slide is removed and all subsequent slides are renumbered.

6. Position the insertion point between slide #5 and slide #6, then click the **Paste** button. The slides are rearranged and automatically renumbered.

7. Save the changes and leave the presentation open for the next Step-by-Step.

Use Help to Learn How to Change the Slide Layout

As in other Office XP applications, the Office Assistant is available to assist you as you work in PowerPoint. The Office Assistant anticipates when you might need help, and it offers tips, solutions, instructions, and examples to help you work more efficiently.

If you have a specific question, you can go to the Office Assistant to search for help. To access Help for PowerPoint, you must have the application open. You can then ask the Office Assistant for information. If the Office Assistant is not displayed, you can access the tips, instructions, and examples in the Help menu.

STEP-BY-STEP 1.8

1. If the Office Assistant is not displayed on the screen, open the **Help** menu and choose **Show the Office Assistant**.

2. Click the Office Assistant. An Office Assistant dialog box similar to Figure 1-9 appears. Your dialog box will look different depending on the information last requested of the Office Assistant.

FIGURE 1-9
The Office Assistant dialog box

3. The text in the text box under *What would you like to do?* should already be selected. Key the following search text: **change slide layout**. As you begin to enter the new text, the selected text disappears.

4. Click **Search**. A list of topics that provide related information is displayed.

5. Click the topic *Apply a slide layout*. Read the information about the topic which displays in the right pane of the Help window.

6. Click the link **task pane**. A definition of the term *task pane* displays in a box on the screen. Click the link again to hide the definition.

7. Click the **PowerPoint** button in the taskbar to switch to the presentation or click any visible part of the PowerPoint window to make it the active window.

 Hot Tip

Sometimes the Office Assistant gets in the way. To move the Office Assistant, simply drag it to a new location on the screen.

8. Go to the Normal view of slide #2 by either double-clicking it or by selecting it and then choosing Normal view.

9. Using the information provided in the Help screen, change the layout of the slide so that the text is on the left side of the slide and the clip art image is on the right. (*Hint:* Click the slide layout to the left of the current design. The ScreenTip displays *Text & Clip Art*.)

10. Do not be concerned that the clip art image is now smaller. You will learn about resizing graphics in the next lesson. Save the changes and close the Help screen.

 Did You Know?

You can change the way the Office Assistant provides help by right-clicking the Office Assistant, choosing **Options**, selecting the **Options** tab, and then making selections.

View the Presentation

Now that you have formatted and sequenced the slides in your presentation, you probably want to see what it will look like for your audience. You can see how it will look in full-screen view by choosing Slide Show View. As you view the presentation, you can click the left mouse button or press the spacebar to advance to the next file. You can also use the arrow keys or the PageUp and PageDown keys on the keyboard to advance forward or backward.

When you move your mouse across the screen in Slide Show view, an arrow appears on the screen so you can point out parts of the slide. A triangle is displayed in the bottom left corner of the screen. When you click this triangle, a menu is displayed. Choosing Pen from this menu changes the mouse pointer to a pen. You can then draw or write on the screen. The pen marks overlay the slide and are temporary. They are automatically erased when you advance to the next slide.

Computer Concepts

To display your speaker notes as you run the presentation, right click the screen in Slide Show view and then choose **Speaker Notes**.

STEP-BY-STEP 1.9

1. Go to slide #1 in Normal view.

2. Click the **Slide Show View** button in the lower left corner, just above the status bar. The first slide shows in full-screen view.

Hot Tip

You can start the slide show on any slide by displaying or selecting the slide you want to begin with before switching to Slide Show view.

3. Click the left mouse button to advance to the next slide.

4. Explore using the arrow keys and the PageUp and PageDown keys to move from slide to slide.

Did You Know?

If you don't want a slide to appear when you run the presentation, you can hide the slide. Select the slide in Normal view or Slide Sorter view. Then open the **Slide Show** menu and choose **Hide Slide**. To restore the slide so it does display when you run the presentation, select the slide, open the **Slide Show** menu, and choose **Hide Slide** again to toggle the feature off.

5. Move the mouse pointer across the screen. When the triangle appears in the lower left corner, click it to display a menu. Choose **Pointer Options**, then choose **Pen**. Experiment writing on the screen with the pen, then advance to the next slide.

6. To end the slide show, press **Esc**. The current slide will display in Normal view. If you reach the end of the presentation, you can follow the screen directions and click to exit.

7. Click the application close box at the top right corner of the screen to close the presentation and the application.

Computer Concepts

If the Help screen is still open it will also close automatically unless you have other Office applications open, in which case the Help screen will not close.

Summary

In this lesson, you learned:

- When you start PowerPoint, you can choose to create a new presentation or open an existing presentation.

- PowerPoint offers three different views to display a presentation. You work in either Normal view or Slide Sorter view as you create and edit your presentation. In Slide Show view, the current slide fills the full computer screen. You use this view when you present the show to your audience.

- In addition to using the Outline pane to move to a different slide, you can also use the scroll bar or shortcut keys to navigate through a presentation in Normal view.

- The slide design automatically formats slides with color schemes, bullet styles, and graphics. The slide design ensures that all slides in a presentation have a consistent look. You can apply a slide design at any time without affecting the contents of the slides.

- You can add a new slide in Normal view or Slide Sorter view. When you add a new slide, you must select a slide layout.

- To add or edit text, the slide must be displayed in Normal view. When you add text or edit text, the slide contents are automatically updated in the Outline pane.

- It is easy to delete, copy, and rearrange slides in Slide Sorter view. You can use the Cut, Copy, and Paste commands, or you can utilize drag-and-drop editing to rearrange the order of the slides.

- The Office Assistant anticipates when you might need help, and it offers tips, solutions, instructions, and examples to help you work more efficiently. If you have a specific question, you can use the Office Assistant to search for help.

VOCABULARY REVIEW

Define the following terms:

Clipboard	Placeholders	Slide Show view
Normal view	Slide design	Slide Sorter view
	Slide layout	

LESSON 1 REVIEW QUESTIONS

TRUE/FALSE

Circle T if the statement is true or F if the statement is false.

T F 1. You can use the Outline pane to quickly navigate through a presentation.

T F 2. You can add new slides in Slide Show view.

T F 3. To move to the first slide in a presentation, you can press Ctrl + Home.

T F 4. To see your presentation as a slide show, you use Normal view.

T F 5. You can rearrange slides using either the Cut and Paste toolbar buttons or drag-and-drop editing.

FILL IN THE BLANK

Complete the following sentences by writing the correct word or words in the blanks provided.

1. To add text to a slide or to edit a slide, you must display the slide in _____ view.

2. _____ view displays a miniature version of each of the slides in the presentation.

3. A(n) _____ specifies a uniform color scheme, background, bullet style, text format, and graphics for a presentation.

4. _____ provide(s) guides for adding text, pictures, tables, and charts.

5. _____ view allows you to see slides in full view.

LESSON 1 PROJECTS

PROJECT 1-1

1. Open **Project1-1** from the data files. Save the presentation as **Gettysburg** followed by your initials.

2. Change to Slide Sorter view. Move slide number 2 to the end of the presentation.

3. Change to Normal view and navigate to the first slide in the presentation.

4. Click in the title placeholder and position the insertion point in front of the word Gettysburg. Key **Battle of** and a space.

5. Click in the subtitle placeholder and key **Three Days in July**.

6. Move to slide number 3 (*Day 2—July 2*). Position the insertion point at the end of the last bullet item and press **Enter**. Key the final bullet point **34,000 Confederates vs. 33,000 Federals engaged**.

7. Choose and apply a slide design to the presentation.

8. Save your changes, view the presentation, and then close the presentation.

PROJECT 1-2

1. Open **Project1-2** from the data files. Save the presentation as **Searching** followed by your initials.

2. Change the color scheme of the current slide design to the scheme in the Color Scheme dialog box that has a purple title.

3. Change the layout of slide number 2 to **Title Only**.

4. Copy slide number 2 and paste the copy after slide number 3. Change the title text on this slide (slide number 4) to **Then, Choose a Tool.**

5. Add a slide at the end of the presentation with the Title and Text layout. In the title placeholder, key the title **Other Resources**.

6. Key the following items in the text placeholder:
    Resource lists
    Guides
    Clearinghouses
    Virtual libraries

7. Delete slide number 7.

8. Save your changes, view the presentation, and then close the presentation.

WEB PROJECT

SCANS

In this lesson, you worked on a presentation that offered information on copyright law as it applies to using materials on the Internet. Use Web search tools to find out more about copyright violations that can happen when Internet users "borrow" materials from the Internet. What types of violations occur most frequently? What are the penalties for such violations? Add one or more slides to the The 3Rs presentation you worked on in the Step-by-Steps in this Lesson to present the information you discover.

TEAMWORK PROJECT

SCANS

One of the best uses of a PowerPoint presentation is to persuade an audience to adopt a particular point of view. With a classmate, explore both sides of a specific issue. Follow these steps:

1. As a class, brainstorm some topic issues of interest to the entire class (such as a proposal for a new community park). Or, your instructor may have a list of issues already prepared.

2. Team members should gather information on the issue from surveys or research and then create a presentation to support their particular points of view.

3. If possible, present the slide shows for each issue and have the class vote on which is the most persuasive.

CRITICAL THINKING

SCANS

You have applied a design template to a presentation. Several of the slides in the presentation need special emphasis so your audience will really pay attention. You wonder if you can change the color scheme for those particular slides. Can you do this in PowerPoint?

Use the Help files in PowerPoint to find the answer. Write a brief summary of what you learn.

ENHANCING POWERPOINT PRESENTATIONS

OBJECTIVES

Upon completion of this lesson, you should be able to:

■ Create a new presentation.

■ Use the Slide Finder to copy slides from one presentation to another.

■ Format text.

■ Use Undo and Redo.

■ Insert pictures.

■ Check spelling and use AutoCorrect.

🕐 **Estimated Time: 1 hour**

VOCABULARY

Clip Organizer

Font

Points

Select text

Sizing handles

To create an effective presentation, you must consider all the text and graphics you enter on the slides. Changing the color of the text or changing the style for the text can make the slides easier to read. Adding pictures can help communicate your message and help your audience remember the information you present. It is also important, of course, to make sure you do not have any spelling errors in your slides.

Create a New Presentation

You have several options for creating a new presentation in PowerPoint:

■ You can create a new blank presentation and apply a design template. The design template provides a preformatted slide design with colors, styles, and layouts. If you want to create a presentation without a preset design and without any existing content, you can create a new blank presentation. You can then apply your own design and slide layouts.

■ You can choose the AutoContent Wizard to guide you through a series of questions about the presentation you want to create. Based upon your answers, the Wizard will organize ideas and create a presentation customized from your responses. You will not be instructed to use the AutoContent Wizard to create a presentation in this lesson, but you will have the opportunity to experiment with the feature in the Teamwork Project at the end of this lesson.

- PowerPoint provides several presentations when you choose General Templates in the New Presentation task pane. These presentations already contain content that was previously organized and formatted on slides. You can modify the content to customize the presentation for your needs.

- You can create a new presentation based on an existing presentation. All the slides from the existing presentation are opened in a new document. Save the new presentation with a new filename.

Computer Concepts

PowerPoint provides numerous design templates from which you can choose. Some of the templates are not installed during a typical installation. If you choose a design that is not installed, you may be able to open the design from the application CD.

You will not practice all of the options in this lesson, but you may want to experiment with the features on your own. Regardless of the way you create your presentation, PowerPoint provides placeholders for easy insertion of text, graphics, and other presentation elements.

STEP-BY-STEP ▷ 2.1

1. Start PowerPoint. Or, if PowerPoint is already open, display the New Presentation task pane. (*Hint*: Open the **View** menu and choose **Task Pane.** If the task pane is open but not showing the New Presentations options, click the down arrow in the title bar of the task pane and choose **New Presentation.**)

2. Click the link **From Design Template**. The Slide Design task pane is displayed. Select the **Ocean** template.

3. The slide pane shows a slide layout for a Title Slide. Click in the first placeholder and key **A New Country**. Press **Enter**, then key **A New Experience**.

Speech Recognition

If your computer has speech recognition capability, enable the Dictation mode. Then, dictate the title, click in the placeholder for the subtitle, and then dictate the subtitle.

4. Click in the second placeholder and key your first and last names.

5. Save the document as **Global Students** followed by your initials. Leave the document open for the next Step-by-Step.

Use the Slide Finder

The Slide Finder enables you to quickly find and copy slides from one presentation to another. You can copy selected slides one at a time or you can copy all of the slides at once. When slides are copied to a second presentation, they automatically adopt the format applied to the second presentation. You can access the Slide Finder either in Slide Sorter view or in Normal view.

1. Switch to Slide Sorter view. The current slide is selected.

2. Open the **Insert** menu and choose **Slides from Files**. The Slide Finder dialog box shown in Figure 2-1 is displayed.

FIGURE 2-1
Slide Finder dialog box

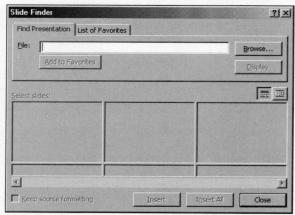

3. Click the Browse button in the dialog box. The Browse dialog box shown in Figure 2-2 is displayed. Locate and select the file Step2-2a in the data files.

4. Click **Open** in the Browse dialog box. Miniature versions of the first three slides in the **Step2-2a** presentation are displayed at the bottom of the Slide Finder dialog box.

5. Click slide number 2 to select it. Then click the **Insert** button. You can probably see that in the screen behind the dialog box, the slide is inserted into your *Global Students* presentation after the first slide. (You can also see that the inserted slide converts to the design template for the current presentation.)

6. The Slide Finder dialog box remains open. Click slide number 2 again to deselect it. Then click slide number 3 to select it, and click **Insert**.

FIGURE 2-2
Browse dialog box

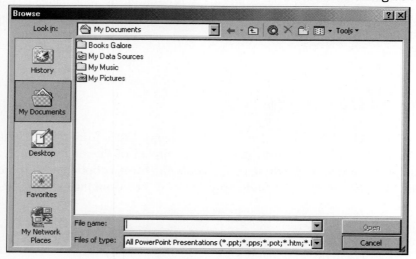

7. Click the **Browse** button and locate and select the file **Step2-2b**. Click **Open**.

8. Click the **Insert All** button. All the slides in the Step2-2b file are inserted in the *Global Students* presentation after the current slide.

9. Click the **Close** button in the Slide Finder dialog box to close it.

10. Notice that there are now ten slides in the presentation. Save the changes and leave the document open for the next Step-by-Step.

Format Text

When you use a design template, the format of the text on each of the slides is predetermined. There may be occasions, however, when you want to alter the text format. You may want to change the *font* style or point size. A font is the general shape and style of a set of characters. Fonts are available in a variety of styles and sizes, and you can use multiple fonts in one document. The size of the font is measured in *points*. The higher the point size is, the larger the font size is. One inch equals approximately 72 points.

You can quickly change font style and point size by using the Formatting toolbar. However, when you open the Font dialog box to change the font, you can also apply other font options such as color, outline, superscript, and shadow. The Font dialog box is also more useful if you want to make several font changes at one time or if you want to explore what options are available and what they would make the text look like.

Use Help to Learn about How to Select Text

To change the text, you must first select the text to be able to change the font, point size, or to apply any other text format such as boldface. When you *select text*, you identify text or blocks of text for editing or formatting. You can select a single character, several characters, a word, a phrase, a sentence, one or more paragraphs, or even the entire document. Once you select text, you can delete it, replace it, change its appearance, move it, copy it, and so on.

You can use the mouse or the keyboard to select text. In the next Step-by-Step we will go to the Help screens to learn more about how to select text. Instead of using the Office Assistant to get help, you will access Help by opening the PowerPoint Help dialog box.

Computer Concepts

You can leave Help screens open as you work with your presentation so you can reference the Help information quickly. Click the buttons in the taskbar to switch between the presentation document and the Help screens.

1. If the Office Assistant is displayed, point to the Office Assistant and right-click. Then choose **Options** in the shortcut menu. Clear the check box for Use the Office Assistant and click **OK**.

2. Open the **Help** menu and choose **Microsoft PowerPoint Help**. If necessary, click the **Show** button on the toolbar to display the Contents, Answer Wizard, and Index tabs.

3. If necessary, click the **Answer Wizard** tab to display the dialog box shown in Figure 2-3.

4. Click in the text box below *What would you like to do?* The text that is in that box is selected. With the text selected, key **select text**, then click **Search**.

5. Under *Select topic to display,* click the topic **Select text**. Read the information that appears at the right that details how to select a word, a paragraph, and all text on a slide.

6. Click in the text box under *What would you like to do?* Key **keyboard shortcuts**, and then click **Search**.

7. A list of topics is displayed in the *Select topic to display* box. Select **Keyboard shortcuts**. In the list that appears at the right, click the link **Select text and objects**. The topic expands to display several keyboard shortcuts and a description of each. Read them all.

8. Study the list of keys in the Help screen. Then click the **Global Students button** in the taskbar to switch back to the presentation document. The Help screen will remain open, so you can refer to the list of keys and practice selecting text. When you're done practicing selecting text, close the Help screen.

FIGURE 2-3
Answer Wizard in the Microsoft PowerPoint Help window

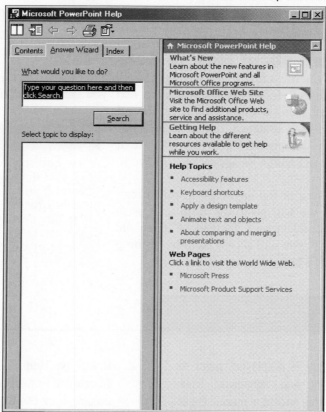

Change the Appearance of Text

You can change the appearance of the text in your presentation by changing the font style, the font size, and the font color. You can also add special emphasis by changing the text to italics, bold, or small capitals. However, using too many fonts or too many different formats generally makes the text harder to read. You want to use formats in moderation.

 Did You Know?

Serif typefaces (such as Times Roman) have embellishments or curls at the ends of the letters. Sans serif typefaces (such as Arial) have plain strokes with clear and simple curves. Serif typefaces are easiest to read and should be used when there are many words on a screen. Sans serif typefaces are usually heavier and bolder and should be used for titles and subtitles.

S TEP-BY-STEP ⟐ 2.4

1. Go to slide number 1 and display the slide in Normal view.

2. Triple-click the text in the first placeholder in the slide pane to select it. *(A New Country A New Experience)*.

3. With the text selected, click the down arrow next to the **Font** box on the Formatting toolbar. Select **Arial** in the drop-down list.

4. With the text still selected, click the down arrow in the **Font Size** box on the Formatting toolbar. Scroll down and select **54** in the drop-down list. The selected text is enlarged to the bigger font size.

 Did You Know?

You can position the insertion point in the Font size box, key the size, and press Enter. This method enables you to enter font sizes that do not appear in the list. However, there is a limit to the maximum and minimum size you can enter.

 Hot Tip

To quickly increase the font size to the next increment in the Font Size box, select the text and press **Ctrl +]** (closing square bracket). Continue pressing the keys for additional increases. Press **Ctrl + [** (opening square bracket) to decrease the font size to the previous increment. This is quite helpful when you want to grow or shrink the text to fit within a specified area on the slide.

5. With the text still selected, open the **Format** menu and choose **Font**. The dialog box shown in Figure 2-4 will display.

FIGURE 2-4
Font dialog box

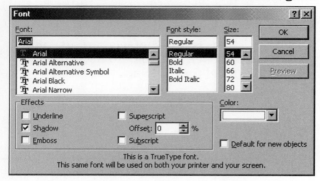

6. Click the down arrow in the box beneath *Color*. A box of color options is displayed. The set of colors shown here are all used in the template design and are, therefore, good choices.

7. Select the gold color. Then, click **OK** to close the Font dialog box.

8. Click anywhere on the slide to deselect the text so you can see the change in the font color. Do not save the changes, but leave the document open for the next Step-by-Step.

Computer Concepts

Too many font styles can make the slides difficult to read, and the mix of fonts can even be distracting. Limit your font styles to two.

Hot Tip

If the Redo button is not displayed on the Standard toolbar, you can click the Toolbar Options button at the right side of the toolbar. Then click the Redo button. The Redo button will appear on the toolbar until you close PowerPoint.

Use Undo and Redo

As you work with a presentation, you may accidentally change some text. Or you may change your mind and want to undo your edits. The Undo command will reverse one or more of your recent actions. You can keep choosing the Undo command to continue reversing actions. Or you can click the down arrow next to the Undo button on the Standard toolbar to see a drop-down list of your recent actions. When you choose an item in this list, all the actions listed above it will also be reversed.

There may be times when you want to redo an edit. The Redo command is similar to the Undo command. You use the Redo command to reverse an Undo action. As with the Undo command, when you click the down arrow next to the Redo button, a list of recent Undo actions appears. You can select one or more actions from the list that appears. When you save the document, the Undo and Redo lists are cleared.

S TEP-BY-STEP ➡ 2.5

1. Click the **Undo** button on the Standard toolbar. The last edit—changing the text color—is reversed to its original color.

2. Click the **down arrow** next to the Undo button. The list of previous actions (*Font Size* and *Font*) is displayed in a drop-down list.

3. Click **Font** in the list. The font change and the font size change are both reversed.

4. Click the **Redo** button on the Standard toolbar. The last undo (changing the font) is reversed and the text is restored to Arial font.

5. Save the changes and leave the document open for the next Step-by-Step.

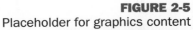

Speech Recognition

If your computer has speech recognition capability, enable the Command mode and say the command to save the document.

Did You Know?

Sometimes photos, clip art, and graphics can be much more powerful than words. Can you think of a time when a picture was more meaningful than words? Share ideas with your classmates.

Insert Pictures

There may be times when you want to add clip art and graphics to your presentation. Often times, pictures help your audience remember your message. PowerPoint allows you to place pictures inside special graphic placeholders. When you insert a picture in a placeholder, the picture replaces the placeholder. You can insert pictures from the *Clip Organizer* (a wide variety of pictures, photographs, sounds, and video clips that you can insert in your documents). You can also insert a picture from a scanned photo or from a file.

When a clip art image is selected, eight small squares called *sizing handles* appear on the border of the graphic. When it is selected, you can cut, copy, paste, delete, move, and resize the picture. To resize the picture, drag a sizing handle. You will see the effects on the screen as you drag. If you drag a corner sizing handle, the picture will be resized proportionally.

STEP-BY-STEP 2.6

1. Go to slide number 2 and display it in Normal view. Notice that the slide layout includes title, content, and text. The content placeholder on the left displays six different icons as shown in Figure 2-5.

2. Point to each of the icons to display the ScreenTip. Notice that you can insert tables, charts, clip art, pictures, diagrams or organization charts, and media clips.

FIGURE 2-5
Placeholder for graphics content

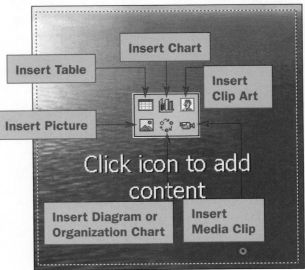

3. Click the **Insert Clip Art** icon. A Select Picture dialog box similar to the one shown in Figure 2-6 is displayed. Do not be concerned if the clip art images in your dialog box are different.

FIGURE 2-6
Select Picture dialog box

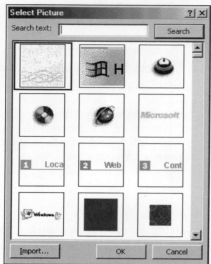

4. Click in the **Search text** box and key **globe**, then click **Search**. PowerPoint will search the Clip Organizer for all pictures related to this word. A dialog box will display images that match the word.

5. Click the picture of the image illustrated in Figure 2-7, or find one that is similar. You may need to scroll down through the pictures or even click the **Keep Looking** link at the bottom of the window.

Speech Recognition

If your computer has speech recognition capability, enable the Command mode and say the command to open the Select Picture dialog box. Then, say the commands to search for and insert the clip art image.

FIGURE 2-7
Search results

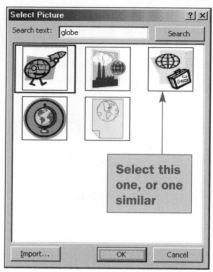

Select this one, or one similar

6. With the clip art image selected, click **OK**. The image is inserted in the slide and the Select Picture dialog box closes.

7. Eight sizing handles should appear around the picture, similar to Figure 2-8. Point to the sizing handle at the top left corner of the image. When the pointer changes to a two-headed arrow, drag the sizing handle up and to the left to make the picture bigger.

FIGURE 2-8
Selected picture with sizing handles

8. Point to the center of the picture. The pointer will change to a four-headed arrow. If necessary, drag the picture to reposition it to the left of the bulleted list.

9. Save the changes and leave the document open for the next Step-by-Step.

Check Spelling and Use AutoCorrect

As you create a presentation, PowerPoint automatically checks for misspelled words. If the words you enter are not in PowerPoint's dictionary, the words will display with a wavy red line. The PowerPoint spellchecker makes it easy to correct spelling mistakes. However, you must also proofread all of your work, because the spellchecker will not identify all spelling errors. For example, if you use the word "too" instead of "two," the incorrect word will not be identified.

Sometimes you make the same spelling errors over and over. For example, you may frequently key "teh" instead of "the." The AutoCorrect feature in PowerPoint can automatically correct this error as you key text in a presentation. You can set the options for the AutoCorrect feature in the AutoCorrect dialog box.

> **Did You Know?**
>
> You can add words to the AutoCorrect list during a spellcheck by clicking the AutoCorrect option in the Spelling and Grammar dialog box.

1. Go to slide number 7 in Normal view. Notice that there is a wavy red line under the word *Austrailia*.

2. Point to the word *Austrailia* and right-click. A shortcut menu is displayed and two correctly spelled words that are likely substitutes for the misspelled word are displayed at the top of the menu. See Figure 2-9.

FIGURE 2-9
Spelling shortcut menu

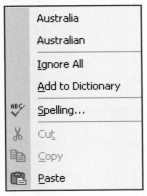

3. Click *Australia* in the shortcut menu. The correct spelling replaces the original spelling in the slide.

4. Go to slide number 5 in Normal view. Position the insertion point in the second placeholder (*Click to add text*). Key the following three lines of text exactly as shown, pressing **Enter** at the end of each line. (*Note:* Watch carefully as you press the **Spacebar** after the word *foriegn*. Notice that PowerPoint automatically corrects the misspelled word.)

```
Study abroad.
Live with a host family.
Speak the foriegn language.
```

5. Save the changes and close the presentation. If the Help screens are still open, close them as well.

Summary

In this lesson, you learned:

- PowerPoint offers several ways to create a new presentation including blank presentations and design templates, the AutoContent Wizard, presentations with content, and existing presentations.

- The Slide Finder enables you to quickly and easily find and copy one or more slides from one presentation to another.

- If you want to change the way text looks on a slide, you can select the text and apply different formats. For example, you can change the font style, font size, and font color.

- The Undo command allows you to reverse the last action. If desired, you can undo multiple actions at one time. The Redo command reverses an undo action.

- Pictures help to clarify the message of your presentation. Often times, pictures help your audience remember your message. PowerPoint makes it easy for you to add a picture to a slide.

- The Spelling and AutoCorrect features in PowerPoint make it easy to correct spelling and keyboarding errors.

VOCABULARY REVIEW

Define the following terms:

Clip Organizer	Points	Sizing handles
Font	Select text	

LESSON 2 REVIEW QUESTIONS

TRUE/FALSE

Circle T if the statement is true or F if the statement is false.

T F 1. To reposition a graphic or picture on a slide, the sizing handles must be displayed.

T F 2. PowerPoint automatically checks for misspelled words as you create a presentation.

T F 3. When you apply a design template to a slide, you cannot change the font of any text on the slide.

T F 4. When you insert a picture in a placeholder, the picture replaces the placeholder.

T F 5. The font dialog box provides many font options that are not available on the standard (default) toolbars.

FILL IN THE BLANK

Complete the following sentences by writing the correct word or words in the blanks provided.

1. The _____ enables you to copy slides from one presentation to another.

2. To change the font size of text, you must first _____ the text.

3. The _____ command will reverse one or more of your recent actions.

4. You can find pictures, photographs, sounds, and video clips in the _____.

5. The _____ feature in PowerPoint automatically corrects common spelling errors as you key them.

LESSON 2 PROJECTS

PROJECT 2-1

1. If necessary, start PowerPoint. Create a new presentation with the **Stream** design template. Accept the Title Slide layout for the first slide. Save the presentation as **Refuge Inn** followed by your initials.

2. In the *title* placeholder, key **Refuge Inn**.

3. In the *subtitle* placeholder, key the following text exactly as shown: **Yuor Refuge from Stress**. PowerPoint will correct the misspelling for you.

4. You've thought of a better phrase for the subtitle. Click **Undo** to remove all but the first word.

5. Key **Island Retreat** as the new subtitle. The subtitle should now read *Your Island Retreat*.

6. Add a new slide and change the slide layout to Title and Text, if necessary. Key the title **About the Refuge Inn**. Key the following bullet items in the text placeholder:
Family owned since 1952
Double rooms, suites, and efficiencies
Excellent restaurants nearby
Hiking, boating, and biking in the Massassoit National Wildlife Refuge

7. Use the Slide Finder to open **Project2-1** from the data files. Insert slides 2, 3, and 4 to your presentation.

8. Add a Title and Text slide at the end of the presentation and key the title **Visit Us Soon!** Key the following bullet items on the slide:
Open year round
Packages available
Call 555-555-4509 for more information

9. Save your changes and close the presentation.

PROJECT 2-2

1. Open **Project 2-2** from the data files and save the presentation as **Refuge Inn 2** followed by your initials.

2. If necessary, switch to Normal view. Beginning with slide number 1, review each slide and check for words with red, wavy underlines. Right-click the misspelled words and select the correct spellings. The name *Massassoit* is spelled correctly. (Choose **Ignore All** to remove wavy red underlines from all instances of the word.)

3. On slide number 1, format the title as Times New Roman, 48 pt., bold and change the color to pale yellow. Format the subtitle as Times New Roman and change its color to the same pale yellow as the title.

4. Format the title on each slide as Times New Roman, 48 pt. bold, and pale yellow. (*Hint:* If you learned how to use the Format Painter in Word, you can use it the same way in PowerPoint to complete this task quickly.)

5. Choose appropriate clip art pictures for slides 3 and 4. Resize and position the pictures as needed.

6. Save your changes and close the presentation.

WEB PROJECT

In this lesson, you created a presentation that offered information about studying abroad. The Web is a good place to locate more information on this subject. Use a search tool to find specific information about a student exchange or foreign study program. What countries can you visit in this program? What are the requirements for joining the program? How do you apply for the program? What courses of study are available? After completing your research, create a PowerPoint presentation that summarizes the information you have gathered.

TEAMWORK PROJECT

In the first two lessons of this unit, you have worked with fairly simple presentations. If you wanted to make a more complex presentation on a specific subject, you could use the AutoContent Wizard in PowerPoint to create the slides for you. With a classmate, explore the AutoContent Wizard using these steps:

1. With your classmate, begin the AutoContent Wizard. Select a presentation type from the list of all presentations. Choose a presentation type with a subject you know a little bit about, such as Selling Your Ideas or Communicating Bad News. It will also be helpful to imagine a particular situation that matches your presentation type. For example, if you choose the Communicating Bad News presentation, imagine that you and your teammate are the management team of a small company, and you each have to tell your employees that none of them will receive bonuses this year.

2. Answer the questions the Wizard asks you. If necessary, use the Help feature in PowerPoint to find out what options the Wizard is giving you.

3. After the presentation appears, examine the sample slide material in the outline pane. You will need to replace the sample text with your own text.

4. Replace the text as necessary to fit the situation you have imagined. Both classmates should contribute in creating new text (you can alternate slides to share the work). Delete any unnecessary slides and add slides if necessary.

5. Run your presentation for the class or make it available on your network.

CRITICAL THINKING

You have created a presentation of almost 30 slides and have applied a design template to all the slides. You really like the background and graphics of this design, but you think the font used throughout is not very attractive. You think a different font could give your presentation a more professional appearance. Is there an easier way to replace one font with another throughout an entire presentation?

Use the Help feature in PowerPoint to find the answer to this question. Write a brief report on what you learn.

WORKING WITH VISUAL ELEMENTS

OBJECTIVES

Upon completion of this lesson, you should be able to:

- Apply animation schemes and preview animation.
- Create custom animation.
- Add sound effects to animations.
- Change the animation sequence.
- Format the animation timing.
- Modify an animation effect.
- Format slide transitions.
- Add animated clip art graphics and sound clips.
- Print the presentation.

⏱ **Estimated Time: 1 hour**

VOCABULARY

Animation

Animation schemes

Emphasis effect

Entrance effect

Exit effect

Sound effect

Transitions

Trigger

Adding special effects is the fun part of creating a presentation. PowerPoint offers several features to help you control the flow of information in your presentation. You can also use sound clips and animated clip art graphics to draw attention to the information and to hold the interest of your audience. However, these features must be used effectively if they are to enhance your presentation.

When you add *animation*, you add special visuals or sound effects to text or an object. Animations add visual appeal and when used effectively, they can help keep the audience interested in your presentation. Without animation, text and objects automatically appear when a slide is displayed. However, when you add animation, you can determine how and when the text or graphics will appear on each slide. For example, you can have text fly in from the left, and you can have a picture zoom out from the center. As you format the animations, you can preview them to see how they work.

Apply Animation Schemes and Preview Animation

PowerPoint offers several *animation schemes,* which are pre-designed sets of visual effects. To see the available animation scheme options, you must display the Animation Schemes task pane. The schemes are organized and listed in three categories: Subtle, Moderate, and Exciting. An animation usually includes an effect for the slide title, bulleted lists and paragraphs of text, and objects on the slide. You can apply these animation schemes to selected slides or to all the slides in the presentation.

After you format animations, you can preview them for one slide or for the whole presentation. The AutoPreview option in the Animation task pane allows you to see a preview of animation effects automatically when you add or modify an effect. To see the preview again, you can click the Play button. When you preview a slide using the Play button in the Animation Schemes task pane, you do not need to click the mouse to *trigger* (start) the animation. However, the default trigger setting to start an animation in Slide Show view is to click the mouse. So, even though the animation played automatically in the preview, you may need to click the mouse button to trigger the animation in Slide Show view.

Computer Concepts

You can apply an animation scheme in Slide Sorter view, but you will not be able to preview the animation unless you are working in Normal view.

S TEP-BY-STEP ▷ 3.1

1. Open **Step3-1** from the data files. Save the presentation as **3 Days** followed by your initials. If necessary, switch to Normal view.

2. Open the **Slide Show** menu and choose **Animation Schemes**. The Slide Design task pane shown in Figure 3-1 is displayed. Do not be concerned that your list under *Recently Used* does not match the list in the figure.

Speech Recognition

If your computer has speech recognition capability, enable the Command mode and say the commands to display the Animation Schemes task pane.

3. Make sure the **AutoPreview** option at the bottom of the task pane is turned on. When it is turned on, the box will have a checkmark.

4. Scroll down to view the *Moderate* list and select **Zoom**. Because AutoPreview is turned on, you should see the animation in the slide pane as soon as you select the scheme. The animation scheme is applied to the first slide only.

FIGURE 3-1
Slide Design task pane

5. Click the **Play** button at the bottom of the task pane to see the animation again. The Play button previews the current slide only.

6. Go to slide number 2 and apply the **Fade in one by one** scheme listed under *Subtle*.

7. Go to slide number 3 and select the **Zoom** scheme. (*Hint*: The scheme is now listed near the top of the task pane under *Recently Used*.)

8. Go to slide number 4. Explore the other schemes and apply a scheme of your choice.

9. Go to slide number 5 and select the **Big title** scheme under *Exciting*.

10. Click the **Apply to All Slides** button at  the bottom of the task pane. The *Big title* scheme is applied to all slides in the presentation.

11. Go to slide number 1. Click the **Slide Show** button at the bottom  of the task pane. Slide Show view launches, starting with the current slide. Click the mouse button to trigger each animation and then to advance to the next slide. Press **Esc** to end the slide show.

Computer Concepts

To remove an animation scheme, select No Animation in the Slide Design task pane.

12. Save the changes and close the presentation.

Create Custom Animations

Instead of using a preset animation scheme, you can apply custom animation to your PowerPoint presentation. You can select which text and objects you want to animate on each slide. However, if you want the effects applied to all slides, it would be easier to use an animation scheme. You can only apply custom animations to the text and objects on a single slide at a time, not to all slides in the presentation at once.

To apply custom animation, you must display the slide in Normal view. Then you display the Custom Animation task pane and select the effects you want. The effects options include Entrance, Emphasis, Exit, and Motion Path. All effects are organized in four categories: Basic, Subtle, Moderate, and Exciting.

To apply an effect, you must first select the text or object you want to format. The effects you can choose from appear in the Custom Animation list in the order you apply them. A green star in front of the item indicates that an *entrance effect* has been applied. An entrance effect controls how the text or object animates as it appears on the slide. A yellow star indicates an *emphasis effect*. An emphasis effect controls the animation effects after the text or object appears. A red star indicates an *exit effect* An exit effect controls the animation effects at the end of the animation sequence. To apply the same effect to multiple items, select all the items before choosing the effect.

If you have several items on a slide, you can have a variety of animations applied. PowerPoint makes it easy to review the animations you have applied. All animated items are referenced on the slide with a number tag that indicates the sequence in which the animation effects will occur. However, this tag will not display in Slide Show view, and it will not print. When the Custom Animation task pane is displayed, the title for each animation appears in a list. An icon is displayed next to the title to represent the type of animation selected. If you click a title in the list, the settings for the start, color, and speed for that animation will display.

Computer Concepts

If an animation scheme has been applied, you must remove the scheme before you can apply custom animations.

Apply an Entrance Effect

You can apply an entrance effect to help focus your audience's attention on a particular item on a slide. For example, you can apply an entrance effect to text in a bulleted list so that the list is introduced one bulleted item at a time. When this type of animation is applied, each bulleted item is tagged and listed separately in the Custom Animation list. However, in a bulleted list, only the first bulleted item appears in the list. The remaining bulleted items are collapsed and do not display unless you expand the list.

STEP-BY-STEP ▷ 3.2

1. Open **Step3-2** from the data files and save the presentation as **Exchange Student** followed by your initials.

   Speech Recognition

   If your computer has speech recognition capability, enable the Command mode and say the commands to open the file and save it with a new name (and path if necessary).

2. Go to slide number 2. If necessary, switch to Normal view.

3. Open the **Slide Show** menu and choose **Custom Animation**. The task pane shown in Figure 3-2 is displayed. If necessary, turn on the **AutoPreview** option. Note that most of the options in the task pane are dimmed because no text or objects have been selected.

   Hot Tip

   You can also access the Custom Animation pane by clicking the down arrow at the top of the task pane and selecting Custom Animation in the drop-down list.

4. Click the clip art image on the slide to select it. Then  click the **Add Effect** button in the task pane to display the menu shown in Figure 3-3.

FIGURE 3-2
Custom Animation task pane

FIGURE 3-3
Add Effect menu

203

5. Click **Entrance** to display a submenu similar to the one shown in Figure 3-4.

FIGURE 3-4
Entrance submenu

6. Click **More Effects** to display the Add Entrance Effect dialog box shown in Figure 3-5. Make sure that the **Preview Effect** option is turned on. Notice that the options display with green stars and that some of the stars reflect movement or a change in size.

FIGURE 3-5
Add Entrance Effect dialog box

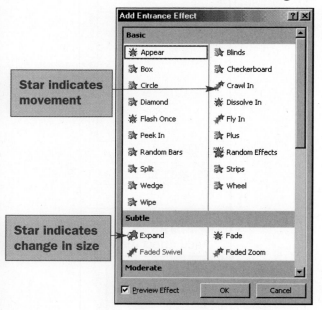

7. Point to the title bar in the dialog box and drag the box to the side of the screen so you can see the clip art graphic. Scroll down to the *Exciting* category and click **Pinwheel**. The animation will preview in the slide pane.

8. Click **OK** to apply the effect and close the dialog box. Notice that there is now a number tab (*1*) next to the clip art image on the slide. Also notice that the animated item is now displayed in the Custom Animation list in the task pane.

Computer Concepts

To remove an effect, select the animation item in the Custom Animation list and click the **Remove** button.

9. Position the insertion point in the first bulleted item on the slide.

10. Click the **Add Effect** button in the task pane, select **Entrance**, and then select **More Effects**. Under *Moderate*, select **Stretch** and then click **OK**.

11. Notice that there are now three tags correlating the items on the slide to the Custom Animation list in the task pane. However, item number 3 (the second bulleted item in the text box) does not appear in the Custom Animation list, as is shown in Figure 3-6. Click the double arrows below the number 2 item in the list to expand the contents of the list.

12. Save the changes and leave the document open for the next Step-by-Step.

FIGURE 3-6

Custom Animation task pane with two items in the Custom Animation list

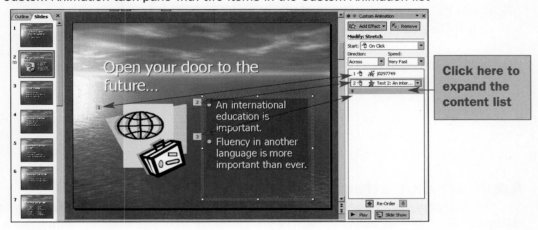

Apply an Emphasis Effect

You can also apply an emphasis effect to draw attention to text or an object on a slide. For example, you can create an animation that will change the fill color or font color of text. The procedures for applying an emphasis effect are the same as for applying an entrance effect. However, the effect options available for emphasis depend on whether you are applying the animation to an object or to text.

S TEP-BY-STEP ⇨ 3.3

1. Go to slide number 3 in Normal view.

2. Position the insertion point in the first bulleted item.

3. Click the **Add Effect** button in the task pane, choose **Emphasis**, and then select **More Effects**. The Add Emphasis Effect dialog box shown in Figure 3-7 displays. If necessary, turn on the **Preview Effect** option.

4. In the Subtle category, select **Color Wave** and then click **OK**. Notice that there are three animation tags on the slide.

5. Click the *Color* box in the task pane and select the **gold** color.

6. Save the changes and leave the presentation open for the next Step-by-Step.

FIGURE 3-7
Add Emphasis Effect dialog box

Apply an Exit Effect

You can apply an exit effect to make text or objects leave the slide. For example, you can make text disappear very subtly by fading it away, or you can make an object disappear with a much more dramatic exit such as making it disappear quickly.

S TEP-BY-STEP ➭ 3.4

1. Go to slide number 10 in Normal view.

2. Click the title *Global Students* to select it. Hold down **Shift** and click the subtitle containing the URL. Both items should be selected.

Speech Recognition

If your computer has speech recognition capability, enable the Command mode and say the commands to navigate to slide number 10. (*Hint*: Say Page Up or Page Down to move from one slide to another in the Outline pane.)

3. Click the **Add Effect** button in the task pane, choose **Exit**, and then select **More Effects**. The Add Exit Effect dialog box shown in Figure 3-8 is displayed. If necessary, turn on the **Preview Effect** option.

FIGURE 3-8
Add Exit Effect dialog box

4. Under the Basic category, select **Peek Out**. Click **OK** to apply the effect and close the dialog box. Notice there are two number tags on the slide, but they both have the same number. This is because you applied the effect to both items at the same time.

5. Save the changes and leave the presentation open for the next Step-by-Step.

Extra Challenge

You can apply or draw a motion path effect to control where text or objects appear on a slide. Explore the Motion Path effect feature by first selecting some of the preset paths and then by drawing your own paths. To get more information about the feature, search the help screens for the key words **motion paths**.

Add a Sound Effect to an Animation

When you animate text and objects, you also have the option of adding *sound effects* to them. A sound effect is a recorded sound that can be added to animated text or objects on a PowerPoint slide. The sound can be stored in a file on your computer, a network, the Internet, or the Microsoft Clip Organizer. To add a sound effect, the text or object must already have an animation applied to it.

STEP-BY-STEP ⟹ 3.5

1. The title and subtitle should still be selected in the slide pane and in the Custom Animation task pane.

2. Click the down arrow for the second selected item in the Custom Animation list and select **Effect Options**.

3. If necessary, click the **Effect** tab to display the Peek Out dialog box shown in Figure 3-9.

FIGURE 3-9
Effect tab in the Peek Out dialog box

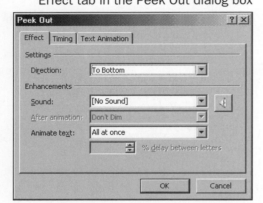

4. Click in the *Sound* box to display the list of options. Scroll down and select **Chime** and then click **OK**.

Hot Tip

If this is the first time sound effects have been applied on your computer, you may be prompted to install the Sound Effects feature. To complete the installation process, you will need the Microsoft Office XP CD-ROM.

5. Click the **Play** button to preview the slide with the sound effect. Notice that both lines of text exit at the same time.

6. Save the changes and leave the presentation open for the next Step-by-Step.

Hot Tip

To adjust the sound effect volume, click the speaker button in the Peek Out dialog box (Effect tab) and then drag the control button up or down to the desired setting.

Format the Animation Timing

As stated earlier, by default, animations are set to trigger when you click the mouse. However, the animation can be formatted to occur automatically. You can set timing options that will determine when the animation begins and the speed at which the animation occurs. You can even format the animation to repeat a specified number of times.

STEP-BY-STEP ⟹ 3.6

1. Click the task pane to deselect the items in the Custom Animation list, then click the URL item to select only that item.

2. Click the down arrow next to the item in the task pane and select **Timing**. The Timing tab in the Peek Out dialog box is displayed. See Figure 3-10.

FIGURE 3-10
Timing tab in the Peek Out dialog box

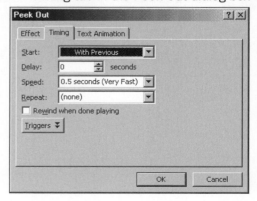

3. Click the *Start* box and select **After Previous**.

4. Click the *Delay* box and either key or select **1.5**.

5. Click the *Speed* box and select **3 seconds (Slow)**.

6. Click in the *Repeat* box and select **Until Next Click**. Then click **OK**.

7. Click the **Play** button to preview the new timing. Note that the URL animation will only repeat one time in the preview.

8. Click the **Slide Show** button to view the slide in full screen. Click to trigger the animation. First the title will exit very quickly with a sound effect. Then, 1.5 seconds later, the URL will exit a bit slower with a sound effect. The URL exit repeats, but the sound effect is not repeated. After the URL has exited a few times, click the mouse to end the animation.

9. Switch to Normal view. Save the changes and leave the presentation open for the next Step-by-Step.

Change the Animation Sequence

There may be times when you want to rearrange the order of animations after you apply the effects. You can change the order of your animations at any time by using the Custom Animation list in the task pane.

STEP-BY-STEP ⇨ 3.7

1. Go to slide number 2 and click the **Play** button to preview the current sequence. Notice the order in which the text and object appear. The object appears before the bulleted list.

2. Select Item number 2 in the Custom Animation list.

3. Click the **Up arrow** for the Re-Order but- tons at the bottom of the task pane twice. Notice that order and numbers change in the task pane and the number tags on the slide also change.

4. Click the **Play** button to preview the new sequence. The bulleted items now appear before the object.

5. Save the changes and leave the presentation open for the next Step-by-Step.

Modify an Animation Effect

When the animation involves movement, you can format the direction and/or the speed of the movement. When the animation involves a change in size, you can specify the percentage of the change in size, and you can also specify the speed for the change in size.

S TEP-BY-STEP ▷ 3.8

1. Click the **Play** button to preview the current sequence. Notice the direction in which the bulleted list stretches across the slide.

2. If necessary, select item number 1 in the Custom Animation list.

3. Click the down arrow in the Direction box above the Custom Animation list in the task pane and select **From Left**.

4. Click the down arrow in the *Speed* box above the Custom Animation list in the task pane and select **Fast**.

5. Click the **Play** button to preview the new sequence.

6. Go to slide number 10. Select item number 1 in the Custom Animation list. Hold down **Shift** and select the second item in number 1. Then click the **Remove** button. All the animations from the slide (including the exit effects and the sound effect) are removed.

7. Save the changes and leave the presentation open for the next Step-by-Step.

Format Transitions

Slide *transitions* determine the changes in the display that occur as you move from one slide to another in Slide Show view. For example, you can format the transition so the current slide fades to black before the next slide is displayed. Or you can choose to have the next slide automatically appear after a designated number of seconds. You can even choose a sound effect that will play as the transition occurs. You can apply the transition choices to a single slide or to all the slides in the presentation. To apply a slide transition, you must work in the Slide Transition task pane.

STEP-BY-STEP 3.9

1. Open the **Slide Show** menu and choose **Slide Transition**. The Slide Transition task pane shown in Figure 3-11 is displayed. Make sure **AutoPreview** is turned on.

FIGURE 3-11
Slide Transition task pane

 Hot Tip

You can also open the Slide Transition task pane by clicking the down-arrow at the top of the task pane and choosing Slide Transition in the menu.

2. Under *Apply to selected slides*, scroll down and select **Strips Right-Down**.

3. Under *Modify transition*, in the *Speed* drop-down box, select **Medium**.

4. Under *Advance slide*, deselect **On Mouse Click**. Then, select **Automatically after**. In the box below, key or select **00.03**.

5. Click the **Apply to All** Slides button.

6. Go to slide number 1 and then click the **Slide Show** button to view the presentation in full screen. Each slide should automatically advance after three seconds.

7. Press **Esc** to exit the slide show. Save the changes and leave the presentation open for the next Step-by-Step.

COMMUNICATION SKILLS

Individuals most likely to be promoted and succeed have something in common—they have good oral and written communication skills. The ability to make formal presentations is an increasingly important skill for many. In fact, communication skills can greatly enhance one's success in the classroom or on the job.

Many jobs require that an employee be able to organize, analyze, and communicate information. Moreover, employees are often called upon to formally present information. The audience may be as small as one or two persons, or it may be a much larger group. To deliver an effective presentation, you must possess the confidence to deliver the presentation competently.

Add Animated Clip Art Graphics and Sound Clips

Animated clip art, sound, and music add an extra dimension to a presentation. You can use sound and video at any point in a presentation to add emphasis or set the mood for the audience. Animated clip art graphics and sound clips are available in the Clip Organizer. You can also use clips from other sources.

Add an Animated Clip Art Graphic

You insert the animated clip art graphic where you want it to play during a slide show. The slide must be displayed in Normal view before you can insert the clip. The clip is inserted in the slide as an object and is displayed with a graphic. You can choose to have the animation play automatically when you move to the slide, or you can format the animation to play only when you click its image during the slide show.

S TEP-BY-STEP ▷ 3.10

1. Go to slide number 10.

2. Open the **Insert** menu and choose **Movies and Sounds**. Select **Movie from Clip Organizer** in the submenu. Results similar to those shown in Figure 3-12 are displayed. Notice that each thumbnail displays a yellow star in the bottom right corner, indicating that the clip is animated.

> **Did You Know?**
>
> If you are connected to the Internet, you can search for available clips online by clicking the Clips Online link at the bottom of the task pane.

3. Point to the thumbnail showing the two computers and the globe (or find a similar clip) to preview the movie clip. When you see the down arrow for the thumbnail, click the arrow and then select **Preview/Properties** in the menu. Click the **Close** button in the Preview/Properties dialog box to close the preview.

FIGURE 3-12
Task pane for inserting Movies from the Clip Organizer

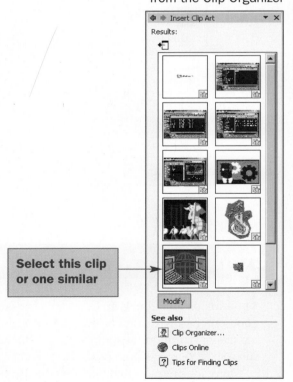

Select this clip or one similar

4. Click the thumbnail. The movie clip is inserted on the slide as an object.

5. Resize and reposition the clip at the bottom of the slide below the URL.

6. Open the **Slide Show** menu and choose **Slide Transition**.

7. In the task pane under *Advance slide*, deselect **Automatically after** so this last slide will not advance without a mouse click. If necessary, turn on the option **On mouse click**.

8. Click the **Slide Show** button to view the slide in full screen. Notice that the movie clip continues to play until you click the mouse button.

 Did You Know?

Web sites supported by various branches of the U.S. government are good sources of images, sounds, and video clips. Make sure the site allows you to use their multimedia materials.

9. Press **Esc** to exit the slide show and return to Normal view. Save the changes and leave the presentation open for the next Step-by-Step.

Add a Sound or Music Clip

In addition to applying sound effects, you can also add a sound or music clip. Adding a sound or music clip is very similar to adding an animated graphic clip. You can add sound and music clips provided in the Clip Organizer or you can add sound or music from a file or CD audio track. The slide must be displayed in Normal view before you can insert the clip. The sound or music clip is represented on the slide by an icon. You can choose to have the clip play automatically or you can set the option so the clip only plays when you click the object icon. If you do not want the sound clip icon to show during your slide show you can hide it behind the movie clip.

STEP-BY-STEP ⟹ 3.11

1. In Normal view, with Slide number 10 displayed, open the **Insert** menu and choose **Movies and Sounds**. Select **Sound from Clip Organizer** in the submenu.

2. Point to a thumbnail, click the down arrow, and preview the sound clip. When you find an appropriate clip, insert it in the document. When prompted to automatically play the sound in the slide show, click **Yes**.

3. Drag the sound clip icon to the bottom right corner of the slide.

4. Right-click the sound clip icon and choose Custom Animation in the shortcut menu.

5. Click the down arrow for the item in the Custom Animation list and select Timing. Click the down arrow in the *Repeat* box and select Until Next Click. Click OK.

6. Click the **Slide Show** button in the task pane to view the slide in full screen. The sound clip will continue to play until you click the mouse. Exit the slide show to return to Normal view.

7. If necessary, display the Drawing toolbar. Select the sound icon and click **Draw** on the Drawing toolbar. Choose **Order** in the pop-up menu, and then select **Send to Back**. Then, drag the icon to the middle of the movie clip image.

8. Save the changes and leave the presentation open for the next Step-by-Step.

Hot Tip

To edit or remove the sound clip, you will need to select the movie clip image, choose the Order command, and send that image to the back. Then you will see the sound icon.

Use Help to Learn about Ways to Print the Presentation

PowerPoint offers several options for printing your presentation. You can print the outline, individual slides, handouts, and more. The Help screens will allow you to learn about the available options.

STEP-BY-STEP ⟹ 3.12

1. If the Office Assistant is not displayed, open the **Help** menu and choose **Show the Office Assistant**.

2. Click the Office Assistant. Key **print** in the text box, then click **Search**.

3. A list of topics is displayed. Select **About printing**.

4. Read the paragraph of text and then click the link **Outline, notes pages, and handouts**.

5. Read the paragraph about printing an outline.

6. If the *Contents*, *Answer Wizard*, and *Index* tabs are not displayed, click the **Show** button on the Help toolbar. Note: If you click the Show button and the Help panel displays without the tabs, click the **Options** button on the Help toolbar and then select **Show Tabs** in the menu.

7. Click the **Answer Wizard** tab if necessary. In the *What would you like to do?* box, key **print outline** and then click **Search**.

8. Read the steps for printing an outline. In Step 3, click the link **Print from Microsoft PowerPoint**.

9. Read the three steps and leave the Help screen open. Then click in the PowerPoint window.

10. Open the **File** menu and choose **Print Preview**. Click the down arrow in the *Print What* box on the Print Preview toolbar, and then select **Outline View**. The outline is displayed as it would print.

11. Click the **Close** button on the Print Preview toolbar.

12. Click the application close box to close the presentation and the Help screen. If other applications are open, the Help screen will not close.

Summary

In this lesson, you learned:

■ Animation effects help make your presentation more interesting. You can set effect options to control how text and objects appear on your slides.

■ An animation scheme provides pre-designed sets of visual effects that can be applied to selected slides or to all slides in the presentation.

■ You can preview animations for one slide or for the whole presentation using options that are available in the task pane.

■ Custom animations enable you to select the text and objects you want to animate. You can apply effects that determine how text or objects enter, display, and exit the slide.

■ Sound effects can be added to enhance the animation of text and objects.

■ Timing options allow you to determine when the animation begins and the speed at which the animation occurs.

■ Once animations are applied, you can rearrange the order in which animated text and objects appear.

■ The slide transition affects how each new slide appears. You can apply transition settings to a single slide or to all the slides in the presentation.

■ Animated clip art, sound or music clips can add a new dimension to a presentation. The clips can be formatted to play automatically or to play when clicked by the mouse.

■ PowerPoint provides several options for printing a presentation, including the outline, notes pages, handouts, and transparencies.

VOCABULARY REVIEW

Define the following terms:

Animation	Entrance effect	Transitions
Animation schemes	Exit effect	Trigger
Emphasis effect	Sound effect	

LESSON 3 REVIEW QUESTIONS

TRUE/FALSE

Circle T if the statement is true or F if the statement is false.

T F 1. By default, animations are set to trigger when you click the mouse.

T F 2. To add a sound effect, the text or object must already have an animation applied to it.

T F 3. You can insert a sound effect from the Clip Organizer or from any other source of sound files.

T F 4. When you format a slide transition, it must be applied to all slides in the presentation.

T F 5. When you create custom animations, you can apply the effects to all slides in the presentation.

FILL IN THE BLANK

Complete the following sentences by writing the correct word or words in the blanks provided.

1. A(n) _____ effect controls the animation effects after the text or object appears.

2. A(n) _____ effect controls how the text animates as it appears on the slide.

3. A(n) _____ effect controls the animation effects at the end of the animation sequence.

4. A slide must be displayed in _____ view before you can insert an animated graphic or sound clip.

5. When you apply a(n) _____ to a slide or group of slides, the visual effects are already formatted.

LESSON 3 PROJECTS

PROJECT 3-1

1. Open **Project3-1** from the data files. Save the presentation as **Rain Forest** followed by your initials.

2. In the subtitle placeholder on slide number 1, key **A Report by** and then key your name.

3. Go to slide number 2. Customize the animation for the bulleted list to enter the slide with a Peek In format from the bottom. Choose an appropriate speed for the Entrance effect. The text should appear on a mouse click.

4. Go to slide number 3. Customize the animation for the items on the slide as follows:
    A. Format an Emphasis effect so that the clip art image grows by 150%. The animation should start on a mouse click.
    B. Format an Entrance effect of your choice for the title. The animation should start after the animation for A.
    C. Format an Entrance effect of your choice for the bulleted list. The animation should start after the animation for B.

5. Go to slide number 4. Customize the animation for bulleted list and the title as follows:
   A. Format an Exit effect so items in the bulleted list leave the slide with the Spiral Out effect.
   B. Set the speed at 2 seconds (Medium).
   C. Format an Exit effect so the title exits with the Stretchy effect.

6. Go to slide number 3. Change the order of the animation sequence so that the title is the first item in the animation sequence.

7. Preview the slide show from the beginning.

8. Save the changes and leave the presentation open for the next project.

PROJECT 3-2

Creating such a variety of effects from one slide to the next can be distracting. If you get too creative with animation features, your audience may have trouble focusing on the content of your presentation. In this project you will create a more consistent flow for all the slides in your presentation.

1. Save the presentation as **Rain Forest 2** followed by your initials.

2. Go to slide number 1 and insert an appropriate sound clip to play automatically. Position the sound icon in the lower right corner of the slide.

3. Apply an animation scheme of your choice to all slides in the presentation.

4. Choose an appropriate slide transition. Set the speed for the transition to medium. Format the slides to advance automatically after five seconds. Apply the transition formats to all slides in the presentation.

5. Preview the entire slide show and save the changes.

6. Display the presentation outline in Print Preview.

7. Close the presentation.

WEB PROJECT

In this lesson, you inserted animated objects and sound clips in your presentations. You can also insert video clips and movies in slides as objects. Video clips are short movies that play when you display the slide during a presentation. Suppose you intend to create a presentation about hurricanes and want to include a video of hurricane movement taken from space. Go to the NASA web site (www.nasa.gov at the time this text was published) and navigate links to the multimedia video gallery. Locate a link that will show you videos of hurricanes. Choose a hurricane and then click the movie link for that hurricane. What type of "player" do you have to use to view the video? How large is the video file? Could you store a presentation that includes this video on a floppy disk? Play the video on your computer, if possible.

The presentations you created in this lesson would work well as Web sites on the Internet. As with most other Office XP applications, PowerPoint presentations are easy to save as Web pages. In this project, explore with a teammate how to publish a PowerPoint presentation on the Web.

1. With your teammate, choose a topic for your Web presentation, or open one of the presentations you have created in this unit.

2. Both teammates should read the Help material in PowerPoint about creating Web presentations. There are two ways to prepare a presentation for Web viewing: You can save the presentation as a Web page or you can publish the presentation. Make sure you both understand the differences between these two ways of putting PowerPoint material on the Web.

3. One teammate should try publishing the presentation while the other should simply save the presentation as a Web page. Describe your experience to your teammate and compare the processes for both approaches. How does the process differ for each approach? Which approach gives you more control over the presentation's appearance on the Web? Which is easiest?

4. View your presentations in your browser and navigate the slides using the options available. After you have explored how a presentation would look on the Web, close your browser and your presentation.

CRITICAL THINKING

You have created a presentation to convince fellow citizens to support a local clean-up campaign. You have included as the last slide a list of several phone numbers and contact names for more information on the campaign. You anticipate that your audience will want to see this information a number of times during the presentation. It will be time-consuming to click through the slides each time to reach the last slide. PowerPoint offers several ways that you can jump directly to a specific slide during a presentation. Research this topic using Help and write a brief report discussing at least two methods of moving between slides. Create a short presentation to demonstrate the two methods.

COMMAND SUMMARY—POWERPOINT

FEATURE	MENU COMMAND	KEYSTROKE	TOOLBAR BUTTON	LESSON
Add slide	Insert, New Slide	Ctrl + M		1
Animation effect, add	Slide Show, Custom Animation			3
Animation scheme, add	Slide Show, Animation Schemes			3
Color scheme, change	Format, Slide Design, Color Schemes			1
Copy slide	Edit, Copy	Ctrl + C		1
Custom animation, apply	Slide Show, Custom Animation			3
Cut slide	Edit, Cut	Ctrl + X		1
Design template, apply	Format, Slide Design, Design Templates			1
Font, change	Format, Font			2
Font color, change	Format, Font			2
Font point size, change	Format, Font	Ctrl + [(to decrease), Ctrl +] (to increase)		2
Help, get	Help, Microsoft PowerPoint Help	F1		2
Insert clip art	Insert, Picture, Clip Art			2
Insert slides from another presentation	Insert, Slides from Files			2
Movie clip, add	Insert, Movies and Sounds, Movie from Clip Organizer or Movie from File			3
New presentation, create	File, New			2
Normal view	View, Normal			1
Paste slide	Edit, Paste	Ctrl + V		1
Pen, use in show	Click triangle in lower left corner to display shortcut menu,Pointer Options, Pen			1

FEATURE	MENU COMMAND	KEYSTROKE	TOOLBAR BUTTON	LESSON
Redo change	Edit, Redo	Ctrl + Y	⟳	2
Slide layout, change	Format, Slide Layout			1
Slide Show, run	Slide Show, View Show or View, Slide Show	F5	🖵	1
Slide Sorter view	View, Slide Sorter		⊞	1
Slide transition, apply	Slide Show, Slide Transition			3
Sound clip, add	Insert, Movies and Sounds, Sound from Clip Organizer or Sound from File			3
Undo change	Edit, Undo	Ctrl + Z	↺	2

REVIEW QUESTIONS

TRUE/FALSE

Circle T if the statement is true or F if the statement is false.

T F **1.** To apply custom animation, you must display the slide in Normal view.

T F **2.** You can add a new slide in Slide Sorter view or in Normal view.

T F **3.** An easy way to reorganize slides is to drag them into place in Slide Sorter view.

T F **4.** Unless you specify otherwise, animations are set to trigger when you click the mouse.

T F **5.** When using the Slide Finder, you must choose to insert all slides.

T F **6.** The Redo command repeats an action you just performed.

T F **7.** With custom animation, you can choose to animate any or all of the text and objects on a slide.

T F **8.** To insert a sound clip, the slide must already have animation effects applied to it.

T F **9.** A design template provides a preformatted slide design with colors, fonts, and layouts.

T F **10.** As you create a presentation, PowerPoint automatically checks for and corrects mis-spelled words.

MATCHING

Match the correct term in Column 1 to its description in Column 2.

Column 1   **Column 2**

____ 1. Slide Finder   **A.** Area where you can add text, a picture, a table, or a chart.

____ 2. Slide Sorter view   **B.** Changes the way text or objects look on a slide.

____ 3. Design template   **C.** View that shows you a slide pane, an outline pane, and a notes pane.

____ 4. Entrance effect   **D.** Determines the changes in the display that occurs as you move from one slide to another in Slide Show view.

____ 5. Clip Organizer   **E.** Feature that lets you select and insert slides from another presentation into the current presentation.

____ 6. Slide Show view   **F.** View that allows you to rearrange slides using the drag-and-drop edit feature.

____ 7. Normal view   **G.** Collection of pictures, photographs, sounds, and videos.

____ 8. Placeholder   **H.** Specifies a color scheme, text formats, backgrounds, and bullet styles.

____ 9. Emphasis effect   **I.** Controls how text and objects animate as they appear on the slide.

____ 10. Slide transition   **J.** View that shows you a full view of the slide.

CROSS-CURRICULAR PROJECTS

MATH

The United States is one of the few countries in the world that has not adopted the metric system of measurement, although the metric system is studied in school and most containers and packages offer metric equivalents for standard English measurements. Research the topic and create a PowerPoint presentation that gives pros and cons for adopting the metric system throughout the country. Your presentation should include at least six slides, and should use many of the concepts you learned in this Unit.

SOCIAL STUDIES

Choose a country in the world that you would like to know more about. You might want to pick a country currently in the news, a country you have visited, or a country from which your ancestors came. Use an almanac or Web search tools to find information on the geography, industries, climate, and population of the country. Create a PowerPoint slide show with a minimum of seven slides to present the results of your research.

SCIENCE

The twentieth century saw many breakthroughs in the field of medicine, from the discovery of penicillin to open-heart surgery to gene therapy. Using an almanac, encyclopedia, or Web search tools, make a list of the important medical discoveries in the twentieth century. Arrange your list by decade. In a PowerPoint presentation, use a separate slide (or more than one slide, if you need the room) for each decade and list the medical discoveries you researched.

LANGUAGE ARTS

Choose a novelist, playwright, or poet whose work you admire. Use an encyclopedia or Web search tools to find out about the writer's life and work. Create a PowerPoint slide show that gives biographical information about the writer and lists his or her major works. Include dates for each major work. If the writer's works have been adapted as films, include information on the films as well.

PROJECT 1

1. Open **Project1** from the data files and save the presentation as **Everest** followed by your initials.

2. Apply the **Mountain Top** design template.

3. On slide number 1, click to the left of the first word in the title placeholder. Key **Mt. Everest:** and then press **Enter**.

4. Change the font of the title to **Times New Roman 54 pt**. Change the font size and format of the text that states the author of the quote (*—Ed Viesturs*) to **24 pt** and **Italic**.

5. Change the titles of the remaining slides in the presentation to **Times New Roman 54 pt**.

6. Change the layout of slide 6 to **Title and 2-Column Text**. In the new right-hand column, key the following text:

   First ascent by an American: Whittaker, 1963
   First ascent by an American woman: Allison, 1988

7. Go to slide number 1 and then run the presentation. After you have finished viewing the slides, save your changes and close the presentation.

PROJECT 2

1. Start a new presentation in PowerPoint using the **Maple** design template. Accept the Title Slide layout for the first slide. Save the presentation as **Recreation** followed by your initials.

2. Key the title **Oak Creek Recreation Commission** and the subtitle **Fall Programs**. Change the font size for the subtitle to **48 pt**.

3. Add new slide with the **Title and Text** layout. Key the title **Something for Everyone**. Then key the following bullet items:
   Adult Programs
   Youth Programs

4. Add a new slide with the **Title Only** layout and key the title **Adult Programs**.

5. Using the Slide Finder, insert all slides from the data files **Project2a**, **Project2b**, and **Project2c** (in that order).

6. In Slide Sorter view, copy slide number 3 and paste it at the end of the presentation.

7. You realize you have inserted too many slides. Delete slide number 4 and slide number 6, and then delete slide number 9. Then move the copied slide (*Adult Programs*) from the end of the presentation to become slide number 9.

8. Display slide number 9 in Normal view and change the word *Adult* to **Youth**.

9. Go to slide number 6 and add the following to the bulleted list:
   Body Attack

10. Check spelling throughout the presentation.

11. Change the slide layout for slide number 11 *Teen Programs* to **Title, Text, and Content**. Then insert an animated or other clip art object relating to any of the topics in the bullet list. Position and resize the object as needed. If you insert an animated clip, specify that the clip play automatically.

12. Animate text on the slides as desired and apply a slide transition to all slides.

13. Run the presentation. After you have finished viewing all the slides, save your changes and close the presentation.

Your community will vote in November on a tax levy for the purpose of building another rail-trail to tie in with existing trails. Your rail-trails organization has asked you to create a persuasive presentation to be shown at a rally for support.

JOB 1

1. Start a new PowerPoint presentation with the **Slit** design template. Accept the **Title Slide** layout as the first slide. Save the presentation as **Rails Yes** followed by your initials.

2. Change the color scheme to a color of your choice.

3. Key the title **Rails Issue 2** and the subtitle **Vote Yes on November 6**.

4. Add a new slide with the **Title, Text, and Content** layout. Key the title **Rail-Trails Benefits**. Key the following items in a bulleted list:
   Economic benefits
   Social benefits
   Environmental benefits

5. Insert clip art relating to the contents of the slide in the clip art placeholder. (Examples: biking, walking, money, people, environmental, and so forth.) Resize and position the object as needed.

6. A colleague has already done some preliminary work on the presentation. Use the Slide Finder to insert all slides from the data file **Job1** into the current presentation.

7. Display slide number 3 in Normal view and change the title to read **Environmental Benefits**. Change the title on slide number 4 to read **Social Benefits**. Change the title on slide number 5 to read **Economic Benefits**.

8. The slides you added are not in the same order as the bulleted list on slide number 2. In Slide Sorter view, move the slides to arrange them in the correct order.

9. Add a **Title and Text** slide at the end of the presentation. Key the title **Costs to You**. Key the following bullet items:
   You pay an additional $10 per year in taxes.
   The tax is retired after 3 years.

10. Add another **Title and Text** slide at the end of the presentation. Key the title **More Information**. Key the following bullet items:
    Call Liz Storey at 555-7890.
    Contact your state representative Dan Rach at 555-555-4512.

11. Check spelling throughout the presentation.

12. Save your changes and leave the presentation open for the next Job.

JOB 2

1. Display slide number 1 in Normal view. Change the size of the title text to **48 pt**.

2. Change the slide layouts on several slides and insert appropriate clip art (or animated pictures) on several slides in the presentation. Use images that relate to wildlife, biking, exercise, nature, telephone, money, and so on. Position and resize the objects as needed.

3. Display slide number 1 and animate the subtitle so it enters with an *Exciting* effect of your choice. If necessary, modify the speed of the animation and format the animation to start on a mouse click.

4. Display slide number 2 and animate the bulleted items with an *Emphasis* effect of your choice. Format the animation to begin after the previous.

5. On slide number 6, add an *Entrance* effect of your choice to to the title. Format the animation to begin after the previous. Add the **Cash Register** sound effect (or another appropriate sound effect) to the title animation.

6. Format the bulleted list on slide number 6 to enter with the *Peek In* effect after the title animation. Start the animation on a mouse click.

7. Choose an appropriate slide transition and apply the transition to all slides.

8. Run your presentation. If any timings need to be adjusted after you have viewed your slides, modify the animation times.

9. Add a new slide at the end of the presentation with the **Title Only** layout. Key the title **The End** and format an *Exit* effect of your choice.

10. Preview the changes, then save your changes and close the presentation.

PORTFOLIO CHECKLIST

Include the following files from this unit in your portfolio.

_____ The 3Rs   _____ Exchange Student

_____ Searching   _____ Rain Forest

_____ Global Students   _____ Rain Forest 2

_____ Refuge Inn   _____ Recreation

EXCEL

CREATING AND FORMATTING A WORKSHEET

OBJECTIVES

Upon completion of this lesson, you should be able to:

■ Identify the parts of the Excel screen.

■ Create and navigate through a worksheet.

■ Use the AutoCorrect and AutoComplete features in Excel.

■ Change column width.

■ Format the contents of a cell.

■ Merge cells.

■ Use the Undo and Redo features.

■ AutoFormat the worksheet.

🕐 **Estimated Time: 1 hr.**

VOCABULARY

Active cell

Cell

Cell reference

Font

Merge

Range

Spreadsheet

Workbook

Worksheet

Excel is an electronic spreadsheet application designed to replace the tedious work of using pencils, paper, and calculators. A *spreadsheet* is the document that you use to store and work with data in Excel. The worksheet is a grid of rows and columns into which you can enter numbers, text, and formulas. The spreadsheet is used to gather, organize, and summarize text and numeric data. Generally, the spreadsheet is also used to perform calculations. In the past, people manually created ledgers that served the same function as today's electronic spreadsheets. So when changes were necessary, the process of making corrections to the ledger was painstaking. With an electronic spreadsheet, changes are relatively easy.

Identify the Parts of the Excel Screen

When you first launch the Excel application, a blank *worksheet* is displayed. Excel refers to the spreadsheet as a worksheet. The new worksheet is titled *Book1*. This filename will remain until you choose Save As from the File menu and assign the document a new filename. The worksheet is always stored in a *workbook* which contains one or more worksheets. Excel has its own unique menus, screen parts, and toolbars. The mouse pointer displays as a thick plus sign when it is within the worksheet. When you move the pointer to a menu, it turns into an arrow.

The New Document task pane is also displayed. This task pane enables you to quickly open workbooks that you have recently accessed or to create a new workbook. After you open an existing workbook or create a new workbook, the task pane will disappear. If Excel is already launched, you can click the New button on the Standard toolbar to create a new blank worksheet.

The worksheet is divided into columns and rows. Columns of the worksheet appear vertically and are identified by letters at the top of the worksheet window. Rows appear horizontally and are identified by numbers on the left side of the worksheet window. The intersection of a single row and a single column is called a *cell*. The *cell reference* identifies the column letter and row number (for example, A1 or B4).

Computer Concepts

You can open additional workbooks on top of the blank Book1. Thus, you can have multiple Excel documents open at the same time.

Computer Concepts

When you open a new workbook using the Blank Workbook option in the task pane, the document contains default settings to create a traditional printed worksheet. Default settings are preset options or variables. You can change the default settings as you work with the document.

S TEP-BY-STEP ▷ 1.1

1. Start Excel.

2. Compare your screen with Figure 1-1.

3. Note the various components of the Excel screen and their names. Leave the workbook open for the next Step-by-Step.

FIGURE 1-1
Main Excel window

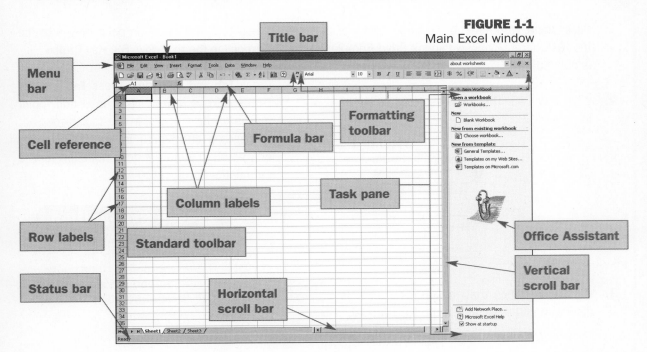

Create and Navigate through a Worksheet

To create a worksheet, you enter information into the cells. Before you can enter data into a cell, you must first select the cell. When the cell is selected, a dark border appears around the cell. You can select a cell using either the mouse or the keyboard. When a cell is selected, it is called the **active cell**. The active cell is identified in the Name Box at the top of the worksheet screen. You can change the active cell by using the mouse or the keyboard.

Enter and Edit Data in a Worksheet

You enter data by keying text or numbers in the active cell and then either pressing Enter on the keyboard or clicking the Enter button (green check mark) on the Formula Bar. You can also press Tab to enter the information and then move to the next cell. By default, Excel displays approximately eight characters in each cell. As you begin keying text, you will see the insertion point indicating where the next character of text will appear. When text is too long for a cell, it will spill over into the next cell—if the next cell is empty. If the next cell is not empty, the text that does not fit into the cell will not be displayed—but it is still contained within the cell.

You can edit, replace, or clear existing data in the worksheet cells. You can edit the data directly in the cell, or you can make the necessary changes to the cell contents in the Formula Bar. To replace cell contents, select the cell and key the new data. To clear the cell contents, select the cell and then press the Delete key or the Backspace key.

> ### Hot Tip
> If you choose not to enter the data you have keyed, you can press ESC or click the Cancel button (red X) in the Formula Bar.

STEP-BY-STEP ▷ 1.2

1. Click **Blank Workbook** in the New section of the task pane. A new workbook titled Book2 is opened.

2. Click in cell A3. The cell is selected as shown in Figure 1-2.

FIGURE 1-2
Active cell in worksheet

3. Key **Days**. Notice that the text you enter is displayed in the cell and in the Formula Bar.

4. Press **Tab**. The insertion point moves to the next cell in the third row, B3. Key **Cruise**.

5. Press **Tab** and key **Price**. Press **Tab** and key **Dates**. Press **Enter**. The insertion point moves to the first cell in the fourth row, A4. (The green checkmark in the Formula Bar only enters the data. It does not allow for the automatic movement to A4.)

> ### Speech Recognition
> If your computer has speech recognition capability, enable the Dictation mode and dictate the text and navigation commands to move from cell to cell and enter the data.

6. Click in cell A3. It currently displays *Days* in the cell and in the Formula Bar. To edit the text in the Formula Bar, click in the Formula Bar and position the insertion point in front of the word *Days*. See Figure 1-3.

FIGURE 1-3
Insertion point positioned in the Formula Bar

Did You Know?

You can choose to have text wrap within a cell in the same way text wraps within a word-processing document. The row height will automatically adjust to show all of the lines of text within the cell. To turn on the text wrap option, select the cell(s) and open the **Format** menu and choose **Cells**. Click the **Alignment** tab and turn on the **Wrap text** option.

7. Key # and then press the **Spacebar**. Click the **Enter** button on the Formula Bar. The change is made in the Formula Bar and in cell A3.

Hot Tip

The Enter and Cancel buttons will not display in the Formula Bar unless you enter data in a cell or position the insertion point in the Formula Bar.

8. Click in cell B3. It currently displays *Cruise*. Key **Destination** and press **Enter**. The contents of the cell are replaced with the new text you entered.

9. Click in cell C3. It currently displays *Price*. Press **F2**. Notice that the insertion point is now positioned at the end of the text in the cell.

10. Use the **Backspace** key to delete the existing text and key **Cost**, then press **Enter**. All the contents in the cell are replaced with the new text you entered, and the cell below, C4, becomes active.

11. Click in cell A4. Key **6** and press **Enter**. The cell below, A5, becomes active.

12. Key the following numbers, pressing **Enter** after each number. When you are done, your worksheet should look like Figure 1-4.

4
5
7
4

FIGURE 1-4
Worksheet with data entered

Speech Recognition

If your computer has speech recognition capability, turn on the Speak On Enter option to hear the value of the cell immediately after you enter data in each cell.

13. Edit the contents of cell A4. Double-click in the cell to display the insertion point. Then, change the contents to **7**, and press **Enter**.

14. Save the worksheet as **Cruises** followed by your initials. Leave the worksheet open for the next Step-by-Step.

Use Help to Find More Ways to Move the Insertion Point and Select Cells

You've already learned a few ways to position the insertion point and select cells. In the following Step-by-Step, you will use the Help feature to find a list of shortcut keys for navigating through a worksheet and selecting cells.

STEP-BY-STEP ⟹ 1.3

1. Click the Office Assistant.

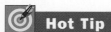
Hot Tip

You can also open the Help menu and choose Microsoft Excel Help, or click F1. You should then use the Index tab and its text box.

2. In the text box, key **shortcut keys** and then click **Search**.

3. When the Office Assistant displays a list of topics, select the topic **Keyboard shortcuts** (or something similar). The Help dialog box shown in Figure 1-5 suggests several topics. Your dialog box may not match exactly.

4. When you point to any of the topics in the list (a link), your mouse pointer will change to a hand. Notice there is a blue triangle just to the left of each link.

5. Click the link **Select cells, row and columns, and objects**. The blue triangle just to the left of the link now points downward to indicate that the content is expanded.

Hot Tip

To expand all the content at once, click the Show All link at the top of the list of topics. The link will then display Hide All. When you click the Hide All link, all the content will collapse at once.

6. Use the vertical scroll bar if necessary to see and read all of the shortcuts in the list.

7. Click the same link again to collapse the content. The blue triangle now points to the right.

8. Click the Close box on the Help dialog box.

9. Leave the worksheet open for the next Step-by-Step.

FIGURE 1-5
Microsoft Excel Help dialog box

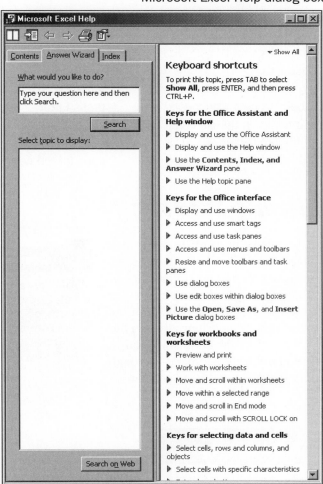

Use the AutoCorrect and AutoComplete Features in Excel

The AutoCorrect feature in Excel corrects common mistakes as you enter data. For example, if you key *adn*, Excel will automatically change the text to read *and*. With the AutoComplete feature, Excel compares the first few characters you key in a cell with existing entries in the same column. If the characters match an existing entry, Excel proposes the existing entry. You can press Enter to accept the proposed entry.

1. Click in cell B4. Key **Caribbean** and press **Enter**.

2. Key **Bahamas** and press **Enter**.

3. Key **C**. Notice that Excel suggests *Caribbean* because you entered it earlier in the column. Press **Enter** to accept the proposed text.

4. Key **Alaska** and press **Enter**.

5. Key **Belize adn**. Then look at the active cell as you press **Spacebar**. Excel automatically corrects the spelling of *and*. Key **Cozumel** and press **Enter**.

6. Save the changes and leave the worksheet open for the next Step-by-Step.

Change Column Width

Sometimes the data you enter in a cell is wider than the column. When the data is too wide for the cell, Excel displays a series of number signs (####), cuts off the data, or allows the data to run outside of the column. You can widen the column in two ways. You can drag the right edge of the column heading to the desired size. Or, an alternative way to change the column width is to select the cells you want to change and then use the Column Width command. Through this method, you can specify the exact width, or you can let Excel find the best fit.

Computer Concepts

You can also use the AutoFit Selection feature to reduce the width of a column to eliminate unnecessary white space in a column.

1. Point to the boundary on the right side of the column heading B. When the pointer changes to a double-headed arrow, drag the boundary to the right about one-half inch to widen the column. See Figure 1-6.

2. Click the column heading B to select the entire column.

FIGURE 1-6
Dragging a column boundary
to change the column width

Drag the column border to resize a column

	A	B	C
1			
2			
3	#Days	Destination	Cost	Dates
4	7	Caribbean	
5	4	Bahamas	
6	5	Caribbean	
7	7	Alaska	
8	4	Belize and Cozumel	
9			
10			

B9 — Width: 15.43 (113 pixels)

3. Open the **Format** menu and choose **Column**, then select **AutoFit Selection** in the submenu. Excel automatically adjusts the cells in the column to fit the cell with the most content—in this case, *Belize and Cozumel*.

Hot Tip

You can also find the best fit by positioning the mouse pointer on the right edge of the column heading and double-clicking when the double-headed arrow appears.

Speech Recognition

If your computer has speech recognition capability, enable the Command mode and say the command to open the **Format** menu, choose the **Column** command, and select the **AutoFit** option.

4. Click anywhere in the worksheet to deselect the column. Save the changes and leave the worksheet open for the next Step-by-Step.

Format the Contents of a Cell

Formatting the contents of a cell changes the way it appears. For example, you may want to change the alignment of the text or use commas in numbers to separate the thousands. To apply formats, you must first select the cell(s) containing the data to be formatted.

Change Fonts and Font Sizes and Align Text

The *font* is the design of the typeface in your document. Fonts are available in a variety of styles and sizes, and you can use multiple fonts in one document. The font size is a measurement in points that determines the height of the font. Bold, italic, underline, and color formats can also add emphasis to the contents of a cell.

By default, Excel aligns text at the left of the cell and numbers at the right of the cell. However, you can change the alignment.

When you select a group of cells, the group is called a *range*. All cells in a range touch each other and form a rectangle. The range is identified by the cell in the upper left corner and the cell in the lower right corner, separated by a colon (for example, A1:D4).

Computer Concepts

When you clear the contents of a cell, the formats applied to the contents of that cell are not removed. To remove the formats without removing the data, choose **Clear** from the **Edit** menu and select **Formats** in the submenu.

Hot Tip

To change the font color, choose **Cells** from the **Format** menu, then click on the **Font** tab.

Computer Concepts

After changing the font or font size, you may find it necessary to adjust the column width, even if you previously used the AutoFit feature.

235

1. Click in cell A3, then drag to the right to select a range of cells containing the other three cells in the same row (B3, C3, and D3). The range A3:D3 is selected.

2. Click the **Italic** button on the Formatting toolbar. The text in each of the cells is formatted with the italic attribute.

3. With the cells still selected, click the down

   Arial

   arrow at the right of the Font box on the Formatting toolbar. Scroll down and select **Times New Roman**.

4. With the cells still selected, click the down arrow at the right of the Font Size box. Select **14**.

5. With the cells still selected, click the **Center** button on the Formatting toolbar. Each of the labels in the row is centered.

6. Click in cell A4 and drag down to cell A8 to select a range of cells. Click the **Center** button.

7. Deselect the cells and save the changes. Leave the worksheet open for the next Step-by-Step.

Format Numbers and Dates

Generally, numbers are displayed with no formatting and are aligned at the right side of a cell. However, dates and times are automatically formatted in the default styles dd-mm-yy and hh:mm respectively.

1. Click in cell C4 and key **599**, then press **Enter**. Notice that the numbers are automatically aligned at the right edge of the cell.

2. Key the following numbers, pressing **Enter** after each number:
   299
   399
   799
   299

3. Click in cell C4 (*599*) and drag down to select the range C4:C8.

4. Open the **Format** menu and choose **Cells**. If necessary, click the **Number** tab to display the dialog box shown in Figure 1-7.

Hot Tip

Ctrl + 1 is a shortcut for accessing the Format Cells dialog box. You can also access the Cells dialog box by right-clicking an active cell or range and then selecting **Format Cells** in the shortcut menu.

FIGURE 1-7
Number tab in the Format Cells dialog box

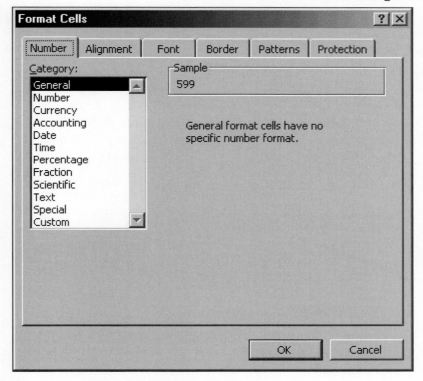

5. Under *Category*, select **Currency**. The dialog box changes to display the currency format options. See Figure 1-8.

6. In the *Decimal places* box, click the down arrow until **0** is displayed. Click **OK**. The numbers are all formatted with dollar signs.

7. Click in cell D4. Key **March 3** and press **Enter**. Notice that Excel automatically changed the format to *3-Mar*.

8. Click in cell D4 (*3-Mar*) and drag down to cell D9 to select the active cell and the five cells below it. (Cell D9, though currently empty, is also formatted so that when you add a new row the format will already be there.)

9. Open the **Format** menu and choose **Cells**. Because you just accessed it, the Number tab should be displayed. If necessary, select the **Number** tab.

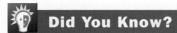

Did You Know?

You can magnify or reduce the view of the worksheet by using the Zoom button on the Standard toolbar. The default magnification is 100 percent. To get a closer view, select a larger percentage from the drop-down list or key in your own percentage and click Enter.

10. Under *Category*, select **Date**. Under *Type*, select **3/14/01** (not *3/14/2001). Click **OK**. The date format in cell D4 changes. Deselect the cells.

FIGURE 1-8
Currency format options in the Format Cells dialog box

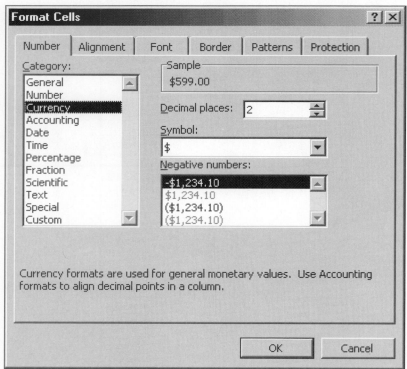

11. Enter the following dates in the remaining cells, pressing **Enter** after each date:
3/10
3/18
3/25
3/31

12. Save the changes and leave the worksheet open for the next Step-by-Step.

Merge Cells

There will be times when you want text to span across several columns or rows. To do this, you can merge cells. When you *merge* cells, you combine several cells into a single cell.

STEP-BY-STEP ➩ 1.8

1. Select cells A1:D1.

2. Click the **Merge and Center** button on the Standard toolbar. Excel combines the four cells into a single cell (A1).

3. Key **La Croix Cruises**, then press **Enter**.

4. Click in cell A1 to select it again. Change the font to **Times New Roman** and change the font size to **16**.

5. With the cell still selected, click the **Bold** button on the formatting toolbar.

6. With the cell still selected, click the down arrow to the right of the **Fill Color** button on the Formatting toolbar and select the color **Yellow**.

7. Deselect the cell and save the changes. Leave the worksheet open for the next Step-by-Step.

Use the Undo and Redo Features

If you make a mistake, or if you change your mind, you can use the Undo command to reverse your most recent changes. If you undo an action and then change your mind, you can reverse the undo action by using the Redo command. You can undo and redo multiple actions at one time by choosing from the Undo or Redo drop-down lists on the Standard toolbar. When you undo or redo an action from the drop-down list, Excel will also undo or redo all the actions listed above it on the list.

1. Click in cell A9. Key **4** and press **Tab**.

2. Key **Baja Mexico** and press **Tab**.

3. Key **299** and press **Tab**.

4. Key **4/2** and press **Enter**.

5. Click the **Undo** button on the Standard toolbar. The date is removed.

6. Click the down arrow to the right of the **Undo** button. The Undo list, similar to that shown in Figure 1-9, is displayed.

FIGURE 1-9
Undo list

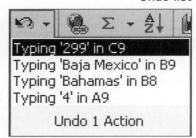

7. Click on the second action in the list (*Typing 'Baja Mexico' in B9*) to undo the last two actions. Cells B9 and C9 are empty now.

Computer Concepts

There is a limit of 16 actions that you can undo and redo. Furthermore, the Undo and Redo actions are cleared from the drop-down list when you save the worksheet. Therefore, you should always undo an action as soon as you realize you have made a mistake.

8. Click the down arrow to the right of the **Redo** button on the Standard toolbar to display the Redo list shown in Figure 1-10. Click on the third action in the list to redo all three. The content in Cells B9, C9, and D9 is restored.

FIGURE 1-10
Redo list

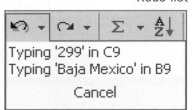

Hot Tip

If the Redo button is not displayed on the Standard toolbar, click the Toolbar Options button (down arrow at the right side of the toolbar) and then click on the Redo button.

9. Save the changes and leave the worksheet open for the next Step-by-Step.

AutoFormat the Worksheet

Excel offers numerous AutoFormats that you can use to give your worksheet a professional look. These AutoFormats instantly format the entire worksheet with borders, shading, and data formatting. To apply an AutoFormat, you must first select the range to be formatted. The AutoFormat may override existing formats that you have applied. If desired, you can modify the formats that are applied.

STEP-BY-STEP ▷ 1.10

1. Select all the cells in the worksheet that contain data (A1:D9). (*Hint*: Click in the left corner of cell A1 and drag down to cell A9.)

2. Open the **Format** menu and choose **AutoFormat**. The dialog box shown in Figure 1-11 is displayed.

3. Scroll down and select the **Colorful 2** option. Click **OK**.

4. Select cells A4:A9, then click the **Center** button on the Formatting toolbar.

5. Click in cell B3 and then click the **Center** button on the Formatting toolbar.

6. Deselect the cells and save the changes. Close the document.

FIGURE 1-11
AutoFormat dialog box

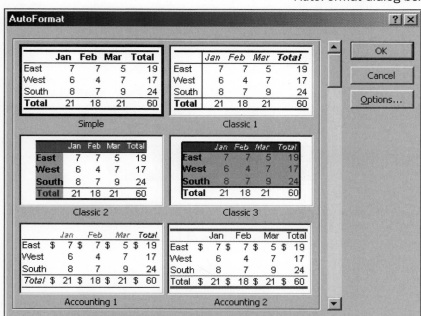

Summary

In this lesson, you learned:

- The Excel screen has its own unique screen parts, menus, and toolbars.

- To enter data in a cell, the cell must be selected. You can use the mouse or the keyboard to move from one cell to another.

- As you enter data, Excel will automatically correct some of your keyboarding errors. If the data you are entering matches characters of existing entries, Excel will propose the existing entry to save you time.

- There are several options for changing the column width. You can drag a column border, use the AutoFit feature, or specify an exact measurement.

- When you format the contents of a cell, you change the appearance of the text or numbers in the cell.

- If you want text to span across several rows or columns, you can merge the cells into a single cell.

- The Undo command reverses a previous action. The Redo command reverses an undo.

- You can quickly and easily give a worksheet a professional look by applying one of the autoformats available.

VOCABULARY REVIEW

Define the following terms:

Active cell	Font	Spreadsheet
Cell	Merge	Workbook
Cell reference	Range	Worksheet

LESSON 1 REVIEW QUESTIONS

TRUE/FALSE

Circle T if the statement is true or F if the statement is false.

T F   1. A worksheet is the same as a spreadsheet.

T F   2. Within the worksheet, the mouse pointer displays as a hand with a pointing finger.

T F   3. When data is too wide for a cell, the part of the data that will not fit is automatically deleted.

T F 4. By default, text aligns at the left of a cell.

T F 5. You use the Merge and Center button to allow text to span several columns.

FILL IN THE BLANK

Complete the following sentences by writing the correct word or words in the blanks provided.

1. The _____ identifies the column letter and row number.

2. The selected cell is called the _____ cell.

3. A selected group of cells is called a(n) _____.

4. The command you use to change a date format is _____.

5. To automatically apply shading, borders, and alignment options to selected cells in a worksheet, use the _____ feature.

LESSON 1 PROJECTS

PROJECT 1-1

1. If necessary, launch Excel. If Excel is already launched, click the New Button on the Standard toolbar to create a new worksheet.

2. In cell A1, key **Running vs. Walking** and press **Enter**.

3. Beginning in cell A3, key the data shown below. If you would like, you can use AutoComplete to help you complete the entries, but you will then have to edit the entry to change *stroll* to **brisk** and **fast**. Do not be concerned if the columns are too narrow for the content. You will fix that in the next step.

Activity	Speed	Calories/Hour
Walking (stroll)	**2 mph**	**120**
Walking (brisk)	**3.5 mph**	**360**
Walking (fast)	**5 mph**	**480**
Jogging	**4 mph**	**600**
Running (moderate)	**10 mph**	**1020**

4. Save the worksheet as **Exercise** followed by your initials.

5. Adjust the column widths to display all text.

6. Merge and center cells A1:C1. Format the range of cells with a fill color of your choice.

7. Edit the speed for Jogging to 5 mph. In cell A1, change the word *vs.* to **versus**.

8. Undo the last change.

9. Format the text in cell A1 as **16-point bold**. Format the range A3:C3 as **12-point bold italic**. (Adjust cell widths as necessary after changing the text size.)

10. Select the cell range B4:B8 and center the content.

11. Select the cell range C4:C8 and apply the **Number** format with the 1000 separator and no decimal places.

12. Save the changes, then close the worksheet.

PROJECT 1-2

1. Open **Project1-2** from the data files. Save the spreadsheet as **Mensa Groups** followed by your initials.

2. Merge and center cells **A1:D1**.

3. Merge and center cells **A2:D2**.

4. Select the range **A1:C22** and apply the **List 2** AutoFormat.

5. Change the main heading text size to **12 point**.

6. Click in cell **A2**. Change the date format to the **March-01** style. Add the **bold** and **italic** formats and **center** the text in the cells.

7. Select the cell range **A4:C4** and add the **center**, **bold**, and **italic** formats.

8. Save your changes. Close the workbook.

WEB PROJECT

SCANS

You have decided you would like to go on a bicycle tour of France. Use Web search tools to locate information on bicycle tours to France. (Your search expression should be similar to *"bicycle tours" AND France*.) Visit several sites to find information from a number of tour operators. Create a worksheet to store the results of your research. Your worksheet should record starting date, ending date, cost, the region of France the tour visits, and level of difficulty of the biking (if supplied). Format the worksheet as you learned in this lesson to make the information about each separate tour company easy to compare.

TEAMWORK PROJECT

Worksheets are excellent tools to organize information so you can make easy comparisons between sets of data. For this project, assume you need to set up a home (or campus) office with new communications equipment. Because you're not yet sure of your budget, you need several price options for each piece of equipment. With a classmate, gather and organize information as follows:

1. Identify a list of at least 16 pieces of equipment a state-of-the-art home office needs. Some of these may be a desktop computer, scanner, printer, fax (or all-in-one unit that includes scanning, copying, printing, and faxing functions), cordless phone, answering machine, and so on.

2. Create a worksheet to store the list of equipment you decide on. Create column headings for "Low End," Moderate," and "High End" so that you can store three prices for each equipment item.

3. Using computer catalogs or Web resources, find low-end, moderate, and high-end options for each equipment item. For example, low-end options for a copier would include 3 pages per minute and black and white copies. Moderate options for a copier would include 8 pages per minute and an automatic document feeder. High-end options would include 12 pages per minute, color copies, and zoom capability. Divide the research work so that you find information on half of the items and your teammate finds information on the other half. Key your results in one worksheet.

4. Format the worksheet so that you can clearly see all data you have entered. Apply AutoFormat to make the data more attractive and readable. Compare your worksheet with those of other teams to see what equipment items are considered most important for a home office.

CRITICAL THINKING

SCANS

While formatting a worksheet, you have changed the default font in a few cell ranges from Arial to Times New Roman. Selecting each cell range is tedious, however. Is there a way you can select an entire worksheet and apply a new font to all cells at one time? Use the Help files in Excel to find the answer and then write a brief report on what you learn.

ORGANIZING THE WORKSHEET

OBJECTIVES

Upon completion of this lesson, you should be able to:

- Insert and delete rows and columns.
- Clear and delete data.
- Copy and move data.
- Fill the same data in adjacent cells.
- Fill a data series in adjacent cells.
- Create multiple worksheets.
- Hide and unhide columns and rows.
- Freeze and unfreeze columns and rows.
- Sort data.
- Change the page setup.
- Print the worksheets.

⏱ **Estimated Time: 1 hour**

VOCABULARY

Ascending order

Clipboard

Descending order

Fill handle

Filling

Header row

Landscape orientation

Portrait orientation

Insert and Delete Rows and Columns

When you insert or delete a row or a column in Excel, it affects the entire worksheet. All existing data is shifted in some direction. For example, when you add a new column, the existing data shifts to the right. When you add a new row, the data shifts down a row. One of the really beneficial features of Excel is that it automatically updates the cell references whenever you do this. What this means is that if the data in one cell is dependent upon the data in another cell, when these cells are adjusted, Excel will keep straight what information is required where. When you delete rows and columns, the cells and all their contents are removed, and the cell references are also automatically updated.

To insert or delete multiple columns and rows in a single step, select the desired number of columns or rows before executing the command.

STEP-BY-STEP ▷ 2.1

1. Open the file **Step2-1** from the data files. Save the worksheet as **Tallest Structures** followed by your initials. (*Note:* This spreadsheet contains data about the tallest towers and buildings built by man. This list is not intended to be an official list, and the data contained in the list may be inaccurate or out of date.)

Extra Challenge

Explore the Internet for up-to-date information about the tallest buildings in the world. Look for details in your search about the standards used for measuring tall buildings, and use this information to evaluate your Internet sources to determine if the data is current, correct, and reliable.

2. Select any cell in column D. Open the **Edit** menu and choose **Delete**. The Delete dialog box shown in Figure 2-1 is displayed.

FIGURE 2-1
Delete dialog box

3. Select the option **Entire column** in the dialog box, then click **OK**. The column and all its contents are deleted from the worksheet. What was labeled *Column E* is now labeled *Column D.*

Speech Recognition

If your computer has speech recognition capability, enable the Command mode and dictate the commands to open the Delete dialog box and select the option.

4. Click in any cell in Row 11. Open the **Insert** menu and choose **Rows**. A new row is inserted above the row you had selected and it becomes Row 11. The existing data shifts down, and the row labels are updated to reflect the change.

5. Key the following information in the new row:
Canadian National (CN) Tower
TV/Tourist tower
Toronto, Canada
1,814

6. Click on the label for Row 12 and drag down to include Row 13 in the selection. Both rows should be selected.

7. Open the **Insert** menu and choose **Rows**. Two new rows are inserted above the selected rows.

8. Key the following information in the new rows:

Ostankino Tower	**TV/Tourist tower**
Moscow, Russia	**1,772**
Oriental Pearl Tower	**TV tower**
Shanghai, China	**1,535**

9. Click on the label for Row 2. The whole row should be selected. Open the **Edit** menu and choose **Delete**. Because you selected the entire row before choosing the Delete command, the Delete dialog box does not display but the entire row is deleted.

10. Click on the column A label to select the entire column. Open the **Insert** menu and choose **Columns**. A new column is inserted to the left of what was column A—which is now column B. The new column is column A and is the active column.

11. Click in cell A1, then click the **Bold** button on the Formatting toolbar to turn on the bold format. Key **Ranking**, and then press **Enter**.

12. Save the changes and leave the workbook open for the next Step-by-Step.

Delete, Copy, and Move Data

Sometimes after entering data in a worksheet, you need to reorganize it. You may even want to remove some of the data and not replace it. Or, you may want to move or copy existing data from one location to another.

Clear and Delete Data

The process for deleting data can be as simple as pressing the Delete or Backspace keys. When you delete the contents of a cell this way, the formats for the cell remain in the cell. Therefore, if you enter new data in the cell, the existing formats will apply to the new contents.

If you want to remove the contents and the formats, you need to clear the cell. Clearing the cell leaves a blank cell in the worksheet. You can clear the contents and the formats from the cell, clear just the contents, or clear just the formats.

When you use the delete feature, you remove the cell entirely. With the delete feature, you have four options. You can delete an entire row or an entire column. You can also shift the cells to the left or shift the cells up. However, use caution when using the shift feature. The results may misalign data in your rows and columns. If this happens, you can always Undo the deletion to return the data to its original position.

1. Click in cell E9. The cell currently displays *1,910*. Press the **Delete** key to remove the contents.

2. With cell E9 still selected, key **1909** and press **Enter**. Notice that the cell contents are automatically centered within the cell and that the comma is automatically added because these formats remained after you deleted the original cell contents.

3. Click in cell E6. The cell currently displays *2,000*. Open the **Edit** menu and choose **Clear**. Select **Formats** in the submenu. The formats are removed from the cell, but the

contents remain. Notice that the numbers align at the right, and the comma is removed.

4. Click the **Undo** button to reverse the action.

5. Click in cell C14. Open the **Edit** menu and choose **Delete**. The Delete dialog box is displayed. Select **Shift cells left** and then click **OK**. The contents in cells D14 and E14 are shifted one cell to the left.

6. Notice that the city name is centered instead of left aligned. This is because the cell formats also shifted to the left. Click in cell D14 and click the **Align Left** button to align the text consistent with the other data in the column.

7. Press **Tab** to move to cell E14 and key **1,362** and press **Enter**. Click the **Center** button if necessary to align the contents with the rest of the column.

8. Save the changes and leave the workbook open for the next Step-by-Step.

Copy and Move Data

Copying data saves you from having to key the same data into another location. The process is easy. First, you must copy the data from one location. To copy the data, select it and then click the Copy button on the Standard toolbar. The data is placed in a temporary storage location in your computer's memory called the *Clipboard*. Then, select the destination cell where you want to place the data, and paste the data into the new location. The data remains in the Clipboard. The Clipboard will hold up to 24 items. If you copy a 25th item, the very first item you placed in the Clipboard is deleted.

Moving data is similar to copying data, except you cut the data from one location and paste it in the destination location. When you move or copy all the data in a cell, the formats are also moved or copied. Unlike a word processing table, if you move data to a cell that already has data in it, that data doesn't move to make room for the new data. If you don't want to lose information, you have to move data into empty cells; otherwise, the data in the destination cells will be replaced.

Did You Know?

If you want to add the same contents to multiple cells, you can select all the cells before you enter the content. After you key the content, press **Ctrl + Enter**. The content you keyed will then be entered into each of the selected cells.

1. Click in cell D2. Click the **Copy** button on the Standard toolbar. The contents (*North Dakota, USA*) of the cell are copied to the Clipboard. Also, an animated border (a dotted-line marquee) is displayed around the selected cell as shown in Figure 2-2.

2. Click in cell D3. Then click the **Paste** button on the Standard toolbar. The contents (*North Dakota, USA*) are pasted in the destination cell.

Hot Tip

If the Paste button is not displayed on the Standard toolbar, click the **Toolbar Options** button at the right end of the toolbar and then select the **Paste** button.

FIGURE 2-2
Marquee around a selected cell

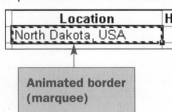

Animated border (marquee)

3. Press **Esc** to remove the marquee around the copied cell.

4. Click in cell C5. The cell currently displays *Radio tower*. Click the **Cut** button on the Standard toolbar. The contents of the cell are stored in the Clipboard and a marquee appears around the cell border.

5. Click in cell C4, then click the **Paste** button on the Standard toolbar. The contents from cell C5 are moved to cell C4.

6. Save the changes and leave the workbook open for the next Step-by-Step.

Hot Tip

If the Cut button is not displayed on the Standard toolbar, click the **Toolbar Options** button at the right end of the toolbar and then select the **Cut** button.

Computer Concepts

You can copy or move multiple cells of data at the same time. First select the range, then click the **Copy** or **Cut** button. Select the first cell in the destination range and click the **Paste** button.

Use the AutoFill Command to Enter Data

The AutoFill command is another time-saving feature that enables you to copy data from one cell to another. AutoFill also provides several options for entering certain kinds of data, such as months, days of the week, or a series of numbers.

Fill the Same Data in Adjacent Cells

Filling data is another method for copying data in a worksheet. It is faster than copying and pasting because filling requires only one step. However, the Fill command can only be used when the destination cells are adjacent to the original cell. You can fill data up or down in the same column, or right or left in the same row.

When you fill a cell, you can choose to copy the cell contents either with or without the formats. Therefore, this feature will save you even more time if you apply formats before using the Fill command.

STEP-BY-STEP ▷ 2.4

1. Click in cell C7. The cell currently displays *TV tower*.

2. Position your mouse point over the small square in the bottom right corner of the active cell. This square, shown in Figure 2-3, is called the *fill handle*. When you point to the fill handle, the pointer changes to a bold plus sign.

FIGURE 2-3
Fill handle in a selected cell

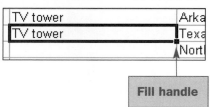

3. Drag the fill handle down to cell C9. The range of cells C7:C9 is selected. A ScreenTip similar to the one shown in Figure 2-4 displays the cell contents that will be copied to the range of cells.

FIGURE 2-4
Copying text to a range of cells

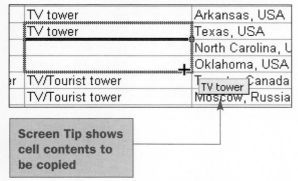

Screen Tip shows cell contents to be copied

4. Release the mouse button, and the contents of C7 (*TV tower)* now appears in cells C8 and C9.

Hot Tip

To quickly fill to the right, click in the destination cell and press the shortcut keys **Ctrl + R**. This copies the contents of the cell to the left. To quickly fill down, click in the destination cell and press the shortcut keys **Ctrl + D**. The contents of the cell above will be copied. To fill multiple cells, select the cell containing the contents, and then drag to create a range of cells before pressing the shortcut keys.

Use Help to Learn How to Fill Other Types of Data

You've already seen how Excel will fill adjacent cells with the same content. The fill command will also allow you to fill a series of numbers and increase or decrease the cell contents in increments based on the pattern of the original contents. You can use the Help screens to learn how to fill series of data.

5. The **AutoFill Options** button displays next to the fill handle for cell C9. Point to the **AutoFill Options** button and the button will expand to show a down button. Click the down button to display the dialog box shown in Figure 2-5. Notice that you can choose to copy the content of the cells, fill the selected cells with formatting only, or fill the cells without the formatting.

FIGURE 2-5
AutoFill Options menu

| ● Copy Cells |
| ○ Fill Formatting Only |
| ○ Fill Without Formatting |

6. The Copy Cells option is already selected, and that is the option you want. Click outside the menu to close the menu without making any changes. Do not be concerned that the AutoFill Option button is still displayed.

7. Click in cell C6, then point to the fill handle. Drag up to select cell C5. When you release, the cell contents from C6 (*TV tower)* are copied to cell C5.

8. Click in cell C2 and fill the contents to Cell C3.

9. Deselect the cells and save the changes. Leave the workbook open for the next Step-by-Step.

Did You Know?

You can press **F1** to quickly access the Help screens. If the Office Assistant is displayed, you can enter your question in the text box. If the Office Assistant is turned off, the opening Help screen will display.

1. If the Office Assistant is displayed, point to the Office Assistant and right-click. Then choose **Options** in the shortcut menu. Clear the check box for *Use the Office Assistant* and click **OK**.

2. Open the **Help** menu and choose **Microsoft Excel Help**. If necessary, click the **Show** button on the toolbar to display the Contents, Answer Wizard, and Index tabs.

3. Click the **Index** tab to display the dialog box shown in Figure 2-6.

4. With the insertion point positioned in the text box below *1. Type keywords,* key **fill**. As you enter the text, the list in the section below (*2. Or choose keywords*) will scroll to display the keywords beginning with those characters.

5. Under *2. Or choose keywords*, double-click **fill** to open a list of topics. Under 3. *Choose a topic*, make sure the topic **About filling in data based on adjacent cells** is selected. Read the information in the first two paragraphs displayed at the right.

6. Scroll down if necessary so you can see all of the section with the heading **Fill in a series of numbers, dates, or other items**.

7. Read the information and look at the examples of series that can be extended. The examples illustrate that you can fill times, days of the week, months, quarters, and text. Notice, too, that if the initial selection includes the months January and April, the extended series will indicate a span of four months. July is the third month after April, and October is the third month after July.

FIGURE 2-6
Index tab in Microsoft Excel Help

8. Click the **Close** button in the top right corner of the screen to close the Help screens.

9. To turn the Office Assistant back on, open the **Help** menu and choose **Show the Office Assistant**. Leave the workbook open for the next Step-by-Step.

Fill a Data Series in Adjacent Cells

You can also use the fill feature to quickly fill in a series of numbers and dates. To fill in a series, a pattern must be established in the initial selection of cells. Then when you drag, the pattern is continued. When you drag the fill handle down or to the right, the series increases. However, if you drag the fill handle up or to the left, the series will decrease.

S TEP-BY-STEP ▷ 2.6

1. Click cell A2. Key **1** and then press **Enter**.

2. Cell A3 is now the active cell. Key **2** and press **Enter**. You have now established a pattern where your numbers increase in increments of 1.

3. Select cells A2 and A3, then click the **Center** button to center the cell contents.

4. With the cells still selected, point to the fill handle at the bottom of cell A3. When the pointer changes to a bold plus sign, drag down to cell A22 to select a range of cells. When you release the mouse button, Excel fills the cells with the numbers 3 through 21. The numbers are also centered within the cells.

Computer Concepts

If you click the AutoFill Options button, a new option called Fill Series will be available and selected in the menu. This option is now available because the original selected cells indicated a pattern.

---

5. Deselect the cells. Then, select cells A2:A20 and press **Delete**.

6. Select cells A21 and A22. Point to the fill handle at the bottom right corner of cell A22 and drag up to cell A2. The cells will fill with a series of numbers in decreasing order from 21 through 1.

 Did You Know?

To continue selecting cells that are below the last visible row on the screen, hold down the mouse button as you reach the bottom (or top) of the screen. The worksheet will scroll and new rows will display.

---

7. Deselect the cells. Notice that in rows 5 and 6, the towers are exactly the same height. Click in cell A6 and change the ranking from *5* to **4** and press **Enter**.

8. Save the changes and leave the workbook open for the next Step-by-Step.

Create Multiple Worksheets

Whenever you open a new worksheet in Excel, you automatically open a workbook with three sheets in it. To switch to a different worksheet, simply click on the worksheet tab at the bottom of the screen.

Excel automatically assigns the name Sheet and a sequential number to each new worksheet. If desired, you can rename the worksheet. You can also add additional worksheets to a workbook.

1. Click the **Sheet2** tab at the bottom of the screen as shown in Figure 2-7. A new blank worksheet is displayed.

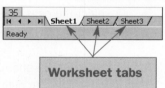

FIGURE 2-7
Worksheet tabs

2. Double-click the **Sheet2** tab. The tab name is selected. Key **Buildings** and press **Enter**.

Hot Tip

An alternative way to rename a worksheet is to right-click the worksheet tab, select **Rename** in the shortcut menu, key the new name, and press **Enter**.

3. Double-click the **Sheet1** tab and rename the worksheet **Towers**.

4. Click on the Buildings worksheet tab to switch back to that worksheet.

5. Enter the data shown in Figure 2-8.

6. Center and bold the column headings and center the numbers in the third column. Select all three columns and then format the columns to AutoFit Selection.

Speech Recognition

If your computer has speech recognition capability, enable the Command mode and say the commands to select the column heading and then say the command to apply the bold and center formats.

7. Save the changes and leave the workbook open for the next Step-by-Step.

FIGURE 2-8
Data for Buildings worksheet

Building	Location	Height in Feet
Empire State Building	New York, USA	1,250
World Trade Center One	New York, USA	1,368
World Trade Center Two	New York, USA	1,362
Sears Tower	Illinois, USA	1,454
Bank of China Tower	Hong Kong, PRC	1,209
Central Plaza	Hong Kong, PRC	1,227
Petronas Tower 2	Kuala Lumpur, Malaysia	1,483
Petronas Tower 1	Kuala Lumpur, Malaysia	1,483
Jin Mao Building	Shanghai, PRC	1,379
The Centre	Hong Kong, PRC	1,149
Emirates Tower #1	Dubai, UAE	1,149

Hide and Unhide Columns and Rows

Hiding columns and rows temporarily removes them from display. This feature is especially helpful if you are working with a wide spreadsheet and you do not need to view all of the columns or rows. For example, you may need to see the first column and another column at the far right. You can hide the columns in the middle so you can view the two columns side by side. This feature is also helpful if you choose to print the worksheet, but you do not want all the content to show in the hard copy.

STEP-BY-STEP ▷ 2.8

1. Click in cell D1 and label the column **Year Constructed**.

2. Click in cell E1 and label the column **# Stories**.

3. If necessary, bold and center these headings, and autofit the column widths for selection.

4. Click the label for column B and drag to the right until both columns B and C are selected.

5. Open the **Format** menu, choose **Column**, and then select **Hide** in the submenu. The selected columns are no longer visible on the screen.

6. Enter the data illustrated in Figure 2-9. Center the data in the columns. (*Note:* This list is not intended to be an official list, and the data contained in the list may be inaccurate or out of date.)

7. Select columns A and D. Open the **Format** menu, choose **Column**, and then select **Unhide** in the submenu. Columns B and C are now visible on the screen.

Speech Recognition

If your computer has speech recognition capability, turn on the **Speak On Enter** feature so you can hear the value of the cell spoken immediately after you enter the data in each cell. Note that you can choose to have the computer read by rows or by columns.

8. Save the changes and leave the workbook open for the next Step-by-Step.

FIGURE 2-9
Data for Buildings worksheet

	A	D	E
1	**Building**	**Year Constructed**	**# Stories**
2	Empire State Building	1931	102
3	World Trade Center One	1972	110
4	World Trade Center Two	1973	110
5	Sears Tower	1973	110
6	Bank of China Tower	1989	70
7	Central Plaza	1992	78
8	Petronas Tower 2	1997	88
9	Petronas Tower 1	1997	88
10	Jin Mao Building	1997	88
11	The Centre	1998	73
12	Emirates Tower #1	1999	54

Enter the data in these two columns

Freeze Columns and Rows

Sometimes a worksheet becomes so large that you cannot view the entire worksheet on the screen. As you scroll to the bottom of the worksheet, column labels at the top of the worksheet disappear. As you scroll to the right, row labels at the left of the screen disappear. Freezing a column or row enables you to keep the column or row visible as you scroll. You can execute the Freeze command for all columns to the left of a selected column, or all rows above a selected row. Or, you can execute the Freeze command around a specific cell, which will freeze the row(s) above the active cell and the column(s) to the left of the active cell.

STEP-BY-STEP ▷ 2.9

1. Click the **Towers** worksheet tab at the bottom of the screen to switch to that worksheet.

2. Click the column C label to select that column.

3. Open the **Window** menu and choose **Freeze Panes**.

4. Click the right scroll arrow on the horizontal scroll bar. Notice that as you scroll to the right, the first two columns do not move.

5. Open the **Window** menu and choose **Unfreeze Panes**.

6. Click in cell B2. Then open the **Window** menu and choose **Freeze Panes**. The row above the active cell and the column to the left of the active cell are now frozen.

7. Click the down arrow on the vertical scroll bar. Notice that the row with the column headings does not move.

8. Click the right arrow on the horizontal scroll bar. Notice that the first column with the ranking information does not move.

9. Open the **Window** menu and choose **Unfreeze Panes**. Leave the workbook open for the next Step-by-Step.

Sort Data

You can quickly sort data in a worksheet. To sort Excel data, you must indicate the column you want to base your sort on. The information in that column will be sorted, and all the data in corresponding rows will also move appropriately. Excel lets you sort alphabetically or numerically. *Ascending order* sorts alphabetically from A to Z or numerically from the lowest to the highest number. *Descending order* sorts alphabetically from Z to A or numerically from the highest to the lowest number.

Excel has two toolbar buttons (Sort Ascending and Sort Descending) that make sorting quick and easy. You simply click in the column you want to sort by and then click one of the sort buttons. Excel will automatically determine if you have a *header row* (headings at the top of your columns), and it will not include this row in the sort.

If you have a worksheet with multiple columns of data, you can base the sort on data in three different columns. For example, you can sort first by height, then by building name, and then by city. When you want to sort by multiple criteria, you must open the Sort dialog box.

S T E P - B Y - S T E P ▷ 2.10

1. Switch to the **Buildings** worksheet.

2. Click in any cell in column A. Then click the **Sort Ascending** button on the Standard toolbar. The building names are arranged in ascending alphabetical order, and the data in the other columns moves with the building name.

3. Click the **Sort Descending** button on the Standard toolbar. The building names are now arranged in descending alphabetical order, and the building data again moves with the building name.

> ⊚ **Hot Tip**
>
> If the Sort Descending button is not displayed on the Standard toolbar, click the Toolbar Options at the right side of the toolbar and then select the Sort Descending button.

4. Open the **Data** menu and choose **Sort**. All the data in the worksheet (except the headings) is selected and the dialog box shown in Figure 2-10 is displayed.

5. Select **Height in Feet** in the list box under *Sort by*. If necessary, select **Descending** at the right of the *Sort by* option.

6. Click the down arrow in the list box under the first *Then by* option. Select **Location** and then, if necessary, select **Ascending** at the right of the *Then by* option.

FIGURE 2-10
Sort dialog box

7. Click the down arrow in the list box under the second *Then by* option. Select **Building** and then, if necessary, select **Ascending** at the right of the *Then by* option.

8. Click **OK**. The worksheet data is rearranged from highest to lowest. If any two buildings are the same height, they are sorted in alphabetical order by the city. If the two buildings are in the same location, they are sorted in alphabetical order by building name.

9. Save the changes and leave the workbook open for the next Step-by-Step.

Print the Worksheet

Before you print the worksheet, you will want to look at it in Print Preview. Print Preview enables you to preview the worksheet on the screen to see what it will look like when it is printed. This can save you time and paper. If the worksheet does not display correctly on the page, you can make adjustments in the Page Setup dialog box.

Change the Page Setup

If the worksheet is large and the columns or rows wrap to a second page, you can sometimes fit the worksheet on one page by changing the page orientation. *Portrait orientation* formats the content of the document with the short edge of the page at the top. This is the default setting. You can change to landscape orientation in the Page Setup dialog box. *Landscape orientation* formats the document sideways with the long edge of the page at the top.

Another option for fitting the worksheet on one page is to turn on the *Fit to* command. This feature scales the worksheet up or down as necessary so it fits on the number of pages you designate.

Computer Concepts

The page setup settings apply to the current worksheet. They do not apply to all the worksheets in the workbook.

S TEP-BY-STEP ▷ 2.11

1. Switch to the **Towers** worksheet.

2. Click the **Print Preview** button on the Standard toolbar. Notice that the Height in Feet column displays on page 2.

3. Click the **Close** button in the toolbar at the top of the screen to close Print Preview.

4. Open the **File** menu and choose **Page Setup**. If necessary, click the **Page** tab to display the dialog box shown in Figure 2-11.

5. Under *Scaling*, turn on the **Fit to** option and accept the default settings of 1 page wide by 1 page tall.

6. Click the **Print Preview** button in the dialog box. Notice that the image of the worksheet is slightly smaller, but it all fits on one page in portrait orientation. Close the Print Preview screen.

7. Open the **File** menu and choose **Page Setup**. Under *Orientation*, select **Landscape**. Under *Scaling, select* **Adjust to** and change the percentage in the **% normal size** box to **100**.

FIGURE 2-11
Page tab in the Page Setup dialog box

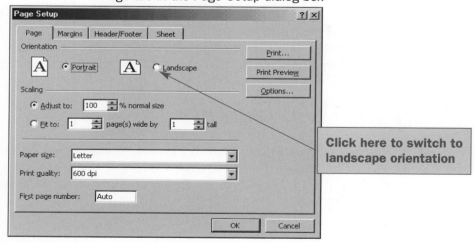

Click here to switch to landscape orientation

8. Click the **Margins** tab to display the dialog box shown in Figure 2-12.

9. Under *Center on page* at the bottom of the dialog box, select **Horizontally**. Click the **Print Preview** button in the dialog box. Notice that this time the preview of the worksheet shows the image in normal size. The page is turned sideways, and the columns are centered horizontally. Close the Print Preview screen.

10. Switch to the **Buildings** worksheet and change the page orientation to landscape and center the worksheet horizontally on the page.

11. Save the changes and leave the workbook open for the next Step-by-Step.

FIGURE 2-12
Margins tab in the Page Setup dialog box

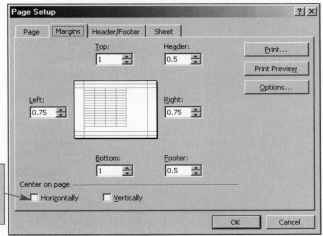

Click here to center worksheet on page horizontally

Print the Worksheets

When you click the Print button on the Standard toolbar, Excel prints the active worksheet with the default print settings. If you want to change any of the print options, you need to open the Print dialog box.

 **Hot Tip**

If you don't want to print the entire worksheet, you can select the range you want to print. Open the **File** menu and choose **Print Area**, and then select **Set Print Area** in the submenu.

 Computer Concepts

When the worksheet is more than one page in length, Excel determines where to break the page and begin a new one. If you don't like where Excel has split the data between pages, you can create your own page break by dragging the page break to a new location.

1. Open the **File** menu and choose **Print** to display the Print dialog box.

2. Under *Print what*, select **Entire workbook** as shown in Figure 2-13. Your dialog box will probably not match exactly.

3. If you are permitted to print, click **OK** to print both worksheets in the workbook. If you are not permitted to print, click **Cancel** to close the Print dialog box.

4. Close the workbook.

Did You Know?

The options available in the Print dialog box vary according to the type of printer available.

FIGURE 2-13
Print dialog box

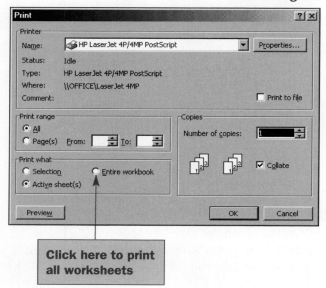

Click here to print
all worksheets

Summary

In this lesson, you learned:

■ When you insert or delete rows and columns, all existing data is shifted up, down, left or right.

■ To reorganize a worksheet, you can delete, copy, or move the data.

■ The AutoFill command enables you to copy data from one cell to another, or enter certain kinds of data such as months, days of the week, or a series of numbers.

■ You can add one or several worksheets to a workbook, and you can rename each worksheet.

■ Hiding columns and rows temporarily removes them from the display. This can be helpful when you are working with a wide spreadsheet or you do not need to view all of the columns or rows.

■ Freezing a column or row enables you to keep the column and row labels visible as you scroll through a worksheet.

■ The sort feature provides options for organizing worksheet data numerically or alphabetically. You can sort the data based on a single column, or you can sort the data based on multiple criteria.

■ Before you print, you can preview the worksheet on the screen to see what it will look like when it is printed. You can change the page orientation or use the Fit to feature to fit all the data on one page.

■ You can choose to print the active worksheet only, or you can choose to print all worksheets in the workbook.

VOCABULARY REVIEW

Define the following terms:

Ascending order
Clipboard
Descending order

Fill handle
Filling
Header row

Landscape orientation
Portrait orientation

LESSON 2 REVIEW QUESTIONS

TRUE/FALSE

Circle T if the statement is true or F if the statement is false.

T F 1. When you fill a cell, you can choose to copy the cell contents either with or without the formats.

T F 2. Using the Delete key will remove both text and formats from a cell.

T F 3. Hiding columns and rows temporarily removes them from display.

T F 4. A workbook can only contain a maximum of three worksheets.

T F 5. Excel usually decides where to break pages when printing a worksheet.

FILL IN THE BLANK

Complete the following sentences by writing the correct word or words in the blanks provided.

1. After you click the Copy button to copy the contents of a cell, the cell is surrounded by a(n) _____ border.

2. The _____ command enables you to copy data from one cell to a number of cells above, below, to the left, or to the right.

3. A collection of related worksheets is called a(n) _____.

4. _____ a column or row enables you to keep the column or row visible as you scroll.

5. To sort from the largest number to the smallest, you would sort in _____ order.

LESSON 2 PROJECTS

PROJECT 2-1

1. Open **Project2-1** from the data files. Save the worksheet as **Classes** followed by your initials.

2. Rename *Sheet1* as **Languages**. Rename *Sheet2* in the workbook as **Fitness**.

3. Switch to the Languages worksheet. Select the cell range A4:F9 and AutoFit the column width to selection.

4. Someone has mistakenly formatted the class numbers with 1000s separators. Use the Clear command on the Edit menu to clear only the formats from these cells. Then center the values again.

5. Copy the cell range A1:F4. Switch to the Fitness worksheet. With cell A1 selected, paste the copied cells.

6. Enter the following fitness class information:

Class	Class #	Winter	Spring	Summer	Fall
Low Impact Aerobics	5105	10	12	15	9
Bench Step Aerobics	5100	9	11	14	12
Combo Aerobics	5290	8	11	13	11
Nautilus	5309	13	14	18	15
Beginning Yoga	4380	10	9	8	7
Tai Chi Chuan	4300	11	9	8	12

7. Switch to the Languages worksheet. Insert a new column to the left of column B. The new column will be very wide since it defaults to the width of the column before it. Do not be concerned. You will adjust the width later. In cell B4, enter the column heading **Fee**.

8. Click in cell B5 and enter the value **120**. Format this value as currency with zero decimal places and center the value in the cell.

9. Fill cells B6:B9 with the value in cell B5. Select the cell range B5:B9 and autofit the column to selection.

10. Insert a row above row 8. Insert the following information in the new row:

    German for Beginners $120   7044   18   17   19   15

11. Switch to the Fitness worksheet. Insert a new column to the left of column B and enter the column heading **Fee**.

12. The fee for all fitness classes is $95. Enter that value in cell B5. Format the cell for Currency with 0 decimal places. Then fill the value in the cell range B6:B10. Select the cell range A5:B10 and AutoFit the column to selection.

13. Select the range C5:G10 and center the values.

14. Center both worksheets horizontally on the page. Preview each worksheet in Print Preview.

15. Save your changes. If you are permitted to print, print both worksheets in the workbook. Close the workbook.

PROJECT 2-2

1. Open **Project2-2** from the data files. Save the presentation as **Tutoring** followed by your initials.

2. Click in cell G1 and key **September**. Use the AutoFill handle to automatically fill cells H1:J1 with the month names **October, November,** and **December**. Select the cell range A1:J15 and adjust column widths to display the content.

3. You decide that last names should come first in this worksheet:
    A. Insert a new column to the left of column A.
    B. Select all data in column C (the Last Name column) and move it into the new column A. Adjust the width of column A to display all data.
    C. Delete the now empty column C.

4. To make it easier to find information about specific students, sort the data in the worksheet. Use the Sort dialog box and specify a sort by last name and then by first name, both in ascending order.

5. Harris Patrick has decided not to continue in the tutoring program. Delete the row that contains his data.

6. Hide the Rate column.

7. Click in cell C1 and freeze panes. Then scroll horizontally so you can easily see how many hours each student is committed to per month.

8. Unfreeze panes and preview the worksheet. Even with the Rate column hidden, the data will not all fit on a page.

9. Change the orientation to landscape and center the worksheet horizontally on the page.

10. Unhide the Rate column.

11. Check the worksheet in Print Preview. If you have permission to print, print the worksheet.

12. Save your changes and close the workbook.

WEB PROJECT

You need to give a talk about earthquake hazards. Use Web search tools to locate information about damage caused by earthquakes. Create a worksheet to hold the information you locate. Use one worksheet in the workbook to hold information on five or six large U.S. earthquakes, and another sheet to hold information on several large earthquakes elsewhere in the world. Your worksheets should record the date, magnitude, and location of the quake, property damage (if you can find it), and persons killed or injured in the quake. Sort the data you find by date or magnitude.

TEAMWORK PROJECT

With a classmate, explore voting statistics for your state in Presidential elections from 1980 through the most recent Presidential election. Follow these steps:

1. Create a worksheet to hold your data. In column A, key **1980** in one cell and then **1984** in the cell below it. Use AutoFill to add the remaining Presidential election years up to and including the most recent Presidential election.

2. Create columns for **Republican**, **Democrat**, and **Independent** candidates.

3. Using an almanac or Web search tools, find information on the popular vote for Republican, Democrat, and Independent candidates for your state in each election. If there is more than one Independent candidate, add together all the votes for all Independent candidates. Collect data from 1980 through the most current Presidential election. Divide the research assignment evenly so that both you and your partner gather the data.

4. Add a column to your worksheet and title it **Winning Party**. Insert the political party of the President who won each election. Use the fill command to insert parties if the same party won two or more consecutive presidential elections. What party won most often in the years you studied?

CRITICAL THINKING

SCANS

You have created a very large worksheet. You would like to be able to work in several parts of the worksheet simultaneously and be able to scroll in each part. You discover you cannot scroll in each part if you simply freeze panes. Is there another way to create panes in a worksheet that would allow you to scroll in each pane independently? Use the Help files in Excel to discover the answer to this question and then write a brief description of what you learn.

CREATING WORKSHEET FORMULAS

OBJECTIVES

Upon completion of this lesson, you should be able to:

- Understand formulas.

- Create a formula.

- Identify and correct formula errors.

- Use the AutoSum feature.

- Use the AutoFill command to enter formulas.

- Use absolute cell references.

- Audit formulas on the worksheet.

⏱ **Estimated Time: 1 hour**

VOCABULARY

Absolute cell reference

Argument

Dependent cells

Formula

Function formula

Mixed cell reference

Operand

Operator

Order of evaluation

Precedent cells

Relative cell references

One of the primary uses of a spreadsheet is to solve problems that involve numbers. The worksheet is often used to complete complex and repetitious calculations accurately, quickly, and easily. Instead of using a calculator to perform mathematical calculations, Excel will perform the calculations for you.

Understand Formulas

The equations used to calculate values in a cell are known as *formulas*. A formula uses numbers and cell references to perform calculations such as addition, subtraction, multiplication, and division. A formula consists of two components: an *operand* and an *operator*. The operand is a number or cell reference. The operator is a symbol that tells Excel what mathematical operation to perform with the operands. For example, in the formula =B5+6, the operands are B5 and 6; the operator is the plus sign. Figure 3-1 lists some of the mathematical operators used in Excel.

Figure 3-2 provides examples to illustrate the order of evaluation.

FIGURE 3-1

Operators used in Excel

Mathematical Operation	Operator
Addition	+ (plus sign)
Subtraction	— (minus sign)
Multiplication	* (asterisk)
Division	/ (forward slash)
Percent	% (percent sign)

All formulas begin with the equal sign. This tells Excel that you are entering a formula instead of a numeric value.

A formula can be as simple as a single cell reference. For example, if you enter the formula =B3 in cell C4, the cell will display the same contents as cell B3. If you then change the value in cell B3, cell C4 will automatically be updated to reflect the change.

Formulas containing more than one operator are called complex formulas. For example, the formula =A4*B5+10 will perform both multiplication and addition. The sequence used to calculate the value of a formula is called the ***order of evaluation***.

FIGURE 3-2

Examples of order of evaluation

Formula	Result
=6+4*4	6+16=22
=6*4+2	24+2=26
=6-4/2	6-2=4
=6/2+4	3+4=7
=(6+4)*4	10*4=40
=(6*4)-(10/2)	24-5=19

Formulas are evaluated as follows:

- Multiplication and division are performed before addition or subtraction.

- Calculations are performed from the left side of the formula to the right side.

- You can change the order of evaluation by using parentheses. Calculations enclosed in parentheses are performed first.

Create a Formula

There are two ways to enter a cell address into a formula. You can key the cell address or you can point to the cell. When entering the cell reference, the column letter can be keyed in either uppercase or lowercase. In the Step-by-Steps in this text, the column letters you must key are shown in lowercase. As you enter the cell references, Excel color-codes the borders around the cells and the cell references in the formula.

The formula is displayed in the Formula Bar as you enter it in the cell. However, once you press Enter or click the Enter button on the Formula Bar, the result of the formula will display in the cell. To see the formula, you must click in the cell and then view the formula in the Formula Bar.

HISTORICALLY SPEAKING

Imagine driving from Michigan to Georgia and needing five different currencies for your trip. To purchase items during your journey, you must convert your Michigan dollars to Ohio marks, Kentucky pounds, Tennessee lira, and Georgia francs. Not only would it be inconvenient, it would also be costly. Each time you converted the money, the money changers would charge you a fee. This is what tourists traditionally experienced when they traveled in Europe. Each time they entered a different country, they had to convert their money to that country's currency.

In January 1999, 11 European countries embraced one currency unit—the euro. The transition to the euro occurred over a three-year period and gradually came to be in general use. The euro was first introduced in electronic trading—business transactions completed without cash. In January 2002, euro notes and coins started circulating.

The changeover to a single currency affects banks, businesses, and consumers. The euro symbol now appears in banks, on financial statements, and on retail price tags. Office XP provides full support for entering, displaying, and printing the euro symbol and for working with values in euro currency.

STEP-BY-STEP ▷ 3.1

1. Open **Step3-1** from the data files. Save the workbook as **Regional Sales** followed by your initials.

> **Speech Recognition**
>
> If your computer has speech recognition capability, enable the Command mode and say the commands to open and save the file.

2. Click in cell E3. Key **=b3+c3+d3**. Compare your screen to Figure 3-3. Notice that each cell you referenced in the formula is selected with a color, and the color matches the color of the cell reference in the formula. Also, notice that the formula is displayed in the cell and in the Formula Bar.

3. Press **Enter** or click the **Enter** button on the Formula Bar. The result of the formula *$50,313* is displayed in cell E3.

4. Click in cell E3. Compare your screen with Figure 3-4. Notice that the formula is still displayed in the Formula Bar.

5. Click in cell E4. Key **=**. Then click in cell B4. Notice that the cell reference B4 now displays following the = in both the Formula Bar and in cell E4.

6. Key **+** and then click in cell C4. Key **+** and click in cell D4. Both the cell and the Formula Bar now display the formula *=B4+C4+D4*.

7. Press **Enter** or click the **Enter** button on the Formula Bar. The result *$51,476* is displayed in cell E4.

8. Double-click in cell B4. Change the amount to **16,750**.

FIGURE 3-3
Entering a formula in a cell

	A	B	C	D	E	F
	SUM ▾ ✗ ✓ *fx* =b3+c3+d3					
1			Sales by Region			
2		July	August	September	Total	
3	Eastern Region	$15,888	$14,645	$19,780	=b3+c3+d3	
4	Central Region	$17,750	$15,404	$18,322		
5	Southern Region	$18,931	$17,932	$20,003		
6	Western Region	$20,050	$21,435	$23,112		
7	Total					
8						

Formula Bar   Formula   Cell references are color coded

FIGURE 3-4
Result of a formula displayed in a cell

	A	B	C	D	E	F
	E3 ▾ *fx* =B3+C3+D3					
1			Sales by Region			
2		July	August	September	Total	
3	Eastern Region	$15,888	$14,645	$19,780	$50,313	
4	Central Region	$17,750	$15,404	$18,322		
5	Southern Region	$18,931	$17,932	$20,003		
6	Western Region	$20,050	$21,435	$23,112		
7	Total					
8						

Formula   Result

269

9. Press **Enter** or click the **Enter** button on the Formula Bar. Notice that the result in cell E4 changes to *$50,476* to reflect the change.

10. Save the changes and leave the workbook open for the next Step-by-Step.

Computer Concepts

Cell references are used in formulas rather than the actual value in the cell. That way, if the value in the cell changes, the formula does not need to be updated.

Identify and Correct Formula Errors

When Excel cannot properly perform a calculation, an error value will display in the cell where you entered the formula. The error may exist because the cell contains text instead of a numeric value. Or, an error value will display if the cell referenced in the formula contains an error. An error value will also display if the cell is not wide enough to display the result.

Did You Know?

Excel has an AutoCorrect feature that automatically checks a formula for common keyboarding mistakes. Sometimes Excel is able to identify the error. If so, a suggested correction appears in an alert box.

Use Help to Learn How to Troubleshoot Formulas and Error Values

If an error value displayed in your worksheet, would you know what to do to correct the problem? You can go to the Help screens to learn about how to troubleshoot the error.

STEP-BY-STEP ⟩ 3.2

1. Click in cell E5. Enter the following formula: **=a5+c5+d5**.

2. Press **Enter** or click the **Enter** button on the Formula Bar. *#VALUE!* is displayed in cell E5. This is the error value. Excel cannot perform the calculation because cell A5 does not contain a numeric value.

3. Open the **Help** menu and choose **Microsoft Excel Help**. If the Office Assistant is displayed, point to the Office Assistant and right-click. Then choose **Options** in the shortcut menu. Clear the check box for **Use the Office Assistant** and click **OK**. Then open the **Help** menu and choose **Microsoft Excel Help**.

4. If necessary, click the **Show** button on the toolbar to display the **Contents**, **Answer Wizard**, and **Index** tabs.

5. If necessary, click the **Contents** tab to display a dialog box similar to the one shown in Figure 3-5. (*Hint:* If you click a plus symbol, the list will expand to display another level of topics.)

FIGURE 3-5
Contents tab in Microsoft Excel Help

6. Click the plus sign (**+**) to the left of the topic *Creating and Correcting Formulas*. The list of topics expands to show a new list of subtopics.

7. Click the plus sign to the left of the subtopic *Correcting Formulas*. Then select the subtopic **Find and correct errors in formulas**.

 Did You Know?

If the entire topic title is not displayed in the Contents pane, you can point to the topic title and a ScreenTip displaying the entire title will appear.

8. The topic information is displayed in the pane at the right. Click the link **Correct an error value, such as #NAME?**. The topic is expanded.

9. Click the link **#VALUE**. Read the information about why the error message is displayed, then follow the suggested steps:

   a. Click in cell **E5** in the worksheet.

   b. Point to the **Trace Error** button that is displayed to the left of the cell.

   c. A ScreenTip displays, showing *A value used in the formula is of the wrong data type*.

   d. Click the down arrow on the **Trace Error** button to display the menu shown in Figure 3-6.

FIGURE 3-6
Error menu

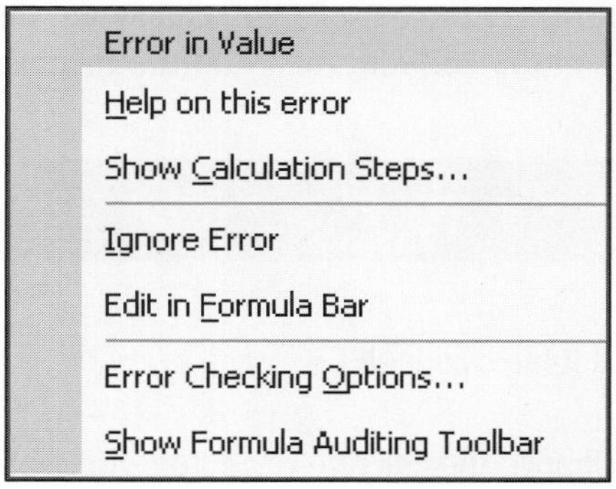

Error in Value
<u>H</u>elp on this error
Show <u>C</u>alculation Steps...
<u>I</u>gnore Error
Edit in <u>F</u>ormula Bar
Error Checking <u>O</u>ptions...
Show Formula Auditing Toolbar

e. Select **Show Calculation Steps**. The Evaluate Formula dialog box shown in Figure 3-7 is displayed. Now you can clearly see that the problem is that you are trying to add text (*Southern Region*) with numbers.

10. Click the **Close** button in the Evaluate Formula dialog box and then close the Help dialog box. Leave the workbook open for the next Step-by-Step.

FIGURE 3-7
Evaluate Formula dialog box

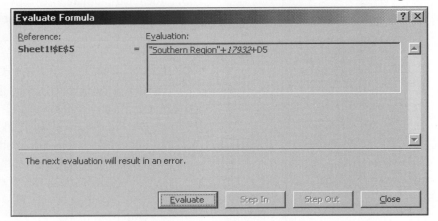

Edit a Formula

You can choose from three methods to edit a formula: 1) you can double-click the cell and then edit the formula in the cell, 2) you can select the cell, press F2, and then edit the formula in the cell, or 3) you can select the cell and then edit the formula in the Formula Bar.

1. Double-click cell E5.

2. Change the cell reference from *A5* to **b5**. Press **Enter** or click the **Enter** button on the Formula Bar. The result (*$56,866*) displays in cell E5.

3. Save the changes and leave the workbook open for the next Step-by-Step.

Use the AutoSum Feature

Although it is easy to enter a formula, if the formula consists of several cells it could take you a long time to enter all the cell references. A shortcut for entering cell references is to identify a range of cells. For example, B5:D5 includes the cells B5, C5 and D5.

The AutoSum feature enables you to quickly identify a range of cells and enter a formula. When you use the AutoSum button, Excel scans the worksheet to determine the most logical column or row of adjacent cells containing numbers to sum. Excel identifies those cells as a range. For example, if the active cell is E7 and there are numbers in cells A7 through D7, Excel will identify the range A7 through D7.

After identifying the range of cells, the AutoSum feature creates a `function formula` to calculate the sum of the range. A *function formula* is a special formula that names a function instead of using operators to calculate a result. In this case, the function is SUM. The SUM function formula is the most frequently used type of function formula. Figure 3-8 illustrates the parts of the SUM function formula. A function contains three parts—the equal sign, the function name, and the arguments. The equal sign tells Excel that a formula follows. The function name tells Excel what to do with the data. The *argument* is a value, cell reference, range, or text that acts as an operand in a function formula. The argument is enclosed in parentheses after the function name. You will learn about other function formulas in the next lesson.

FIGURE 3-8
Parts of a function formula

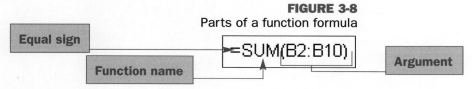

Sometimes Excel does not identify the correct range when you use the AutoSum feature. To identify a different range of cells, drag to select the desired cell range. Then click Enter to display the sum in the cell.

STEP-BY-STEP 3.4

1. With cell E6 selected, click the **AutoSum** button on the Standard toolbar. Excel displays a marquee (an animated border) around the cell range E3:E5 and proposes the formula *=SUM(E3:E5)*. A ScreenTip also displays showing that the formula involves adding numbers. See Figure 3-9.

2. Click in cell B6 and drag to select cells C6 and D6. Excel places a marquee around the new range B6:D6. The proposed formula changes to *=SUM(B6:D6)* to reflect the cell references in the new selection.

FIGURE 3-9
Proposed AutoSum formula

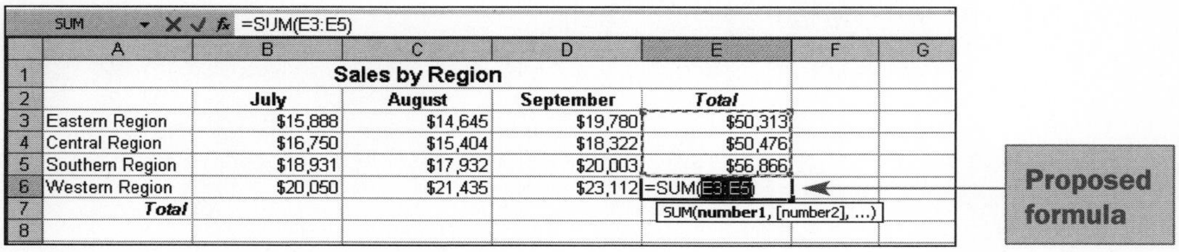

	A	B	C	D	E	F	G
SUM		=SUM(E3:E5)					
1		Sales by Region					
2		July	August	September	Total		
3	Eastern Region	$15,888	$14,645	$19,780	$50,313		
4	Central Region	$16,750	$15,404	$18,322	$50,476		
5	Southern Region	$18,931	$17,932	$20,003	$56,866		
6	Western Region	$20,050	$21,435	$23,112	=SUM(E3:E5)		
7	Total				SUM(number1, [number2], ...)		
8							

Proposed formula

3. Press **Enter** or click the **Enter** button on the Formula Bar to accept the new formula. The result *$64,597* is displayed in cell E6.

4. Click in cell B7. Click the **AutoSum** button and, since it is correctly summing the cell range B3:B6, press **Enter** or click the **Enter** button on the Formula Bar. The result *$71,619* displays in cell B7.

5. Use the **AutoSum** button to enter a formula to calculate the column totals in cells C7, D7, and E7.

Speech Recognition

If your computer has speech recognition capability, enable the Command mode. Then position the insertion point in the designated cell and say the command to calculate the total using the AutoSum feature. Say **Enter** to accept the proposed formula.

6. Insert a new row between the Central Region and Southern Region. Key the following information in the new row. Notice that as you enter the new data, Excel automatically adjusts the results in cells B8, C8, and D8.
Midwest Region 14505 16112 17341

Computer Concepts

When you insert or delete a new row or column that affects a range of cells identified in a formula, Excel will automatically update the range in the formula to reflect the change(s) in the range.

7. Click in cell B8. Look at the formula in the Formula Bar. Notice that Excel automatically updated the range in the formula. The formula now shows the range B3:B7 instead of B3:B6.

8. Click in cell E5, then click the **AutoSum** button. Change the range in the formula to **b5:d5**. Then press **Enter** or click the **Enter** button on the Formula Bar. (Notice that the value in cell E8 changes to reflect the new total added in the column.)

Computer Concepts

Note that the value in cell E8 did not change until you entered a new value in cell E5. This is because the formula calculated the range E3:E7. However, if the formula in cell E8 had instead calculated the range B7:D7, the value in cell E8 would have been adjusted at the same time cells B8, C8, and D8 changed.

9. Notice that there is a triangle in the top left corner of cell E5. Click in the cell, and then point to the **Trace Error** button that displays to the left. The ScreenTip indicates that the formula in this cell differs from the formulas in this area of the spreadsheet. If you click in any of the other cells in the column, you will see that most of the formulas use plus signs instead of the sum feature to calculate the total. The formula in cell C5 is, however, accurate.

$47,958

10. Compare your screen to Figure 3-10. If necessary, edit the formulas to correct any errors. When the values in your worksheet match those illustrated in Figure 3-10, save the changes and close the workbook.

Hot Tip

To quickly preview the sum of a range of cells, select the range of cells. The sum is displayed in the status bar at the bottom of the screen.

FIGURE 3-10
Completed worksheet

	A	B	C	D	E	F
	E20	▼	fx			
1			Sales by Region			
2		July	August	September	Total	
3	Eastern Region	$15,888	$14,645	$19,780	$50,313	
4	Central Region	$16,750	$15,404	$18,322	$50,476	
5	Midwest Region	$14,505	$16,112	$17,341	$47,958	
6	Southern Region	$18,931	$17,932	$20,003	$56,866	
7	Western Region	$20,050	$21,435	$23,112	$64,597	
8	Total	$86,124	$85,528	$98,558	$270,210	
9						

Use the AutoFill Command to Enter Formulas

In this Unit's Lesson 2, you learned how AutoFill can copy data to adjacent cells or fill a range of cells with a data series such as numbers 1 through 10. You can also use AutoFill to copy formulas. You can fill formulas up, down, left, and right.

By default, when you create formulas, the cell references are formatted as ***relative cell references***. That means when the formula is copied to another cell, the cell references will be adjusted relative to the formula's new location. This automatic adjustment is helpful when you need to repeat the same formula for several columns or rows.

STEP-BY-STEP ⇒ 3.5

1. Open **Step3-5** from the data files. Save the workbook as **Mileage Report** followed by your initials.

2. Click in cell D3. Enter the formula **=c3-b3**. Press **Enter** or click the **Enter** button in the Formula Bar. The result *81* displays in cell D3.

3. Click in cell D3. Point to the fill handle in the lower right corner of cell D3. When the pointer changes to a bold plus sign, drag down to cell D7. The results of the formula display in each of the selected cells.

4. Click in cell D4. Notice the formula in the Formula Bar displays *=C4-B4*.

275

5. Click in cell D5. Notice the formula in the Formula Bar displays *=C5-B5*.

6. Save the changes and leave the worksheet open for the next Step-by-Step.

Use Absolute Cell References

There are times, though, when you don't want the cell reference to change when the formula is moved or copied to a new cell. For example, you may be calculating expenses for auto mileage. The number of miles should always be multiplied times a fixed amount that represents the cost per mile. To create this formula, you format an absolute cell reference. An *absolute cell reference* does not change when the formula is copied or moved to a new location.

To create an absolute cell reference, you insert a dollar sign ($) before the column letter and/or the row number of the cell reference you want to stay the same. To illustrate, =A1 is a formula with an absolute reference.

A cell reference that contains both relative and absolute references is called a *mixed cell reference*. For example, you can have an absolute column reference and a relative row reference. Or, you can have a relative column reference and an absolute row reference. To illustrate, =$A1 is a formula with a mixed cell reference. The column reference is absolute and the row reference is relative. When formulas with mixed cell references are copied or moved, the row or column references that are preceded by a dollar sign will not change. However, the row or column references that are not preceded by a dollar sign will adjust relative to the cell to which they are moved.

Hot Tip

Another method for creating an absolute cell reference is to key the cell reference and then press **F4**. This toggles the display of a dollar sign in front of the column letter and/or the row number. When you press **F4** once, Excel will insert a dollar sign in front of the column letter and another dollar sign in front of the row number. If you press **F4** a second time, Excel will insert a dollar sign in front of the row reference only. If you press **F4** a third time, Excel will insert a dollar sign in front of the column reference only.

STEP-BY-STEP 3.6

1. Click in cell E3. Enter the formula **=d3*c10**.

2. Press **Enter** or click the **Enter** button on the Formula Bar. Excel multiplied the value in cell D3 (*81*) times the value in cell C10 (*$0.33*). The result is *$26.73*.

3. Click in cell E3. Drag the fill handle down to cell E7. The results display in each of the selected cells.

4. Click in cell E4. Notice the formula in the Formula Bar displays *=D4*C10*. When you filled the formula down, Excel automatically changed the cell references for D3 in the original formula. However, because the cell reference for C10 was absolute, Excel did not change that cell reference.

5. Click in cell E8. Click the **AutoSum** button, then press **Enter** or click the **Enter** button on the Formula Bar.

6. Save the changes and keep the workbook open for the next Step-by-Step.

Audit Formulas on the Worksheet

Because Excel performs the calculations, spreadsheet users (even experienced ones) often assume that the results in the worksheet are accurate. However, the results are only accurate if the user has entered accurate data and correct formulas. Therefore, data and formulas should be checked to assure the accuracy of the results.

If your worksheet contains several formulas, it would be a tedious task to click each cell in order to view and proofread each formula. Fortunately, there is an easier way to display formulas. Simply hold down **Ctrl** and press the single left quotation mark (generally located in the upper-left corner of the keyboard). You can also display formulas in a worksheet by opening the Tools menu and choosing Options. Then click the View tab and turn on Formulas under *Window options*.

Likewise, it could be very time-consuming to verify all the cell references in the formulas. The Formula Audit toolbar offers some tools that make it easy to trace these cell references and display both ***precedent cells*** and ***dependent cells***. The cells that provide data to a formula are called precedents. Formulas that reference a particular cell are called dependents.

STEP-BY-STEP ⟹ 3.7

1. Press **Ctrl + '** (single left quotation mark). The number formats are removed from the cells, and the formulas display instead of the results.

2. Compare your worksheet with the one illustrated in Figure 3-11. If your formulas do not match those in the figure, click the cell and edit the formula. If the Formula Auditing toolbar is displayed, drag it to the side. You will use it later.

FIGURE 3-11
Worksheet with formulas displayed

	A	B	C	D	E
	E9 ▼ fx				
1			JULY MILEAGE REPORT		
2	Date	Odometer Start	Odometer End	Total Miles	Expense
3	36708	78541	78622	=C3-B3	=D3*C10
4	36709	78904	78991	=C4-B4	=D4*C10
5	36714	79106	79165	=C5-B5	=D5*C10
6	36715	80155	80352	=C6-B6	=D6*C10
7	36716	80394	80457	=C7-B7	=D7*C10
8	Total				=SUM(E3:E7)
9					
10		Cost per mile	0.33		
11					

3. Click in cell E8. The cells referenced in the formula are highlighted.

4. Press **Ctrl + '** to hide the formulas and display the results.

5. If necessary, display the Formula Auditing toolbar shown in Figure 3-12. Open the **View** menu, choose **Toolbars**, and select **Formula Auditing**.

6. Click cell D7. Then click the **Trace Precedents** button on the Formula Auditing toolbar. An arrow displays through cells B7 and C7 to trace the cells that provide data to the formula.

7. Click in cell C10. Click the **Trace Dependents** button on the Formula Auditing toolbar. Several arrows display pointing to the cells in column E that depend on the data in cell C10.

8. Compare your worksheet with the one illustrated in Figure 3-13.

9. Click the **Remove All Arrows** button on the Formula Auditing toolbar to remove the arrows from the worksheet.

Speech Recognition

If your computer has speech recognition capability, enable the Command mode. Position the Insertion point in the designated cells and then say the commands to trace the precedents and dependents.

10. Close the workbook. Click **Yes** if you are prompted to save changes.

FIGURE 3-12
Formula Auditing toolbar

FIGURE 3-13
Arrows show precedents for cell D7 and dependents for cell C10

	A	B	C	D	E	F
1			JULY MILEAGE REPORT			
2	Date	Odometer Start	Odometer End	Total Miles	Expense	
3	1-Jul	78,541	78,622	81	$26.73	
4	2-Jul	78,904	78,991	87	$28.71	
5	7-Jul	79,106	79,165	59	$19.47	
6	8-Jul	80,155	80,352	197	$65.01	
7	9-Jul	80,394	80,457	63	$20.79	
8	Total				$160.71	
9						
10		Cost per mile	$0.33			
11						

Summary

In this lesson, you learned:

- One of the primary uses for Excel spreadsheets is to perform calculations. Formulas are equations with numbers, cell references, and operators that tell Excel how to perform the calculations.

- All formulas begin with =. To enter the cell references in a formula, you can key the cell address or you can point and click the cell you want to reference.

- If Excel cannot perform a calculation, an error value will display. The Trace Error button will display and can help guide you in troubleshooting the problem. Then, you can edit the formula directly in the cell or in the Formula Bar.

- The AutoSum feature enables you to quickly identify a range of cells and enter a formula.

- The AutoFill feature enables you to quickly copy formulas to adjacent cells. The cell references are adjusted relative to the formula's new location.

- If you do not want the cell reference to change when the formula is moved or copied to a new location, the cell reference must be formatted as an absolute cell reference.

- Displaying formulas in the worksheet can make it easier to view and proofread the formulas.

- Tracing the precedents and dependents of a formula make proofing formulas quicker and easier.

VOCABULARY REVIEW

Define the following terms:

Absolute cell reference	Function formula	Order of evaluation
Argument	Mixed cell reference	Precedent cells
Dependent cells	Operand	Relative cell reference
Formula	Operator	

LESSON 3 REVIEW QUESTIONS

TRUE/FALSE

Circle T if the statement is true or F if the statement is false.

T F   1.   A formula must consist of more than one cell reference.

T F   2.   You can enter a cell reference in either uppercase or lowercase.

T F   3.   If you do not include a closing parenthesis in a formula, Excel will display an error message.

T F 4. You can only fill formulas down.

T F 5. An absolute cell reference will automatically adjust when moved or copied.

FILL IN THE BLANK

Complete the following sentences by writing the correct word or words in the blanks provided.

1. A complex formula consists of two components: a(n) _____ and a(n) _____.

2. The _____ determine(s) the sequence calculations are performed in a complex formula.

3. The _____ feature enables you to quickly find the total of a range of cells.

4. Cell references that contain both relative and absolute references are called _____.

5. _____ provide data to a formula.

LESSON 3 PROJECTS

PROJECT 3-1

1. Open **Project3-1** from the data files. Save the workbook as **Deer** followed by your initials.

2. Click in cell G6 and create a formula that will add the numbers for all four days of the survey.

3. Use Fill to copy the formula to the cell range G7:G14.

4. Click in cell H6 and create a formula that will divide the total in cell G6 by the square miles value in cell B6. (*Hint:* The operator for division is / (forward slash). Format the cell with the Number format using one decimal place.)

5. Use Fill to copy the formula to the cell range H7:H14.

6. The Division of Wildlife in your state suggests that for deer herds to remain healthy, there should be no more than 25 deer per square mile. Find out how the deer herds in your state county parks compare with this suggested density by calculating the percent over or under for each park:
   A. Click in cell I6 and type the formula **=h6/25**. Format the resulting value as a Percentage with no decimal places.
   B. Fill down the formula in each cell in the range I7:I14.
   C. Which parks meet the suggested density figures (are under 100%)? Which parks have a serious overpopulation problem (are over 130%)?

7. Check your formulas by displaying all the formulas in the worksheet.

8. Hide the formulas again. Save the changes and close the workbook.

PROJECT 3-2

1. Open **Project3-2** from data files. Save the workbook as **Pies** followed by your initials.

2. Click in cell E6 and create a formula that will multiply the total number of Deep-dish apple pies by the price for all fruit pies in cell C5. (*Hint:* The formula should include an absolute cell reference for cell C5.)

3. Use Fill to copy the formula for the other fruit pies.

4. In cells D11 and E11, use AutoSum to sum the total number of fruit pies and the fruit pie revenue.

5. Using the same procedure, calculate revenues and subtotals for the remaining pie categories.

6. In cell D33, create a formula that will add each of the subtotal values in the D column (cells D11, D17, D24, and D31).

7. In cell E33, create a formula that will add each of the subtotal revenue values in the E column (cells E11, E17, E24, and E31).

8. In cells D35 and E35, create formulas to subtract last year's numbers and revenues from the Grand Total amounts for this year. Is Melissa gaining or losing business?

9. Change the price for Tropical Treats to $15.00. How did the change impact Melissa's gain/loss?

10. Save the changes and close the workbook.

WEB PROJECT

You plan to visit Europe in the coming summer and would like to know what kind of exchange rate you can expect when changing dollars to euros. Search the Web for a site that gives a current exchange rate for euros. Then create a worksheet that contains a cell in which to type a dollar amount, a cell that contains the current euro exchange rate, and a cell that will display the result of the calculation to convert dollars to euros.

TEAMWORK PROJECT

SCANS

At some time in your future, you will probably consider the purchase of a car, either new or used. It is easy to overlook the fact that there are other expenses associated with a car besides the initial purchase price. With a classmate, explore the costs of buying, running, and maintaining a car in this project. Follow these steps:

1. With your teammate, decide what kind of car you want to purchase. It can be either new or used.

2. Establish the expenses you expect to be associated with the car. For example, you will have the purchase price, insurance, regular fillups of gasoline, and regular maintenance. Divide this list of expenses with your partner.

3. Find a representative price for your car in a newspaper or on a Web site. You can locate insurance information on the Web or by calling car insurance agencies. Establish an average price per gallon of gas. Ask friends or family about yearly regular maintenance costs such as tuneups, new tires, oil changes, and so on.

4. Create a worksheet to store the data you gather. In part of the worksheet, figure out about how many gallons of gas your car might use in 12 months and add that sum to the values you have established for purchase, car insurance, and regular maintenance.

5. How much do you figure it will cost you to purchase and use your automobile for a year?

CRITICAL THINKING

SCANS

Open a new worksheet. In cell B2, key **25**. Press **Enter** and key **30**. Press **Enter** and key **35**. Press **Enter** and key **40**. Suppose you wanted to add up these numbers and then multiply the total by **2**.

In cell D2, key the following formula: **=b2+b3+b4+b5*2**. In cell D3, key the following formula: **=(b2+b3+b4+b5)*2**.

Are the values in cells D2 and D3 the same? Why not? Write a brief report to explain why the formula results are different.

USING FUNCTION FORMULAS

OBJECTIVES

Upon completion of this lesson, you should be able to:

- Understand function formulas.

- Use the Average and Sum functions.

- Use the Count function.

- Use the Minimum and Maximum functions.

- Use the Now functions.

- Use logical functions.

⏱ **Estimated Time: 1 hour**

VOCABULARY

Logical functions

Mathematical functions

Statistical functions

Trigonometric funcitons

Understand Function Formulas

Excel has more than 300 built-in functions for performing calculations. In fact, you have already used one of Excel's built-in mathematical and trigonometric functions—the SUM function. *Mathematical* and *trigonometric functions* perform calculations that you could do using a scientific calculator. When you used the AutoSum button, Excel used the SUM function to calculate the results. *Statistical functions* are functions that describe large quantities of data. For example, a statistical function can determine the average of a range of data.

Table 4-1 describes some of the most common mathematical and statistical functions.

TABLE 4-1
Common Excel functions

MATHEMATICAL AND TRIGONOMETRIC FUNCTIONS

=PRODUCT	Multiplies values in the specified cells
=ROUND	Rounds the value to the nearest value in one of two ways: with the specified number of decimal places or to the nearest whole number
=ROUNDUP	Rounds the value up to the next higher positive value (or the next lower negative value) with the number of specified decimal places
=ROUNDDOWN	Rounds the value down to the next lower positive value (or to the next higher negative value) with the number of specified decimal places
=SUM	Adds the values in the specified range of cells

STATISTICAL FUNCTIONS

=AVERAGE	Totals the range of cells and then divides the total by the number of entries in the specified range
=COUNT	Counts the number of cells with values in the specified range
=MAX	Displays the maximum value within the specified range of cells
=MEDIAN	Displays the middle value in the specified range of cells
=MIN	Displays the minimum value within the specified range of cells

Figure 4-1 illustrates an example of a formula containing an Average function. The equal sign tells Excel that a formula follows. The function name AVERAGE tells Excel to calculate an average of the three cells included in the argument—B4, B6, and B8.

Computer Concepts

When the function formula contains more than one argument, commas are used to separate the arguments.

FIGURE 4-1
Average function formula

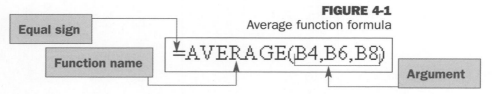

Equal sign

Function name

=AVERAGE(B4,B6,B8)

Argument

There are several methods for entering functions in the worksheet. If you know the function name and argument, you can key an equal sign, the function name, and the argument. Or, if you want help entering the formula, you can use the Insert Function button and the Function Arguments dialog box to guide you through the process of building a formula that contains a function.

Did You Know?

It is not necessary to key the function name in all caps.

Use the Average and Sum Functions

The Average function is a statistical function. It displays the average of the range identified in the argument. For example, the function =AVERAGE(B2,G2) calculates the average of the values contained in cells B2 and G2. As you already know, the Sum function is a mathematical function. If you used the Sum function instead of the average function, the total (instead of the average) of the values contained in cells B2 and G2 would be calculated.

STEP-BY-STEP ▷ 4.1

1. Open **Step4-1** from the data files. Save the workbook as **Weather** followed by your initials.

Speech Recognition

If your computer has speech recognition capability, enable the Command mode and say the commands to open the file and then save it with a new filename.

2. You want to calculate the average low temperature for the week. Click in cell B13. Key **=average(b2:b8)**. This formula tells Excel to calculate the average of the values in the cell range B2:B8.

3. Press **Enter** or click the **Enter** button on the Formula Bar. The result *9* is displayed in cell B13.

4. Now you want to calculate the average high temperature for the week. Click in cell D13. Click the **Insert Function** button on the Formula Bar. An Insert Function dialog box similar to the one shown in Figure 4-2 is displayed. Do not be concerned if your dialog box looks a little different.

FIGURE 4-2
Insert Function dialog box

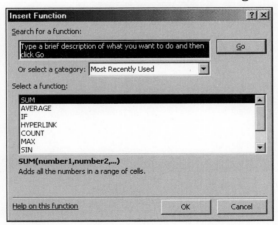

285

5. In the *Search for a function box*, key **calculate average** and click **Go**. The display of options under *Select a Function* changes and **AVERAGE** is already selected. Notice that a brief explanation of the Average function is displayed at the bottom of the dialog box.

Hot Tip

If you do not know which category to choose from, click the down arrow in the *Or select a category:* list box and then select **All**. The complete list of function names will display.

Computer Concepts

The Insert Function dialog box makes it easy for you to browse through all of the available functions to choose the one you want. Furthermore, when you select a function, a brief explanation of that function is displayed. If you want help on the function, click the link at the bottom of the dialog box.

6. Click **OK**. The Function Arguments dialog box shown in Figure 4-3 is displayed. Notice that Excel identified the range D10:D12 in the *Number 1* text box. Also, Excel proposes a formula with the AVERAGE function in the Formula Bar. The result *25* is displayed at the bottom of the Function Arguments dialog box.

Computer Concepts

The purpose of the Function Arguments dialog box is to help you construct a function formula.

FIGURE 4-3
Function Arguments dialog box

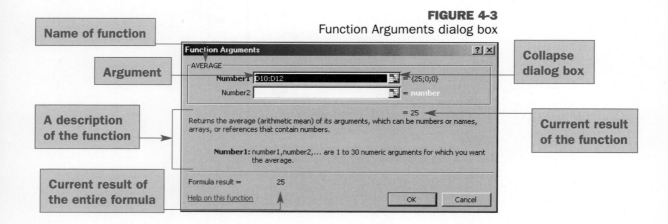

7. The range in the *Number 1* text box is not cor-rect. Click in the text box and change the range to **d2:d8**. Notice the result at the bottom of the dialog box now displays *24*.

8. Click **OK**. The result *24* is displayed in cell D13.

9. Save the changes and leave the workbook open for the next Step-by-Step.

Hot Tip

You can also use the Formula Palette to edit functions in existing formulas.

Use the Count Function

The Count function is a statistical function that displays the number of cells with numerical val-ues in the argument range. For example, the function =COUNT(B4:B10) displays the number 7 when all the cells in the range contain a numeric value.

You can edit a range of cells in the Function Arguments dialog box by selecting the cells. Although the intent of the Function Arguments dialog box is to guide you in creating formulas, the dialog box can get in the way when you are creating the formula. That is why the collapse and expand features are avail-able in the Function Arguments dialog box. They allow you to minimize and maximize the dialog box as you work with it.

1. Click in cell **B12**.

Speech Recognition

If your computer has speech recognition capability, enable the Command mode and say the commands to navigate to the specified cells.

2. Click the **Insert Function** button to display the Insert Function dialog box. Under *Select a function*, select **COUNT**.

3. Click **OK**. The Function Arguments dialog box is displayed. Because you chose a different func-tion, the information looks slightly different. The text boxes are now labeled *Value 1* and *Value 2*. Excel proposes the range B10:B11 in the *Value 1* text box and the result is *1*. The range, however, is not correct.

4. Click the **Collapse Dialog** button at the right side of the *Value 1* text box. The dialog box minimizes so that you only see its title bar and the range of cells. See Figure 4-4. The proposed formula is still dis-played in the Formula Bar.

FIGURE 4-4
Minimized Function Arguments dialog box

5. If necessary, drag the minimized dialog box out of the way and then select the range B2:B8. The formula in the dialog box is updated and now shows the new range you selected. Notice, too, that the formula in the Formula Bar is also updated.

6. Click the **Expand Dialog** button at the right side of the Function Arguments title bar, or press **Enter**. The dialog box is maximized. Notice that the *Value 1* text box now displays the range *B2:B8*.

7. Click **OK**. The result *7* is displayed in cell B12.

8. Click in cell B16. Click the **Insert Function** button and select **SUM** under *Select a function*. Click **OK**.

9. The Function Arguments dialog box displays. The range in the *Number 1* text box is not correct. Minimize the Function Arguments dialog box. Click in cell F2 and drag to select the range F2:F8. Then maximize the dialog box and click **OK**. The result *12* displays in cell B16.

10. Save the changes and leave the workbook open for the next Step-by-Step.

Use the Minimum and Maximum Functions

The Minimum (MIN) and Maximum (MAX) functions are also statistical functions. The MIN function displays the smallest number contained in the range identified in the argument. The MAX function displays the largest number contained in the range identified in the argument.

STEP-BY-STEP 4.3

1. Click in cell B14. Click the **Insert Function** button to display the Insert Function dialog box.

2. In the *Search for a function* box, key **minimum**. Under *Select a function*, select **MIN** if necessary and click **OK**.

3. Collapse the Function Arguments dialog box and then select the range B2:B8.

4. Expand the dialog box and then click **OK**. The result *–2* is displayed in cell B14.

5. Click in cell B15. Click the **Insert Function** button to display the Insert Function dialog box.

6. Under *Select a function*, select **MAX** and click **OK**.

7. Collapse the dialog box and select the range D2:D8.

8. Expand the dialog box and click **OK**. The result *30* is displayed in cell B15.

9. Save the changes and leave the workbook open for the next Step-by-Step.

Use the Now Function

Sometimes you may want to insert the current date or the current time in a cell. The Now function is a Date and Time function you can use to enter the current date and time. You can then format the results in the desired date format. When you format the results, you can choose to show the date and time, just the date, or just the time.

If you want to enter just the current date or just the current time, you can save time by using shortcut keys. The shortcut to enter the current date is Ctrl + ; (semicolon). The shortcut to enter the current time is Ctrl + Shift + ; (semicolon).

Did You Know?

You can also display the Insert Function dialog box by opening the **Insert** menu and choosing **Function**.

STEP-BY-STEP ▷ 4.4

1. Click in cell B17. Click the **Insert Function** button. The Insert Function dialog box is displayed.

Speech Recognition

If your computer has speech recognition capability, say the command to open the Insert menu, then say the command to choose the Function command. Continue to say the commands to select the options in the Insert Function dialog box and in the Function Arguments dialog box.

2. In the *Search for a function* box, key **date and time** and click **Go**. NOW is highlighted under *Select a function*.

3. Press **Enter** or click **OK**. The Function Arguments dialog box is displayed.

4. Click **OK**. The current date and time are displayed in cell B17. Notice that the time is based on the 24-hour clock.

Computer Concepts

When you use the NOW function, the format for the date or time will display depending on the cell formats. The date and time are not updated continuously, but they will be updated when you perform a calculation in the worksheet, and also when the worksheet is reopened.

5. With cell B17 still selected, open the **Format** menu and choose **Cells**. Select the **Number** tab and under *Category* select **Time**. Under *Type*, select **1:30 PM**.

6. Click **OK**. Now only the time is displayed. The current time based on the 12-hour clock is displayed, followed by either AM or PM.

7. With cell B17 still selected, open the **Format** menu and choose **Cells**. The Number tab should already be displayed. Under *Category*, select **Date**; and under *Type*, select **3/14/01**. Click **OK**. The result in the cell changes to display only the current date.

289

8. Click in cell B18. Hold down **Ctrl** and **Shift**, then press **;**. Press **Enter**. The current time based on the 12-hour clock is displayed.

9. Save the changes and leave the workbook open for the next Step-by-Step.

Computer Concepts

When you use the shortcut keys to enter the current time or current date, they are entered as absolute values. In other words, the values will not change when other calculations are performed or when the worksheet is reopened.

Use Logical Functions

One of the most powerful and useful features of spreadsheets is their ability to perform different calculations based on changing values. *Logical functions* are special functions that display predetermined text or values when certain conditions exist. You can use logical functions either to see whether a condition is true or false, or to check for multiple conditions.

Use the IF Function

The most used logical function is the IF function. You can use the IF function to determine whether a condition is true or false. If the condition is true, a value (such as the text YES) is given. If the condition is false, a value (such as the text NO) is displayed.

An example of a formula containing an IF function is illustrated in Figure 4-5. The IF function has three parts: the logical test, the IF function, and the value.

The logical test can include operators or qualifiers that help to evaluate the range of numbers or results. In Table 4-2, the logical test is B2>100.

FIGURE 4-5
Formula with a logical function

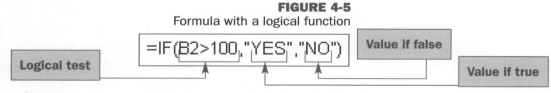

Table 4-2 describes some of the qualifiers you can use for a logical test.

TABLE 4-2
Qualifiers for a logical text

LOGICAL TEST QUALIFIERS	
=	Equal to (or the same as)
>	Greater than
<	Less than
>=	Greater than or equal to
<=	Less than or equal to
<>	Not equal to

The second part of the IF function is called value if true. It contains values or functions that result when the logic test is true. For example, in the IF function illustrated in Figure 4-5, if the logical test is true, then the text *YES* will result.

The value if false is the third part of the IF function. It contains values or functions that result when the logic test is false. For example, in the IF function illustrated in Figure 4-5, if the logical test is false, then the text *NO* will result.

In the next Step-by-Step, you will use the IF function to determine if the daily low temperatures were below the normal low and if the daily high temperatures were above the normal high.

S TEP-BY-STEP ▷ 4.5

1. Click in cell C2. Click the **Insert Function** button to display the Insert Function dialog box.

2. Under *Select a function*, select **IF**. Click **OK**. The Function Arguments dialog box shown in Figure 4-6 is displayed. It looks different than the previous function dialog boxes because the IF function requires different information.

FIGURE 4-6
Function Arguments for the IF function

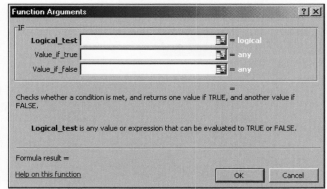

291

3. In the *Logical_test* text box, key **b2<b10**. This logical test determines if the value in cell B2 is lower than the value in cell B10 (the normal low temperature). Remember you learned in Lesson 3 that the dollar signs indicate that the column and row references are absolute.

4. Click in the *Value_if_true* box and key **YES**. This tells Excel to enter the text *YES* when the logical test is true.

5. Click in the *Value_if_false* box. Notice that Excel put quotes around the word *YES* in the box above. Key **NO**. This tells Excel to enter the text *NO* when the logical test is false.

Computer Concepts

If you do not enter a value in the Value_if_true box, Excel will display the result *TRUE*. If you do not enter a value in the Value_if_false box, Excel will display the result *FALSE*.

6. Click **OK**. Excel determines that the value in cell B2 is not below the normal low temperature; therefore, the result displayed in the cell is *NO*.

7. Fill down the function from cell C2 through C8.

8. Click in cell E2. Click the **Insert Function** button, then select **IF** under *Select a function* and click **OK**.

9. In the *Logical_test text* box, key **d2>d10**. In the *Value_if_true* text box, key **YES**. In the *Value_if_false* text box, key **NO**. This formula tells Excel to determine if the value in cell D2 is greater than the value in cell D10 (the normal high temperature).

10. Click **OK**. The value *NO* is displayed in cell E2.

11. Fill down the formula from cell E2 through E8. Deselect the cells.

12. Save the changes and leave the workbook open for the next Step-by-Step.

Did You Know?

You can click the down arrow to the right of the Function button to display other functions you have used.

Use Help to Learn about Other Logic Functions

The IF function is just one example of a logic function. The Help screens can help you learn about some of the other logic functions that Excel provides.

STEP-BY-STEP ⟹ 4.6

1. Open the **Help** menu and choose **Microsoft Excel Help**. If the Office Assistant is displayed, point to the Office Assistant and right-click. Then, choose **Options** in the shortcut menu. Clear the check box for **Use the Office**

Assistant and click **OK**. Then, open the Help menu and choose **Microsoft Excel Help**.

2. If necessary, click the **Show** button on the toolbar to display the *Contents, Answer Wizard,* and *Index* tabs.

3. If necessary, click the **Answer Wizard** tab to display the dialog box shown in Figure 4-7.

FIGURE 4-7
Answer Wizard tab of the Help screen

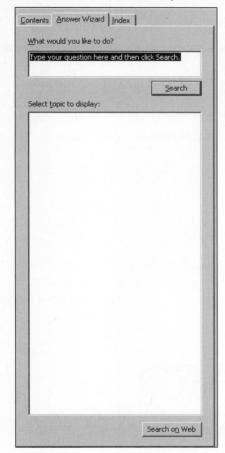

4. In the *What would you like to do?* text box, key **learn more about logical functions**. Then click **Search**.

5. Under *Select topic to display*, select **AND worksheet function**.

6. Click the link **See Also** displayed at the top of the information at the right. The Topics Found dialog box shown in Figure 4-8 is displayed.

FIGURE 4-8
Topics Found dialog box

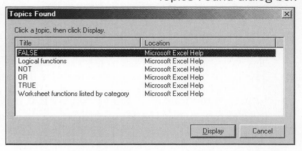

7. Select **Logical functions**, then click **Display** in the dialog box.

8. Click any one of the links to read about a logical function available in Excel.

9. Click the **Back** button on the Help toolbar to go back to the previous Help screen. If desired, click another link under the topic *Logical Functions* to read about another logical function available in Excel.

10. Close the Help screens and close the workbook.

Computer Concepts

The examples of functions presented in this lesson are very simple. As you can see by reviewing the topics related to logical functions in the Help screens, function formulas can perform very complex calculations that would be extremely difficult to perform manually.

Summary

In this lesson, you learned:

- Functions are special formulas that do not require operators. Excel provides more than 300 built-in functions to help you perform mathematical and trigonometric, statistical, and logical functions.

- The Average function displays the average of the range identified in the argument. The Sum function totals the values in the specified range of cells.

- The Count function displays the number of cells with numerical values in the argument range.

- The Minimum and Maximum functions display the smallest or the largest number contained in the range identified in the argument.

- The Now function can be used to enter the current date and/or current time.

- Logical functions are used to display text or values when certain conditions exist. The most used logical function is the If function.

VOCABULARY REVIEW

Define the following terms:

Logical functions   Statistical functions   Trigonometric functions
Mathematical functions

LESSON 4 REVIEW QUESTIONS

TRUE/FALSE

Circle T if the statement is true or F if the statement is false.

T F   1.   A function contains two parts: the function name and the arguments.

T F   2.   When entering a function name, you must use all capital letters.

T F   3.   The Function Argument dialog box displays only when you have an error in a function formula.

T F   4.   To enter the current date in a worksheet cell, use the Now function.

T F   5.   The If function has three parts: the logical test, the value if true, and the value if false.

FILL IN THE BLANK

Complete the following sentences by writing the correct word or words in the blanks provided.

1. _____ functions are used to describe large quantities of data.

2. If you wanted to display the smallest number contained in a range of cells, you would choose the _____ function.

3. The _____ function displays the number of cells with numerical values in the argument range.

4. To quickly enter the current time in a cell, use the shortcut keys _____.

5. _____ functions are used to display text or values when certain conditions exist.

LESSON 4 PROJECTS

PROJECT 4-1

1. Open **Project4-1** from the data files. Save the workbook as **Grades** followed by your initials.

2. In cell B4, use a function to display the current date in the format 3/14/01.

3. In cell F7, use a function to average the test scores in cells B7:E7. Format the resulting value with no decimal places. Fill the formula down to average the tests for the remaining classes.

4. You want to keep track of your current grade in each class in column G. If your test average is above 90, you will receive an "A." If it is not above 90, you will receive a "B." (You're a very good student!). Use the IF function to display your current grades as follows:
   A. The logical test for the IF function is **f7>90**.
   B. The value if true is "A."
   C. The value if false is "B."

5. Fill the formula down for the other classes and then center the grades in column G. In what classes are you currently receiving an "A?"

6. Save your changes and close the workbook.

PROJECT 4-2

1. Open **Project4-2** from the data files. Save the workbook as **Birds** followed by your initials.

2. In cell J6, use a function to sum the number of blue jays observed at all stations. Fill the formula down to sum the totals for the other bird species.

3. In cell A25, enter **Species Counted** and boldface the text.

4. In cell B25, use the Count function to total the number of species observed at Station 1. (Hint: Your count should equal *14*.) Fill the formula across to count the number of species observed at each of the other stations, but do not fill the formula into column J. Boldface cell range B25:I25.

5. The Audubon Society would like to know if too many birds of any one species are visiting each station and, therefore, driving other birds away. In cell A27, key **Maximum Counted** and boldface the text.

6. In cell B27, use a formula to find the maximum number of birds counted at Station 1. Fill the formula across for all stations and boldface the values.

7. The Society would also like to know the minimum number of birds counted. Low numbers of individual species could indicate stress in the bird population. In cell A29, key **Minimum Counted** and boldface the text.

8. In cell B29, use a formula to find the minimum number of birds counted at Station 1. Fill the formula across for all stations and boldface the values.

9. Save your changes and close the workbook.

WEB PROJECT

In this lesson, you worked with some representative weather data to learn how to analyze the data using statistical and logical functions. Use Web search tools to locate information on the weather in your area. Choose any month and find the actual high and low temperatures and precipitation amounts (in rain or snow) for that month. Record the temperatures and precipitation amounts in a worksheet. Locate information on normal high temperatures, low temperatures, and monthly precipitation amounts for your area and record those on your worksheet. Use functions to analyze the data you have gathered. During the month you chose, were the temperatures in your area higher or lower than normal? How many days recorded precipitation? Was the precipitation amount higher or lower than normal for the month?

TEAMWORK PROJECT

As you have learned in this lesson, functions can help you analyze data in a number of ways. Excel includes hundreds of functions to help you with financial, statistical, mathematical, and other problems. In this project, explore two functions of your choice with a teammate to learn how they can be applied to specific data analysis situations. Make sure your functions are not covered in this or the previous lesson. Follow these steps:

1. In a blank Excel worksheet, open the Insert Function dialog box. Review the functions in each category to find two you are interested in exploring with your teammate. (Your functions should come from two different categories.)

2. Read the Microsoft Excel Help files for the functions you have chosen to find out what kind of data the function can analyze, and what kinds of information you must supply as arguments for the functions.

3. Construct worksheets containing data appropriate for each function and then use the functions to analyze the data.

4. After you are sure you are using the function correctly, make a team presentation to the class to share what you have learned about your functions.

CRITICAL THINKING

SCANS

You want to buy a used car that costs $5,000. You can scrape up $2,000 of the total, but you will need to borrow the rest of the money. Your uncle has offered to loan you the additional money at a modest 5% interest per year, but only if you can pay the money back in four years. He has agreed to let you make a payment once a year for the four years.

Create a worksheet that contains the following information:

Rate	5%
Nper (number of payments)	4
PV (principal)	$3000

Using Excel's PMT function, plug in the information shown above from your worksheet to find out how much you will have to pay your uncle each year if you accept the loan. (The yearly payment will appear in red and in parentheses in the cell where you insert the PMT function.)

USING THE WORKSHEET TO COMMUNICATE INFORMATION

OBJECTIVES

Upon completion of this lesson, you should be able to:

■ Apply conditional formats.

■ Insert a cell comment.

■ Insert a picture in a worksheet.

■ Resize and position pictures.

■ Create a chart.

■ Edit chart data.

■ Edit chart formats and options.

⏱ **Estimated Time: 1 hour**

VOCABULARY

Cell comment

Chart

Clip art

Conditional formats

Embedded chart

Sizing handles

Excel comes with a number of tools that can help you communicate worksheet data more effectively. Features such as formats, comments, pictures, and charts can help to enhance the information contained in a worksheet. The features are easy to use and often make the worksheet more useful.

Apply Conditional Formats

Conditional formats are built-in format features in Excel which apply various formats to cell contents when certain conditions are met. These special formats make it easy for you to monitor worksheet results. For example, you may want to bring attention to values that fall below a minimum requirement or flag a date that indicates a passed deadline. The format is applied only when the value meets specified conditions. If the value changes, the format will also change. To illustrate, if the minimum requirement for inventory falls below 500, the value in the cell will be formatted in a red format. When the value for inventory rises above the minimum requirement, the red format is removed.

S TEP-BY-STEP ▷ 5.1

1. Open the file **Step5-1** from the data files. Save the workbook as **Quality Control** followed by your initials.

2. Select the range D4:D8.

3. Open the **Format** menu and choose **Conditional Formatting**. The dialog box shown in Figure 5-1 is displayed.

4. The first text box displays *Cell Value Is*. This condition is correct. Click in the second text box and then select **greater than** in the drop-down list.

5. Click in the third text box and key **3.00%**.

6. Click the **Format** button in the dialog box. The Format Cells dialog box shown in Figure 5-2 is displayed.

FIGURE 5-1
Conditional Formatting dialog box

FIGURE 5-2
Format Cells dialog box

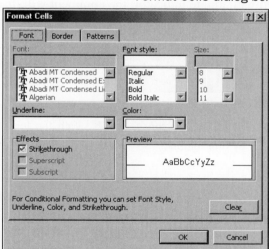

7. Click the down arrow in the list box under *Color*. Select the color **Red**.

Hot Tip

If you point to a color in the color palette, a ScreenTip will display with the name of the color.

8. Click **OK** to close the Format Cells dialog box. Then click **OK** to close the Conditional Formatting dialog box.

9. Click outside the selected range. Notice that only one of the values in the *% Defective* column exceeds the 3.00% limit you set.

10. Click in cell C4, key **7**, and press **Enter**. Now that the percentage in cell D4 exceeds the limit, the font color for that value changes to red.

11. Save the changes and close the workbook.

Insert a Cell Comment

A cell comment is a message that helps explain the information contained in the cell. Cell comments can be used to help you remember details about the data, or they can be used to help others understand the data.

When you insert a comment, Excel creates a text box and inserts a user name. The user name is the same as the user information provided in the General sheet in the Tools Options dialog box. A red triangle (note indicator) appears in the corner of the cell to indicate that it contains a comment. However, this triangle will not print when you print the worksheet.

When you point to a cell with a note indicator, the comment will display in a ScreenTip. If necessary, you can edit or delete the cell comment.

STEP-BY-STEP ⟹ 5.2

1. Open the file **Step5-2** from data files. Save the workbook as **News** followed by your initials.

2. With the insertion point positioned in cell A1, open the **Insert** menu and choose **Comment**. The comment box shown in Figure 5-3 is displayed.

FIGURE 5-3
Cell Comment text box

	A	B	C	D	E	F
1	Where People Get the News			Student Name:		
2						
3	# Surveyed	2142				
4						
5	Television	1278	60%			
6	Newspapers	531	25%			
7	Radio	179	8%			
8	Internet/online	133	6%			
9	Magazines	21	1%			
10			100%			
11						

Cell comment box

Hot Tip

You can also insert a comment by right-clicking on the desired cell and then choosing **Insert Comment** from the shortcut menu.

Did You Know?

If the text box is not large enough to display your comment, you can resize the cell comment text box by pointing to a corner sizing handle. When the pointer changes to a two-headed arrow, drag the sizing handle to enlarge the box.

3. Key **Overall findings have a margin of error of plus or minus 3.6%.**

Speech Recognition

If your computer has speech recognition capability, enable the Dictation mode and dictate the comment.

4. Click anywhere outside the cell comment text box to close the display. Notice that a red triangle appears in the top right corner of cell A1. This mark indicates that the cell contains a comment.

5. Click in cell C10 and insert the comment **Total may not add up to 100% due to rounding.**

6. Click anywhere outside the cell comment text box to close the display.

7. Point to cell A1 and rest the mouse pointer over the cell. The cell comment text box will display next to the cell.

8. With the cell comment still displayed, right-click to display a shortcut menu. Choose **Edit Comment** from the shortcut menu. The cell comment text box is selected and the insertion point appears in it.

9. Edit the text in the cell comment text box to read **3.8%** instead of *3.6%*. Then click outside the comment box.

10. Point to cell C10 and right-click. Choose **Delete Comment** from the shortcut menu. The comment box and the red triangle are removed.

11. Save the changes and leave the workbook open for the next Step-by-Step.

Computer Concepts

To print the comments with the worksheet, choose Page Setup from the File menu. Click the Sheet tab and choose one of the options in the Comments box.

Insert a Picture in a Worksheet

Adding a picture to your worksheet can make it more visually appealing. For example, you can add a company logo or a photograph related to the worksheet data. Or, you can insert images from the Office Clip Gallery.

Insert a Clip Art Image

Pictures can help communicate worksheet data. **Clip art** is pictures and other artwork that is ready to insert in a worksheet. Excel has numerous clip art images and photos that are stored in the Clip Art folder. You can also insert picture files from other sources or from scanned images.

S TEP-BY-STEP ⟧ 5.3

1. Click in cell A11.

2. Open the **Insert** menu and choose **Picture**, then select **Clip Art** from the submenu. The Insert Clip Art task pane similar to that shown in Figure 5-4 is displayed.

FIGURE 5-4
Insert Clip Art task pane

Hot Tip

If the Add Clips to Organizer dialog box appears, click **Later** in order to proceed with these steps.

3. Click in the *Search text:* text box and key **computer**, then click **Search** or press **Enter**. Excel will search the Clip Art gallery for all pictures related to this key word.

Did You Know?

If your computer has an Internet connection, you can click the link **Clips Online** at the bottom of the Insert Clip Art task pane and locate images on the Web.

4. Select a picture of a computer (or other picture related to the contents of the worksheet, such

    ![Modify]

    as TV, newspaper, Internet, and so forth). (*Note:* If you can't find a picture related to computer, click the Modify button at the bottom of the task pane and search for key words TV, radio, Internet, and so forth, until you find a picture that fits with the content of the worksheet.)

5. Click the picture to insert it in the worksheet.

6. Close the task pane. If the Picture toolbar is in the way, dock it at the top, bottom, or side of the screen.

7. Save the changes and leave the workbook open for the next Step-by-Step.

Did You Know?

You can leave the Insert Clip Art task pane open as you work so you can quickly access additional Clip Art images. If you know you might use a clip art image again, add it to the Favorites folder in the Clip Organizer to save time in finding it again.

Resize and Position Pictures

Once you have inserted a picture in a worksheet, there are many ways to manipulate the picture. To work with the picture, you must click it to select it. You will know it is selected when you see eight small circles on the border of the graphic. These circles are called *sizing handles*. Once a picture is selected, you can resize it and reposition it.

The easiest way to change the size of a picture is to drag one of the sizing handles. As you drag the sizing handle, you can see the effects of the change on your screen. When you resize a picture proportionally, you change all dimensions of the graphic approximately equally. You can also resize a picture just vertically or just horizontally, but that will distort the image.

Computer Concepts

Resizing and repositioning pictures in Excel is the same as resizing and repositioning pictures, text boxes, and other objects in other Office applications.

S TEP-BY-STEP ▷ 5.4

1. If necessary, click the picture you selected to display the sizing handles. Eight sizing handles appear on the outside border of the image as shown in Figure 5-5.

FIGURE 5-5
Worksheet with picture selected

	A	B	C
1	**Where People Get the News**		
2			
3	# Surveyed	2142	
4			
5	Television	1278	45%
6	Newspapers	531	22%
7	Radio	179	8%
8	Internet/online	133	24%
9	Magazines	21	1%
10			100%

Sizing handles

2. Point to the sizing handle in the lower right corner of the picture. When the pointer changes to a two-headed arrow, drag the sizing handle up and to the left. When the bottom picture border extends down to cell B16, release the mouse button.

3. Point to the center of the picture. When the pointer changes to a four-headed arrow, drag the picture to the right to center it under the columns of data. Click outside the picture to deselect it.

4. Save the changes and leave the workbook open for the next Step-by-Step.

Did You Know?

You can also use the drawing tools to add graphics to your worksheet.

Create a Chart

A *chart* is a graphic representation of your worksheet data. Charts help to make the data more interesting and easier to read and understand. Before you can create a chart, you must decide what type of chart you want to create. Excel provides several options for chart types. The chart type you select will depend on the data you want to represent. Table 5-1 lists some of the Excel chart types and a description of the types of data you can illustrate with each chart.

TABLE 5-1
Chart types

Area chart		Effective for emphasizing trends because it illustrates the magnitude of change over time.
Bar chart		Helpful when you want to make comparisons among individual items.
Column chart		Useful in showing changes over a period of time, or for making comparisons among individual items.
Doughnut chart		Similar to a pie chart in that it shows comparisons between the whole and the parts. However, a doughnut chart enables you to show more than one set of data.
Line chart		Illustrates trends in data at equal intervals.
Pie chart		Compares the sizes of portions as they relate to a whole unit, and it illustrates that the parts total 100 percent. Effective when there is only one set of data.
Scatter chart		Illustrates scientific data, and it specifically shows uneven intervals – or clusters – of data.

After you decide which chart type you want to create, you must decide which chart options you want to use. To do this, you must first understand the parts of a chart. Figure 5-6 describes the parts of a chart. Take time to study this illustration and become familiar with the various parts.

FIGURE 5-6
Parts of a chart

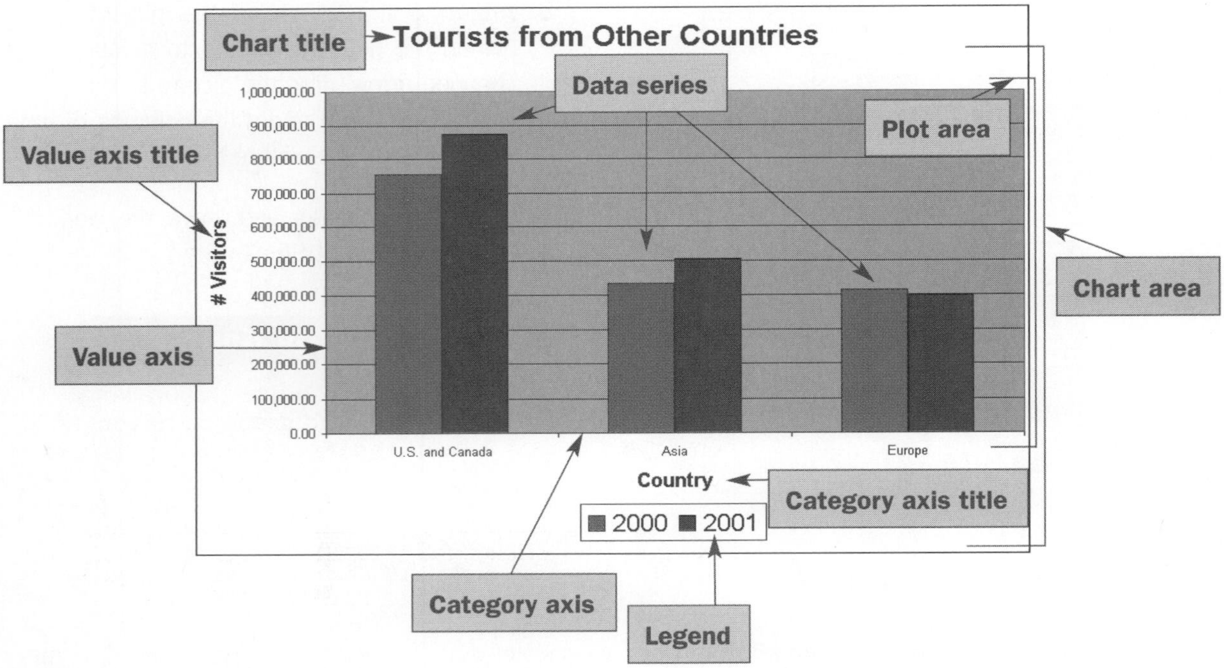

Use the Chart Wizard to Create a Chart

The Chart Wizard in Excel makes it easy for you to create professional-looking charts. The Chart Wizard will ask you questions about several chart options. You can create the chart on a separate sheet, or you can create the chart on the worksheet that has the data you want to chart. If the chart will not fit on the same sheet with the data, or if you want to create more than one chart from the same data, you will probably want to create the chart on a separate sheet. An *embedded chart* is a chart created on the same sheet as the data used in the chart. One advantage of embedding a chart on the same page as the data is that the data and the chart can be viewed at the same time.

Before you begin the Chart Wizard, you must first select the data you want to be represented in the chart. You do not always need all the worksheet data to create the chart, so you need to select the range of cells that you want to illustrate in the chart before you use the Wizard.

Computer Concepts

With the exception of the pie and doughnut type charts, all chart types have a horizontal and a vertical axis.

STEP-BY-STEP 5.5

1. Select the range A5:B9.

2. Click the **Chart Wizard** button on the Standard toolbar. The dialog box shown in Figure 5-7 is displayed.

FIGURE 5-7
Chart Wizard—Step 1 of 4—Chart Type dialog box

3. Under *Chart type*, select **Pie**, then select the second chart sub-type in the first row (Pie with a 3-D visual effect).

Speech Recognition

If your computer has speech recognition capability, enable the Command mode and say the command to start the Chart Wizard. Then, say the commands to navigate through the steps in the Chart Wizard and select the options. Use the keyboard to enter chart and axis titles.

4. Click and hold the **Press and Hold to View Sample** button in the dialog box. A preview of the chart is displayed.

5. Release the button and click **Next**. The dialog box shown in Figure 5-8 is displayed. A preview of the chart is shown in the Chart Source Data dialog box. Notice also that the data range you selected is displayed in the Data range text box.

Hot Tip

Click the **Back** button to return to the previous Chart Wizard dialog box if, for instance, you want to make a change to a previous selection.

FIGURE 5-8
Chart Wizard—Step 2 of 4—
Chart Source Data dialog box

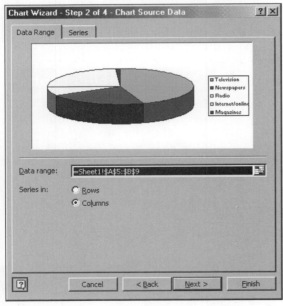

6. Click the **Next** button to display the dialog box in Figure 5-9.

FIGURE 5-9
Chart Wizard—Step 3 of 4—
Chart Options dialog box

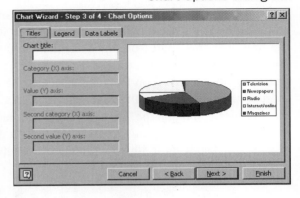

7. Click in the *Chart title:* text box and key **Where People Get the News**.

8. Click the **Data Labels** tab to change the dialog box options. Under *Label Contains*, select the option **Percentage**. The preview of the chart is updated to show the labels. Compare your screen to Figure 5-10.

FIGURE 5-10
Data Labels tab in Step 3 of 4—
Chart Options dialog box

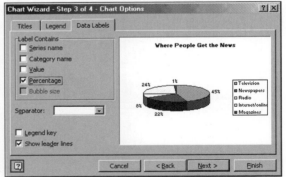

9. Click **Next**. The dialog box shown in Figure 5-11 is displayed.

FIGURE 5-11
Chart Wizard—Step 4 of 4—
Chart Location dialog box

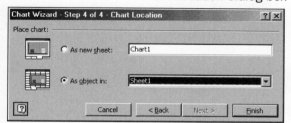

10. Select the **As new sheet** option to place the chart on a sheet by itself. The new sheet will be named *Chart1*.

11. Click **Finish** in the Chart Wizard dialog box. The wizard closes and the chart is displayed in a new sheet in the workbook.

12. Save the changes and leave the workbook open for the next Step-by-Step.

> **Hot Tip**
>
> You can create an instant chart by selecting the data you want to chart and then pressing F11. A two-dimensional column chart is created. However, notice that there are no chart or axis titles in this chart.

Edit Chart Data

There may be occasions when the data used to create the chart changes—after the chart has been created. Fortunately, you do not need to create a new chart. When you edit the data in the worksheet, Excel will automatically update the chart to reflect the changes.

S TEP-BY-STEP ⟹ 5.6

1. Notice that the chart currently displays 24% for Internet/online.

> **Hot Tip**
>
> If you point over a data series in a chart, Excel displays the related worksheet data in a ScreenTip.

2. Click the **Sheet1** tab to switch to the worksheet containing the data for the chart.

3. Click cell B8 and key **555**, then press **Enter**. The value in cell C8 is updated from *24%* to *25%*.

4. Click the **Chart1** tab. Notice that the chart has also been updated and it now shows 25% for Internet/online. (Also note that the other percentages changed accordingly.)

5. Save the changes and close the workbook.

Edit Chart Formats and Options

You've already seen that you can easily update chart data, even after the chart is created. But can you change the chart options after you create a chart?

Edit Chart Formats

Many of the parts of the chart such as the chart title and the axis titles are positioned on the chart in a text box. If you click the part of the chart you want to change, the text box will display and then you can change the formats.

S TEP-BY-STEP ▷ 5.7

1. Open the file **Step5-7** from the data files. Save the workbook as **Demographics** followed by your initials.

2. You do not want the information from column C included in the chart, so hide column C. Then select the range A2:E7.

3. Click the **Chart Wizard** button. Under *Chart type:*, select **Bar**. Under *Chart sub-type:*, select the first option in the second row (Clustered bar with a 3-D visual effect).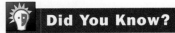

4. Click **Next**. For *Series in:*, Columns is the correct option.

5. Click **Next**. If necessary, click the **Titles** tab to display the Titles sheet. In the *Chart title:* text box, key **Centerville Demographics**. In the *Category (X) axis:* text box, key **Year**. In the *Value (Z) axis:* text box, key **Census Count**.

> ### Computer Concepts
>
> The value Z axis is used for three-dimensional charts.

6. Click **Next**. Leave the option *As object in:* selected. Then click **Finish**. The chart is displayed below the worksheet data. Do not be concerned if the chart overlaps some of the worksheet data.

7. Point to any white area in the chart. When a ScreenTip displays *Chart Area*, click and drag the chart down to the bottom left corner just below the worksheet data.

> ### Did You Know?
>
> The chart is an object, just like a clip art image or a graphic. You can resize the chart by dragging a sizing handle. Be sure to drag a corner handle if you want to resize the chart proportionally.

8. Click the chart title. The text box surrounding the title is displayed.

9. With the text box selected, click the down arrow in the *Font Size* box on the Formatting toolbar and select **14** (or a font size not already selected). The text box is resized to accommodate the new font size.

10. Right-click the category axis title *Year*. Select **Format Axis Title** in the shortcut menu. The Format Axis Title dialog box is displayed.

11. If necessary, click the **Font** tab. Change the font size to **12** and click **OK**.

12. Right-click the value axis title *Census Count*. **Select Format Axis Title** in the shortcut menu. From the Format Axis Title dialog box, change the font size to **12**.

13. Save the changes and leave the workbook open for the next Step-by-Step.

Edit Chart Options

The Chart Options command enables you to change many of the chart features. For example, you can change the text in the chart title, or you can change the position of the legend.

STEP-BY-STEP ⟹ 5.8

1. If necessary, click the chart to select it. (*Hint:* It is selected when you see the eight sizing handles around the border of the chart.)

2. With the chart selected, open the **Chart** menu and choose **Chart Options**. The Chart Options dialog box shown in Figure 5-12 is displayed.

3. Click the **Legend** tab. Select **Bottom** in the Placement section. The preview in the dialog box now shows the legend below the chart.

4. Click the **Titles** tab. Under *Chart title:*, change the title in the text box to **Centerville Growth Trends**.

5. Click **OK**. The chart title is changed, and the legend is repositioned at the bottom of the chart.

6. Save the changes and leave the workbook open for the next Step-by-Step.

FIGURE 5-12
Chart Options dialog box

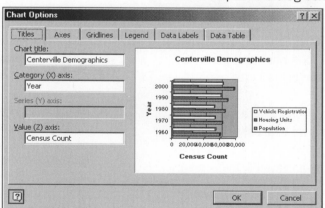

Change the Chart Type

Now that you have created a bar chart and edited some of the chart parts, you realize a bar chart is not the best chart type for displaying the demographic data. A line graphic would be more effective for illustrating trends in data. Fortunately, you can change the chart type easily—and without starting over!

STEP-BY-STEP ▷ 5.9

1. With the chart selected, open the **Chart** menu and choose **Chart Type**. The Chart Type dialog box opens.

2. Under *Chart type:*, select **Line**. Under *Chart sub-type:*, the first option in the second row is already selected.

3. Click **OK**. The bar chart is converted to a line chart.

4. Save the changes and leave the workbook open for the next Step-by-Step.

Speech Recognition

If your computer has speech recognition capability, enable the Command mode and say the commands to open the Chart Type dialog box and select the new chart type. Then say the command to save the changes.

Use Help to Learn How to Change an Embedded Chart to a Chart Sheet

You decide the chart would be much easier to read if it were enlarged. However, there is no room to expand the chart when it is embedded on the worksheet. Go to the Help screens to see if you can move the embedded chart to a new chart sheet.

STEP-BY-STEP ▷ 5.10

1. Click in the *Ask a Question* box at the right side of the menu bar and key **move an embedded chart**. Then press **Enter**.

2. In the list of topics, click **Place a chart on a worksheet or on its own chart sheet**.

3. Read the information displayed in the screen.

4. Close the Help screen.

5. With the chart selected, open the **Chart** menu and choose **Location**. Select **As new sheet** in the Chart Location dialog box. Click **OK**.

 Hot Tip

If the chart is not displayed full screen, open the **View** menu, choose **Zoom**, and select **100%** under *Magnification* in the Zoom dialog box.

6. Right-click the axis title *Census Count*, then choose **Format Axis Title** in the shortcut menu. When the Format Axis Title dialog box is displayed, click the **Alignment** tab.

7. The dialog box shown in Figure 5-13 is displayed. In the *Orientation* box, point to the red diamond and drag it up to the top of the radius. When the *Degrees* box displays **90**, release and click **OK** to close the Format Axis Title dialog box.

8. Right-click the axis title *Year*, then choose **Format Axis Title** in the shortcut menu. Again, drag the red diamond in the *Orientation* box until the *Degrees* box displays **0**. Click **OK**.

9. Click the **Sheet1** tab and unhide column C. Deselect the cells.

10. Save the changes and close the workbook.

FIGURE 5-13
Alignment tab in the Format Axis Title dialog box

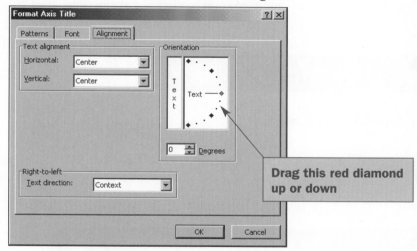

Summary

In this lesson, you learned:

- Conditional formats help you monitor worksheet results because you can apply various formats to cell contents when certain conditions are met.

- Cell comments can be added to the worksheet to help the creator and other users understand the data contained in the worksheet.

- Not only do pictures enhance the appearance of the worksheet, they also help to communicate the worksheet data.

- Clip art can be repositioned and resized as needed in a worksheet for an attractive presentation.

- A chart displays the worksheet data visually and often helps the audience understand and interpret the information more clearly.

- When the worksheet data is changed, the chart is automatically updated to reflect those changes.

- Chart formats, options, and types can be changed at any time, even after the chart has been created.

VOCABULARY REVIEW

Define the following terms:

Cell comment	Clip art	Embedded chart
Chart	Conditional formats	Sizing handles

LESSON 5 REVIEW QUESTIONS

TRUE/FALSE

Circle T if the statement is true or F if the statement is false.

T F 1. The red triangle that indicates a comment is inserted in a cell will also show when the worksheet is printed.

T F 2. Once you create a chart using the chart wizard, you cannot edit the chart.

T F 3. All chart types can be used to graph any kind of data.

T F 4. If the data changes after the chart is created, you must create a new chart.

T F 5. You can reposition a chart easily by dragging the selected chart to another section of the worksheet.

FILL IN THE BLANK

Complete the following sentences by writing the correct word or words in the blanks provided.

1. To emphasize data in a cell when certain conditions are met, you can apply _____.

2. You know a picture is selected when you see the _____ on the border of the graphic.

3. A chart created on the same sheet with the data is called a(n) _____ chart.

4. To change the position of a chart label, select the chart and then choose _____ from the Chart menu.

5. To change a column chart to a bar chart, you would select the column chart and then choose _____ from the Chart menu.

LESSON 5 PROJECTS

PROJECT 5-1

1. Open **Project5-1** from the data files. Save the workbook as **Reorders** followed by your initials.

2. In cell K7, insert a formula to subtract the Current Inventory value in cell J7 from the Beginning Inventory value in cell E7.

3. Apply conditional formatting to cell K7 as follows:
   A. In the Conditional Formatting dialog box, specify the condition *Cell Value Is* less than **5**.
   B. Click the **Format** button. On the **Font** tab, select **Bold**.
   C. Click the **Patterns** tab. Select the pink color that is the first color in the fifth row from the top of the color palette.

4. Fill the formula and conditional formatting down through cell K16.

5. Sales figures are in for the fourth quarter of the year. Insert the following values, beginning in cell I7, to see what items must be reordered immediately (i.e., any items with fewer than 5 left in inventory).

   15

   17

   18

   8

   10

   18

   5

   8

   8

   5

6. Insert the following comment in cell B14: **This item discontinued; no reorder.**

7. Insert a clip art picture relating to sports, exercise, or recreation. Resize the picture so that it will fit in the first five rows of the worksheet to the left of the title information.

8. Save your changes. Close the workbook.

PROJECT 5-2

1. Open **Project5-2** from the data files. Save the workbook as **Tree Sale** followed by your initials.

2. Use the Chart Wizard to chart the data in cell range A5:E12 as follows:
   A. In the Step 1 of 4 dialog box, select the first column chart in the second row of chart options (Clustered column with a 3-D visual effect).
   B. In the Step 2 of 4 dialog box, select the **Rows** option to chart the data by rows.
   C. In the Step 3 of 4 dialog box, key the Value (Z) axis label **Total Sales**. Click the **Legend** tab and select the **Bottom** placement option.
   D. In the Step 4 of 4 dialog box, accept the default option to embed the chart on the same sheet.

3. Position the chart so that it is below the worksheet data. Enlarge the chart if space permits, but do not make the chart wider than the last column of data.

4. Rotate the Value (Z) axis label (*Total Sales*) to **90** degrees so it reads from bottom to top and change its point size to **10**.

5. You have just noticed an error in the data. Change the value for Tulip poplar in Week 1 to **$4,150** and observe the change in the chart.

6. You have decided that this chart would look better on a sheet by itself. Move the chart to a new sheet.

7. Display the Chart Options dialog box and add the title **Fall Tree Sale** to the chart. Change the title point size to **16**.

8. Click the legend and increase the size of the legend text to **12** point.

9. Save your changes. Close the workbook.

WEB PROJECT

With the increasing popularity of the Internet as a source of sales revenue, many retailers and other merchandisers are offering a wide variety of products for sale online. Online sales have increased greatly over the past several years. Using Web search tools, locate information about online sales for at least two recent years. (*Hint:* Target your search for news articles and current events.) Try to find specific information on categories such as books, music, apparel, computers and peripherals, toys, and so on. Record the sales figures you find in a worksheet and then chart the data.

TEAMWORK PROJECT

Increasing entertainment options have led some people to wonder if the era of mass-market professional sports is on the wane. Do people still go out to the ballgame, or do they stay at home watching satellite TV, playing video games, or surfing the Internet? With a teammate, track attendance figures for several professional sports franchises to see if you can identify a trend. Follow these steps:

1. With your teammate, choose a professional sport that you both want to research, such as baseball, basketball, football, or hockey. Select five teams from large and small cities.

2. Using Web search tools or other sources of information, locate the season attendance figures for your five teams for the previous five years (or as many as you can find).

3. Record your data in a worksheet and then chart the data. Do you see a pattern of rising or decreasing attendance for the teams you chose?

CRITICAL THINKING

You have created a three-dimensional pie chart with a number of slices. Some of them are hard to see because the three-dimensional chart is rather flat. Can you tilt the chart in any way so you can see the pie slices better? Use the Help files in Excel to find the answer and then write a summary on what you learned.

Excel

COMMAND SUMMARY

FEATURE	MENU COMMAND	KEYSTROKE	TOOLBAR BUTTON	LESSON
Absolute cell reference		F4		3
AutoFill, options			⊞	3
AutoFormat, apply	Format, AutoFormat			1
AutoSum			Σ ▾	3
Bold	Format, Cells, Font tab, Bold	Ctrl + B	**B**	1
Cell comment, insert	Insert, Comment		🖉	5
Cell, clear contents	Edit, Clear, Contents	Delete or Backspace		1
Cell, clear formats	Edit, Clear, Formats			2
Cell, shading	Format, Cells, Patterns		◌ ▾	1
Cell, Center align	Format, Cells, Alignment tab, Center		≣	1
Cell, Left align	Format, Cells, Alignment tab, Left		≣	1
Cell, Right align	Format, Cells, Alignment tab, Right		≣	1
Chart options, edit	Chart, Chart Options			5
Chart type, change	Chart, Chart Type			5
Chart, create	Insert, Chart		📊	5
Clear, clear all	Edit, Clear, All			2
Clip art, insert	Insert, Picture, Clip Art		🖼	5
Column, change width	Format, Column, Width			1
Column, delete	Edit, Delete			2
Column, hide	Format, Column, Hide			2
Column, insert	Insert, Columns			2
Column, unhide	Format, Column, Unhide			2
Conditional formats	Format, Conditional Formatting			5

FEATURE	MENU COMMAND	KEYSTROKE	TOOLBAR BUTTON	LESSON
Copy cells	Edit, Copy	Ctrl + C		2
Currency format, apply	Format, Cells, Number tab		$	1
Cut cells	Edit, Cut	Ctrl + X		2
Date format, apply	Format, Cells			1
Date, insert current	Insert, Function, NOW	Ctrl + ;		4
Fill down	Edit, Fill, Down	Ctrl + D		2
Fill right	Edit, Fill, Right	Ctrl + R		2
Font size, change	Format, Cells, Font tab			1
Font, change	Format, Cells, Font tab		Arial	1
Formulas, show in worksheet	Tools, Options, View tab	Ctrl + `		3
Freeze columns and rows	Window, Freeze Panes			2
Function, Arguments, collapse				4
Function, Arguments, expand				4
Help	Help, Microsoft Excel Help	F1		2
Insert function formula	Insert, Function		fx	4
Italics	Format, Cells, Font tab, Italics	Ctrl + I	I	1
Merge and center cells	Format, Cells, Alignment, Center, Merge cells			1
Number format, apply	Format, Cells, Number tab			1
Page setup, adjust	File, Page Setup			2
Paste cells	Edit, Paste	Ctrl + V		2
Preview worksheet	File, Print Preview			2

FEATURE	MENU COMMAND	KEYSTROKE	TOOLBAR BUTTON	LESSON
Print worksheet	File, Print	Ctrl + P	🖨	2
Redo	Edit, Redo	Ctrl + Y	↻ ▾	1
Remove all arrows	Auditing, Tools, Formula Remove All Arrows		ℛ	3
Right align	Format, Cells, Alignment tab, Right		≣	1
Row, delete	Edit, Delete			2
Row, insert	Insert, Rows			2
Set print area Set Print Area	File, Print Area,			2
Sort data (ascending)	Data, Sort		ᴬ↓	2
Sort data (descending)	Data, Sort		ᶻ↓	2
Time, display current		Ctrl + Shift+ ;		4
Trace dependents	Tools, Formula Auditing, Trace Dependents		⬦	3
Trace error	Tools, Formula Auditing, Trace		◇	3
Trace precedents	Tools, Formula Auditing, Trace Precedents		⬦	3
Undo	Edit, Undo	Ctrl + Z	↶ ▾	1
Unfreeze columns and rows	Window, Unfreeze Panes			2
Wrap text in cell	Format, Cells, Alignment tab, Wrap text			1

REVIEW QUESTIONS

TRUE/FALSE

Circle T if the statement is true or F if the statement is false.

T F 1. When data is too wide to fit in a cell, Excel displays a series of asterisks (*****).

T F 2. By default, numbers are aligned at the right of a cell.

T F 3. To remove only the formats from a cell, you can use the Delete key.

T F 4. When you sort numbers in descending order, the number 1 will always be at the top of the list.

T F 5. A formula can be as simple as =E4.

T F 6. When you use AutoSum, you should always check the suggested cell range.

T F 7. Unlike formulas, functions begin with an @ sign.

T F 8. You can use an If function to check whether a condition is true or false.

T F 9. Conditional formatting is used to show negative numbers in a worksheet.

T F 10. You can easily change a column chart to a bar chart if you wish.

MATCHING

Match the correct term in Column 1 to its description in Column 2.

Column 1	Column 2
___ 1. Cell reference	**A.** A group of selected cells
___ 2. Operand	**B.** A grid of rows and columns containing text, numbers, and formats
___ 3. Argument	**C.** A collection of related worksheets
___ 4. Logical test	**D.** Small circle on the border of the active cell
___ 5. Embedded chart	**E.** The part of an If function that evaluates whether a condition is true
___ 6. Range	**F.** Chart that appears on the same sheet with the data it charts
___ 7. Chart options	**G.** Identifies the column letter and row number of a cell
___ 8. Fill handle	**H.** A value, cell reference, range, or text that acts as an operand in a function formula
___ 9. Absolute cell reference	**I.** Dialog box you would open to change the position of a chart legend
___ 10. Workbook	**J.** Cell reference that does not change when moved
	K. A number or cell reference used in a formula

MATH

Create a worksheet with three worksheets. One worksheet should display common units of measurement for length (inch, foot, yard, mile), another common units of weight (ounce, pound, ton) , and the last common volumes (ounce, quart, gallon). On each sheet, supply the metric equivalents for units if they exist (for example, the equivalent for inch is centimeter and the equivalent for yard is meter, but there is no direct equivalent for foot). If necessary, use your math book or other references to help you. Create formulas to convert all your measurements to metric equivalents. Set up all three worksheets so that you can enter a value for which you want the metric equivalent and see the equivalent immediately in another cell.

SOCIAL STUDIES

Take a survey in your class to find out the origins of your classmates' families. Create a worksheet that lists a number of European, Asian, African, and South American countries. Set up column headers for Parents, Grandparents, Great-grandparents, and Distant Ancestors. Record in the worksheet the origins of students' families. For example, if a classmate's parents are from Korea, insert 2 where the Parents column and the Korea row intersect. If another classmate's parents also were born in Korea, add the number 2 to the existing number in that cell. Those students who do not know what countries their ancestors came from can ask their parents for information. Add or remove countries as necessary. Create totals for each country and see which country is best represented in your class. Chart your results.

SCIENCE

Science fiction is full of descriptions of space travel to distant planets and stars. Using the Web or other source of information, find out how far the other planets in our solar system are from Earth (in miles). Also find the distance to at least one close star in another solar system. Record the information in a worksheet. Also find out how fast our most recent space vehicles (such as Mars exploration vehicles) can travel. Create a formula that will determine how long it would take you to travel to the planets in the solar system and the "closest" star at the best speed we can currently manage.

LANGUAGE ARTS

Gather a number of your language arts assignments for the current school year. Tally the number and types of errors you have made (for example, in subject-verb agreement, spelling, dangling participles, awkward phrasing, and so on). Create a worksheet and list the language errors in the first column. Create additional columns for each month of the school year. Enter into the worksheet your errors by month and type. Record the average, maximum, and minimum errors for each month. Do you see any reduction in errors over the course of the year?

PROJECT 1

1. Start Excel (or open a new document) and save the blank workbook as **Shady** followed by your initials.

2. Create the worksheet shown in Figure UR-1. Use AutoFill to insert the days of the week. Adjust column widths as necessary to display all data.

FIGURE UR-1
Project 1 worksheet

Shady Acres Stables
Employee Info

Name	Address	Phone	Rate	Monday	Tuesday	Wednesday	Thursday	Friday	Saturday
Tanner, Pam	7809 Fox Run	555-3301	6	4			4	4	
Jackson, Tom	12 Charingford	555-1030	8.5	8	8	8	8	8	
Chambers, Val	909 Portsmouth	555-6780	8.5		8	8	8	8	8
Lakshmi, Ari	2270 Wincasset	555-4390	6	4			4		
Dellivan, April	579 Chester	555-8080	6				4	3	4
Rogers, Kris	12790 Farmcrest	555-2804	6	4					6

3. Format the numbers in the Rate column as currency with two decimal points.

4. Insert a column to the right of the Rate column and name it **Status**. Enter the status of each employee as **Part-Time** or **Full-Time**. The employees who make $6.00 are part-time, and the employees who make $8.50 are full-time. Let AutoComplete help you insert the data in this column.

5. Hide the Rate column.

6. In cell L4, enter the heading **Total Hours**. Create a formula for cells L5:L10 to calculate the hours each employee works throughout the week.

7. Freeze the first column and scroll so that you can see both the employee names and the Friday hours side by side.

8. Change April Delivan's hours for Friday from 3 to **4**. Unfreeze the column.

9. Sort the worksheet so that the employee names are in ascending alphabetical order.

10. Your boss wants to know how many employees are working on each day the stables are open. In cell E12, enter **Staff/day** and apply the bold format. Use the COUNT function in cell F12 to show the number of employees working on Monday. Use Fill to copy this formula to cells G12:K12.

11. Center the contents in cells F5:L12.

12. Unhide the Rate column.

13. Merge and center the heading *Shady Acres Stables* across columns A through L. Then, merge and center the subheading *Employee Info* across the same columns.

14. If necessary, deselect cells and then save your changes and close the workbook.

PROJECT 2

Your boss at Shady Acres would like to revise the employee worksheet. She wants to see information for part-time and full-time employees on separate sheets, and she wants to see her total payroll each week for each group of employees.

1. Open the file **Project2** and save the workbook as **Shady2** followed by your initials.

2. Delete the Rate column. Then delete the last two rows of data (the row containing the COUNT formulas and the blank row above it). Delete the Status column.

3. Change the text in cell A2 to **Part-Time Employees**. Rename Sheet1 **Part-Time**. In cell A3, insert the rate for part-time employees (**$6.00**).

4. Copy cell range A1:J4 and paste it in cell A1 on Sheet2 of the workbook.

5. Change the text in cell A2 on Sheet2 to **Full-Time Employees**. Change the rate in cell A3 to **$8.50**. Rename Sheet2 **Full-Time**.

6. Return to the Part-Time sheet and cut the data for the first full-time employee (Val Chambers) to the Clipboard task pane. Switch to the Full-Time sheet, and paste the item into row 5.

7. Return to the Part-Time sheet and cut the data for the second full-time employee (Tom Jackson). Switch to the Full-Time sheet, and paste the item into row 6. Adjust column widths to show all data.

8. In cell K4, key **Pay**. Center the new heading and make sure the bold format is applied. In cell K5, create a formula to multiply the total in cell J5 by the full-time rate in cell A3. Fill the formula to cell K6.

9. In cell K7, use AutoSum to total the Pay column.

10. Switch to the Part-Time sheet and delete the two blank rows left behind when you cut the text in step 6.

11. Apply the *3D Effects 1* AutoFormat to both sheets. Adjust the column widths to their best fit. Center the main heading and the subheading. Center the column headings and then center the hours and total hours worked.

12. Save your changes and close the workbook.

PROJECT 3

1. Open **Project3** from the data files. Save the workbook as **Invoice** followed by your initials.

2. Merge and center the text in cell A1 across columns A through E. Format the text in cell A1 as the Footlight font (or a font of your choice) and 18-point bold. Then merge and center the text in cell A2 across columns A through E. Format the text in cell A2 as 12-point bold italic.

3. Boldface and right-align the text in cell range D19:D25. Center column C.

4. In cell E4, insert a function to display the current date in the format 3/14/01.

5. In cell E7, create a formula to multiply the value in C7 times the value in D7. Fill the formula down to cell E18.

6. In cell E19, use AutoSum to sum the values in column E. In cell E20, insert the following formula to calculate sales tax on the amount in cell E19: **=E19*0.05**.

7. In cell E22, create a formula that adds the values in cells E19 and E20.

8. Rhodes' policy is to give a 15% discount on all purchases over $500.00. In cell E23, enter the following IF function formula: **=IF(E22>500,E22*.15,0)**.

9. In cell E25, create a formula that subtracts the value in cell E23 from the value in cell E22.

10. Show the formulas in your worksheet and check them for accuracy. Trace the precedents and dependents, then remove all the arrows. Hide the formulas.

11. Insert the following text in rows 7 and 8:

| 1765 | **Red Oak (3-inch)** | 4 | 125 |
| 4080 | **Pieris Japonica (Red Mill)** | 3 | 45 |

12. Insert an appropriate clip art picture. If necessary, resize the picture and position at the top of the worksheet.

13. Preview your invoice to make sure it will fit on one page. If necessary, fit the worksheet to print on one page.

14. Save your changes. Close the workbook.

PROJECT 4

1. Open **Project4** from the data files. Save the workbook as **Creamery Sales** followed by your initials.

2. The Creamery wants all of its ice cream flavors to generate at least $4,000 in revenue each quarter. Apply conditional formatting to the cell range E5:E11 to display any totals less than $4,000 in blue text.

3. Create formulas in cell range E5:E11 to sum the monthly sales.

4. You know that the Fresh Strawberry sales were low in September because of a failure in the strawberry crop. Insert a comment in cell D9 that reads **Fresh strawberries are not available**.

5. Create formulas to find the average, minimum, and maximum sales for each month.

6. Chart the monthly sales data for the ice cream flavors. (Do not include the totals.) Use these options:
   A. In the Step 1 of 4 dialog box, choose the first Column chart in the second row of options (Clustered column with a 3-D visual effect).
   B. In the Step 2 of 4 dialog box, choose the Rows option.
   C. In the Step 3 of 4 dialog box, key the chart title 3rd Quarter Sales. Click the Legend tab and select the Bottom placement option.
   D. In the Step 4 of 4 dialog box, choose to insert the chart on a new sheet.

7. Format the chart title size as 18 point. Format the legend text size as 12 point.

8. You just discovered that the September sales for Rich Vanilla ice cream were reported incorrectly. The correct sales were **$1,790**. Make the change in the data on Sheet 1 and then verify that the changes are updated in the average sales and in the chart.

9. Save your changes. Close the workbook.

SIMULATION

JOB 1

At your volunteer job at Rail Trails, you are always being asked about rail trails in neighboring states. You have decided to prepare a fact sheet about current and projected trails in the five-state area.

1. Open **Job1** from the data files. Save the workbook as **Trail Miles** followed by your initials.

2. Widen columns as necessary to display all the information.

3. Apply the Number format with the 1000 separator and zero decimals to the number values.

4. Insert a row above row 4. In cell B4, enter the heading **Open**. Merge and center this data over cells B4 and C4. In cell D4, enter the heading **Projected**. Merge and center this data over cells D4 and E4.

5. In cell A12, key **Totals**. In cells B12:E12, total the numbers of trails and miles.

6. Sort the data in ascending order by state.

7. Apply the List 2 AutoFormat to the worksheet. Then center the two lines in the title.

8. Save your changes. Close the workbook.

JOB 2

You have been asked to pull together membership data for the local Rail Trails organization to see how membership revenues compare to the year's goal. You have data for three quarters of the year, and you expect to receive the fourth quarter data at any time.

1. Open **Job2** from the data files. Save the workbook as **Memberships** followed by your initials.

2. Merge and center the text in cell A1 across columns A through J. Format the text as 16-point Arial Black (or another font of your choice). Merge and center the text in cell A2 across columns A through J and format the text as 12-point bold.

3. Click in cell C4 and use AutoFill to fill cells D4:F4 with the remaining Qtr headings. Boldface and center all headings in row 4 and adjust column widths to display all text.

4. Format cell ranges B5:B8 and H5:I8 for currency with zero decimals. Center all values in the cell range B5:I8.

5. In cell G5, create a formula that will sum the membership values for the four quarters. Center the cell contents, then fill the formula down to cells G6:G8.

6. Notice that Excel displays green triangles in the Memberships cells and a symbol with an exclamation point. Excel is suggesting the formula may have a potential error because not all the cells with numbers were included in the formula. To hide the green triangles and the exclamation point, click the down arrow next to the arrow and select **Ignore error**.

7. In cell H5, create a formula that will multiply the membership value times the cost of each membership type (use absolute cell references in the formula). Fill the formula down to cells H6:H8.

8. In cell J5, use an IF formula as follows: If the Revenues value is greater than the Goal value, display **We did it!** If not, display **Not quite!** Fill the formula down to cells J6:J8.

9. You have received the fourth quarter membership figures. In cells F5:F8, enter the following values:
   48
   55
   42
   28

10. Boldface and right-align the text in cells A10:A11. Move the data to cells B10:B11. In cell C10 create an average formula to find the average donation in each of the four quarters. In cell C11 create a maximum formula to find the maximum donation in each of the four quarters. Center the averages and maximums.

11. Save your changes. Leave the workbook open for the next Job.

JOB 3

1. When memberships of any type exceed 50 in a quarter, your local organization gets a bonus. Find out how many bonuses you will receive this year by applying conditional formatting to the cell range C5:F8. When the value in these cells is greater than 50, display the text in pink.

2. You're sure someone will wonder about the 68 Family memberships in Qtr 3. Insert a cell comment to remind yourself that the **Family Cycle Outing took place in July**.

3. You'd like to see a graphic depiction of the membership data. Create a pie chart as follows:
   A. Hide columns B through G and create a pie chart from the data in the cell range A4:H8.
   B. Choose a pie chart you like, and chart the data in columns rather than rows.
   C. Change the chart title to **Membership Revenues**. On the Data Labels tab, select the **Category name** and **Percentage** options. On the Legend tab, click the *Show legend* check box to deselect it so no legend is displayed.
   D. Display the chart on a new sheet. Format the chart title as 18 point bold. Then format the data labels (the percent and membership options) as 12 point bold.

4. Return to the worksheet and unhide the columns. Insert an appropriate clip art picture related to hiking or biking somewhere on the worksheet.

5. Change the page setup to landscape orientation. Center the worksheet on the page horizontally. Look at the worksheet in Print Preview and then close the preview.

6. Save your changes. Close the workbook.

PORTFOLIO CHECKLIST

Include the following files from this unit in your learner portfolio.

_____	Cruises	_____	Weather
_____	Genius	_____	Birds
_____	Tallest Structures	_____	News
_____	Tutoring	_____	Quality Control
_____	Regional Sales	_____	Tree Sales
_____	Deer		

ACCESS

UNIT 5

Estimated Time for Unit: 4 Hours

udios
Minooka dori 472
a-ku, Kobe 687
PAN

WORKING WITH DATABASES

A *database* is a collection of related information organized for rapid search and retrieval. Databases can contain all types of data from an address list to schedules for a soccer tournament. Access is the Microsoft Office database program that enables you to organize and manipulate data in many ways.

You might wonder what the difference is between a spreadsheet and a database. Actually, they are very similar. Like spreadsheets, databases are composed of rows and columns. Both enable you to organize, sort, and calculate the data. Although a spreadsheet is great for calculating data, a database offers much more comprehensive functions for manipulating the data. Access is a powerful program that offers many features, most of which are beyond the scope of this course. The lessons in this unit will introduce you to some of the basic features for entering, organizing, and reporting data in Access. Then as you continue to learn and use Microsoft Office, you will have the building blocks you need for utilizing this powerful program.

Identify the Parts of the Access Screen

The Access screen is similar to other Office XP applications—displaying a title bar, a menu bar, and a status bar. Unlike Word and Excel, Access does not have a standard document view. The Access screen changes based on the features you are using as you work with the database. Furthermore, many of the menu options and toolbar buttons are unique to Access.

S TEP-BY-STEP ▷ 1.1

1. Launch Access. The Microsoft Access window and the New File task pane shown in Figure 1-1 are displayed. Do not be concerned that the files listed in the *Open a file* section of your task pane are different.

2. In the task pane, under *Open a file*, select **More Files** (or just **Files**).

 Did You Know?

The files listed above More Files at the top of the task pane in Access are the documents most recently accessed.

Computer Concepts

In all other units in this text, you have saved learner data files using a new file name. However, you can only use the Save As command for naming and saving parts of an Access database. You cannot use the File Save As command to save the entire database under a new name. To rename an Access file, double-click on My Computer on the desktop. Then locate and select the filename, open the **File** menu, and choose **Rename**. Another alternative is to open the **Tools** menu, choose **Database Utilities**, and select the **Compact and Repair Database** command. You can then locate the existing database file that you want to rename and assign it a new name. If desired, you can save the file in a new location.

FIGURE 1-1
Microsoft Access window with the New File task pane

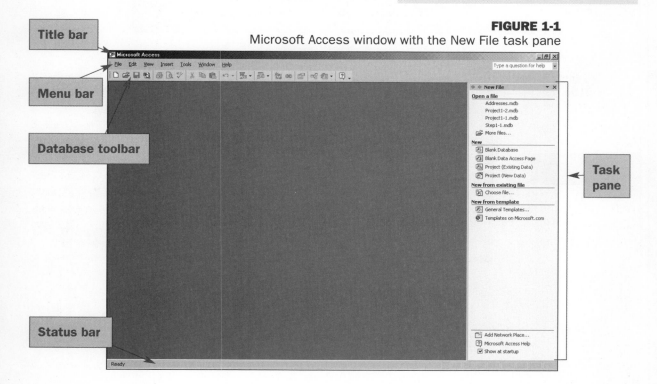

3. The Open dialog box shown in Figure 1-2 is displayed. Do not be concerned if the folders displayed in your dialog box are different.

4. Locate and open the file **Step1-1** from the data files. The Step1-1: Database window, similar to that shown in Figure 1-3, is displayed.

Compare your screen with Figure 1-3 and identify the parts of the Access screen to familiarize yourself with the program.

5. Leave the database open for the next Step-by-Step

FIGURE 1-2
Open dialog box

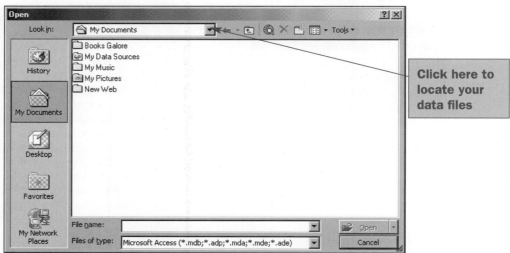

FIGURE 1-3
Step 1-1: Database window displayed

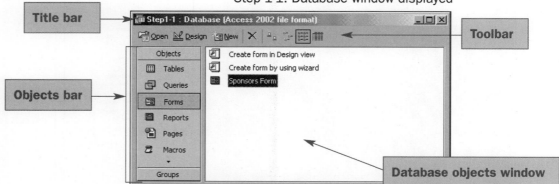

Understand the Purpose of the Database Objects

Notice that the Objects bar displays several objects: Tables, Queries, Forms, Reports, Pages, Macros, and Modules. These objects work together to help you organize and report the information that you store in the database. Every database file contains each of these objects. Tables are the primary objects in the database, and each of the objects and everything you do in a database relies on the data stored in the tables. A database can contain multiple tables.

The following list describes the purpose of each of the objects. You will learn to create tables in this lesson, and you will learn to create queries, forms, and reports in Lessons 2 and 3. Although you will not learn how to create pages, macros, or modules in the scope of this course, the following explanations help to describe the potential of the features that are available to you in Access.

■ Tables –Tables store data in columns and rows. All database information is stored in tables, and all other database objects rely on the existence of the table(s).

■ Queries – A query is a way to ask question about the information stored in the table. Access searches for and retrieves data from the database table(s) to answer your question.

■ Forms – Forms make it easy for you to enter data into a table.

■ Pages – Pages enable you to design other database objects so they can be published on the Web.

■ Macros – Macros enable you to perform a series of operations with a single command.

■ Modules – Modules enable you to perform more complex operations that cannot be completed with macros.

STEP-BY-STEP ▷ 1.2

1. Select **Tables** on the Objects bar if necessary. The Sponsors table in the Database objects window will already be selected.

2. Click the **Open** button in the Database window toolbar. The Sponsors: Table shown in Figure 1-4 is displayed.

FIGURE 1-4
Sponsers: Table

Company	Address	City	State	ZIP	Phone	Fax	Email	Contact	Years	
Al's Trucking	2460 North Road	Fenton	MI	48430	555-1910	555-1915	BigAl@area.net	Al Polidan	3	Gol
Gould Projections	3234 West Thompson Road	Fenton	MI	48430	555-0700	555-8976	Gouldproj@quest.com	Jack Crooks	1	Bro
T2 Designs, Inc.	266 North Alloy Drive	Fenton	MI	48430	555-9870	555-9875	T2@brightnet.com	Kirsten Lucas	0	Pro
Kasper's Pizzeria	1534 North Leroy Street	Fenton	MI	48430	555-0877	555-0879		E.J. Daros	5	Silv
The WaterSports Shop	17084 Silver Parkway	Fenton	MI	48430	555-6554	555-6540	Watersports@ecr.net	Lori Jenkins	5	Gol
Dragon's Pearl Take-Out	403 Rounds Drive	Fenton	MI	48430	555-4335	555-4312	Dragon@tir.net	Cheryl Godmar	2	Gol
Genesee Fitness & Athletic Center	4281 Owen Road	Fenton	MI	48430	555-1232	555-1233	Genfit@flash.com	Andy Brown	0	Pro
Thomas Transit Mix	4036 Owen Road	Fenton	MI	48430	555-4354			Judy Perry	1	Bro
Andrea's Boutique	233 West Caroline Street	Fenton	MI	48430	555-3801	555-3645	Andrea's@quest.com	Keith Barnett	0	Pro
Bill's Gravel Company	10024 Bennett lake Road	Fenton	MI	48430	555-8856	555-8804		Bill Lashley	3	Silv
Fisher Enterprises, Inc.I	17114 Silver Parkway	Fenton	MI	48430	555-9908	555-9905	Fisher@brightnet.com	Mary Rising	1	Silv
Gould Sports Center	1471 Torrey	Fenton	MI	48430	555-8661			Tom Gould	0	Pro
									0	

3. Click the right arrow on the horizontal scroll bar (at the bottom of the screen) to view the columns to the right. This table provides data about companies that currently provide sponsorship for a club as well as companies that potentially could become sponsors.

4. Open the **File** menu and choose **Close** to close the table. The Database window is visible again.

Did You Know?

You can also close the table by clicking the close box in the top right corner of the Sponsors: Table title bar. Be sure you click the table close box and not the Access application close box, which is at the top right side of the Microsoft Access title bar.

5. Click **Queries** on the Objects bar. There is one query object named *Prospective Sponsors Query*, and it should already be selected.

6. Double-click the query object to open it. This query locates and displays the companies that are considered to be prospective sponsors. The information comes from the Sponsors table.

7. Open the **File** menu and choose **Close** to close the query. The Database window is still displayed.

8. Click **Forms** on the Objects bar. There is one form object named *Sponsors Form*, and it should already be selected.

9. Double-click the form object to open it. This form makes it easy to enter information about each of the club sponsors. When you enter information in this form, the information is stored in the Sponsors table. Open the **File** menu and choose **Close** to close the form. The database window is still displayed.

10. Click **Reports** on the Objects bar. There is one report object named *Prospective Sponsors Report*, and it should already be selected.

Speech Recognition

If your computer has speech recognition capability, enable the Command mode and say the commands to open and close the database objects.

11. Double-click the report object to open it. The report displays the data contained in the Prospective Sponsors Query.

12. Open the **File** menu and choose **Close** to close the report, then open the **File** menu again and choose **Close** to close the Database window. Leave Access open for the next Step-by-Step.

Create a Table

When you create a new database, the first object you need to create is a table. It is the primary object because it contains the data. You can create as many tables as you need to store the information. An Access table contains fields and records. A *field* is a single piece of database information, such as a first name, a last name, or a telephone number. A *record* is a group of related fields in a database, such as all the information about the person, including first and last name, address, postal code, telephone number, and so forth.

When you create a table in Access, you will be prompted to create a primary key. The *primary key* uniquely identifies each record in a table. The primary key tells Access how your records will be sorted, and it prevents duplicate entries. For example, you may have a student ID number, and no other student has exactly the same number as you.

You can display the table in Datasheet view or in Design view. *Datasheet view* displays the table data in a row-and-column format. *Design view* displays the field names and what kind of values you can enter in each field. It is in Design view that you can define or modify the field formats.

If this sounds like a lot to remember, do not be concerned. Access provides a wizard that simplifies the task of creating and entering data in the table.

Create a Table Using a Wizard

When you create a table using a *wizard*, you respond to a series of questions about how you want to set up the table. The wizard guides you through the process and formats the table based on your answers.

STEP-BY-STEP ▷ 1.3

1. Click the **New** button in the Database toolbar. The New File task pane displays at the right.

2. In the task pane under *New*, select **Blank Database**. A File New Database dialog box similar to the one shown in Figure 1-5 is displayed. Your dialog box may look different.

FIGURE 1-5
File New Database dialog box

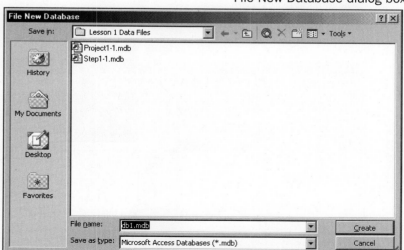

3. Locate the folder where you save your documents. Then delete the proposed file name in the File name: box and key **Addresses** followed by your initials. Click **Create**. A new database window like the one shown in Figure 1-6 is displayed.

4. Double-click **Create table by using wizard**. The Table Wizard dialog box opens. Select **Personal** to display the dialog box shown in Figure 1-7.

Computer Concepts

A default setting tells Access 2002 to save files in the Access 2000 file format. A file in Access 2000 file format can be opened in both Access 2000 and Access 2002. You can choose to save your Access files in Access 2002 file format, but then you will be able to open those files only with Access 2002. To change the default setting, an Access file must be open. Open the **Tools** menu, choose **Options**, and then click the **Advanced** tab. In the *Default File Format* box, select the desired Access file format.

FIGURE 1-6
Addresses: Database window

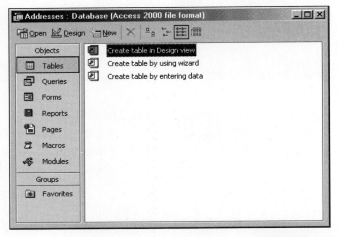

FIGURE 1-7
Table Wizard dialog box

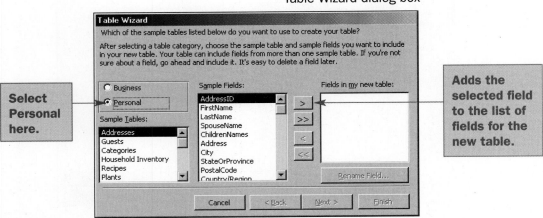

5. Identify the fields to be included in the table. In the *Sample Fields:* list, select **FirstName.** Then click the single right arrow to add the field in the *Fields in my new table:* list.

Did You Know?

If you click the right double arrows, all the fields are added to *Fields in my new table.* If you click the left single arrow, the selected field will be removed from *Fields in my new table* list. If you click the double left arrows, all the fields will be removed from the *Fields in my new table* list.

6. Using the same procedure, select the following fields in the *Sample Fields:* list and add them to the *Fields in my new table:* list.
LastName
Address
City
StateOrProvince
PostalCode
Country/Region

7. Click **Next**. The wizard will ask you to name your table. The proposed name *Addresses* is displayed, and this name is appropriate. This step of the wizard also asks if you want the wizard to set a primary key for you. The answer *Yes, set a primary key for me.* is already selected. Click **Next** to accept the settings on this page of the wizard.

8. The wizard then asks what you want to do after the wizard creates your table. If necessary, select *Enter data directly into the table.* and click **Finish**.

9. The table is created and the columns display the field names. Because there are no records entered in the table, a single blank row is displayed. See Figure 1-8.

10. Notice that in the first row in the AddressesID field, *(AutoNumber)* is displayed. This field contains the primary key, and Access will automatically number each record that you enter.

11. Click the **Save** button on the Database toolbar and leave the table open for the next Step-by-Step.

FIGURE 1-8
Addresses: Table displayed in Datasheet view

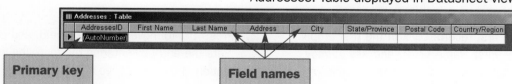

Enter Records in Datasheet View

The Addresses table is currently displayed in Datasheet view. In this view, the table display is similar to a spreadsheet. The intersection of a row and a column is called a **cell**. Fields appear as columns, and each column has a **field name**. The field name is a label that helps you identify the fields. Each row in the table contains one single record of the entire database.

When you enter data into a cell, it is called an **entry**. To move from one cell to another, you can use the mouse to click in a cell. You can also use the keyboard to navigate in a table. Table 1-1 describes the keys you can use to move around in a table in Datasheet view.

Speech Recognition

If your computer has speech recognition capability, enable the Command mode and say the commands to navigate through the table.

TABLE 1-1
Keys for navigating in Datasheet view

KEY	DESCRIPTION
Enter, Tab, or right arrow	Moves the insertion point to the next field.
Left arrow or Shift + Tab	Moves the insertion point to the previous field.
Home	Moves the insertion point to the first field in the current record
End	Moves the insertion point to the last field in the current record.
Up arrow	Moves the insertion point up one record and stays in the same field.
Down arrow	Moves the insertion point down one record and stays in the same field.
Page Up	Moves the insertion point up one screen.
Page Down	Moves the insertion point down one screen.

STEP-BY-STEP ▷ 1.4

1. Enter the first record. Click in the first empty cell, (the *First Name* field), and key **Jaimey**. Notice that as you enter the text in the first field, Access automatically assigns the primary key *1* in the *AddressesID* field.

2. Press **Tab** to move to the next field, and complete the entry by entering the following information in the respective fields:

Last Name	**McGuirk**
Address	**610 Brae Burn**
City	**Mansfield**
State/Province	**OH**
Postal Code	**44907-9122**
Country/Region	**USA**

3. Press **Tab** twice to move to the *FirstName* field in the next row. Enter the following data for two more records:

First Name	**Jesse**
Last Name	**Bain**
Address	**288 Silvercrest Drive**
City	**Lexington**
State/Province	**OH**
Postal Code	**44904-9007**
Country/Region	**USA**

First Name	**Matt**
Last Name	**Smith**
Address	**4645 Rule Road**
City	**Bellville**
State/Province	**OH**
Postal Code	**44813-0987**
Country/Region	**USA**

4. Click the **Save** button to save the changes and leave the database open for the next Step-by-Step.

Modify a Table

Although it is usually easier to change your table design before you enter data, you can refine the design at any time. You can modify the table in Datasheet view or Design view.

Use Help to Learn How to Change the Column Width

The default column widths are often too wide or too narrow for the data in the table. This is the case with your database. The Address field is not wide enough to display all the text in the street address, and there's a lot of white space in the StateOrProvince field. Go to the Help screens to learn how to adjust the column width.

1. In the Ask a Question text box, key **change column width** and then press **Enter**.

2. When the list of topics displays, select the link **Resize a column or row.** If you do not see this topic, click the **See more...** link.

3. Under Step 2 in the Help screen, click the link **Resize a column** to expand the content. Study the illustration and read the information about dragging the right edge of the column to change the column width. Be sure to read the note at the bottom of the screen about undoing the changes to the width of columns.

4. Click the **Close** box on the Help window to close the Help screen.

5. Point to the right edge of the Address column. The pointer changes to a two-headed arrow as illustrated in the Help screen. Drag the column border to the right to increase the width of the column. Continue to drag the column border until you get the correct width so that the complete address for all entries is visible.

Did You Know?

You can leave the Help screen open and click the database button in the taskbar to return to the database. That way you can quickly switch to the Help screen if you need to refer to it again as you work with the database.

6. Point to the right edge of the *State/Province* column and drag the border to the left to decrease the width of the column so there is no wasted space in that column. Do not be concerned that the entire field name does not display after you resize the column width.

7. Point to the field name *First Name*. When a down arrow displays, click and drag to the right until all the columns in the table are selected.

8. Open the **Format** menu and choose **Column Width**. The dialog box shown in Figure 1-9 is displayed.

9. Click **Best Fit**. Notice that the width of each column is adjusted to accommodate the contents within the column, including the field name at the top of each column.

10. Save the changes and leave the database open for the next Step-by-Step.

FIGURE 1-9
Column Width dialog box

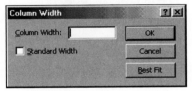

Add and Delete Fields in Design View

Often, after you create a table and enter data, you decide you want to add or delete fields. You can add fields in either Datasheet view or Design view. Design view, however, provides toolbar buttons that make the task easier.

S TEP-BY-STEP ⟹ 1.6

1. Click the **View** button on the Table Datasheet toolbar. The table is displayed in Design view as shown in Figure 1-10.

Computer Concepts

The View button is a toggle button. This means when you're viewing the table one way, the button changes to make it easy to switch quickly to the other view. So, when the table is in Datasheet view, the View button shows Design view. If you click the View button, the table switches to Design view and the View button now indicates Datasheet view. The View button makes it very easy to switch between these two ways of viewing the table.

2. Click in the first blank row directly below the field name *Country/Region*.

3. Key **Birthdate** and press **Enter**. The new field is entered.

4. Click the **Country/Region** field. A right-pointing arrow displays to the left of the field name. This arrow indicates that the row is the current row.

5. Click the **Insert Rows** button on the toolbar. A new row is inserted above the selected row.

7. Select the row containing the *Country/Region* field. Click the **Delete Rows** button on the toolbar.

Speech Recognition

If your computer has speech recognition capability, enable the Command mode and say the toolbar button name to insert the new row.

Computer Concepts

Use caution when deleting rows in Design view. Once you confirm the deletion, you cannot undo the deletion.

---

6. Key **e-mail** and then press **Enter**.

8. When prompted to delete the field and all the data in the field, click **Yes**. The field and all the data entered in the field are removed from the table.

9. Save the changes and leave the database open for the next Step-by-Step.

FIGURE 1-10
Addresses: Table displayed in Design view

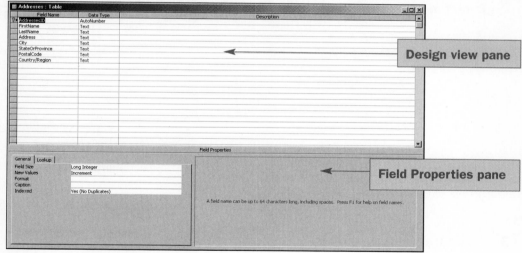

Change Field Properties

In Design view, you can specify the data type for each field. For example, you can specify text, numbers, currency, and even Yes/No. The default data type for a field is regular text, which is appropriate for most of the fields in your table. However, when users enter data for the Birthdate field, you may want to specify that the data type be formatted to hold date and time data instead of text.

When you select a data type, a dialog box displays several options for field properties. *Field properties* are specifications that allow you to customize the data type settings. The field properties available depend on the data type selected. One of the most common field properties is field size. The default field size is 50 characters, but you can specify that the field allow up to 255 characters. Another common field property is format. The format specifies how you want Access to display numbers, dates, times, and text.

S TEP-BY-STEP ▷ 1.7

1. Your database should still be displayed in Design view. Click in the **Data Type** cell next to the field Birthdate. The current data type is Text, and when you click in the cell, a down arrow will display.

2. Click the down arrow to display the options shown in Figure 1-11 and then select **Date/Time**.

FIGURE 1-11
Data Type options

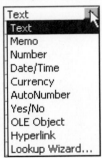

3. Notice that the Field Properties that are displayed in the pane at the bottom of the Design view window change to show the values for the Date/Time data type.

4. In the Field Properties pane at the bottom of the window, click in the text box next to *Format*. When the down arrow displays, click it to display the list of options shown in Figure 1-12.

FIGURE 1-12
Date/Time format options

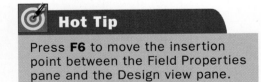

5. Select **Short Date**.

Hot Tip

Press **F6** to move the insertion point between the Field Properties pane and the Design view pane.

6. In the Design view pane, click in the **Data Type** cell for the *StateOrProvince* field. The data type is set for Text.

7. Click in the *Field Size* text box in the Field Properties pane. The field size is currently set at *20*. Change the field size to **2**. This will require that the user use two-letter state abbreviations when entering the state name in the table.

8. Click the **View** button on the tool-bar to switch to Datasheet view. When prompted to save the changes, click **Yes**. When prompted that data may be lost, click **Yes** to continue.

9. Enter the following data in the Birthdate and e-mail fields. Notice that as you enter the birthdate data, Access will automatically format the date using the short date format you specified.

First Name	e-mail	Birthdate
Jaimey	**JMcGuirk@ nets.com**	**March 13, 1978**
Jesse	**JBain@ LFSC.com**	**April 11, 1979**
Matt	**MSmith@ qry.com**	**June 18, 1980**

10. Enter the following new record. Remember that as you enter the state name, Access will not permit you to enter more than two characters.

You will need to enter the two-letter state abbreviation for Ohio.

First Name	**Kelsey**
Last Name	**Erwin**
Address	**2038 Leiter Road**
City	**Lucas**
State/Province	**Ohio**
Postal Code	**44843-9880**
e-mail	**KErwin@csfa.com**
Birthdate	**October 6, 1979**

11. Format the e-mail and Birthdate columns width for best fit. (*Hint*: Open the Format menu, choose Column Width, and then select Best Fit in the dialog box.) Save the changes.

12. Open the **File** menu and choose **Close**. The Datasheet objects window is displayed. Notice that your Addresses table is now displayed as an object in the Database objects window.

13. Open the **File** menu and choose **Close** to close the database file.

Computer Concepts

Access offers several other ways to create a table. You can create a table in Datasheet view or you can use the Table Wizard.

Summary

In this lesson, you learned:

- Many parts of the Access screen are similar to other Office XP applications. However, Access also has several different toolbar buttons and menus to perform tasks unique to Access.

- Database objects work together to help you organize and report the information stored in the database.

- Tables are the primary objects in a database. All other objects are based on data stored in tables.

- You use Datasheet view to enter records in a table.

- A table can be modified after it is created, even after data records have been entered into it. You can edit a table in Datasheet view or in Design view.

- In Design view, you can specify the data type for each field. The field properties are specifications that allow you to customize the data type settings. Text is the default field property for a cell.

VOCABULARY REVIEW

Define the following terms:

Cell	Entry	Primary key
Database	Field	Record
Datasheet view	Field name	Wizard
Design view	Field properties	

LESSON 1 REVIEW QUESTIONS

TRUE/FALSE

Circle T if the statement is true or F if the statement is false.

T F 1. All database information is stored in tables.

T F 2. You cannot add or delete fields after you have entered data in a table.

T F 3. Tables are the primary objects in a database because they store the data.

T F 4. Databases are similar to spreadsheets.

T F 5. Unlike Excel, you cannot adjust Access column widths.

FILL IN THE BLANK

Complete the following sentences by writing the correct word or words in the blanks provided.

1. A(n) _____ is a single piece of information in a database, such as a first name, a last name, or a telephone number.

2. _____ view displays the table data in a row-and-column format.

3. The _____ uniquely identifies each record in a table.

4. _____ are specifications that allow you to customize a field beyond choosing a data type.

5. A(n) _____ is a group of related fields, such as all the information about an employee.

LESSON 1 PROJECTS

PROJECT 1-1

1. Open **Project1-1** from the data files. This database stores membership information and the current video collection of the Oak Creek Film Society (OCFS), a club for lovers of classic films.

2. Notice that this database contains two tables: Collection and Members. Open the **Collection** table to see the films the OCFS has collected so far.

3. Close the table and click the **Forms** object in the Objects bar. Open the **Members** form to see the form used to insert member data.

4. Close the form and click the **Queries** object in the Objects bar. Double-click the **Suspense** query to see the films in the collection that belong to the Suspense category. Close the query.

5. You need to create a new table for the database to store information on special events the OCFS sponsors. Create a new table using the wizard:
   A. Select the **Business** category if necessary and then select the sample table **Events**.
   B. Add the following sample fields to your new table: **EventName**, **Location**, **StartDate**, and **EventDescription.**
   C. Accept the table name **Events**.
   D. Let the wizard set a primary key for you.
   E. There is no relationship between this new table and existing tables. So, when prompted about the relationship, simply click **Next**.
   F. When prompted about what you want to do after the wizard creates the table, select **Enter data directly into the table**, if necessary and click **Finish**.

6. Enter the following data in Datasheet view:

Event Name	Location	Start Date	Event Description
Holiday Classics	**Odeon Theatre**	**12/15/02**	**Christmas theme**
Horror Classics	**Odeon Theatre**	**1/17/03**	**Horror theme**
Hitchcock Classics	**Odeon Theatre**	**2/22/03**	**Suspense theme**

7. You decide your table needs some modifications. With the **Events** table open, switch to Design view.

8. The *EventDescription* field doesn't add much to the table because the subject of each event is clear from the event name. Delete the **EventDescription** field and all contents.

9. It would be helpful to see the time for each event. Insert a new field following the *StartDate* field named **Start Time** with the **Date/Time** data type. Specify the **Medium Time** field property.

10. Each event includes clips from classic films. Insert a new field named **Films** following the *StartTime* field. Because each event includes more than one film, change the field size for the Films field to **200**.

11. Save your changes to the design and return to Datasheet view. Insert the following data in the new fields.

Event	Start Time	Films
Holiday Classics	**7:00 PM**	**A Christmas Story, A Christmas Carol**
Horror Classics	**7:00 PM**	**Dracula, Frankenstein**
Hitchcock Classics	**6:30 PM**	**The Birds, Vertigo**

12. Add one more event with the following information. Note that all three movies fit in the Films field now that you have changed the field size.

Event:	**Spoofing the Classics**
Location:	**Odeon Theatre**
Start Date:	**3/17/03**
Start Time:	**4:00 PM**
Films:	**The Pink Panther, Young Frankenstein, Dr. Strangelove**

13. Adjust the column widths to display all text in the fields. Save your changes.

14. Close the Events table and the Project1-1 database.

PROJECT 1-2

1. Open **Project1-2** from the data files. This database stores statistics for the Pistons Softball Team.

2. Open the **Stats** table and switch to Design view. Notice that the default value for the Number Data Type is *0*. That explains why the last row in the table shows zeros when the table is displayed in Datasheet view.

3. Add the following new fields after the HP field:

Field Name	Data Type	Description
SOL	Number	Strike out looking
SOS	Number	Strike out swinging
OBE	Number	On by error
SACF	Number	Sacrifice fly

4. Save your changes. Switch to Datasheet view and update the existing records by entering the following data in the new fields:

Player	SOL	SOS	OBE	SACF
Reardon	3	8	7	6
Erwin	6	6	4	2
Caulfield	4	8	13	10
Chen	8	12	1	3
Winters	1	11	8	1

5. Switch to Design view and change the format for the Date/Time Data Type in the *Joined* field to **Short Date**.

6. Select the entire table and format the column widths for best fit.

7. Save the changes to your database. Close the Stats table and the Project 1-2 database.

WEB PROJECT

Films of all types are such popular forms of entertainment that many sites on the Internet are dedicated to film information. A good source of information about movies is the Internet Movie Database. Think of a movie you have seen recently (or one you saw in the past that still interests you). Use a Web search tool to locate the current URL of the Internet Movie Database. If that site is not available, locate a site that provides movie information. Use the search box on the home page to key the name of the movie and then display information about the movie. If you were going to create your own database about films you like, what fields would you use to store the information?

TEAMWORK PROJECT

Databases are ideal for storing statistics such as those of sports teams. With a classmate, create a database to record stats for one of your school's sports teams. Follow these steps:

1. With your teammate, choose one of your school's teams for further study.

2. Collect the statistics you will need for your database. Some of the pieces of information you might collect would be players' names, number of games, and statistics for each game. You can probably get this information from the team's coach or from the players themselves. Divide up the players and/or games with your teammate so you each have half the work to do.

3. Create a database to store the data you collect.

CRITICAL THINKING

You want to insert two new fields in a database. One field—named Notes—will hold complete sentences of text. In some cases, the sentences are fairly lengthy. The other field, named Values, has to hold numbers containing decimals. However, it is important that these numbers are not rounded off during calculations. What data types and field properties will you need to specify in order to display data properly in these new fields? Experiment in Access to find the answers, and then check your answers using the Access Help screens.

EDITING RECORDS AND USING FORMS

OBJECTIVES

Upon completion of this lesson, you should be able to:

■ Edit records in Datasheet view.

■ Add and delete records in Datasheet view.

■ Cut, copy, and paste data in Datasheet view.

■ Change the datasheet layout.

■ Hide columns in a table.

■ Create a form.

■ Enter and edit data in a form.

Estimated Time: 1 hour

VOCABULARY

Clipboard
Field selector
Record selector

Edit Records in Datasheet View

It is common for data to change after you've entered it in your database. For example, people move, so you have to change their addresses and probably their phone numbers. Access provides several navigation features that make it easy for you to move around in a datasheet table so you can make necessary edits. These features are especially useful when you're working in large databases. Figure 2-1 shows the navigation buttons that are displayed at the bottom of a table shown in Datasheet view.

FIGURE 2-1
Navigation buttons

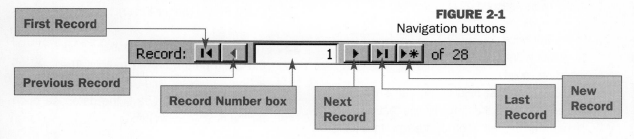

First Record

Previous Record

Record Number box

Next Record

Last Record

New Record

If you make a mistake adding or editing data, you can choose the Undo command to reverse your last action. As soon as you begin editing another record, however, the Undo command is no longer available.

1. If necessary, launch Access and then open the file **Step2-1** from the data files.

2. If necessary, click Tables in the Objects bar, and then double-click the **Classics** table in the Database objects window to open the table. The table is displayed in Datasheet view.

3. The first cell in the table *(ID number 1)* is selected. The right-pointing arrow to the left of the first row indicates that this is the current row.

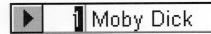

4. Click the **Next Record** button in the bottom left corner of the screen. The selection moves to the ID number 2 in the second row in the table.

5. Click the **Previous Record** button. Notice that even though the selection changes rows, the selection remains in the same field – *ID*.

6. Select the number *1* in the Record Number box and key **22**. Press  **Enter** (or **Tab**). The selection moves to the ID *22* in the twenty-second row in the table.

7. Press **Tab** twice to position the insertion point  in the *Author First* field in the same row. Key **James** to change the entry. Notice that a pencil displays at the left edge of the row, indicating that the record is being edited.

8. Click the **Next Record** button. The selection (or insertion point) moves to the next row in the table. Notice that the selection stays in the *Author First* field. Also notice that the pencil is

no longer displayed to the left of row 22. This is because when you pressed Next Record, the edit was completed. (This is true whether you press a navigation button, press the **Enter** key, use the **Tab** key to move to the next row, use the arrow keys, or the mouse. As soon as you move out of the row, the entry is completed.)

Computer Concepts

When you edit a record in Datasheet view, Access automatically saves the changes to the record.

9. Click the **First Record** button. The insertion point moves to the *Author First* field in the first row in the table.

10. Click the **Last Record** button. The insertion point moves to the *Author First* field in the last row in the table.

11. Press **Tab** twice to move to the *Cover* field in the same row. Key **Paperback** to replace the current entry.

12. Click the **Previous Record** button to move to the row above. Key **Paperback** to replace the entry. Press **Tab** (or **Enter**).

13. The change was not necessary. Click the **Undo** button on the toolbar. The action is reversed and the cell should display *Hardcover*. Leave the database open for the next Step-by-Step.

Did You Know?

You can also execute the Undo command by pressing **Ctrl + Z** or opening the **Edit** menu and choosing **Undo**.

Add and Delete Records in Datasheet View

To add a record, you must enter the data in the blank row at the end of the table. To delete a record, you must first select the record. To select a record, point to the *record selector*, which is the box located at the left edge of each row. You use the record selector to select the row. When you see a right-pointing arrow in the record selector, you can click, and the entire row is selected. You can select more than one record by dragging down several rows. This means you can delete multiple rows at once.

Hot Tip

You can also select multiple, consecutive records by selecting the first record, holding down the **Shift** key, and then clicking on the last record. All the fields in between the first selected record and the last record will be selected.

After a record is selected, you can press the **Delete** key to remove the data. Access will display a message box to ask you if you are sure about the deletion. Once you've deleted a record, you cannot use the Undo command to restore it.

STEP-BY-STEP ▷ 2.2

1. Click the **New Record** button. The insertion point is positioned in the first available blank row at the end of the table.

2. Press **Tab** to move to the *Title* field. Access will automatically insert an ID number for the primary key when you begin to enter data. Enter the following data for the new record:

   Title: **Crime and Punishment**
   Author First: **Fyodor**
   Author Last: **Dostoyevsky**
   Cover: **Hardcover**
   # Pages: **499**
   Publisher: **HarperCollins Publishers, Inc.**
   Price: **6.99**

3. Point to the left of the ID field 26. (The record is fourth from the bottom in the table.) When the pointer changes to a right-pointing arrow, click to select the entire row.

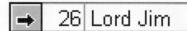

4. Press **Delete**. When prompted to confirm the deletion of the record, click **Yes**. The record is deleted from the table. Leave the database open for the next Step-by-Step.

Cut, Copy, and Paste Data in Datasheet View

Selected data can be copied or moved from one location in an Access table to a new location within the same table, or to a different table. The Copy command duplicates the data in a new location. The Cut and Paste commands relocate selected data.

Computer Concepts

You can access the Cut, Copy, and Paste commands by clicking the appropriate buttons on the toolbar. You can also access the commands by right-clicking on the selected data to display a shortcut menu and then choosing the desired command from the menu.

When you use the Cut, Copy, and Paste commands, Access stores the selected text in the Clipboard. The *Clipboard* is a temporary storage place in your computer's memory. You send selected contents of your database to the Clipboard by using the Cut or Copy commands. Then you can retrieve those contents by using the Paste command. Pasting the contents of the Clipboard does not delete the contents from the Clipboard. Therefore, you can paste Clipboard items as many times as you want. When you turn off the computer, the Clipboard contents are lost.

As items are added to the Clipboard, the items are displayed as icons of the application (i.e., the Access icon or the Excel icon) in the Clipboard task pane. Along with the icon there is a thumbnail of the copied graphic or copied text. The Clipboard will store up to 24 items. The newest entry is always added to the top of the gallery. When you copy or cut a 25th item, the first item you placed in the Clipboard is deleted.

Hot Tip

As in all Office applications, the shortcut keys for Cut are **Ctrl + X**; for Copy, **Ctrl + C**; and for Paste, **Ctrl + V**. The Cut, Copy, and Paste commands can also be found on the Edit menu; and there are Copy, Cut, and Paste buttons on the Standard toolbar.

Computer Concepts

When you cut data from a table, you will get a warning about deleting the record. However, when you cut data, the data is stored in the Clipboard. Thus, if you change your mind and want to restore the data, you can paste the data in the table. When you paste data in a table, the data will overwrite the existing data.

STEP-BY-STEP ▷ 2.3

1. Open the **Edit** menu and choose **Office Clipboard**.

2. Click the **Clear All** button in the Clipboard task pane to clear the contents of the Clipboard. (If you have not copied or cut any items, the Clipboard will already be cleared and this step will not be necessary. Your Clear All button will be greyed out and not available.) Your Clipboard task pane should now look like the one shown in Figure 2-2.

Speech Recognition

If your computer has speech recognition capability, enable the Command mode and say the command to display the Office Clipboard task pane, and then say the command to clear all the contents on the Clipboard.

3. Go to record 7 (*Oliver Twist*) and select the entire row.

4. Click the **Copy** button on the toolbar to copy the record data to the Clipboard. An Access icon and the first portion of the text is added to the Clipboard task pane to indicate contents from an Access database are stored in the Clipboard.

FIGURE 2-2
Empty Clipboard task pane

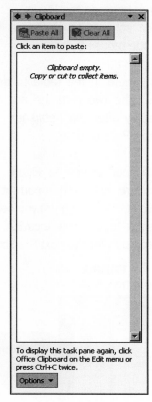

6. Click the **New Record** button. The new row is selected.

7. Click the first object at the top of the list (*Wuthering Heights*) in the Clipboard toolbar. The contents of the object are pasted into the new record row. Notice that the contents still remain in the Clipboard.

8. Click the **New Record** button. Paste the contents of the second object (*Oliver Twist*) in the new record row. Then, close the Clipboard task pane.

Speech Recognition

If your computer has speech recognition capability, enable the Command mode and say the commands to navigate in the table in Datasheet view. Note that the commands you can use include Up, Down, Left, Right, Page Down, Page Up, Home, End, and New Record.

9. Edit the fields in the Oliver Twist record (*31*) as follows: Change *Paperback* to **Hardcover**, change the page count to **325**, and change the price to **4.99**. Press **Enter**.

5. Go to record 12 (*Wuthering Heights*) and select the entire row. Then click the **Copy** button to copy the record data to the Clipboard. A second Access icon is added to the Clipboard task pane to indicate another item is stored in the Clipboard.

10. Edit the fields in the Wuthering Heights record (*30*) as follows: Change *Hardcover* to **Paperback**, change the page count to **225**, and change the price to **3.49**. Press **Enter**. Leave the database open for the next Step-by-Step.

Change the Datasheet Layout

If you want to rearrange the fields in Datasheet view, you can drag them to a new location. To select a field, point to the field name at the top of the column. The box containing the field name is also a *field selector*. You use the field selector to select the column. When you see a down-pointing arrow in the field selector, click, and the entire column is selected. After you select the field, point to the field selector and drag the selection to the new location. As you drag, a vertical bar will follow the mouse pointer to indicate where the field will be moved. When you release the mouse button, the field is inserted in its new location.

1. Scroll to the right until the *Cover* column, the *# Pages* column, the *Publisher* column, and the *Price* column are all visible on the screen.

2. Point to the field name *Cover*. When the pointer changes to a down-pointing arrow, click and drag to the right to select the *Cover* and *# Pages* columns.

3. Release the mouse button when the two columns are selected. Then point to either of the field names and drag the columns to the right. As you drag, a bold vertical line will display. When that vertical line is positioned on

the border between the *Publisher* column and the *Price* column as shown in Figure 2-3, release the mouse button.

4. Click anywhere in the table to deselect the columns. The two columns are moved and now display after the *Publisher* column and before the *Price* column.

5. Compare your screen to Figure 2-4. If the columns are not in the correct order, try again. Select the column(s) you need to move and drag it to the new location. Leave the database open for the next Step-by-Step.

FIGURE 2-3
Dragging columns to a new location

Last	Cover	# Pages	Publisher	Price
	Hardback	477	HarperCollins Publishers, Inc.	$5.99
	Hardcover	573	Fellows Press	$6.99
eare	Paperback	125	HarperCollins Publishers, Incorporated	$1.59
	Paperback	288	Warner Books, Incorporated	$2.79
	Paperback	480	Bantam Books, Incorporated	$3.49
	Paperback	292	Doubleday Dell Publishing Group	$2.59
	Paperback	228	HarperCollins Publishers, Inc.	$1.00
n	Hardcover	228	Price Thomas	$2.29
k	Hardcover	578	Price Thomas	$6.99
d	Paperback	240	Landover Press	$2.59
	Hardcover	288	Fellows Press	$2.79
	Hardcover	248	Courage Books	$4.59
	Hardcover	592	Oxford University Press, Inc.	$7.49
	Hardcover	266	Bantam Doubleday Dell Publishing Group	$4.99

Drag pointer to here

FIGURE 2-4
Table with columns rearranged

ID	Title	Author First	Author Last	Publisher	Cover	# Pages	Price
1	Moby Dick	Herman	Melville	HarperCollins Publishers, Inc.	Hardback	477	$5.99
2	Little Women	Louisa	Alcott	Fellows Press	Hardcover	573	$6.99
3	Romeo & Juliet	William	Shakespeare	HarperCollins Publishers, Incorporated	Paperback	125	$1.59
4	To Kill a Mockingbird	Harper	Lee	Warner Books, Incorporated	Paperback	288	$2.79
5	Uncle Tom's Cabin	Harriet	Stowe	Bantam Books, Incorporated	Paperback	480	$4.59
6	The Adventures of Huckleberry Finn	Mark	Twain	Doubleday Dell Publishing Group	Paperback	292	$2.59
7	Oliver Twist	Charles	Dickens	HarperCollins Publishers, Inc.	Paperback	228	$1.00
8	The Scarlet Letter	Nathaniel	Hawthorn	Price Thomas	Hardcover	228	$2.29
9	The Grapes of Wrath	John	Steinbeck	Price Thomas	Hardcover	578	$6.99
10	The Great Gatsby	F. Scott	Fitzgerald	Landover Press	Paperback	240	$2.59
11	Pride and Prejudice	Jane	Austen	Fellows Press	Hardcover	288	$2.79

Use Help to Learn How to Hide Columns

When all the columns in a table cannot display on the screen at one time, you must scroll horizontally to view all the columns. This can make it difficult to enter data in Datasheet view because you cannot see all of the fields.

If you completed the lessons in the Excel unit, you learned to hide columns in a spreadsheet. Go to the Help screens to see if you can hide columns in an Access table as well.

STEP-BY-STEP ▷ 2.5

1. Click the **Office Assistant**, or open the **Help** menu and choose **Microsoft Access Help**.

Hot Tip
The shortcut for accessing the **Help** command is F1.

2. In the text box, key **hide columns** and then press **Enter** or click **Search**.

3. When the assistant displays a list of topics, select the topic **Show or hide columns in a datasheet**.

4. Read the directions for hiding a column. Be sure to also read about how to show hidden columns.

Did You Know?
If the Office Assistant is in the way, point to the Office Assistant and drag it to the side of the screen. To turn off the display of the Office Assistant, right-click, and choose Hide in the shortcut menu.

5. Click the **Classics: Table** button in the taskbar to view the database table.

6. Hide the *Author First*, *Author Last*, *Publisher*, and *Cover* columns.

Hot Tip
If you can't remember all the steps for a certain task, click the **Microsoft Access Help** button in the taskbar and review the information presented in the Help screen. Then switch back to the database and complete the task.

7. Only four columns should now display. Compare your screen with Figure 2-5. You should see only four fields displayed in the table.

FIGURE 2-5
Table with columns hidden

ID	Title	# Pages	Price
1	Moby Dick	477	$5.99
2	Little Women	573	$6.99
3	Romeo & Juliet	125	$1.59
4	To Kill a Mockingbird	288	$2.79
5	Uncle Tom's Cabin	480	$3.49
6	The Adventures of Huckleberry Finn	292	$2.59
7	Oliver Twist	228	$1.00
8	The Scarlet Letter	228	$2.29
9	The Grapes of Wrath	578	$6.99
10	The Great Gatsby	240	$2.59
11	Pride and Prejudice	288	$2.79
12	Wuthering Heights	248	$4.59

8. Edit the following records as follows:

Record 5:	Uncle Tom's Cabin	Change the price to **$4.59**
Record 14:	My Antonia	Change the price to **$6.99**
Record 16:	Great Expectations	Change the price to **$5.99**

9. To unhide the columns, open the **Format** menu and choose **Unhide Columns**. The Unhide Columns dialog box shown in Figure 2-6 will display.

10. The boxes without checkmarks indicate the columns that are currently hidden. Click each of the empty boxes to select them. (You may notice the columns reappearing in the database behind the dialog box as you check them.) When all the boxes in the dialog box have checkmarks, click the **Close** button in the dialog box.

11. Open the **File** menu and choose **Close** to close the table. When prompted to save the changes to the layout of the table, click **Yes**.

12. Click the **Microsoft Access Help** button in the task bar and then close the Help window. Leave the database open for the next Step-by-Step.

FIGURE 2-6
Unhide Columns dialog box

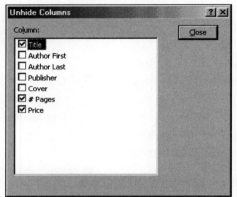

Create a Form

Access offers another way to enter data in a table. You can create a data-entry form. A form offers a more convenient way to enter and view records. When you create a form, you are adding a new object to the database. Although you can create a form manually, the Form Wizard makes the process easier. The wizard asks you questions and formats the form according to your preferences.

STEP-BY-STEP ▷ 2.6

1. Click **Forms** in the Objects bar.

2. Double-click **Create form by using wizard** in the Database Objects window. The Form Wizard dialog box shown in Figure 2-7 is displayed.

3. Notice that *Table: Classics* is already selected under *Table/Queries*. Also notice that all the fields available in the table are listed under *Available Fields*.

4. You need to identify the fields you want on your form. Click the double arrows button (>>). All of the field names are displayed in the *Selected Fields* list. This tells Access to include all the fields in the form.

FIGURE 2-7
Form Wizard dialog box

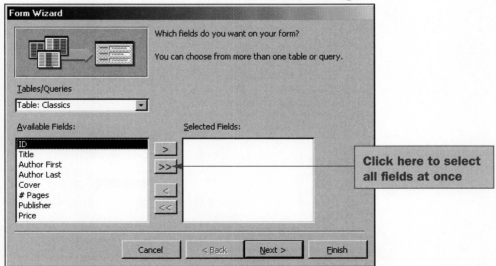

5. Click the **Next** button. The Form Wizard dialog box changes so you can select a layout for the form, as shown in Figure 2-8.

6. If necessary, select **Columnar** for the layout, then click **Next**. The dialog box changes so

you can select a style for the form, as shown in Figure 2-9.

7. If necessary, select the **Standard** style. The preview box shows you what this form style looks like.

FIGURE 2-8
Selecting a layout for a form

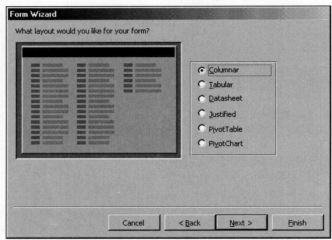

FIGURE 2-9
Choosing a style for a form

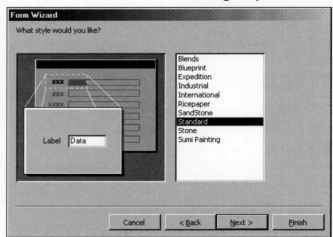

8. Select some of the other styles to see what they look like. Then select **Stone** and click **Next**. The final Form Wizard dialog box changes so you can create a title for the form, as shown in Figure 2-10.

9. Key **Classic Books**.

10. If necessary, click the **Open the form to view or enter information.** option to select it. Then click **Finish**. Access creates and displays the form similar to that shown in Figure 2-11. Notice that data from the first record is displayed in the form. Leave the form and the database open for the next Step-by-Step.

FIGURE 2-10
Creating a title for a form

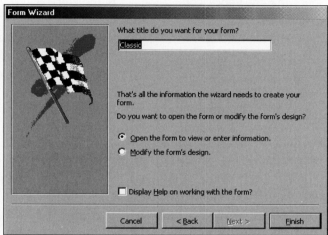

FIGURE 2-11
Customized form

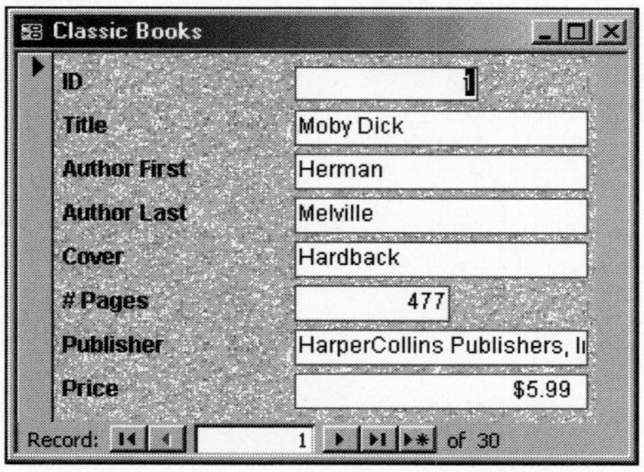

Enter and Edit Data in a Form

Entering data in a form is similar to entering data in a table in Datasheet view. You use the same keys to move the insertion point among the fields. Furthermore, the same navigation buttons are available at the bottom of the form. To add a new record, go to the blank record at the end of the database or click the New Record button. To edit an existing record, display the record and make the changes in the fields of the form.

1. Click the **New Record** button at the bottom of the form. A new form is displayed with labels, but there is no data entered in the form.

2. Press **Tab** to position the insertion point in the field *Title*. Access will assign an ID number when you begin to enter data. Key **A Room with a View**. Notice that the Pencil icon is displayed at the top left corner of the form, indicating that you are editing the record.

3. Press **Tab** and key **E. M.**

4. Press **Tab** and enter the following information into the form:

   Author Last: **Forster**
   Cover: **Paperback**
   # Pages: **355**
   Publisher: **Bagshot Press**
   Price: **5.99**

Speech Recognition

If your computer has speech recognition capability, enable the Dictation mode, position the insertion point in the field, and dictate the entry. Or, enable the Command mode and say the commands to navigate from one field to another.

5. Press **Enter** (or **Tab**). A new blank form is displayed.

6. Select the number **32** in the Record Number box, key **8**, and press **Enter**. A form containing the data for the eighth record is displayed.

7. The author's last name is misspelled. It should be Hawthorne. Click in the *Author Last* field, position the insertion point at the end of the entry, and key the letter **e**.

8. Open the **File** menu and choose **Close**. Notice that the Database objects window displays the new form *Classic Books* in the list of objects.

9. Click the **Tables** button in the Objects bar, then double-click the **Classics** table to open it.

10. **Scroll** down to the end of the table. Notice that the new record has been added to the table. Go to record 8. Notice that the name Hawthorne has been corrected.

Computer Concepts

When you enter or edit a record in form view, Access automatically updates the records in the table.

11. Close the table and the Database.

Summary

In this lesson, you learned:

■ Access provides several navigation buttons to make it easy for you to move around in a table. If you make a mistake adding or editing data, you can choose the Undo command to reverse your last action.

■ You can add and delete records in a table while working in Datasheet view. New records are added at the end of the table. To delete a record, you must first select the entire row containing the record.

■ Selected data can be copied or moved from one location in an Access table to a new location within the same table, or to a different table.

■ The Clipboard task pane displays copied and cut items, and it also enables you to paste items.

■ To rearrange database fields in Datasheet view, you must select the columns containing the fields and then drag them to a new location.

■ If you have several fields in a table, you can hide some of the columns so you can display the fields with which you need to work. You can unhide these columns when you are done.

■ The Form Wizard helps you create a professional-looking, customized form for entering data.

■ Entering and editing data in a form is similar to entering and editing data in a table in Datasheet view. You use the same navigation buttons to move from one record to another.

VOCABULARY REVIEW

Define the following terms:

Clipboard   Field selector   Record selector

LESSON 2 REVIEW QUESTIONS

TRUE/FALSE

Circle T if the statement is true or F if the statement is false.

T F 1. You can use the Undo command any time after you have entered a record to reverse changes.

T F 2. You must add new records at the end of the table.

T F 3. You cannot save changes to the datasheet layout.

T F 4. A form makes it easy to enter new data into a table.

T F 5. You use the same navigation controls in a form as you use in a datasheet.

FILL IN THE BLANK

Complete the following sentences by writing the correct word or words in the blanks provided.

1. To go to record 35 in a database, you would key 35 in the _____ box and then press Enter.

2. The box at the left edge of a row is called the _____.

3. The box containing the field name is called the _____.

4. The easiest way to create a new form is to use the _____.

5. To insert new data in a form, click the _____ button to display a blank form.

LESSON 2 PROJECTS

PROJECT 2-1

1. Open **Project2-1** from the data files. Open the **Collection** table.

2. Hide the *Year*, *Length*, *MPAA*, and *Director* columns.

3. Make the following corrections to the data in the table:
   A. Go to record 20 (*King Solomon's Mines*) and change the *Category* field to **Adventure**.
   B. Go to record 24 (*The Haunting*). You think the title of this film is incorrect. It should be *The Haunting of Hill House*. Key **of Hill House** in the *Title* field.
   C. Whoops, you were wrong. That was the title of the book, not the film. Your original title was correct after all. Click Undo to return the title to The Haunting.
   D. Go to record 26 (*Casablanca*) and scroll, if necessary, so you can see the *Awards* field. To save space, you are not including the word *Best* for all Academy Awards. Delete the word *Best* and the space that follows in this field.

4. Unhide the hidden columns.

5. You need to add several films that were acquired for recent events. (You do not have to enter a number in the *ID* field; Access will supply a number automatically when you key an entry in the *Title* field.)

Title:	**Vertigo**	Title:	**Dr. Strangelove**
Year:	**1958**	Year:	**1964**
Length:	**128**	Length:	**93**
MPAA:	**NR**	MPAA:	**NR**
Color/BW:	**Color**	Color/BW:	**BW**
Director:	**Hitchcock**	Director:	**Kubrick**
Category:	**Suspense**	Category:	**Comedy**
Actor:	**James Stewart**	Actor:	**Peter Sellers, George C. Scott**
Actress:	**Kim Novak**		

6. You have another new film to add. To save time, copy record *29* (*Star Wars*) and paste it in a new record. Change the title to **The Empire Strikes Back**, the year to **1980**, the Length to **124**, and the Director to **Kershner**. Remove *Alec Guinness* from the list in the Actor field and add **Billy Dee Williams** to the list. Delete the existing text in the *Award* field and then enter **Special Effects**.

7. You have discovered that the 1969 version of Hamlet is damaged. Delete this record (*14*) from the table.

8. Move the *Category* column to the right of the *Title* column.

9. Close the table and save changes when prompted.

10. Exit the database.

PROJECT 2-2

1. Open **Project2-2** from the data files.

2. Select **Forms** in the Objects bar. Use the Form Wizard and the following information to create a new form using the Members table: select all fields, the Columnar format, the Sumi Painting style. Finish using the Form Wizard by naming the form **OCFS Members**.

3. Add a new record using the form. (You do not need to enter a number in the *Member ID* field. Simply press **Enter** or **Tab**. Access will add the Member ID automatically after you key an entry in the *First Name* field.)
   First Name: **Sam**
   Last Name: **Martin**
   Address: **Old Ferry Rd**
   City: **Oak Creek**
   State: **OH**
   Zip: **43211**
   Phone: **555-1216**

4. Go to record *8* and change Judith Schuyler's phone number to **555-5005**.

5. Go to record *14*. Brian Tannenbaum has moved. Change his street address to **7140 Cascade Street** and leave all other information the same.

6. Close the form and the database.

SCANS

Every year, financial publications create lists of the richest people in this country and the world. Use Web search tools to find the most recent list of wealthy Americans. Record each person's wealth ranking, first name, last name, and current wealth for each of the first ten people listed. Also record the current job title, if any, and how each person achieved his or her current wealth if you can easily determine this information. (For example, William Gates acquired his wealth through ownership of Microsoft stock.) Create a database to store your information. You'll want to cite your references, so be sure to include a resources field where you can record the Web site(s) where you found the information. If you identify any other items you want to record, modify the database structure and add the information.

SCANS

Create a roster for your computer class to record the names, addresses, phone numbers, e-mail addresses, and other information about your classmates. Follow these steps:

1. With your teammate, determine what information you want to gather and organize.

2. Divide the names of your classmates so that each of you will gather information for half the class.

3. After you have gathered the information, create a new database and a table with the fields you identified in Step 1. Then use the Form Wizard to create a form to make data entry easier. Select the options you think will present the information you've collected in the best way, and give your form a relevant title.

4. Enter the information into the form.

SCANS

You want to create new records using data from some fields in other records. For example, you want to use a company name from one record, a city from another record, and a product from a third record. It would be tedious to copy and paste all three records and then delete the material you don't need. Is there any way to copy only a single field entry to the Clipboard and then paste it into a new record? Experiment with an Access table and the Clipboard. Use the Help screens if you're unable to figure it out. Write a brief report about what you discover.

ORDERING AND FINDING DATA AND CREATING REPORTS AND MAILING LABELS

LESSON 3

OBJECTIVES

Upon completion of this lesson, you should be able to:

■ Sort data in Datasheet view.

■ Find and replace data in Datasheet view.

■ Create a query.

■ Create a report.

■ Create mailing labels.

🕐 **Estimated Time: 1 hour**

VOCABULARY

Ascending order

Descending order

Landscape orientation

Orientation

Portrait orientation

Query

Report

As the amount of data in a database increases, it becomes more difficult to manage records and find information. Access has several useful features that help you work with larger databases. These features help you order the data, find the data, and summarize and report the data.

In this lesson, you will work with the same database you edited in the previous lesson. However, instead of opening the file you saved in Lesson 2, you will start again by opening a new data file created for this lesson. This ensures that the database file you are working with matches the illustrations and examples presented in this lesson.

Sort Data in Datasheet View

Often you will want records in a database to appear in a specific order so you can access data easier and more quickly. Databases often contain numerous records. Access provides toolbar buttons that will help you sort the records in a table quickly. You can sort text and numbers in either ascending or descending order. *Ascending order* sorts alphabetically from A to Z and numerically from the lowest to the highest number. *Descending order* sorts alphabetically from Z to A and numerically from the highest to the lowest number.

Unfortunately, the Undo command is not available after you perform a sort. However, if you change your mind after sorting data, you can open the Records menu and choose Remove Filter/Sort.

363

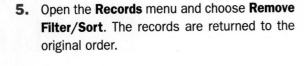
1. Open the file **Step3-1** from the data files.

> ### Speech Recognition
>
> If your computer has speech recognition cabability, enable the Command mode and say the command to open the data file.

2. Click **Tables** in the Objects bar, then double-click **Classics** in the list of objects to open the table.

3. Click in any row in the field *Title*.

4. Click the **Sort Ascending** button on the toolbar. The records in the table are rearranged and placed in alphabetical order from A to Z by book title.

5. Open the **Records** menu and choose **Remove Filter/Sort**. The records are returned to the original order.

6. If necessary, scroll to the right and click in any row in the *Price* field.

7. Click the **Sort Descending** button on the toolbar. The records are rearranged in numerical order with the highest priced book listed first.

8. Click in any row in the *Author Last* field, then click the **Sort Ascending** button. The records are arranged in alphabetical order from A to Z by the author's last name. Leave the database open for the next Step-by-Step.

Find and Replace Data in Datasheet View

There may be occasions when you need to locate a particular value, one record, or a group of records in a database. Locating this data can be simple if the database is not large. However, if the database is quite large, finding a particular record or value can be tedious.

Use Help to Learn about Scrolling in a Datasheet or Form

If your database is not large, you may find it more expedient to locate data by scrolling in a datasheet or form. Go to the Help screens to learn more about scrolling in order to locate a specific record.

S TEP-BY-STEP ⊳ 3.2

1. Open the **Help** menu and choose **Microsoft Access Help**. If the Office Assistant is displayed, point to the Office Assistant and right-click. Then choose **Options** in the shortcut menu. Clear the check box for Use the Office Assistant and click **OK**. Then, open the **Help** menu and choose **Microsoft Access Help**.

2. If necessary, click the **Show** button on the toolbar to display the *Contents*, *Answer Wizard*, and *Index* tabs.

3. If necessary, click the **Contents** tab to display a dialog box similar to the one shown in Figure 3-1. Do not be concerned if your dialog box looks different.

FIGURE 3-1
Contents tab in
Microsoft Access Help

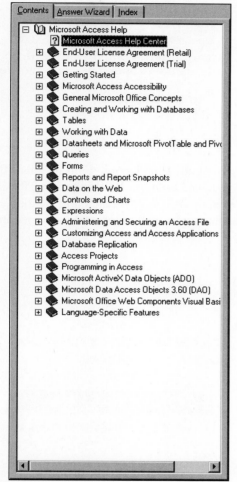

4. If necessary, click all minus signs so that your screen matches the dialog box in Figure 3-1.

5. Click the plus sign next to **Working with Data**. Then click the plus sign next to the subtopic **Finding, Sorting, and Grouping Data**. Then select the plus sign next to the subtopic **Finding and Replacing Data**. Another list of subtopics is displayed.

6. Click the topic **Find a record in a Datasheet or form**.

 Did You Know?

If you only want to search a specific section of the table, you can select the section before you execute the Find command. Access will look for the search text only in the selected cells.

7. Click the link **Find a specific record by scrolling in a datasheet or form** to expand the topic. Click the links for **Datasheet view** and **continuous form** to display the definitions of those terms. Click a second time to hide the definitions. Read all of the information. If you don't know the meaning of a term, click it to read its definition.

8. Click the **Classics: Table** button in the taskbar to view the database table.

9. Use the scroll bars to practice scrolling. Then scroll and locate the following book titles:
The Great Gatsby
Little Women
A Tale of Two Cities
Dr. Jekyll and Mr. Hyde

Computer Concepts

If you click the plus (+) sign next to a topic, the topic will expand to show a list of subtopics. If you click a minus (-) sign next to a topic, the list of subtopics will collapse so that only the topic above the current level is displayed.

10. Click the **Microsoft Help** button in the taskbar and then close the Help screens. Leave the database open for the next Step-by-Step.

Did You Know?

If you have a Microsoft IntelliMouse or Microsoft IntelliMouse Explorer, you can also use the wheel on the mouse to scroll. The wheel eliminates the need to click buttons and scroll bars on the screen.

Speech Recognition

If your computer has speech recognition cabability, enable the Command mode and say the commands to scroll through the database records.

Hot Tip

To turn the display of the Office Assistant back on, open the **Help** menu and choose **Show the Office Assistant**.

Use the Find Command

Let's assume that you want to see if there are any books about Huckleberry Finn included in the database. You could sort the records in alphabetical order by title and then scroll down through the list to look for the title. However, if the database had hundreds, or even thousands of records, this method could be time-consuming. The Find Command provides a much faster way for you to locate specific records or find certain values within fields quickly.

1. Position the insertion point in the first row in the *Title* field. Be careful, though, not to select any text in a cell.

2. Open the **Edit** menu and choose **Find**. The Find and Replace dialog box shown in Figure 3-2 is

displayed. Do not be concerned if your dialog box does not match exactly.

Hot Tip

The shortcut keys for displaying the Find dialog box are **Ctrl + F**.

FIGURE 3-2
Find and Replace dialog box

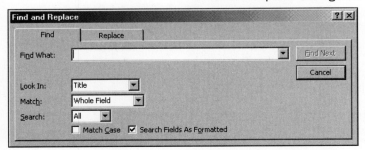

3. With the insertion point already positioned in the *Find What:* text box, key **Huckleberry Finn**. If there is already text in the box, it will be replaced when you key the new search text.

4. Notice that *Title* is displayed in the *Look In:* box. This option is correct as is. It tells Access to look for all occurrences in the *Title* column.

Hot Tip

If you want Access to search the entire database, select the name of the database table in the *Look In:* box.

5. Change the options, if necessary, to match those illustrated in Figure 3-3:

a. Click the down arrow in the *Match:* box and select **Any Part of Field**. Access will locate any book title that has the words *Huckleberry* and *Finn* in it.

b. If necessary, select **All** in the *Search:* box.

c. The *Match Case* and *Search Fields As Formatted* options should not be selected. If they are selected, point to the option and click once to uncheck the box and turn the option off. When these options are turned off, Access ignores capitalization and data formats when searching for matching text.

Speech Recognition

If your computer has speech recognition cabability, enable the Command mode and say the commands to change the options in the Find and Replace dialog box.

FIGURE 3-3
Completed Find and Replace dialog box

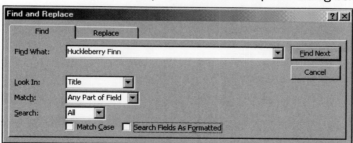

Lesson 3 Ordering and Finding Data and Creating Reports and Mailing Labels

6. Click the **Find Next** button in the dialog box. Access scrolls to the first record that matches the search criteria and highlights the book title in the *Title* field. See Figure 3-4.

7. Click the **Find Next** button again. A message displays indicating that there are no more occurrences of the search text.

8. Click **OK** in the message box to close the message. Then click the **Cancel** button in the **Find and Replace** dialog box. Leave the database open for the next Step-by-Step.

Hot Tip

You can use the shortcut keys **Shift + F4** to execute the Find command without opening the Find and Replace dialog box. Access will search for the text and values that were entered in the *Find What:* box for the last search.

FIGURE 3-4
Search text located in Classics table

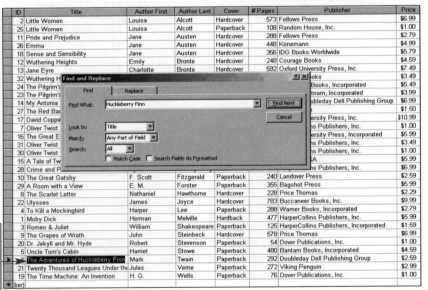

First record that matches the search criteria

Use the Replace Command

If you are working with a large database and you want to replace existing data with new data, the task can be tedious. However, like the Find command, the Replace command makes the task easy. The Replace command locates the search text and replaces it with new text that you specify. For example, in the Classics database there is no consistency in the spelling of the word Incorporated. Sometimes it is spelled out completely, and sometimes it is abbreviated (Inc.). You can search for all the occurrences when the word is abbreviated and then automatically replace those abbreviations with the complete spelling.

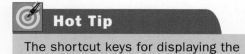

S TEP-BY-STEP 3.4

1. Click in the first row in the *Publisher* field.

2. Open the **Edit** menu and choose **Find**. Click the **Replace** tab to display the dialog box shown in Figure 3-5.

> **Hot Tip**
>
> The shortcut keys for displaying the Replace dialog box are **Ctrl + H**.

3. Notice that the *Find What:* box still contains the text from your last search. Key **Inc.** to replace the old search text.

4. Click in the *Replace With:* box to select it and key **Incorporated**.

5. The *Look In:* box should display *Publisher*. The *Match:* box should display *Any Part of Field*. The *Search:* box should display *All*.

6. Click the **Find Next** button. Access selects the entry *Random House, Inc.* in the second record in the *Publisher* column because it contains the abbreviation *Inc.* Do not be concerned that the entire entry is selected.

7. Click the **Replace** button in the dialog box.

> **Computer Concepts**
>
> If you change your mind about a replacement, you can use the Undo command to reverse the action. Remember, you must choose the Undo command before editing another record.

FIGURE 3-5

Replace tab in the Find and Replace dialog box

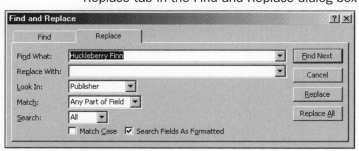

8. If necessary, click the up arrow in the vertical scroll bar so you can see the second record in the Publisher column. Notice that *Inc.* was replaced with *Incorporated*, but the remaining text in the entry (*Random House,*) did not change.

Computer Concepts

There may be times when you do not want to replace the selected text. On those occasions, simply click the **Find Next** button to go to the next occurrence. No changes are made unless you click the **Replace** button.

9. Notice, too, that the next occurrence of *Inc.* is selected. When you pressed the **Replace** button in step 7, Access automatically replaced the appropriate text and performed the Find Next function.

10. Click the **Replace All** button. A message is displayed warning that you will not be able to undo the replace operation. Click **Yes**. Access replaces all occurrences of *Inc.* with *Incorporated* throughout the column.

Replace All

Computer Concepts

When you use the Replace option, you can view each change and confirm the replacements individually. You should use the Replace All option only when you are confident about making all the replacements without reviewing them first. You can use the Match Case option to aid in preventing inadvertent replacements. Match Case allows you to be more specific in what you replace and you won't need to approve each replacement individually.

11. Scroll up and down to view all the entries in the column. Notice that there are no more abbreviations for *Incorporated*.

12. Click the **Cancel** button to close the dialog box, then close the table. When prompted to save the changes to the design of the table, click **Yes**. Leave the database open for the next Step-by-Step.

Create a Query

Although the Find command provides an easy way to find data, you may need to locate multiple records, all containing the same values. If you have a large database, and several records contain the value you are searching for, this is another task that can be tedious. In this case, you can use a *query*, which enables you to locate multiple records matching a specified criteria. Remember, you learned in Lesson 1 that Query is one of the database objects displayed in the Objects bar. The query provides a way for you to ask a question about the information stored in a database table(s). Access searches for and retrieves data from the table(s) to answer your question.

To illustrate, consider the following example. Suppose you just read a book by Charles Dickens. You really enjoyed the book and you would like to read another book authored by him. You could locate the books by Charles Dickens one at a time in the Classics database by using the Find command. But a query makes your task easier, and also creates a list of the titles for you.

When you create a query, you must identify all the fields for which you want to display information. For example, you might want only the title and the author name to display. The order in which you select the fields will be the order in which the information is displayed in the query results.

S TEP-BY-STEP ▷ 3.5

1. Click the **Queries** button on the Objects bar. The query objects are displayed in the Database objects window. Note that there are currently no query objects for this database.

2. Double-click **Create query in Design View**. The Show Table dialog box shown in Figure 3-6 is displayed.

FIGURE 3-6
Show Table dialog box

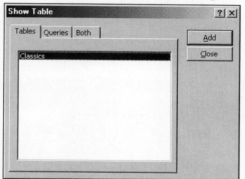

3. Click the **Add** button in the dialog box. This adds the fields from the selected table (*Classics*) to your new query.

4. Click the **Close** button in the dialog box to close the Show Table dialog box.
   The fields available from the *Classics* table are listed in a dialog box and the query grid shown in Figure 3-7 is displayed.

5. In the query grid, click the down arrow in the first column next to *Field*. Choose **Author Last** from the drop-down list.

6. Click in the first column next to *Criteria*. Key **Dickens** and press **Enter**. This tells Access to display any records written by authors with the last name *Dickens*. Access places quotations around the text.

Computer Concepts

Because databases often include more than one table, you can choose the table you want to use for the query. In this case, the database has only one table—Classics—and it is already selected.

FIGURE 3-7
Query window

Fields from the Classics table

Query grid

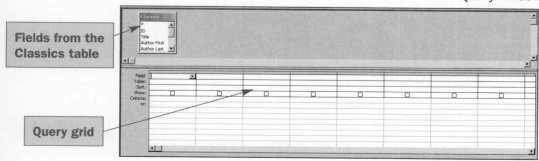

371

7. Click in the second column next to *Field*, click the down arrow, and then select **Title** from the drop-down list. Your screen should match Figure 3-8.

8. Click the **Save** button on the toolbar. Because the query has not yet been saved, the Save As dialog box is displayed. Key **Dickens Query** and click **OK**.

FIGURE 3-8
Completed query grid

9. Open the **File** menu and choose **Close**. The query Design view is closed and the Datasheet window is displayed. The Dickens Query is in the list of Query objects.

10. Select **Dickens Query** in the list of objects and then click the **Open** button in the Datasheet window. The results of the query are displayed as illustrated in Figure 3-9.

11. Close the query. Leave the database open for the next Step-by-Step.

Hot Tip

You can also double-click the query object to open it.

Did You Know?

You can save a table, form, or query as a Web page. Choose **Save As HTML** on the File menu. This command will start the Publish to the Web Wizard. Follow the steps through the wizard to create your Web page.

FIGURE 3-9
Dickens Query

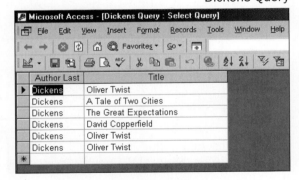

Create a Report

You can print a database in Datasheet view, but when you do, all of the data contained in the database is printed. This can be very cumbersome if the database is large, or if you only need certain information from the database. A *report* is a database object which allows you to organize, summarize, and print all or a portion of the data in a database. You can create a report based on a table or a query.

Although you can prepare a report manually, the Report Wizard provides an easy and fast way to design and create a report. The wizard will ask you questions about which data you want to include in the report and how you want to format that data. Most of the format options that the wizard will present are beyond the scope of this lesson. More than likely, when the options are presented in the wizard dialog boxes, you can ignore most of them.

One of the format options you will apply in the report is page orientation. The orientation determines how the report will print on the page. *Landscape orientation* formats the report with the long edge of the page at the top. *Portrait orientation* formats the report with the short edge of the page at the top.

STEP-BY-STEP ▷ 3.6

1. Click the **Reports** button on the Object bar. The report objects are displayed in the **Database objects** window. There are currently no reports to display for this database.

2. Double-click **Create report by using wizard**. The Report Wizard dialog box shown in Figure 3-10 is displayed. If necessary, click the down arrow in the text box under *Tables/Queries* and select **Table:Classics**.

3. Choose the field names to be included in the report:
   a. Select **Author First**, then click **>** to move the field name to *Selected Fields*. The field name is displayed under *Selected Fields*.
   b. Select **Author Last** and then click **>**.
   c. Select **Title**, then click **>**.
   d. Select **Price** and then click **>**.

FIGURE 3-10
Report Wizard dialog box

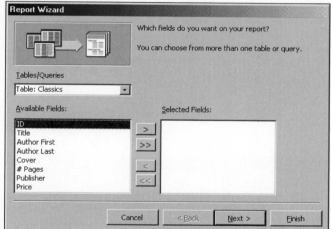

4. Then click the **Next** button. The dialog box shown in Figure 3-11 is displayed and it offers options for grouping a report by fields. With this report, these options are not needed.

5. Click the **Next** button. The dialog box shown in Figure 3-12 is displayed, and it offers options for the sort order of the records. Click

the down arrow in the first box and select **Author Last**. Click the down arrow in the second box and select **Title**. Leave the order at the default setting Ascending. If there are two or more books by the same author, the titles will be ordered first by author last name, then by the book title.

FIGURE 3-11
Grouping level options

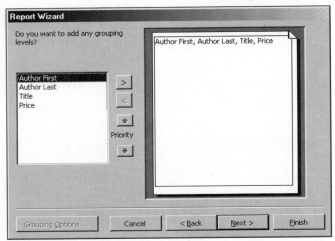

FIGURE 3-12
Sort order options

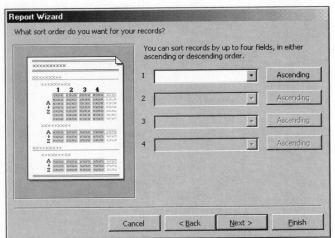

6. Click the **Next** button. The next dialog box, shown in Figure 3-13, offers options for layout and orientation. If it is not already selected, click the Tabular option. Then select the **Landscape** option under *Orientation*. Notice that the option to adjust the field width to fit all fields on a page is selected.

7. Click the **Next** button. The dialog box shown in Figure 3-14 is displayed, and it offers options for styles. Your dialog box may have a different style selected. Select the **Casual** style.

FIGURE 3-13
Layout and orientation options

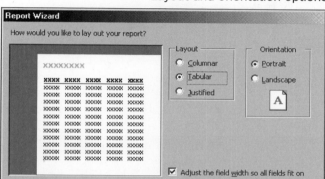

FIGURE 3-14
Style options

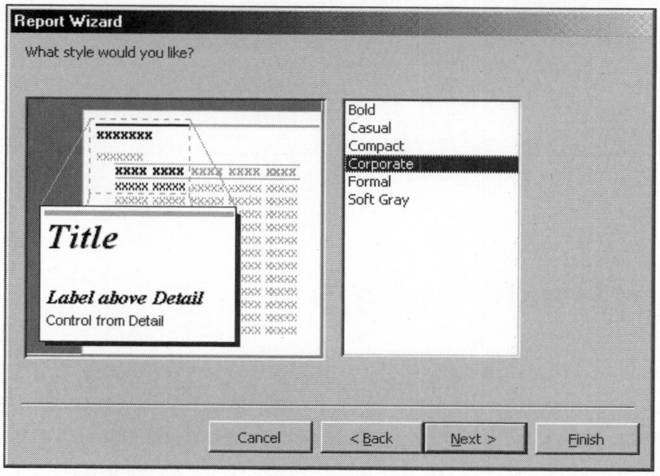

8. Click the **Next** button. The last dialog box for the Report Wizard shown in Figure 3-15 asks you what title you want to use for the report. The title currently displayed is Classics because that is the name of the table. Change the title to **Classic Books**.

9. If necessary, click the option **Preview the report** to select it. Then click the **Finish** button. A preview of the report is displayed in Print Preview.

10. Click the down arrow to the right of the Zoom box on the Standard toolbar and select **75%**. The preview of the report is reduced. If necessary, reduce the zoom more so you can see the entire page.

11. Click the **Close** button on the Print Preview toolbar. The report is displayed in Design view.

12. Click the **Save** button to save the report. Then open the **File** menu and choose **Close** to close the report.

13. Notice that the Classic Books report is listed in the Database objects Reports window. Close the database.

FIGURE 3-15
Title dialog box

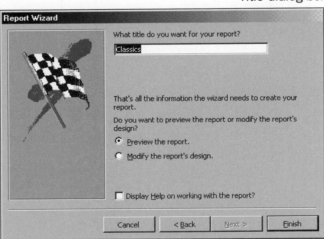

Create Mailing Labels

Because databases often contain data regarding names and addresses, it is common to create mailing labels based on the database information. For example, if you maintain your friends' names and addresses in a database file, you can quickly print labels to mail greeting cards. You can print labels for selected friends or for the entire database. In the next Step-by-Step, you will use the report feature to create mailing labels. You will create a new report using a different wizard.

STEP-BY-STEP 3.7

1. Open **Step3-7** from the data files.

2. If necessary, click the **Reports** button on the Object bar. There are no reports to display for this database.

3. If necessary, Click the **New** button in the Database objects toolbar. The New Report dialog box is displayed.

4. Select **Label Wizard**. Click the down arrow in the list box below and select **Mailing List**. When

your dialog box looks like the one illustrated in Figure 3-16, click **OK**.

5. The Label Wizard dialog box is displayed. If necessary, select **Sheet feed** under *Label Type*. And, if necessary, select **Avery** in the *Filter by manufacturer:* list box. Scroll down in the *first* list box above and select Product number **3110** (or another product number with three labels across and no larger than 1 ¼" x 2 ⅜").

6. When your dialog box looks like Figure 3-17, click **Next**.

FIGURE 3-16
New Report dialog box

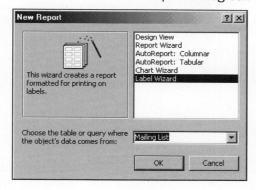

FIGURE 3-17
Label Wizard dialog box displaying selected label options

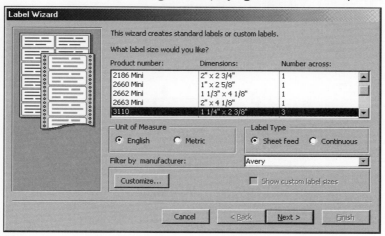

7. The next step in the wizard is to describe the text appearance on the mailing label. If necessary, change the *Font size:* to **10**. If necessary, change the other options so your dialog box looks like the one shown in Figure 3-18. Then, click **Next**.

8. The next step in the wizard is to choose the fields and from the *Available Fields* list construct a prototype (a sample) for the labels. Select the fields as shown in Figure 3-19. (Hint: Select the field name from the *Available Fields* list, and then click **>**. Leave a blank space between fields, and press **Enter** to move to the next line. It is not necessary to key a comma after the field *City*.) When your dialog box looks like Figure 3-19, click **Next**.

FIGURE 3-18

Label Wizard dialog box displaying selected font options

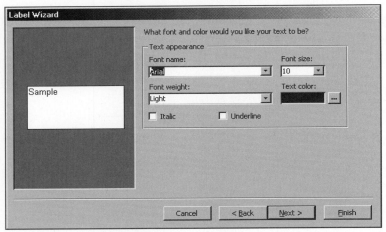

FIGURE 3-19

Label Wizard dialog box displaying a prototype label

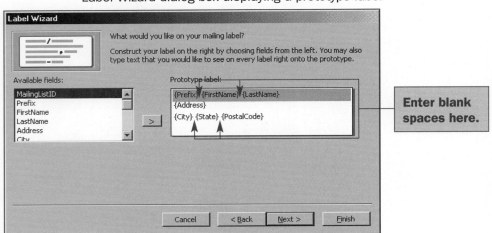

9. The next step in the wizard is to sort the labels. Scroll down and select the **PostalCode** field from the *Available Fields* list and then click **>**. The field name is moved to the *Sort by* list. When your dialog box looks like Figure 3-20, click **Next**.

10. The last step in the wizard is to name the report. You can assign a name to the report if desired, but the proposed name *Labels Mailing List* is good. Click **Finish**. If you get a

message indicating that some data may not be displayed, click **OK**. The labels are displayed as they will print. If you were printing the labels, you would put the label sheets in your printer and choose the command to print.

11. Open the **File** menu and choose **Close** to close the report. Notice that the **Labels Mailing List report** is listed in the Database objects Reports window. Close the database.

FIGURE 3-20
Label Wizard dialog box displaying the selected sort options

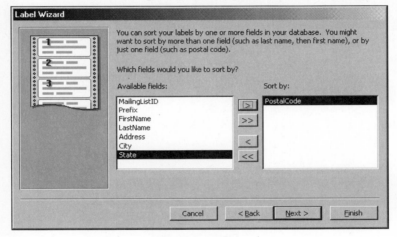

Summary

In this lesson, you learned:

■ You can sort records in Datasheet view in either ascending or descending order.

■ The Find command can save you time looking for records and specific values in a table. The Replace command can save you time finding and replacing specific text.

■ You can create a query to find records that match specified criteria. Access searches for and retrieves data from the table(s) that match the criteria you identify.

■ A report allows you to organize, summarize, and print all or a portion of the data in a database. You can choose a wizard to guide you through the process in creating and formatting a report.

■ When you want to create mailing labels, you create a report object and you use the Label wizard.

VOCABULARY REVIEW

Define the following terms:

Ascending order	Orientation	Query
Descending order	Portrait orientation	Report
Landscape orientation		

LESSON 3 REVIEW QUESTIONS

TRUE/FALSE

Circle T if the statement is true or F if the statement is false.

T   F   1.   If you change your mind after you sort data, you can choose the Undo command to return the data to its original order.

T   F   2.   You can use the Find command to locate specific data in a particular field or anywhere in the table.

T   F   3.   The Replace command replaces existing data with new data.

T   F   4.   You can use the Find command to make a list of multiple records that match specific criteria.

T   F   5.   The Report Wizard guides you through the process of organizing and summarizing data in a database.

FILL IN THE BLANK

Complete the following sentences by writing the correct word or words in the blanks provided.

1. If you have several records in a database, you can easily locate data you are searching for by using the _____ command.

2. If you want to sort data with the most recent date at the top of the list, you would choose _____ order.

3. A(n) _____ enables you to locate multiple records, all matching the same criteria.

4. _____ orientation prints the report with the long edge of the page at the top.

5. You can base a report on either a(n) _____ or a(n) _____.

LESSON 3 PROJECTS

PROJECT 3-1

1. Open **Project3-1** from the data files. Open the **Members** table.

2. You want to make sure that you added a new member to the database. Find the record for *Sam Martin*.

3. Oak Creek is growing rapidly and has earned another Zip code. Find all the 43210 Zip codes in the table and change them to 43213.

4. You would like to have a list of member names and phone numbers to hand out to all members. Create a report as follows:
   A. Start the Report Wizard and choose the **Members** table.
   B. Select only the **First Name**, **Last Name**, and **Phone** fields.
   C. Do not group the report.
   D. Sort the report by **Last Name** in ascending order.
   E. Use the **Tabular** format and **Portrait** orientation.
   F. Choose the **Bold** style.
   G. Name the report **Members Phone List** and preview the report.

5. Close the preview, and then close the database.

PROJECT 3-2

1. Open **Project3-2** database, and then open the **Collection** table.

2. Sort the table by Category in ascending order. How many adventure films do you have in the collection?

3. Sort the table by Length in descending order. What is the longest film in the collection?

381

4. Close the table without saving design changes.

5. For an upcoming society meeting, you want to see the titles, directors, and lengths of all foreign films in the collection. Follow these steps to create your query:
   A. Create a new query in Design view using the **Collection** table.
   B. Add the **Category**, **Title**, **Director**, and **Length** fields to the query, in that order.
   C. In the *Category Criteria* box, key **Foreign**.
   D. Save the query as **Foreign Query**.

6. Open the query. How many foreign titles do you have in the collection? Close the query results.

7. You are considering doing a special event on several directors. Create a report that will show you what films you have by each director. Follow these steps to create the report:
   A. Create a new report using the Report Wizard based on the **Collection** table. Select the **Director**, **Title**, and **Year** fields for the report, in that order.
   B. Do not add any grouping levels.
   C. Sort the report by **Director**.
   D. Choose the **Columnar** layout and **Portrait** orientation.
   E. Use the **Compact** style.
   F. Name the report **Directors Report** and preview the report.

8. Close the preview and then close the database.

PROJECT 3-3

1. Open **Project3-3** from the data files.

2. Use the Label Wizard to create mailing labels. Follow these steps to create the labels:
   A. Base the labels on the **Members** table.
   B. Choose the **Avery** Product number **3612** (or another product number with two labels across and no larger than 2" x 3 ½").
   C. Change the font size to **11** pt.
   D. The prototype should display the following fields in the format shown:
      First Name Last Name
      Address
      City State Zip
      There is no need to add a comma between the city and state.
   E. Sort the labels by **Last Name**.
   F. Name the labels **Members Labels** and preview the report.

3. Close the preview and then close the database.

WEB PROJECT

Use Web search tools to find information on the worst natural disasters of the twentieth century in the United States. These disasters can include earthquakes, tornadoes, hurricanes, winter storms, and so on. Create categories for each type of disaster you identify. Try to find as much information about the disasters as you can: injuries, deaths, property damage, location of the disaster, date and time of the disaster, and so on. Create a database table to store the information you find. Sort the data to find the most injuries and the greatest property damage. Create a query that locates all natural disasters in a particular state, such as California. Create a report from selected data in your table.

TEAMWORK PROJECT

If you have completed any of the Web Projects in this course, you have visited a number of sites and employed a number of useful tools such as search engines, directories, and almanacs. With the help of a classmate, create a database table to store data on some of the tools you have used and sites you have visited. If you have not completed any of the Web Projects, you can still explore the Web now on your own to try out various search tools and locate interesting and useful sites. Or, if you do not have Web access, create a database that stores reference materials you use regularly in your classes, such as encyclopedias, dictionaries, almanacs, and so on. Then create a report from your data.

Follow these steps:

1. With your teammate, make a list of the Web search tools (or other reference materials) you have used in this course. You can categorize them as search engines, directories, or other online resources. Record the URLs of these various resources, and make a few notes about what type of information you can get from each search tool. Create a database table to store the information.

2. Create another table to store information on various sites (or articles) you have visited. Record the URL of the site and what type of data you found there. Have your teammate help you remember the sites.

3. Create a report for each table so that you will have a hard copy of useful tools and sites.

CRITICAL THINKING

Creating a query isn't the only way you can display specific records in a database. You can use what is called a filter. Open the **Project3-1** database and then open the **Collection** table. Click in any Category field that reads *Shakespeare*. Click the toolbar button just to the right of the Sort Descending button. What happens to the table?

Use the Help files in Access to find out what kind of a filter you just applied. How do you redisplay all the records in the table?

383

COMMAND SUMMARY

FEATURE	MENU COMMAND	KEYSTROKE	TOOLBAR BUTTON	LESSON
Clipboard, clear all			Clear All	2
Column, change width	Format, Column Width			1
Copy record	Edit, Copy	Ctrl + C		2
Cut record	Edit, Cut	Ctrl + X		2
Database, create new	File, New	Ctrl + N		1
Database, open		Ctrl + O		1
Datasheet view, change to	View, Datasheet View			1
Design view, change to	View, Design View		Design	1
Find data	Edit, Find	Ctrl + F		3
Find next item	Edit, Find	Shift + F4		3
First Record				2
Form, create new	Insert, Form		New	2
Form, open			Open	1
Help	Help, Microsoft Access Help	F1	Type a question for help	1
Last Record				2
Next Record				2
Paste record	Edit, Paste or Paste Append	Ctrl + V		2
Previous Record				2
Query, new			New	1
Query, open			Open	1
Record, add in Datasheet view	Insert, New Record			2
Record, delete in Datasheet view	Edit, Delete Record	Delete		2
Replace data	Edit, Replace	Ctrl + H		3
Report, new			New	1
Report, open			Open	1

FEATURE	MENU COMMAND	KEYSTROKES	TOOLBAR BUTTON	LESSON
Row, delete in Design view	Edit, Delete Rows		⊟→	1
Row, insert in Design view	Insert, Rows		⊟←	1
Save table design	File, Save	Ctrl + S	🖫	1
Sort records	Records, Sort, Sort Ascending or Descending		↕↓, Z↓	3
Sort, remove	Records, Remove Filter/Sort			3
Table, close	File, Close			1
Table, new			🖽 New	1
Table, open			🗐 Open	1
Undo	Edit, Undo	Ctrl + Z	↜	2

REVIEW QUESTIONS

TRUE/FALSE

Circle T if the statement is true or F if the statement is false.

T F **1.** Databases and spreadsheets are very similar in structure.

T F **2.** The first objects you create in a database are the forms that hold the data.

T F **3.** If you delete a field in Design view, you automatically delete all the contents of that field as well.

T F **4.** You can insert a new record anywhere in an Access table.

T F **5.** To move a column, you must be in Design view.

T F **6.** Data that you enter in a form is automatically stored in the table used to create the form.

T F **7.** If you want records in a table to appear in alphabetical order by last name, you have to enter them that way.

T F **8.** You can often find a record you want to edit by simply scrolling through the database, no matter how large the database is.

T F **9.** To locate all records in a database where the state is California, you would use a query.

T F **10.** A report can be based on either a form or a table.

MATCHING

Match the correct term in Column 1 to its description in Column 2.

Column 1

___ **1.** New Record

___ **2.** Query

___ **3.** Database

___ **4.** Find

___ **5.** Field

___ **6.** Report

___ **7.** Field selector

___ **8.** Entry

___ **9.** Record selector

___**10.** Record

Column 2

A. Feature that allows you to locate specific data in a field or table

B. An object that allows you to select, format, and print only specific fields from a table

C. A group of fields

D. Data keyed in a cell

E. The button you click before adding a new row

F. The box at the left edge of a row

G. An object that allows you to locate multiple records matching specified criteria

H. A single piece of information about an item or person

I. Uniquely identifies each record in a table

J. The box containing the field name

K. A collection of related information organized for rapid search and retrieval

CROSS-CURRICULAR PROJECTS

MATH

Create your own math test using a database to store the math problems. Use a different table for each type of problem (word problems, algebra, simple equations, and so on). Each table should have three fields for three levels of difficulty (easy, average, and difficult). Enter about ten problems at each level of difficulty. Then create reports to print out "tests" that you can use for study. Try mixing the types of problems, creating separate tests for different levels of difficulty, or creating a test with only the problems with which you have difficulty. Ask classmates what sort of tests they might need to aid them with their studies and create tests to meet their specific criteria.

SOCIAL STUDIES

Choose five countries throughout the world that you are interested in knowing more about or that are currently in the news. Create a database to store data on each country, such as what continent it is located on, the land area, head of government, type of government, capital, largest city, principal language, unit of currency, population, literacy rate, principal industries, and so on. You can find this information in an almanac or using a Web search tool. Sort the data by country. Create a report to display data on a particular field of interest to you, such as population or type of government.

SCIENCE

Trees are an important part of the ecosystem. Survey a nearby park or greenbelt area to find out how many and what type of trees are growing there. If necessary, use a field guide to help you identify the types of trees. You can get a field guide from your local library, or you may be able to locate Web sites that provide similar information. (With a field guide, you can determine tree type based on information about the bark, type and shape of the leaves, or the shape of the tree.) Estimate the circumference of each tree and note whether each tree looks healthy or stressed. The field guide will give you criteria for making this evaluation. Create a database to store your data. Sort the table by tree type. Create a report to summarize your data.

LANGUAGE ARTS

In 1999, the Modern Library published a list of the most important books of the twentieth century. Use Web search tools to locate this list. Print the book titles from the Web. Using any other reference tools you need, find out the author's name and date of publication for each book. Create a database to store the data, and add a field to the table with the name **I have read**. Use a Yes/No data type for this field and place a check in this field for all the books on this list you have read. Create a query that lists the books you have read (in the Criteria box of the *I have read* field, key **Yes** to show all records where the check box is checked). Create a report from your query.

PROJECTS

PROJECT 1

1. Open **Project1** from the data files. This database stores information for the Lakeside Wildlife Center, a small zoo in Lakeside.

2. You need a way to store information about the volunteers who work in the gift shops and help the zoo employees. Use the table wizard to create a new table. Choose **Personal** for the table category, and then select the **Addresses** sample table. Add the following fields to your new table:

    Address ID
    First Name
    Last Name
    Address
    City

State/Province
Postal Code
Email Address
Home Phone

3. Name the table **Volunteer Addresses** and let the wizard set a primary key for you. The database is not related to the table *Specimens*.

4. Enter the following records into the table in the correct fields:

Marge Gonzalez
1203 Forest
Lakeside, OH 44131-0987
MGonzalez@sim.net
555-8802

Fran Michaels
368 Warren
Lakeside, OH 44132-0987
Michaels@tir.com
555-5910

Dave Schubert
55 Maxwell
Lakeside, OH 44131-0966
DASchubert@worldnet.net
555-7812

5. You forgot to create a field for the date each volunteer joined the Wildlife Center. Close the table, then go to Design view and insert a field named **Since** at the end of the field list with the Date/Time format. Select the **Short Date** format. Then, save the changes, switch to Datasheet view, and insert the following dates for your volunteers:

Marge Gonzalez   **9/9/95**
Fran Michaels   **7/14/89**
Dave Schubert   **10/18/00**

6. Fran Michaels' husband has just retired and wants to become a volunteer, too. Copy Fran's record and paste it at the end of the table. Change the First Name entry in the new record (Address ID 4) to **Colin** and enter today's date as the Since date.

7. Close the table and then close the database.

PROJECT 2

1. Open **Project2** from the data files. This is a revised database for the Lakeside Wildlife Center, with the volunteer addresses added.

2. You decide a form would help you enter volunteer data more easily. Using the Form Wizard and the following steps, create a form based on the *Volunteer Addresses* table:
   A. Select all fields for the form.
   B. Use the **Columnar** layout and the **Expedition** style.
   C. Name the form **Volunteer Form** and display the form for data entry.

3. Move to a new record in the form and enter the following volunteer information in the appropriate fields:

   Treva Janssen
   340 Kittimer
   Lakeside, OH 44131-0987
   TJ309@ecr.com
   555-9505
   Since: 2/5/96

   Ben Jacobi
   4908 Terrace
   Lakeside, OH 44131-0996
   BJacobi@ix.net.com
   555-2385
   Since: 6/12/98

4. Close the form.

5. Marge Gonazlez has decided to retire. Delete her record.

6. You have entered the wrong phone number for Fran and Colin Michaels. Display both of their records and change the number to **555-5912**.

7. You want to mail some information to each of the volunteers. Create mailing labels for the volunteers following these steps:
   A. Use the Label Wizard.
   B. Use the data in the **Volunteer Addresses** table.
   C. Select the Avery labels, product number 3110 (or another product number with three labels across and no larger than 1 ¼" x 2 ⅜").
   D. If necessary, change the font size to **10 pt**.
   E. Set up the prototype using the appropriate fields for mailing labels.
   F. Sort the labels by last name.
   G. Save the report as **Volunteer Labels**.

8. Preview the report and close it. Then close the database.

PROJECT 3

1. Open **Project3** from the data file, then open the **Specimens** table.

2. Adjust column widths to the best fit for all fields. Move the **Group** column to the right of the **ID** column.

3. In Design view, change the name of the Status field to **Endangered**, and then change the data type for that field to **Yes/No**. At the end of the field list, add a new field titled **Births/Hatchings** with the **Number** data type.

4. Switch to Datasheet view. To make it easy to enter the births and hatchings for each species, hide the *Species Name*, *Order*, *Family*, and then the *Habitat*, *Endangered*, and *Number* columns. Then enter the following new zoo members in the *Births/Hatchings* column:

Sicilian donkey	1	Umbrella cockatoo	2
White-tailed deer	2	Lion-tailed macaque	5
African lion	2	Wild turkey	3
Bald eagle	1	European fallow deer	1
Cougar	1	White-handed Lars gibbon	4
Bison	1		

5. Unhide the hidden columns.

6. The new column entry and the column name change altered the size of the columns. Correct the column widths as necessary for best fit.

7. In the process of entering the data, you noticed some errors in the table. Fix them as follows:
   A. Use Find to locate the entry *Turkey vulture* and change it to **Black vulture**.
   B. *Felidae* has been entered as *Felidea* throughout the table. Use Replace to change *Felidea* to **Felidae** wherever it occurs in the *Family* field.
   C. Go to record 38 and change the *Group* entry to **Birds**. Whoops! That's the wrong record. Undo the change, move to the next record, and replace the *Group* for the Mandarin duck with **Birds**.

8. Close the table and save changes when prompted, then close the database.

PROJECT 4

1. Open **Project4** from the data files and then open the **Specimens** table.

2. Several people have recently asked you some specific questions about the zoo's specimens. Use the sort feature to find the answers to these questions:
   A. How many Reptile specimens does the zoo have?
   B. Does the zoo have any ring-tailed lemurs? If so, how many?
   C. What species has the largest population? (*Hint:* Sort in the Number field in descending order and then find the common name at the top of the table.)
   D. Sort in ascending order on the ID field to return the table to its original order.

3. You want to know how many members of the Carnivora order the zoo currently has. Create a query in Design view for the Specimens table as follows:
   A. Add the **Order**, **Common Name**, **Species Name**, and **Number** fields to the query.
   B. In the *Order* column, click in the *Criteria* box and key **Carnivora**.
   C. Save the query as **Carnivores Query** and close it.

4. Open the **Carnivores Query**. How many different species does the zoo have? How many carnivores altogether? Close the query.

5. Create a report to show all the animals in each group. Follow these steps:
   A. Start the Report Wizard and select the **Specimens** table for the report.
   B. Select the **Group**, **Common Name**, **Endangered**, and **Number** fields for the report.
   C. In the next dialog box, if necessary select **Group** and then click the > button to group the records by this field.
   D. In the next dialog box, choose to sort by **Common Name**.
   E. If necessary, choose the **Stepped** layout and the **Compact** style.
   F. Name the report **Animals by Group** and preview the report. Use the navigation controls at the bottom of the report to view the second page of the report.

6. Close the preview window and then close the database.

SIMULATION

You have created a database to store trail and other information for your local rail-trails organization. In this simulation, you will add a new table to the database, modify an existing table, and create a query and a report from the data.

JOB 1

Your supervisor has asked you to create a table that can be used to store membership data. In this job, you will create the table, set up a form for data entry, and enter a few records to test your fields.

1. Open **Job1** from the data files.

2. Use the Table Wizard to create a new table. Choose the **Business** category and then the sample table **Contacts**. Include the following fields in your new table:

Contact ID
First Name
Last Name
Address
City
State/Province
Postal Code

3. Name the table **Membership** and let the wizard set a primary key for you. The new table is not related to the table *Ohio Trails*.

4. Before you enter any records, switch to Design view and enter the new fields **Type, Level**, and **Paid**. The field properties for the *Type* and *Level* fields should be **Text**. The field properties for the *Paid* field should be **Currency**.

5. While in Datasheet view, make the following changes:
   A. Click the **Paid** field. In the field properties box, click in the *Decimal Places* box and choose **0** in the list.
   B. Click in the **State/Province** field. Specify a field size of **2**.
   C. Click in the **Contact ID** field and edit the field name to **Member ID**.

6. Switch to Datasheet view and enter two sample records using fictitious information for the first name, last name, address, city, state, and postal code. In the first record, specify that the type of membership is **Family**. This member's level is **Committed**, and the member paid **$25**. In the second record, specify that the member type is **Donation**. The donation is **$150**, and the member is a **Competition** level biker.

7. You have decided the *Level* field might be confusing to use, since there are many members whose levels you don't know. Delete the *Level* field and its data.

8. Use the Form Wizard to create a form from the *Membership* table using all fields. Choose the layout and style of the form as desired. Save the form as **Membership**. Close the form.

9. Open the **Membership** table. While you are in Datasheet view, delete your sample records. You are now ready to record the membership data when your supervisor gives it to you.

10. Close the table and leave the database open for the next Job.

JOB 2

1. Open the **Ohio Trails** table from the **Job1** database. This table stores a lot of information about Ohio's rail trails.

2. Adjust column widths to their best fit so you can see all of the data.

3. Three trails have not yet been entered into the table. Copy the last record in the database, and paste a copy of it as a new record. Make the following changes to the record you pasted into the table:
   A. Change the trail name to **Westerville Bikeway**. Change the *Start* entry to **Westerville**.
   B. Change the county to **Franklin**. In the *Uses* column, delete the comma after *bike* as well as the rest of the field entry.

4. Add the remaining two records.

Trail Name:	**Wolf Creek Bikeway**	Trail Name:	**Zanesville Riverfront Bikepath**
Start:	**Trotwood**	Start:	**Zanesville**
End:	**Verona**	End:	
County:	**Montgomery**	County:	**Muskingum**
Length:	**13**	Length:	**2.9**
Surface:	**Asphalt**	Surface:	**Asphalt**
Uses:	**Walk, bike, cc ski**	Uses:	**Walk, bike, skate**

5. You've received a lot of phone queries about wheelchair accessibility on the trails. You decide you'd better add this information to your table. In Design view, insert a field named **Wheelchair** above the *Uses* field and use the Yes/No data type for the new field.

6. Save your change and return to Datasheet view. All trails with an asphalt surface are wheelchair accessible. Insert check marks in the *Wheelchair* column for all trails with Asphalt surfaces. (You should also insert check marks if the surface is a combination, such as Asphalt/crushed stone.)

7. Sort the trails in ascending order by County. Sort the trails in descending order by Length. Sort the trails in ascending order by the ID field to restore the table to the original order.

8. Save design changes and close the table. Leave the database open for the next job.

JOB 3

This job challenges you to create a more complex query and then use it to create a report.

1. Create a query to list trails that are longer than 10 miles and have an asphalt surface. Create the query in Design view and follow these steps to create the query:
   A. Using the **Ohio Trails** table, add the **Trail Name**, **Start**, **Length**, and **Surface** fields.
   B. In the *Trail Name* column, click in the *Sort* box and choose **Ascending**.
   C. In the *Length* column, click in the *Criteria* box and key **>10**.
   D. In the *Surface* column, click in the *Criteria* box and key **Asphalt**.
   E. Close the query. Save the query as **>10 Asphalt Query**.

2. Open the **>10 Asphalt Query**. Your query results should show the trail names in alphabetical order, with all lengths more than 10 miles and all surfaces asphalt. Close the query.

3. Create the report as follows:
   A. Start the Report Wizard and specify the query **>10 Asphalt Query** as the record source if necessary.
   B. Select all fields. You do not have to group the fields, and you have already sorted the data by Trail Name in the query.
   C. Select a layout and style for the report.
   D. Name the report **Long Trails** and preview the report.

4. Close the preview, save the report if necessary, and close the report.

5. Close the database and exit Access.

PORTFOLIO CHECKLIST

Include the following files from this unit in your portfolio.

___ Addresses   ___ Project4

___ Job1   ___ Step2-1

___ Project1-2   ___ Step3-1

___ Project2-2   ___ Step3-7

___ Project3-3

OUTLOOK

lesson 1

Working with Outlook

1 hr

Estimated Time for Unit: 1 hour

WORKING WITH OUTLOOK

OBJECTIVES

Upon completion of this lesson, you should be able to:

- Identify the parts of the Outlook screen.

- Schedule and manage appointments.

- Create and manage contacts.

- Organize and manage tasks.

- Send and receive e-mail.

🕐 **Estimated Time: 1 hour**

VOCABULARY

Ascending order

Contacts

Descending order

Event

Field

Form

Item

Microsoft Outlook is a program that can help you organize your appointments, addresses, tasks, and e-mail messages. Outlook stores information in folders. Each Outlook folder can organize different types of information and makes it easy for you to store many kinds of personal and business information and then display it at the touch of a button. A particular piece of information stored in an Outlook folder is called an *item*.

Identify the Parts of the Outlook Screen

When you launch Outlook, a screen similar to the one shown in Figure 1-1 is displayed. Like other Office programs, Outlook displays both a menu bar and the Standard toolbar. You can display or hide toolbars by opening the View menu, choosing Toolbars, and then selecting the toolbar name. The Preview Pane enables you to preview the content of any item. You can display or hide the Preview Pane by opening the View menu and choosing Preview Pane. You will learn more about each part of the window in this lesson.

Hot Tip

Your Outlook Bar may display different icons than shown in Figure 1-1. You can customize the Outlook Bar by adding or removing shortcut icons. To add a new shortcut, right-click the background of the Outlook Bar, choose **Outlook Bar Shortcut**, and in the Add to Outlook Bar dialog box select the folder you want to add. To delete a shortcut, right-click the shortcut and choose **Remove from Outlook Bar**.

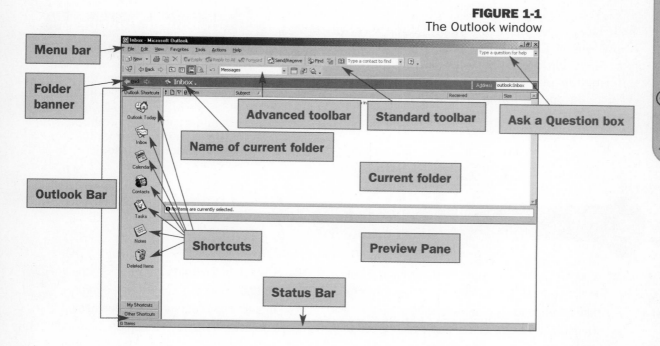

FIGURE 1-1
The Outlook window

There are different Outlook folders, and you use each one to perform a different function. The name of the current Outlook folder appears in the folder banner, which is the shaded area located at the top of the window. Figure 1-1 shows the Inbox folder. If your current folder isn't the Inbox folder, your screen will display a different folder.

Table 1-1 lists some of the Outlook folders and how you use them. You can quickly access different folders using the shortcuts in the Outlook bar at the left of the window. To select what displays in the Outlook window, you can change the view settings for each file folder.

TABLE 1-1
Outlook folders and their functions

OUTLOOK BAR SHORTCUT/FOLDER NAME	USE THIS FOLDER TO
Inbox	Send, receive, and organize e-mail messages
Calendar	Schedule appointments, meetings, and events
Contacts	Store information such as names, addresses, phone numbers, and e-mail addresses
Outlook Today	Get an overview of some of your current Outlook information
Tasks	Create lists of things you need to do
Deleted Items	Store items you have deleted from other folders

You will not use all of Outlook's folders in this lesson, but in the following Step-by-Step you will take a short tour of Outlook by opening several Outlook folders. Most Outlook folders can be customized to display information in a folder in a number of different ways. When you open a folder, you will see the view that was used the last time that folder was opened.

Computer Concepts

Clicking the **Outlook Today** shortcut in the Outlook Bar will show you all tasks and appointments for the current day. It will also indicate how many new e-mail messages you have. You can set this page to be the opening page when you launch Outlook.

STEP-BY-STEP ▷ 1.1

1. Launch Outlook. If your computer is on a network, you may be prompted to enter your profile name and a password when launching Outlook. If a dialog box appears asking you to make Outlook your default program for e-mail, Calendar and Contacts, click **No**.

Hot Tip

You can quickly launch Outlook by clicking the **Outlook** button on the Windows taskbar.

Computer Concepts

AutoArchive is a default feature that automatically clears out old and expired items from folders, such as old e-mails or expired meetings scheduled on the calendar. If a dialog box appears asking you to archive deleted files, check with your instructor regarding what your response should be.

2. Click the **Calendar** shortcut in the Outlook Bar. This folder contains features that help you set up appointments and meetings. If no one has entered any meetings in Outlook yet, this folder will be empty.

3. Click the **Contacts** shortcut in the Outlook Bar. This folder stores information about personal and business contacts. If no one has entered any contacts in Outlook yet, this folder will be empty.

Hot Tip

You can also change folders by opening the **View** menu, choosing **Folder List**, and then selecting the folder name in the Folder List. Or, Open the **View** menu, choose **Go To**, select **Folder**, and then select the folder name.

4. Click the **Tasks** shortcut in the Outlook Bar. This folder displays a grid in which you can enter information about tasks you want to accomplish. If no one has yet entered any tasks in Outlook, this folder will be empty.

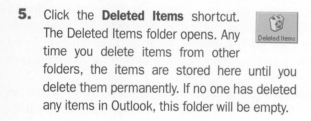

Did You Know?

While working in Outlook, you can view and work with files or folders saved on local or network disks in Outlook. Click **Other Shortcuts** at the bottom of the Outlook Bar to display shortcuts to My Computer, My Documents, and Favorites. When you click one of these short-cuts, Outlook displays the files and folders similar to the way they are displayed in Microsoft Windows Explorer, except that in Outlook, more information is dis-played and there are more ways to view the contents of a folder. You can also use Outlook to view Web pages so you don't have to leave Outlook and open your browser. For example, you can go to a Web page from a link in an e-mail.

5. Click the **Deleted Items** shortcut. The Deleted Items folder opens. Any time you delete items from other folders, the items are stored here until you delete them permanently. If no one has deleted any items in Outlook, this folder will be empty.

Speech Recognition

If your computer has speech recognition capability, enable the Command mode and say the commands to open the folders.

6. Click the **Calendar** shortcut again to return to the Calendar folder. Leave this folder open for the next Step-by-Step.

Hot Tip

You can also open a folder by clicking the folder name in the folder banner to display a list of folder names. To go to a folder on the list, just click the folder name.

Schedule and Manage Appointments

The Calendar folder shown in Figure 1-2 contains three separate areas that help you create and keep track of appointments. You can use the Appointment Book to create and display your appointments. The Date Navigator helps you to locate and display dates in the past or future. The TaskPad displays items from your Tasks list.

FIGURE 1-2
Calendar Folder

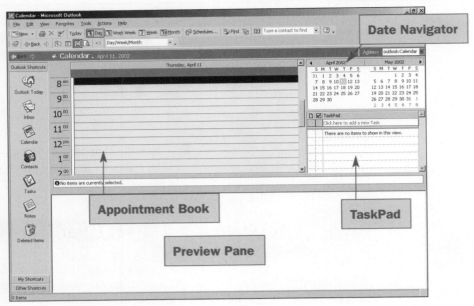

Date Navigator

Appointment Book

TaskPad

Preview Pane

Schedule an Appointment

To schedule an appointment, display the day of the appointment and then select New Appointment from the Actions menu. Outlook provides a *form* with preset controls to help you enter the right information for your appointment. For example, there are controls for subject, location, start time, and end time. Each piece of information in the form is called a *field*. After you save and close the form, the appointment appears in the Appointment Book.

You can view the contents of an item in the Preview Pane without opening the item. However, to edit the item, you must first open the item and make the changes in a form. To open the item, double-click the item.

STEP-BY-STEP ▷ 1.2

1. If necessary, open the **View** menu and choose **Preview Pane** to display the Preview Pane of the Calendar folder.

2. In the Date Navigator, click the date that is one week from today. The date at the top of the Appointment Book changes to that date.

3. Click the New Appointment button on the Standard Toolbar. The Untitled - Appointment form opens.

Hot Tip

You can also right-click at the time for the appointment and select **New Appointment** from the shortcut menu or double-click at the appointment time to display the dialog box. You can also open the Actions menu and choose New Appointment.

4. The insertion point is positioned in the *Subject:* text box. Key **Dr. Savin** in this text box.

5. Click in the *Location:* text box. Notice that the dialog box title bar now displays *Dr. Savin - Appointment*. Key **Lakeside Medical**.

6. Notice that the date you selected is already entered in the first set of *Start Time* and *End Time* list boxes. Click in the second *Start Time* list box (it currently displays *8:00 AM*) to display the drop-down list, and select **10:00 AM**.

7. Outlook always assumes your appointment will take half an hour. Change the length of the appointment by clicking the down arrow of the second *End Time* list box and selecting **11:00 AM (1 hour)**. Your form box should now look like the one shown in Figure 1-3.

Computer Concepts

Notice that the reminder option is checked. Outlook will remind you of your appointment with a sound effect. You can select the reminder sound and specify how far ahead of the appointment Outlook should remind you.

8. Click the **Save and Close** but- ton at the top of 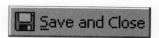 the form to save the appointment information and close the form. The appointment is dis- played in your Appointment Book. The bell symbol indicates that you will receive an audi- ble reminder about the appointment.

FIGURE 1-3
Completed Appointment form

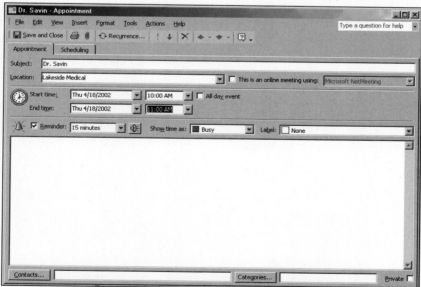

Schedule Recurring Appointments

Some appointments occur repeatedly, such as a weekly club meeting or a monthly board meeting. You can designate these appointments as recurring. You simply indicate how frequently the meeting will occur, and Outlook will set up all the appointments within the time period specified.

1. Open the **Actions** menu and choose **New Recurring Appointment**. The Appointment Recurrence form is displayed.

2. Under *Appointment time*, set the *Start:* time at **7:00 PM** and the *End:* time at **9:00 PM (2 hours)**.

3. In the left side of the Recurrence pattern section, select **Monthly**. Then select the second option on the right beginning with the word *The*. Select **second** in the first text box and select **Tuesday** in the second text box.

4. Compare your form with the completed form shown in Figure 1-4 to make sure you have selected all the correct options. Make any necessary changes. Note that your dates will be different than those shown in the figure.

Speech Recognition

If your computer has speech recognition capability, enable the Command mode and say the commands to open the Appointment Recurrence form and schedule the appointments.

5. Click **OK** to save the recurrence information. The Untitled – Appointment form is still displayed, and the appointment has not yet been saved. For the subject for the recurring meeting, enter **Club Board Meeting**. For the location, enter **Community Center**.

6. Click the **Save and Close** button to save the recurring appointment information and close the form.

7. Notice that the second Tuesday of each month from this point forward is highlighted in the Date Navigator. Click that highlighted date in the Date Navigator to display the appointments for that date. Scroll down to 7:00 PM in the Appointment Book. Notice that the monthly meeting at the Community Center is scheduled. If you check the second Tuesday for any upcoming month, the meeting is scheduled from 7:00 to 9:00 PM. Leave the Calendar folder open for the next Step-by-Step.

FIGURE 1-4
Completed Appointment Recurrence form

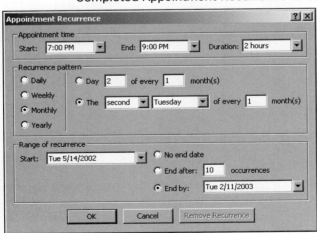

Use Help to Learn How to Schedule an Event

Appointments usually take place on a specific day at a specific time. You can also, however, schedule an event. An *event* is a scheduled item in the Outlook calendar that lasts 24 hours or longer. Examples of events are vacations, or an annual event that occurs every year, such as a birthday or anniversary. You can use Microsoft Outlook Help to learn how to create an event in the Appointment Book.

STEP-BY-STEP ⟹ 1.4

1. Click the Office Assistant or open the **Help** menu and choose **Microsoft Outlook Help**. Key **create an event** in the text box and click the **Search** button.

> **Did You Know?**
>
> You can also quickly access Help screens by entering your search text in the *Ask a Question:* box and then pressing **Enter**.

2. If necessary, click the **Create an all-day event** link to display a Help window about scheduling an all-day event.

3. Read the information on scheduling an event. Close the Help window and then use what you have learned to schedule an event the day after your appointment with Dr. Savin. Key **Jobs Fair** for the subject of the event and **Wilson Center** as the location of the event. Save and close the form.

4. Notice that the all-day event appears at the top of the Appointment Book. Leave the Calendar folder open for the next Step-by-Step.

Change Views and Delete Appointments

All Outlook folders allow you to change your view of the items in the folder. Different views can show you more detail about the items or help you focus on a specific kind of item stored in the folder. For example, you can view the active appointments, the recurring appointments, or the events in your calendar.

In the Calendar folder, you can also change the view of your current appointments and events using the four view buttons on the Standard toolbar. Click these buttons to view your appointments by day, by work week (Monday through Friday), by week (Monday through Sunday), or by month.

You can delete an appointment if you no longer need it. Deleted items are automatically moved to the Deleted Items folder and will stay in that folder until deleted permanently. If you change your mind about a deletion, you can retrieve the item from the Deleted Items folder.

STEP-BY-STEP ⟹ 1.5

1. Open the **View** menu and choose **Current View**. Select **Active Appointments** in the submenu. Your appointments display in a grid so you can easily see all of them at once.

2. Open the **View** menu, choose **Current View**, and then select **Day/Week/Month** to return to the previous view.

3. Click the **Month** button on the Standard toolbar. A monthly calendar displays with your appointments listed on the appropriate days. Click the **Day** button to return to the previous view where you can see the Date Navigator and the Task Pad.

4. Use the Date Navigator to go to the day on which you have an appointment with Dr. Savin. (*Hint:* The date is highlighted.) Click the appointment with Dr. Savin and then click the **Delete** button on the Standard toolbar. The appointment is moved to the Deleted Items folder.

5. Move to the next day and click the jobs fair event name at the top of the Appointment Book. Click the **Delete** button to remove the event.

6. Delete the recurring monthly board meeting. When you click the Delete button, the dialog box shown in Figure 1-5 will display. Select the option **Delete the series.** and then click **OK**. Leave Outlook open for the next Step-by-Step.

FIGURE 1-5
Confirm Delete dialog box

Create and Manage Contacts

The **Contacts** folder allows you to store many kinds of information about people you work with or communicate with on a regular basis. As you insert information about a contact, Outlook creates an address card for that contact. Outlook arranges the address cards in alphabetical order so you can easily locate each one. Figure 1-6 shows two address cards in the Contacts folder.

FIGURE 1-6
Business and personal contacts in the Contacts folder

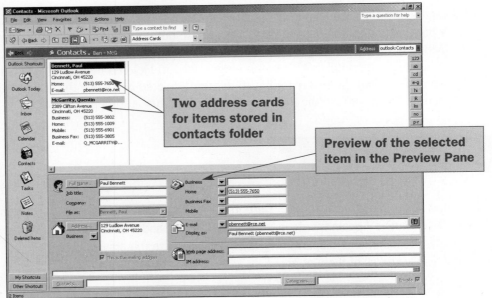

Add a New Contact

To add a new contact, choose New Contact from the Actions menu. Outlook displays a dialog box with a number of tabs. You can fill in as much or as little information on these tabs as you like. After you complete the dialog box, Outlook adds a new address card to the Contacts folder.

STEP-BY-STEP ▷ 1.6

1. Click the **Contacts** shortcut to open the Contacts folder.

2. Open the **View** menu, choose **Current View**, and select **Address Cards** on the submenu, if necessary.

3. Open the **Actions** menu and choose **New Contact**. The Untitled - Contact form opens.

Hot Tip

You can also double-click in any blank space in the **Contacts** folder (not the Preview Pane) to display the Untilted – Contact form or you can click the **New** button on the **Standard** toolbar.

4. Click in the *Full Name* text box and key **Jane Treadway**. This is the way the contact will be filed in the Contacts folder.

Hot Tip

If you click the Full Name button in the Untitled – Contact dialog box, a Check Full Name form will display. This form will help you complete all the necessary information including title, first, middle, and last names, and a suffix if applicable.

5. Press **Tab** to move the insertion point to the next text box. Notice the dialog box name changes to Jane Treadway – Contact and the *File as:* text box below automatically fills in *Treadway, Jane*. Key **Office Manager** in the Job title text box.

6. Press **Tab** to go to the next text box and key **Williston Associates**.

7. Click in the *Address* text box and key the address shown in Figure 1-7. Then key the remaining information shown in the figure.

FIGURE 1-7
Contact information for Jane Treadway

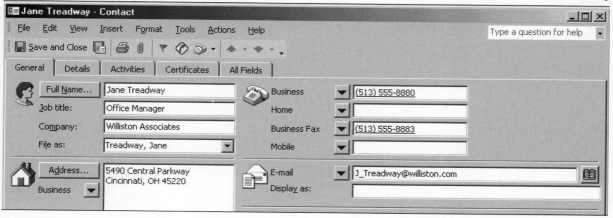

8. When you have finished entering the information, click the **Save and Close** button. If you are prompted to designate the contact as a Small Business Customer Manager contact, click **No**. The form closes and the contact information appears in the Contacts folder.

9. Add another contact from Williston Associates:

a. Open the **Actions** menu and choose **New Contact from Same Company**. The Williston Associates – Contact form is displayed, with the business address and business phone and fax numbers already entered.

b. Enter the name **Penny Cantin**. Penny's job title is **Marketing Manager**. Her e-mail address is **P_Cantin@williston.com**.

c. Click the **Save and Close** button. If prompted to designate the contact as a Small Business Customer Manager contact, click **No**.

10. Notice that as the new contact is entered, Outlook places the address cards in alphabetical order by last name. Leave the Contacts folder open for the next Step-by-Step.

Change Views and Delete Address Cards

You might wonder why Jane Treadway's and Penny Cantin's job title and company name information do not display on their address card. The Address Card view does not show these details. To see all the information you insert for your contacts, you need to use the Detailed Address Cards view.

You can easily remove an address card from the contacts list. In the next Step-by-Step, you will remove one of the contacts you added.

1. Open the **View** menu and choose **Current View**. Select **Detailed Address Cards** in the submenu. You can now see all information on the address cards.

2. Open the **View** menu and choose **Current View**. Select **Address Cards** to return to the original view.

3. Click the address card for Penny Cantin to select it. The bar behind the name changes to a color to indicate it is the active card. (If this contact is the first one in the list, it may already be selected.)

4. Click the **Delete** button on the Standard toolbar to remove the contact. Leave Outlook open for the next Step-by-Step.

Organize and Manage Tasks

The Tasks folder helps you organize things you have to do. You can use the Tasks list as you would a to-do list. You can add tasks, reorganize them if one task suddenly becomes more important than another, and cross each task off as you finish it.

Tasks are displayed in a grid, as shown in Figure 1-8. Depending on the view you are working in, you have a number of columns of information about each task. In Figure 1-8, the Subject and Due Date columns tell you the name of each task and the day it should be completed.

Computer Concepts

You can also enter a new task by opening the **Actions** menu and choosing **New Task** or by clicking the **New Task** button on the Standard toolbar to open the Untitled - Task dialog box. You enter all task information in the dialog box and then click **Save and Close** to add the task to the list.

FIGURE 1-8
Tasks folder with three tasks displayed

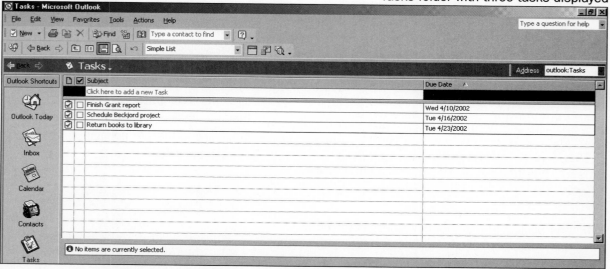

Add and Work with Tasks

The easiest way to add a new task is to display the Tasks folder and click in the box that reads *Click here to add a new Task*. When you do, the Subject box becomes active so you can key the name of the task you want to add. Press Tab to move to the next column, just as you would when entering text in a worksheet or a table, and enter the information required in that column.

As you enter each task, Outlook keeps your tasks in order by due date. You can sort the tasks to display them in a different order. *Ascending order* sorts alphabetically from A to Z and numerically from the lowest to the highest number. *Descending order* sorts alphabetically from Z to A and numerically from the highest to the lowest number. The Subject column header will display a triangle pointing either upward or downward, indicating the sort order.

To sort the tasks, click the heading of the column you want to sort by. For example, to sort tasks by name, click the Subject column header.

1. In the Outlook Bar, click the **Tasks** shortcut to open the Tasks folder.

2. Open the **View** menu, choose **Current View**, and then select **Simple List** from the submenu, if necessary.

3. Click in the box that reads *Click here to add a new Task*. Key **Return books to library** and then press **Tab**. Key the date that is two weeks from today's date and press **Enter**. Outlook will automatically add the day of the week to your date.

Computer Concepts

You can double-click on a task to open the task form and display details about the task. You can use this form to enter information about the status of the task, the number of hours worked, mileage, billing information, and so forth.

4. The Subject box is currently selected so you can enter another task. Key **Schedule Beckjord project** and then press **Tab**. Key the date that is one week from today's date and press **Enter**.

5. Add another new task: Key **Finish Grant report** and then press **Tab**. Key tomorrow's date and press **Enter**.

Did You Know?

If you switch to the Calendar after entering tasks, you will see your tasks in the TaskPad.

6. The tasks are currently displayed in chronological order by due date. To display the tasks in alphabetical order by subject, click the **Subject** column header. The tasks are listed in ascending order and the *Finish Grant report* task now appears at the top of the list. Notice that the Subject column header displays a triangle pointing upward.

7. Click the **Subject** column header again, and the tasks are listed in descending order and the *Finish Grant report* task appears at the bottom of the list. Notice that the Subject column header displays a triangle pointing downward.

8. To display the tasks in order by due date, click the **Due Date** column header. Notice that the tasks appear in descending date order and a triangle pointing downward displays in the column header.

Hot Tip

You can format a reminder so Outlook will display a message to remind you when the task is due. Double-click the task to open the task form. Then check the reminder option and select a date and time.

9. Click the **Due Date** column header again to display the tasks in ascending date order. Leave the Tasks folder open for the next Step-by-Step.

Marking Tasks as Complete and Deleting Tasks

After you have completed a task, you mark it as complete by clicking in the check box to the left of the task name. A check mark appears in the check box and the rest of the task information is crossed out.

You can leave a completed task in the task list or you can remove the task from the list. To remove the task, select it and click the Delete button on the Standard toolbar. You can remove several tasks at one time even if they are not located next to each other in the task list. To do so, select the first task, hold down the Ctrl key, and then click the other tasks you want to delete. If the tasks you want to delete are all grouped together, select the first task, hold down the Shift key and then select the last task in the group of tasks. All tasks in between the first and last tasks are then selected. Regardless of how you select the tasks, click the Delete button to delete them. Like all other Outlook items, deleted tasks go to the Deleted Items folder.

STEP-BY-STEP ▷ 1.9

1. You have returned your books to the library. Click in the empty check box to the left of the task name. A check mark appears in the check box, and the task name and due date are crossed out.

2. Mark each task as complete.

3. Click the last task in the list. Hold down **Ctrl** and click the first task in the list. Both tasks are selected.

4. Click the first task in the list. It should now be the only selected task. Press **Shift** and click the last task to select all of them.

5. Click the **Delete** button on the Standard toolbar to remove all tasks. Leave Outlook open for the next Step-by-Step.

Send and Receive E-Mail

If your computer is set up to handle e-mail, you can use the Inbox folder in Outlook to send and receive e-mail messages. An advantage to using Outlook as your e-mail application is that, as you create messages, you have easy access to the other Outlook folders. You can quickly address the message to someone on your contacts list, check your calendar to make sure you are available for a meeting, or add a task to your task list when a message requests further action.

Computer Concepts

Before you can use Outlook for e-mail, you must have a mail account with an ISP (Internet Service Provider), and Outlook must be configured to send and receive e-mail.

Receiving E-Mail

When Outlook launches, it sends a request to your mail server to find out if you have any messages waiting. If you do, Outlook receives them and displays them in the Inbox folder. The top half of the Inbox folder displays message headers for any new messages. The message header tells you who sent the message, the subject of the message, and the date and time your server received it. The bottom half of the Inbox displays the actual text of the message. If you have a number of messages, you can read each one by clicking its message header to display the message text in the bottom part of the Inbox.

If you are already working in Outlook, you can check your e-mail at any time. Open the Inbox folder and click the Send/Receive button on the Standard toolbar. After you have finished reading your messages, you can delete them by selecting each message header and clicking the Delete button on the Standard toolbar.

Sending E-Mail

Sending e-mail is as easy as clicking a few buttons and keying your message text. If you want to send a message to a contact stored in the Contacts folder, click the To button. A dialog box opens to allow you to select a contact name. Because you have already stored the e-mail address for that contact in the Contacts folder, you do not have to rekey the address. The contact's name appears in the To text box, and the message will automatically be sent to the e-mail address you previously stored. If you want to send a copy of the message to another person, enter that person's e-mail address in the Cc text box. If an e-mail address is not in your address book, you can also type it in the To or the Cc box.

It is good e-mail etiquette to include a subject for your mail message. The subject should be brief, yet it should be descriptive enough to tell the recipient what the message is about. Then key your message.

After you have entered the addresses, subject, and text of your message, just click the Send button in the message window to send the e-mail message. In the next Step-by-Step, you will practice creating an e-mail message, but you will not send it. You can perform the steps even if you do not have an ISP (Internet Service Provider) or if your ISP information is not entered in Outlook.

Computer Concepts

E-mail attachments can contain viruses. Never download or open files from people you don't know. And, most importantly, be sure to keep your anti-virus software up to date.

Computer Concepts

The Instant Messaging feature in Outlook enables you to send messages in real time. In other words, you can send and receive messages while you and the contact are both logged on. In order for the Instant Messaging feature to work, both people must be logged onto the Internet. Each contact must have an Instant Messaging account and you must enter the contact's Instant Messaging address into the IM text box in the General tab of the Contact form.

![STEP-BY-STEP 1.10]

1. Click the Inbox shortcut in the Outlook Bar, or open the **View** menu, choose **Go To**, and select **Inbox** to open the Inbox folder. In the Inbox folder, click the **New Mail Message** button. The Untitled Message – Microsoft Word form shown in Figure 1-9 appears.

New ▾

Hot Tip

If your screen does not match Figure 1-9, you may not have Word selected as your e-mail editor. To choose this option, open the **Tools** menu, choose **Options**, click the **Mail Format** tab, and turn on **Use Microsoft Word to edit e-mail messages**.

FIGURE 1-9
New Message form

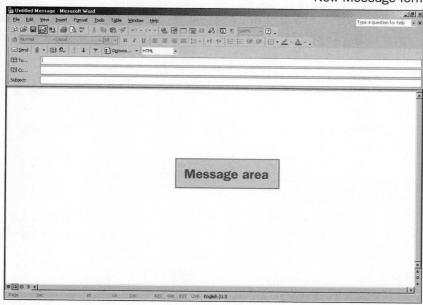

2. You will send a message to Jane Treadway, the contact you added earlier. Click the To... button to open the Select Names dialog box.

3. Jane Treadway's name should appear in the Name list at the left side of the Select Names

dialog box. Click her name to select it, and then click the **To ->** button to add the name to the Message Recipients list. Your Select Names dialog box should look similar to the one shown in Figure 1-10. However, you may have additional contacts listed. Do not be concerned if yours looks different.

FIGURE 1-10
Contact name added to the Message Recipients list

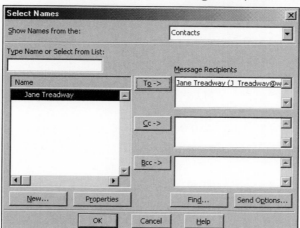

4. Click **OK** to close the dialog box. Jane Treadway's name now appears in the *To...* box in the message window.

5. Click in the **Subject** text box and key **Product Info**.

6. Click in the message area. As soon as you do, the title of the window changes to *Product Info – Message - Microsoft Word*.

Hot Tip

You can insert more than one name in the Message Recipients list for the To... box. The message will go to all the names on the list at the same time. Add people you would like to receive a copy of this e-mail to the Cc... list. If you want someone to receive a copy of the e-mail without letting the other message recipients know who else is receiving the e-mail, add them to the Bcc (blind copy) list.

7. Key the following message:
Hi Jane,
I will have the information you asked for later today. I need to contact a sales rep for the latest figures.

Speech Recognition

If your computer has speech recognition capability, enable the Dictation mode and dictate the message.

8. Press **Enter** twice and key your name to sign the e-mail.

9. Open the **File** menu and choose **Save As**. Save the message with the name **Treadway Message**. Click the **Save** button.

10. Close the message window by clicking the application close button in the title bar (at the top right corner of the screen). Remember, you are not actually sending this message to the recipient.

11. When prompted to save the draft of this message, click **No**.

12. Switch to the Contacts folder and delete the Jane Treadway contact from the Contacts folder.

13. Close Outlook.

Computer Concepts

By default, Outlook saves the file in html format unless you've selected Word as your e-mail editor. If Word is your editor, Outlook saves the files in Word format and you can use the spellcheck and grammar checking features to help you proofread your document. However, if you've formatted for plain text, the file will be saved as a text file.

HISTORICALLY SPEAKING

Did you ever wonder why we always use the @ symbol in e-mail addresses? Sometime in late 1971, Ray Tomlinson, a computer engineer, created the first e-mail program that launched the digital information revolution. Tomlinson was employed by Bolt Beranek and Newman (BBN), a company hired by the United States Defense Department to build ARPANET. He wrote an electronic message progam called SNDMSG, which enabled programmers and researchers to exchange messages. The users could create a text file and deliver the file to a designated mail box on the computer. However, the messages had to be accessed by all users on the same machine. Tomlinson later adapted the application so he could send messages to mailboxes on remote machines. He chose the @ symbol to distinguish between messages addressed to mailboxes in the local machine and messages that were directed out onto a network. Tomlinson said, "I used the @ sign to indicate that the user was "at" some other host rather than being local."

Source: "The History of Email," http://www.swynk.com/friends/janssen/Articles/ History_Of_Email.asp (August 1, 2001)

413

Summary

In this lesson, you learned:

- The Outlook window changes depending on which folder is open. The Outlook Bar displays short-cuts that give you quick access to each of the Outlook folders.

- Each Outlook folder has a number of views you can use to display the information in that folder in different ways.

- The Calendar folder lets you schedule appointments and events. A form makes it easy for you to enter information about your appointments. Each piece of information is called a field.

- Each appointment and event you schedule is displayed in the Appointment Book.

- You can use the Date Navigator to select the day of the appointment.

- The Contacts folder is designed to store information about business and personal contacts with whom you communicate with often.

- You create address cards that hold information such as name, address, phone number, e-mail address, and so on. Address cards are listed in alphabetical order in the Contacts folder.

- The Tasks folder supplies a grid in which you store information about tasks you must complete.

- You can sort the tasks to see them in different orders.

- After you have completed a task, you can mark it as completed or delete it.

- The Inbox folder is an e-mail application you can use to send and receive e-mail messages.

VOCABULARY REVIEW

Define the following terms.

Ascending order	Event	Form
Contacts	Field	Item
Descending order		

LESSON 1 REVIEW QUESTIONS

TRUE/FALSE

Circle T if the statement is true or F if the statement is false.

T F 1. Each Outlook folder organizes a different type of information.

T F 2. Each piece of information in a form is called a field.

T F 3. As you add contacts, Outlook arranges them in alphabetical order.

T F 4. You can sort tasks by subject or by due date.

T F 5. To preview the contents of an item, you must open the form for the item.

FILL IN THE BLANK

Complete the following sentences by writing the correct word or words in the blanks provided.

1. The _____ contains shortcuts you can click to open folders.

2. The _____ helps you to locate and display calendar dates in the past or future.

3. A(n) _____ is a scheduled item in the Outlook calendar that lasts 24 hours or longer.

4. Use the _____ folder to organize things you have to do.

5. A(n) _____ contains a set of controls in which you enter a piece of information to be stored in an item.

LESSON 1 PROJECTS

PROJECT 1-1

1. If necessary, launch Outlook. Open the **Calendar** folder. Enter the following appointments and events:
    A. A week from tomorrow, you have an appointment with **R. Golding**, a career counselor, in **Rhodes Hall**. The appointment is at **10:00 AM** and should last an **hour and a half**.
    B. Your brother Dave's birthday is three days from today. Schedule the birthday as an event.
    C. Your family will get together at **7:00 PM** on that day for a celebration. You expect this celebration to last about two hours.
    D. You promised your friend Marian that you would go to the library with her to do some research. She wants to go next **Tuesday at 9:00 AM** and stay **two hours**.
    E. You've been elected to the board for a volunteer group in your community. The board meets the first Monday of each month. Schedule a recurring appointment for six months.

2. Click the **Month** view button to see all of your appointments.

3. Open the Contacts folder. Enter and save the following personal and business contacts. Use your own city or town, state, and zip code for the addresses.

Full Name:	Marian Teodorescu	Full Name:	Rose Golding
Job Title:		Job Title:	Career Counselor
Company:		Company:	Careers Plus
Address:	18 Baldwin Way	Address:	451 Rhodes Hall
Business Phone:		Business Phone:	555-8825
Home Phone:	555-9834	Home Phone:	
E-mail:	teodorm@netlink.com	E-mail:	rgolding@careers.org

4. Leave Outlook open for the next Project.

415

PROJECT 1-2

1. Open the Tasks folder. Enter the following tasks:
   A. Buy a present for your brother Dave by the day before his birthday. (Check the Calendar if you need to remember what day Dave's birthday is.)
   B. Complete your resume, due a week from today.
   C. You need a new printer cartridge to print your resume. Get one by the day after tomorrow.
   D. You need to confirm your trip to the library with Marian for research within three days.

2. Sort the tasks by subject. Then sort them in descending date order. Sort them again in ascending date order.

3. Switch to Calendar view to see your tasks in the TaskPad.

4. Open the Inbox folder. Create the following e-mail messages:
   A. Create a message to Marian to confirm that you will be going to the library with her next Tuesday. (Hint: Remember to click the **To...** button in the new message window to locate her name in your contacts list.) The subject of the message should be **Library Research**. Key your name at the end of the message. Save the message as **Marian** and do not send it.
   B. Create a message to **Ms. Golding** to confirm your appointment with her at 10:00 next week (use your Calendar to find the exact date and use it in your message). The subject of the message should be **Confirm Meeting**. Thank her for taking the time to see you. Key your name at the end of the message. Save the message as **Confirm Meeting** and do not send it.

5. You have confirmed your trip to the library with Marian and bought a new printer cartridge. In the Tasks folder, mark these tasks as complete.

6. Go back through all the Outlook folders and delete all the items you added in Project 1-1 and Project 1-2.

7. Close Outlook.

WEB PROJECT

Individuals who use e-mail for frequent communication are often annoyed by unwanted e-mail called spam. Spam is unsolicited e-mail messages that can be obnoxious and offensive, and a waste of your time. Some countries have laws against spam. Your Internet service provider may try to block spam before it reaches your mailbox. However, you may still be inconvenienced by junk e-mail.

Using some of the search engines you have used in this course, research the topic "spam" to learn ways you can stop spam. Write a brief summary of your findings.

TEAMWORK PROJECT

You probably noticed when you created e-mail messages in this lesson that your e-mails looked plain and boring. While you don't want your e-mails to be distracting or silly (particularly if you are sending them to business contacts), you can still add some visual interest. Two Outlook features can provide a more professional appearance for your e-mails: stationery and a signature. With a classmate, use the following steps to explore these Outlook features:

1. Using the Help feature in Outlook, one teammate should research "stationery" and the other teammate should research "e-mail signatures."

2. Using what you learned from the Help files, set a new default stationery and create an e-mail signature file. Open new e-mail messages to see your stationery and signature in place.

3. If you have e-mail capability, send a message to your teammate so he or she can see how the message looks when it is received by Outlook.

4. After you have finished experimenting with these features, remove the e-mail signature and the stationery formats that you applied. (Use the Help files in Outlook to help you restore default settings.)

CRITICAL THINKING

The Outlook Today folder displays an overview of some of your current Outlook information. The folder displays a summary of your appointments, a list of your tasks, and a list of new e-mail messages. You can use Outlook Today as your starting point when you work in Outlook. Use the Help feature to learn how to make Outlook Today your default page.

PUBLISHER AND FRONTPAGE

UNIT 7

lesson 1 — 1.5 hrs.
Working with Publisher

lesson 2 — 1.5 hrs.
Working with FrontPage

unit review — 1 hr.

Estimated Time for Unit: 4 hours

WORKING WITH PUBLISHER

OBJECTIVES

Upon completion of this lesson, you should be able to:

- Plan the design for a publication.
- Select a publication design template.
- Create a personal information set.
- Identify parts of the Publisher screen.
- Change the color scheme for a template.
- Replace the text and graphics provided in a template.
- Format text and apply font schemes.
- Delete frames.
- Insert new frames.
- Create a new logo.
- Print a publication.

⏱ **Estimated Time: 1.5 hours**

VOCABULARY

Automatic copyfitting

Frame

Landscape orientation

Layout guides

Mock-up

Portrait orientation

Scratch area

Sizing handles

Smart objects

Templates

Microsoft Publisher is a desktop publishing program you can use to create calendars, invitations, greeting cards, and much more. Publisher provides a variety of tools including sample layouts, clip art, font styles, and color schemes. Using these tools, you can create professional-looking publications quickly and easily.

To use Publisher proficiently, you need a good understanding of formatting text and working with text boxes, graphics, and wrapping text around objects. If you have little or no experience working with these features, you will find it helpful to complete the Step-by-Steps in Lessons 2 and 6 of Unit 2 before beginning this lesson. If you've already completed these lessons, you're ready to proceed.

Plan the Publication Design

Before you begin to create a publication, you should plan the design. There are several factors you should consider. Figure 1-1 lists some questions to help guide you. Your answers to these questions will influence the design elements you choose.

FIGURE 1-1

Questions to answer before designing a publication

- Who is the intended audience?

- What is the purpose of the publication?

- What are the key points you want to emphasize?

- What idea or emotion do you want to convey?

- Will the publication be printed on one side or both sides of the paper?

- Will a mailing label be required on the publication?

- Will you print the publication on white or colored paper stock?

- Will the text and graphics be printed in black and white or color?

- How will the publication be reproduced?

- How many copies of the publication will you reproduce?

To illustrate how you might answer these questions, consider the following scenario. You want to create a trifold brochure to distribute to the members of the Silver Lake Homeowners Association. The purpose of the publication is to inform the homeowners about the scheduled clean-up day for the neighborhood park. The key points to emphasize are the date and time, the rain date, the necessary tools, and a picnic lunch afterward. The theme should revolve around spring, and it should motivate homeowners to help with this annual event. The publication will be printed in color on both sides of white paper stock using an inkjet printer. The brochure will be enclosed in an envelope for mailing.

To help with planning the design, you can create a mock-up. A *mock-up* is a simple sketch of the publication that visually represents what it should look like when completed. The mock-up should be created using the same paper size that you will use for the final publication. This will enable you to experiment with the page orientation and the placement of text and graphics. *Portrait orientation* formats the content of the document with the short edge of the page at the top; *landscape orientation* formats the content of the document sideways with the long edge of the page at the top.

A mock-up is especially helpful if you will be folding the page(s) of your publication. When completed, the mock-up provides a visual guide for positioning text and graphics as you create the publication.

S TEP-BY-STEP ▷ 1.1

1. Use a blank sheet of 8.5" x 11" paper. Turn the paper sideways to represent landscape orientation (the paper should be wider than it is tall).

2. Create a trifold as shown in Figure 1-2. First fold the right ⅓ of the page to the left. Then fold the left ⅓ of the page to the right.

FIGURE 1-2

Folding a page for a mock-up of a trifold brochure

3. Unfold the paper and number each panel as illustrated in Figure 1-3.

4. Fold the paper again. Notice the order in which each panel will be seen as the brochure is opened and read. Panel 6 should be the cover. As readers open the brochure, they will then see panels 1, 4, 2, and 3, in that order. Panel 5 is the center panel on the back of the brochure.

5. Keep this sheet of paper with the numbered panels to use as a visual guide for creating a trifold brochure in this lesson.

FIGURE 1-3
Numbered panels of a trifold brochure

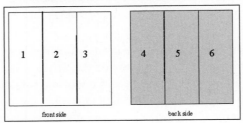

Select a Publication Template

When you start Publisher, the task pane is displayed on the left and the Publication Gallery is displayed on the right. Compare your screen to Figure 1-4. Do not be concerned if your screen does not match exactly – the options you have available may vary.

FIGURE 1-4
Task pane and Publication Gallery

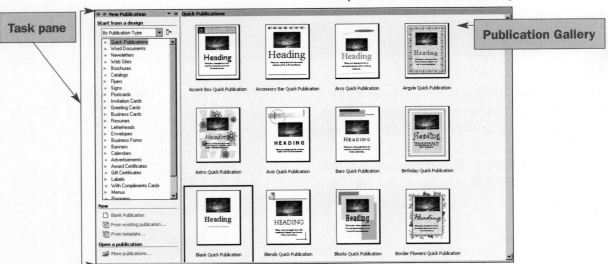

The task pane provides several options for creating new publications or opening existing publications. If you choose to create a new publication from a design, you can select from the many publication templates available in the Publication Gallery. *Templates* are predesigned documents that provide the basic layout and format for a specific publication. Examples of publication templates include a brochure, a flyer, or a certificate.

There are three options for publication templates: *By Publication Type*, *By Design Sets*, and *By Blank Publications*. The *By Publication Type* option lists the templates by category. For example, if you want to create a brochure, you simply select the **Brochure** category to view the available templates. The *By Design Sets* option allows you to apply the same design to a series of related documents. For example, you can create business cards, envelopes, and letterheads incorporating the same design. If you choose a template from one of these two options, you use the template by simply replacing the sample text and graphics with your own content.

The *By Blank Publications* option provides a sample layout to get you started, and then allows you to create your own publication from scratch. To create a blank publication, you must first have an understanding of the various Publisher features available and how to use them. This lesson will introduce you to some of the basic features as you create a publication from a design. Then you will have an opportunity to put your skills to work to create a blank presentation.

S TEP-BY-STEP ⟩ 1.2

1. Launch the Publisher application. Your screen should look similar to Figure 1-4. If necessary, click the **Shows Publication Gallery** button near the upper-right corner of the task pane to display the Quick Publications window.

🎯 Hot Tip

You can display the Publication Gallery at any time by clicking the **Shows Publication Gallery** button in the task pane.

2. In the task pane under *Start from a design*, the option *By Publication Type* should already be selected in the drop-down text box. Select the category **Brochures**. The submenu shown in Figure 1-5 is displayed. The down arrow to the left of the category name **Brochures** indicates that the subtopics are expanded.

FIGURE 1-5
Brochures submenu

3. Select **Fund-raiser** in the submenu. Notice that the display of templates in the Publication Gallery changes. This submenu provided a shortcut to help you quickly scroll down to a specific location in the quite lengthy list of brochure templates that are available.

▦ Computer Concepts

When you select a publication category with a triangle next to it, a submenu appears. The submenu presents more specific projects in that category. Categories with diamonds do not have submenus.

4. Select **Informational** in the submenu to return to the top of the list of brochure templates. If necessary, scroll down and then click the **Borders Informational Brochure** to select it. See Figure 1-6. The Borders Informational Brochure template is displayed on the right side of the screen.

5. Compare the Borders Informational Brochure layout on your screen to your mock-up. The layout on your screen shows the back page of the brochure with three panels. This is the back side of your mock-up, panels 4, 5, and 6. You will view and work with the front side later in this lesson.

Computer Concepts

If you are the first to use the Publisher application, you will be prompted to provide personal information such as your business name or address. If you receive this prompt, click **OK** and then click **Cancel**. You will enter the personal information in the next Step-by-Step.

6. Open the **File** menu and choose **Save As**. Save the document as **Clean-Up** followed by your initials. Leave the document open for the next Step-by-Step.

FIGURE 1-6

Borders Informational Brochure selected in the Informational Brochures window

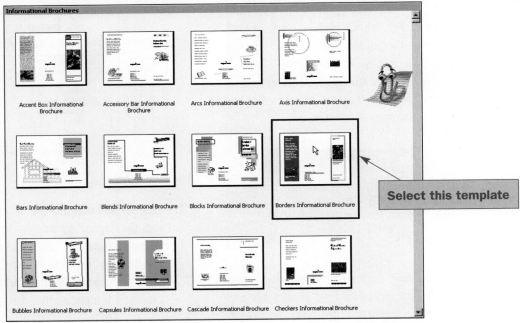

Edit a Personal Information Set

Publisher has a personal information set that stores frequently used information about you, your business, or your organization. When Publisher opens a template, this personal information is automatically inserted into the publication as needed. You can create up to four different information sets. If you have more than one, you can choose which set you want to use for your publication.

1. Open the **Edit** menu and choose **Personal Information**. The Personal Information dialog box, similar to the one shown in Figure 1-7, displays. However, your personal information dialog box will look different because of the personal information already stored on your computer.

2. Under *Select a personal information set to edit:*, select **Other Organization**. Update the personal information as follows:

   a. In the *Name:* box, delete any current text and leave the box blank.

   b. In the *Address:* box, delete the current text and key the following:

   > **P. O. Box 6507**
   > **Marysville, OH 43040-6507**

   c. In the *Phone/fax/e-mail:* box, replace the existing information with the following:

   > **Phone: 937-555-3391**
   > **Fax: 937-555-3395**
   > **E-mail: homeowners@silverlake.com**

   d. In the *Organization name:* box, key **Silver Lake Homeowners Association**.

   e. In the *Tag line or motto:* box, delete the text and leave the box blank.

   f. In the *Job or position title:* box, delete the text and leave the box blank.

3. Click the **Update** button to save the information and close the Personal Information dialog box.

4. Click the **Save** button on the Standard toolbar to save the changes. Leave the document open for the next Step-by-Step.

 Computer Concepts

Publisher enables you to store up to four different personal information sets. To apply a different set to your publication, open the **Edit** menu, choose **Personal Information**, and select the set you want to apply under *Select a personal information set to edit*. Then click **Update**.

FIGURE 1-7
Personal Information dialog box

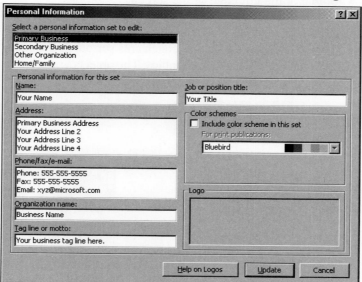

Identify Parts of the Publisher Screen

Once the Publisher document is created, it is displayed on a screen similar to the one shown in Figure 1-8. Your screen may look different because not all of the parts shown in the figure always display. If you look at the middle panel in the publication, you will see that it now displays the information you just entered in the personal information set.

FIGURE 1-8
The Publisher screen with a publication template

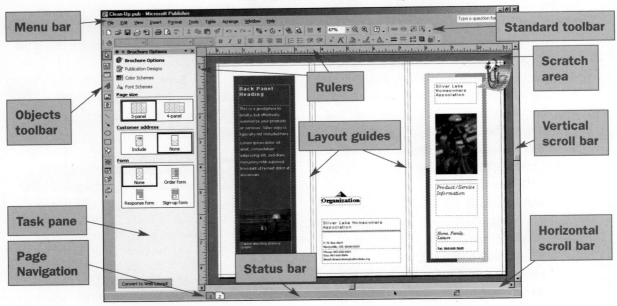

If you're familiar with other Office applications, you'll recognize many parts of the screen, such as the menu bar, the Standard toolbar, the scroll bars, and the taskbar. However, there are several other parts on the screen that are unique to Publisher. The rulers look different, the status bar displays different icons, and there's a new toolbar at the left edge of the screen.

Use the Scratch Area

If you close the task pane, a gray area called the scratch area surrounds the document. The *scratch area* is a place where you can temporarily store text and graphics. The objects you store in this area do not print.

S T E P - B Y - S T E P ▷ 1.4

1. Click the **Close** button at the top of the task pane. The document shifts to the left and is surrounded by the scratch area.

Computer Concepts

Even though you have hidden the task pane, you can show the task pane again at any time by opening the **View** menu and choosing **Task Pane**.

2. Click the number **2** on the **Page Navigation** button on the status bar to switch to the second page of the document. This is the front side of your mock-up, panels 1, 2, and 3.

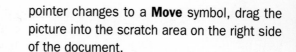

3. Point to the center of the picture of the girl running with a football in the left panel of the page. When the pointer changes to a **Move** symbol, drag the picture into the scratch area on the right side of the document.

4. Save the changes and leave the document open for the next Step-by-Step.

Use Help to Learn about the Layout Guides

Within the display of the document page, there are pink and blue *layout guides*. These guides are nonprinting rules that you can use to help you align objects and maintain a consistent look on all pages of the publication. Publisher automatically formats these lines on every page of the document, but they do not print. Go to the Help screens to learn more about how to use the layout guides.

1. In the Ask a Question text box, key **use layout guides** and then press **Enter**.

2. In the list of topics, select the topic **What's the difference between layout guides and ruler guides?** A screen related to the topic is displayed. Read the information.

3. Click the link **guides** to display a definition of the term. Click the link again to hide the definition.

4. Click the **Close** button in the Microsoft Publisher Help dialog box to close the Help screen.

Did You Know?

You can create ruler guides (green dotted lines) to measure or align design elements. To create a ruler guide, hold down **Shift** and point to either the vertical or horizontal ruler on the screen. When the pointer changes to an Adjust handle, drag the pointer out from the ruler. Release when the ruler guide is positioned where you want it.

Computer Concepts

You can also use the rulers on the screen as guides for positioning items on the screen. You can drag the rulers to position them anywhere within the document. To move the horizontal ruler, point to either the top or bottom edges of the horizontal ruler. When you see a two-headed arrow, drag the ruler up or down the screen. To move the vertical ruler, point to either the left or right edge of the ruler and drag the ruler to the right or left.

Change the Color Scheme

When you select a publication design template, a color scheme with a predefined set of colors automatically applies. However, you can choose a different color scheme in the task pane. The advantage to using the color schemes supplied by Publisher is that the colors complement each other and provide a consistent look throughout the publication. You can apply a color scheme to publications created with the different templates in Publisher, or to those you create from scratch from a blank publication.

S TEP-BY-STEP ▷ 1.6

1. Open the **View** menu and choose **Task Pane** to display the Brochure Options task pane shown in Figure 1-9.

2. Click **Color Schemes** in the task pane. A list of color schemes is displayed. Bluebird is the current color scheme.

3. Experiment with different color schemes. Notice that each time you select a new color scheme, the colors in the document are updated. Select the **Dark Blue** color scheme.

4. Save the changes and leave the document open for the next Step-by-Step.

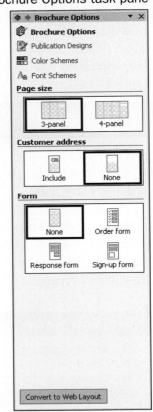

FIGURE 1-9
Brochure Options task pane

Replace Text and Apply New Formats

In Publisher, all text and graphics are objects, and therefore must be placed in a frame. A *frame* is a tool that makes it easy to position objects in a document. There are two kinds of frames. Text frames hold text. Picture frames hold graphics such as pictures, clip art, and WordArt. Regardless of the kind of frame you use, *sizing handles* display on the frame border when the frame is selected. You can drag these sizing handles to resize the frame. If you drag a corner handle, the frame is resized proportionately.

When you use a template, text frames and picture frames are already in place and already contain sample text and graphics. If you create a blank publication, you must insert the text and picture frames yourself. Sometimes, for one reason or another, you also want to insert frames in a publication that already provides them for you. You will learn how to insert frames later in this lesson.

To replace the text in a text frame, simply click inside the frame to select the contents of the frame and then enter the new text. The ***automatic copyfitting*** option automatically resizes the text to fit inside the text frame. To select the automatic copyfitting options, open the Format menu and choose AutoFit text. A submenu will display. The *Shrink Text On Overflow* option continually adjusts the text if you add or remove sections of the text later. The *Best Fit* option shrinks or expands the text to fit in the text box. Automatic copyfitting will also automatically resize the text as needed if you change the formatting (such as making the text bold) or if you resize the text frame. To turn the automatic copyfitting feature off, open the **Format** menu, choose **AutoFit Text**, and select **None**.

After you enter text in a text frame, you can format the text as you do in other Office applications. For example, you can apply formats or change the font style and size using buttons on the Formatting toolbar. When you want to change all the fonts in your publication, you can choose a font scheme in the task pane. A font scheme provides a ready-made set of fonts so you can quickly apply consistent formatting of headings, titles, and headlines throughout your publication. One big advantage to using font schemes is that all the fonts in a set already go together well, which can help make your publication easier to read.

S TEP-BY-STEP ▷ 1.7

1. Click the heading *Main Inside Heading* at the top of the left panel of the page. (This is panel number 1 in your mock-up.) Publisher automatically selects all of the text. You will see eight sizing handles on the border of the text frame as shown in Figure 1-10.

FIGURE 1-10
Selected text frame

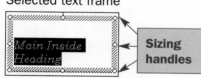

2. Click the **Zoom In** button on the Standard toolbar a few times so you can enlarge the display of text and make it easier to read.

Hot Tip

To enlarge the display of text, you can also click the down arrow to the right of the Zoom box and select a percentage, or you can press **F9** to zoom in and out quickly.

3. With the insertion point positioned within the *Main Inside Heading* text frame, open the **Format** menu and choose **AutoFit Text**. A submenu will display. Make sure the **Shrink Text On Overflow** option is turned on. If there is a checkmark in front of this option, click anywhere outside the shortcut menu to close the menu.

4. With the text within the frame still selected, key **Spring Clean-Up Scheduled for Saturday, April 13**. As you enter the text, it automatically replaces the old text and is resized to fit within the text frame. Press **Enter** and key **9 a.m. – Noon**. (This text should be on a line by itself.) All the text should fit within the text frame.

429

> ### Hot Tip
>
> If the Center button is not displayed on the Formatting toolbar, click the **Toolbar Options** button at the right side of the Formatting toolbar, and then click the **Center** button.

5. Select all of the text inside the text frame. Click the **Center** button on the Formatting toolbar.

6. Click the text below the new heading you just created. With the text selected, key the following paragraph:
Spring has arrived, and that means it's time to enjoy outdoor activities. Silver Lake residents are encouraged to join their neighbors to spruce up the neighborhood park.

> ### Computer Concepts
>
> You can import text from a Word document into a text frame if a converter has been installed to display Word files in Publisher. Select the text box, open the **Insert** menu, and choose **Text File**. In the Insert Text dialog box, locate the Word document you want to import and click **OK**.

7. Press **Enter** and then key **The rain date is scheduled for Saturday, April 18.** Notice that Publisher automatically hyphenates the word "Saturday" and wraps the word to the next line.

8. Select all the new text you just entered and change the point size to 12.

9. Scroll to the right if necessary, and click the heading **Secondary Heading** at the top of the second panel. Key **Bring Tools**. Click the **Center** button to center the heading. Select the heading text and change the point size to 16.

10. Click anywhere within the text under the Bring Tools heading and key:
We'll be raking, sweeping, trimming, painting, and picking up litter. Bring rakes, brooms, pruning shears, and other appropriate tools.

> ### Computer Concepts
>
> If the automatic copyfitting options are turned off and you enter more text than the text box can hold, Publisher will display a message asking if you want the text to flow automatically. If you choose **Yes**, Publisher will create text boxes as needed and then flow the extra text into them. If you choose to resize text boxes yourself, the Text in Overflow indicator **(A...)** will display in the lower-right corner of the text box.

11. Select the text you just entered and change the point size to 12. Click anywhere outside the selected text to deselect it.

12. Click **Font Schemes** in the task pane to display the Font Schemes task pane shown in Figure 1-11. Experiment with the various font schemes and choose a scheme that you think is easy to read and appropriate for the tri-fold brochure.

> ### Hot Tip
>
> If you apply a font scheme and then decide you do not like it, click the **Undo** button on the Standard toolbar.

13. Save the changes. When you are prompted to save changes to the logo in the publication, click **Yes**. (Note that the font style for the logo changed when you applied a new font scheme.) Leave the document open for the next Step-by-Step.

FIGURE 1-11
Font Schemes task pane

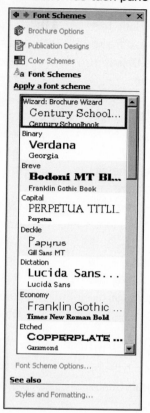

Delete Frames

Y ou already know how to delete text from a text frame, but when you delete the text, the frame does not delete. To remove the text frame, right-click anywhere within the frame and then select **Delete Object** in the shortcut menu. Note that when you remove a text frame, the contents are also removed. You can easily delete graphics by simply clicking on the object to select it and then pressing **Delete**. The graphic and the frame are both deleted.

STEP-BY-STEP ▷ 1.8

1. Click the **Zoom Out** button on the Standard toolbar so you can reduce the display of text. This will make it easier to see the entire layout.

2. Click the text just above the picture in the second panel. The text in the second and third panels is selected because this text box wraps to the third panel. In other words, the two text frames are connected.

3. Press **Delete** to remove the text. Both text frames are still there. Right-click the text frame in the third panel and choose **Delete Object** in the shortcut menu to delete the frame.

4. Click the heading *Secondary Heading* in the second panel, then press **Delete**.

5. Click the picture in the second panel. The picture and the caption below the picture are both selected. Press **Delete** to remove the picture frame, its contents, and the caption.

6. Click the **Page 1** icon in the status bar to switch to that page. If necessary, drag the horizontal scroll box to the left so all of the first panel displays.

7. Click the heading *Back Panel Heading* in the first panel (panel number 4 in your mock-up). Key **Keep Silver Lake Park Beautiful!** Center the heading.

8. Click the text in the frame below the new heading and key:
   Silver Lake Park offers a natural setting for the residents of Silver Lake. Each year the Silver Lake Homeowners Association organizes a spring clean-up to maintain the park. Join your neighbors in this effort to maintain the beauty of Silver Lake Park.

9. Delete the picture frame and caption below the text.

10. Publisher automatically inserted information about the organization on this page. Center the heading *Silver Lake Homeowners Association* at the bottom of the second panel.

11. If necessary, scroll to the right and center the heading *Silver Lake Homeowners Association* at the top of the third panel. Change the point size to 14. If necessary, AutoFit the text for best fit.

12. Click the text *Product/Service Information* in the third panel and key **Annual Park Clean-Up**. Center the new text.

13. Right-click the empty text frame above the telephone number and then select **Delete Object** in the shortcut menu.

Computer Concepts

Publisher generally inserts the business tag line (such as a company slogan) in this empty text box, but your personal information set does not include a tag line or motto.

14. Select the telephone number that appears at the bottom of the third panel and key **Saturday, April 13**. Center the text and change the point size to 12. If necessary, AutoFit the text for best fit.

15. Save the changes and leave the document open for the next Step-by-Step.

Insert Text Frames and Picture Frames

So far you have been replacing text in text frames that are already in place. You can also insert your own text and picture frames into a Publisher document. The Objects toolbar, which displays at the left side of the screen as shown in Figure 1-8, displays several tools that can be used to create and modify frames. If you want to add text or pictures to a document, you must first insert a new text frame or a new picture frame.

STEP-BY-STEP 1.9

1. Click the picture of the cyclist you inserted in the third panel. Replace the existing picture by following these steps:

   a. With the picture frame selected, click the **Clip Organizer Frame** button on the Objects toolbar. The Insert Clip Art task pane, similar to the one shown in Figure 1-12, is displayed. If you are prompted to organize all media files, click **Later** to postpone this task.

FIGURE 1-12
Insert Clip Art task pane

b. If necessary, select the text in the *Search text:* box, then key **lake**. Click **Search**. Images matching the keyword *lake* are displayed.

c. Select an appropriate image. The picture is inserted in the document. If necessary, resize the picture frame to fit in the panel.

 Hot Tip

If the results for your search are minimal, make sure the *All collections* option is selected in the *Search in:* box under Other Search Options. If you still cannot locate an appropriate clip art image, try searching for clips online. Also, additional clip art images are available on the Microsoft Office XP Media Content disk.

2. Point to the center of the new picture. When the pointer changes to a move symbol, drag the picture up to center it vertically between the two text frames already positioned on the panel.

3. Switch to page 2. The Insert Clip Art task pane should still be displayed. Search for a clip art image or photo related to yard tools (for example, rakes, brooms, or watering cans). When you select an image, the image displays eight sizing handles. If necessary, resize the picture frame to fit in the panel.

 Hot Tip

To continue your search using a different keyword, click the **Modify** button near the bottom of the Insert Clip Art task pane and key your new keyword.

 Hot Tip

Another way to display the Insert Clip Art task pane is to open the **Insert** menu, choose **Picture**, and then select **Clip Art** in the submenu.

4. When you select a yard tools-related clip art image, position it under the paragraph of text in the second panel.

5. Click the **Text Box** button on the Objects toolbar. The pointer changes to a crosshair.

Computer Concepts

Depending on the operating system in use on your computer, the Objects Bar may display a Text Frame Tool button instead of a Text Box button. Both buttons function the same way – enabling you to create a new text box.

6. Drag the cross-hair pointer to create a text frame approximately 2 inches wide and 1½ inches high at the top of the third panel.

7. With the new text frame selected, key **Bring a picnic lunch and join us after the work is done. We may even field a couple of flag football teams!** Change the point size of the text to 12.

8. Close the task pane and then drag the picture you placed in the scratch area in Step-by-Step 1.4 and position it below the text frame in the third panel. Resize the picture frame to fill the white space in the panel.

Hot Tip

You may find it easier to drag the picture from the scratch area if you reduce the view first. Try 75% or 50%.

9. Select the text in the picture caption and key **Fun for the entire family!**

10. Click the **Clip Organizer Frame** button and insert an image related to "park" or "spring." Resize the picture frame as needed (remember to do so proportionately) and position it in the white space at the bottom of the first panel.

Did You Know?

You can also insert scanned pictures or imported pictures taken with a digital camera.

11. Save the changes and keep the document open for the next Step-by-Step.

Create a New Logo

Publisher automatically inserted a logo object in the middle panel on the first page of the brochure (panel number 5 in your mock-up). You can easily create your own logo using a Design Gallery smart object. *Smart objects* are preformatted design elements in Publisher that you can customize. For example, you can use a smart object to create a new company or organization logo.

S TEP-BY-STEP ▷ 1.10

1. Switch to page 1 and click the logo in the second panel (panel number 2 in the mockup) of your brochure to select it, as shown in Figure 1-13.

FIGURE 1-13
Selected logo object in
brochure publication

2. Click the **Wizard** button at the bottom of the logo. The Logo Designs task pane shown in Figure 1-14 is displayed.

3. Select the **Open Oval** logo in the task pane. (*Hint*: The logo names appear below each logo design, and the Open Oval logo design is in the middle of the list.) The logo object in the document changes to the new design.

4. Resize the logo object to enlarge the logo. Then reposition the logo in the center of the panel.

5. Select *Organization* and key **Silver Lake Park**. The text will automatically resize to fit within the text frame.

FIGURE 1-14
Logo Designs task pane

6. Save the changes. When prompted to save the changes to the logo in your organizational information, click **Yes**. Leave the document open for the next Step-by-Step.

Print a Publication

Publisher provides several printing options. You can print all pages of the document, or you can print only selected pages. If you designed your publication to be printed on both sides of the paper, you will want to print one page at a time (unless your printer can print both sides of a piece of paper at once). After the first side of a page is printed, place the page back in the paper tray (or in the manual feed tray) to print the other side. The way you position the paper in the paper tray is dependent on your printer.

The directions below are for a printer that cannot print on both sides of a paper. If you do have a printer capable of double-sided printing, then you would need to select the option for two-sided printing in the Print dialog box. (See your printer manual for specific instructions.) The directions in the following Step-by-Step will guide you through the process of manually printing the publication on both sides of the paper. Check with your instructor for permission to print before completing the steps.

1. Open the **File** menu and choose **Print**. A dialog box similar to the one shown in Figure 1-15 is displayed. Your dialog box will vary depending on your printer.

Did You Know?

If you click the **Print** button on the Standard toolbar, Publisher will print one copy of all pages of your document. If you want to print selected pages or multiple copies, you must open the **File** menu and choose **Print**.

2. Under *Print Range*, select **Pages**, then key **1** in both the *from:* and *to:* boxes. Click **OK**.

Hot Tip

To use the Design Checker in Publisher to check your publication before you print, open the **Tools** menu and choose **Design Checker**. Publisher will alert you of potential errors such as empty frames, text or other objects left in the scratch area, spacing between sentences, and so forth.

3. When the first page is printed, return the page to the paper tray. The direction you face the page in the paper tray will depend on your printer model. See your printer manual for specific directions on printing on both sides of a sheet of paper.

4. Open the **File** menu and choose **Print.** Select **Pages** and key **2** in both the *from:* and *to:* boxes. Click **OK**.

5. Close the document.

Did You Know?

If you click the **Print** button on the Standard toolbar, Publisher will print one copy of all pages of your document. If you want to print selected pages or multiple copies, you must open the **File** menu and choose **Print**.

FIGURE 1-15
Print dialog box

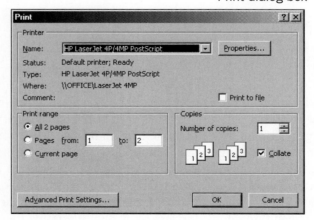

Create a Publication from Scratch

Now that you have worked with some of Publisher's basic features using a design template, creating a new publication from scratch will be easy. The following Step-by-Step will guide you through the process to create a flyer from a blank publication.

STEP-BY-STEP ▷ 1.12

1. If necessary, display the task pane, click the down arrow in the task pane title bar, and choose **New Publication**.

2. Under *Start from a design:*, select **By Blank Publications**. The Blank Full Page window of the Publication Gallery shown in Figure 1-16 is displayed and shows several different document layouts.

3. Select the **Full Page** option. A blank page with layout guides is displayed.

Hot Tip

If the Blank Full Page window is not displayed, click the **Shows Publication Gallery** button near the top right corner of the task pane.

FIGURE 1-16
Publication Designs task pane

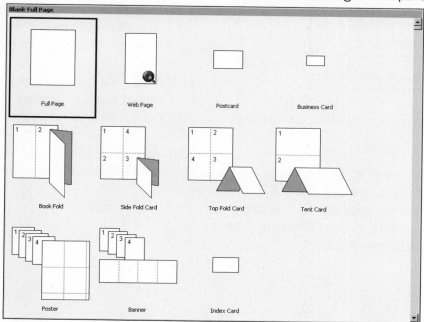

4. Open the **Format** menu and choose **Publication Designs**. The Publication Designs task pane shown in Figure 1-17 is displayed.

FIGURE 1-17
Publication Designs task pane

5. Under *Apply a design*, select the **Bouquet** design.

6. Insert a text frame at the top of the page, approximately 3 inches high and 6 ½ inches wide. Enter the following text in the text frame:
The Flint Institute of the Performing Arts presents Midsummer Nights

7. Center the text and autofit the text for best fit. Format *Midsummer Nights* as bold and italic text. (Open the **Format** menu, choose **Font**, and select **Emboss** under *Effects* to apply this effect.) Then click **OK**.

8. Create a second text frame at the bottom of the page, approximately 1 ½ inches high and 6 ½ inches wide. Enter the following text:
July 26, 27, 28
8 p.m.

9. Center the new text and autofit the text for best fit.

10. Click the **Clip Organizer Frame** button on the Objects toolbar. Search for and insert a clip art image for "music." Position the clip art image in the center of the page and resize as needed to fill the space between the two text boxes.

11. Open the **Format** menu, choose **Color Schemes**, and select a color scheme that complements the clip art image you inserted. Click **Font Schemes** in the task pane and select the Garamond font scheme.

12. Resize and reposition the text boxes and the clip art image to enhance the appearance of the text for an effective presentation.

13. Save the publication as **Midsummer Nights** followed by your initials. Close the document.

Summary

In this lesson, you learned:

■ You should plan the design of your publication before you begin to create a document in Publisher. A mock-up is helpful in planning the placement of text and graphics.

■ Publisher provides several design templates, making it easier to create a professional-looking publication.

■ Publisher stores personal information about your business, address, and so forth. When you create a new publication, Publisher automatically inserts that information as needed. You can store up to four different personal information sets.

■ The Publisher screen has some unique parts such as the Object toolbar and the page navigation button. The scratch area is a space for holding objects temporarily as you work with a document.

■ The task pane simplifies the task of changing the color schemes or font schemes for a publication. When you apply a new scheme, the new formats are applied to the entire document.

■ You need to use frames to position text and graphics in the document. You can resize frames as needed. Automatic copyfitting options automatically resize the text to fit inside the text frame.

■ You can easily remove frames from the document.

■ You use buttons on the Object toolbar to insert new text frames and new picture frames.

■ Publisher provides several smart objects that make tasks such as creating a customized logo easier.

■ Unless you have a printer capable of double-sided printing, when you print a publication on both sides of the paper, you must print the first page and then feed that paper through the printer again to print on the second side.

■ When you create a publication from scratch, you use the same features that are available when you create a publication using a design template.

VOCABULARY REVIEW

Define the following terms:

Automatic copyfitting
Frame
Landscape orientation
Layout guides

Mock-up
Portrait orientation
Scratch area
Sizing handles

Smart objects
Templates

TRUE/FALSE

Circle T if the statement is true or F if the statement is false.

T F 1. Pre-designed templates in the Publication Gallery provide a basic layout and format for a specific publication.

T F 2. To create a publication from scratch, you would choose the *By Blank Publications* option in the New Publication task pane.

T F 3. You can create six different personal information sets.

T F 4. All text in a Publisher document must be inserted within areas called text boxes.

T F 5. You have to know how to use the drawing tools to create a logo in Publisher.

FILL IN THE BLANK

Complete the following sentences by writing the correct word or words in the blanks provided.

1. To help with planning a publication design, you should create a(n) _____.

2. The gray area around the document for holding objects temporarily as you work is called the _____.

3. Pink and blue _____ help you to align objects on the page.

4. When the _____ option is turned on, Publisher will resize text as you type it to fit in a specific area.

5. Graphics in a publication are contained within _____.

PROJECT 1-1

1. If necessary, launch Publisher and display the New Publication task pane. Select the **Postcards** publication type, and then select the **Borders Informational Postcard** template.

2. Use the following information to apply and edit the Other Organization personal information that you created in Step-by-Step 1.3:
    A. Open the **Edit** menu, choose **Personal Information**, and select **Other Organization**. In the *Name:* box, key **Kerry Tolzmann**.

B. Turn on the check box under *Color schemes:* and select the **Dark Blue** color scheme.
C. Click **Update**.

3. Save the publication as **Board Meeting Reminder** followed by your initials.

4. Apply a font scheme of your choice.

5. Select the heading *Product/Service Information* and replace the text with **May Board Meeting**. AutoFit the text frame for **Best Fit**.

6. Click in the paragraph below the new heading. AutoFit the text frame for **Shrink Text On Overflow** and then key the following:
   Next month's board meeting will be held at 7 p.m. Tuesday, May 22, at Joe Knapp's home. Agenda items include a final report on the installation of the new pier and plans for the July watercraft parade. Please let me know if you will not be attending.
   KT

7. Save your changes. When prompted, save your new logo information in the Primary personal information set and close the publication.

PROJECT 1-2

1. Open the New Publication task pane and select **By Publication Type**. Select the **Flyers** category, then select **Informational**. Choose the **Tilt Informational Flyer** design.

2. Choose the **Mistletoe** color scheme.

3. Edit the Primary Business personal information set by clearing any previous information from the Personal Information dialog box and inserting the following:
   Address: **3428 Burney Lane**
                                    Mt. Washington, OH 45230
   Phone: **Phone: 513-555-3390**
                                    Web: www.ocrc.org
   Organization name: **Mt. Washington Recreation Center**

4. Update the information, then save the publication as **Holidays** followed by your initials.

5. If desired, increase the zoom to enlarge the view of the document.

6. At the top of the flyer, change the Mt. Washington Recreation Center font size to 14 point. Click in the empty text frame below the *Mt. Washington Recreation Center* frame and key **An Oak Creek Community Center**.

7. Click the logo at the right of these text frames and start the Wizard by clicking the Wizard button that displays below the logo. Change the logo design to **Foundation Bar** and change the name in the logo to **Oak Creek**.

8. Select the *Product/Service Information* sample text and key **Holiday Aerobics!** Replace the sample photo with clip art or a photo that relates to exercising, aerobics, or fitness.

9. Select the sample text below the graphic and replace it with the following paragraph:

   Holidays can be stressful times, what with all the eating, merrymaking, eating, gift giving, and eating. Maintain your fall fitness level by attending our special Holiday Aerobics sessions. You can attend as many or as few as you like in the six-week period.

10. In the bottom left corner of the frame you just keyed this information in, create a new text frame. Insert the following information in the new text frame:

    Holiday Aerobics
    December 2 – January 10
    Monday, Tuesday, and Thursday
    5:30 – 6:30 p.m.
    $49
    Instructor: Jan Michaels

11. Align the top of your newest text frame with the top of the box that contains Mt. Washington Recreation Center.

12. Save your changes. When prompted, save your new logo information in the Primary Business personal information set and close the publication.

WEB PROJECT

Publisher allows you to create not merely one-page publications, but multipage publications like catalogs. Think of an item or items for which you would like to create a catalog. You can use collectibles, coins, jewelry, books, and so forth. Use the Web to find out current prices for your catalog items so you can set fair prices. You might need to visit a number of Web sites to get all the information you need. Prepare a mock-up and then use a template in Publisher to create the first few pages of your catalog.

TEAMWORK PROJECT

If you have explored the task panes in Publisher, you know that you can create a tremendous variety of different publications, from advertisements to paper airplanes. The fun of working with Publisher lies in how you choose to customize the template publications. Hold a class competition to see which team can customize the same template in the most interesting way. Follow these steps:

1. As a class decide on a simple publication to customize, such as an invitation to an upcoming event (a holiday party, for example).

2. Divide into teams of two or three. Each team should work on the same template and use Publisher's many features to create an attractive and useful publication. Be sure to prepare a mock-up before you begin to create the document in Publisher.

CRITICAL THINKING

You would like to add a logo to a publication design that doesn't contain a sample logo. Will Publisher let you add a logo to any design? Use the Help system in Publisher to find out, and then write a brief report in Word on what you learn.

WORKING WITH FRONTPAGE

OBJECTIVES

Upon completion of this lesson, you should be able to:

- Create a Web page.
- Create a navigation structure.
- Add content and save Web pages.
- Add a theme.
- Add a page banner.
- Insert text from another application to a Web page.
- Insert a link bar and other hyperlinks to a Web page.
- Add graphics to a Web page.
- View and print a Web site.

🕐 **Estimated time: 1.5 hours**

VOCABULARY

HTML

Hyperlink

Home page

Link bar

Marquee

Theme

Web site

Word wrap

Microsoft FrontPage makes it easy to combine text, graphics, audio, video, and animation in a format that can be viewed on the Internet. Although you can create Web pages in other Office applications, FrontPage provides the most complete set of tools for creating and publishing a Web page.

You can create a single Web page in FrontPage, but the best way to take advantage of the features available is to create a Web site. A **Web site** is a series of single Web pages linked together as a unit. Each Web site has a **home page**, which is the main entry page for the entire Web site. Additional Web pages can be accessed from the home page, as well as images and other types of files that are on the Web pages. Because a Web page is the main starting point of any Web site, you must first create that page before creating additional Web pages.

Create a Web

Whien you use FrontPage to create a Web page, it is automatically formatted with HTML tags. *HTML* is an acronym for HyperText Markup Language and is a system for marking text so that it can be published on the World Wide Web. The HTML tags provide information about the navigation structure, appearance, and contents of the page. This information is necessary for a Web browser to display the page.

Identify the Parts of the FrontPage Screen

When you launch FrontPage, a blank Web page is displayed in Page view as shown in Figure 2-1. You can edit your pages in this view. You can change the view by clicking to select a different view on the Views bar at the left side of the screen. You will work with some of the other views in this lesson.

Computer Concepts

In this lesson, when references are made to the web you create in FrontPage (the network of inter-related pages), the word "web" is shown with a lowercase "w." When references are made to Web pages and Web sites, the word "Web" is shown with an initial cap because the page or site can be published on the World Wide Web.

FIGURE 2-1
Blank page in Page view

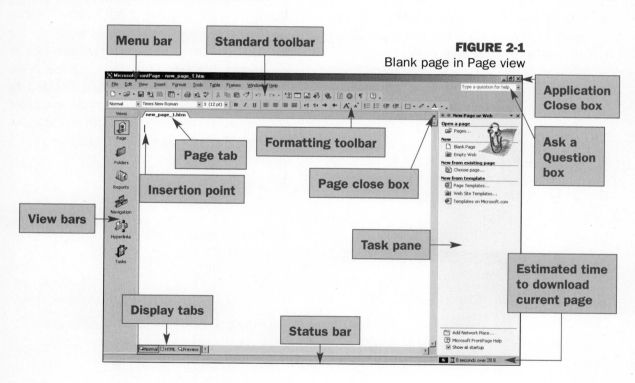

Menu bar · Standard toolbar · Application Close box · Page tab · Formatting toolbar · Ask a Question box · Insertion point · Page close box · View bars · Task pane · Estimated time to download current page · Display tabs · Status bar

The task bar, the menu bar, and both the Standard and Formatting toolbars are similar to those you've seen in other Office applications. However, the status bar at the bottom of the screen is different. In FrontPage, the status bar displays information and messages. For example, in Page view, you will see a message estimating how long the page will take to download at a particular modem speed.

Hot Tip

If your screen does not match Figure 2-1, try clicking the **Page** button in the Views bar to display the page in Page view. If the Views bar is not displayed, open the **View** menu and choose **Views Bar**.

The default pane is the Normal pane. When you click the HTML tab at the bottom of the screen, your page changes to the HTML pane and the content will display in HTML code. If you know HTML code, you can write and edit the page in this view. If you don't know HTML code, you should stay in the Normal pane.

If Microsoft Internet Explorer is installed on your computer, you will also see a Preview tab at the bottom of the screen. You can click this tab to view your pages as others will see them in their Web browser.

Create a Web Based on a Template

FrontPage provides several wizards and templates to help you create professional-looking Web pages. The wizards and templates offer a variety of layouts and formats.

Computer Concepts

If you want to design the page by yourself, you can start with a blank page and not a template.

STEP-BY-STEP ▷ 2.1

1. Launch FrontPage. If the task pane is not displayed, open the **File** menu, choose **New**, and then select **Page or Web** in the submenu.

2. In the task pane under *New*, click **Empty Web**. The Web Site Templates dialog box is displayed.

3. Click **One Page Web** to select it. (Although you will initially begin with a single page, you will be able to add pages later.)

4. Click in the text box under *Specify the location of the new web*. Change the path to the location where you save your solution files as displayed in Figure 2-2. The last folder in the path shold be **Warner Guitars** followed by your initials. FrontPage will create this folder for you. For example, your path may look like *Unit 7\Lesson 2\Warner Guitars smn.*

FIGURE 2-2
Web Site Templates dialog box

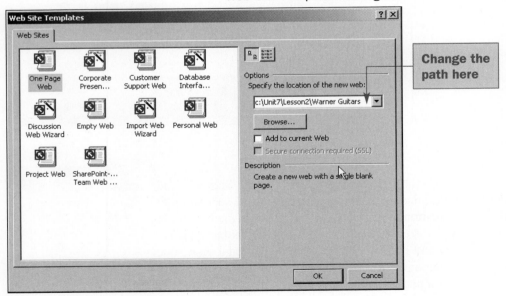

5. Click **OK**. A new page is created. The path and the new folders that FrontPage created for the new page are displayed in the Folder List next to the Views bar. Leave the web open for the next Step-by-Step.

Computer Concepts

The path is the route the computer's operating system uses to locate a document. The path identifies the disk and any folders relative to the location of the document. The filename is generally at the end of the path. When you save a web, however, you identify only the folder and not the filename. If the folder doesn't exist, FrontPage will create it.

Create a Navigation Structure

FrontPage identifies the first page you create as the home page. It saves this page under the filename *index.htm*. When you add additional pages to the home page, you create a web. An easy way to add additional pages is to switch to Navigation view. When you display the page in Navigation view, you can see the navigation structure of your web as you add each new page. You can assign a name to each new page you create.

STEP-BY-STEP ⟹ 2.2

1. Click the **Navigation** button on the Views bar to switch to Navigation view. Your screen should look similar to Figure 2-3. If the Folder List is not displayed, open the **View** menu and choose **Folder List**.

FIGURE 2-3
Navigation view of a page

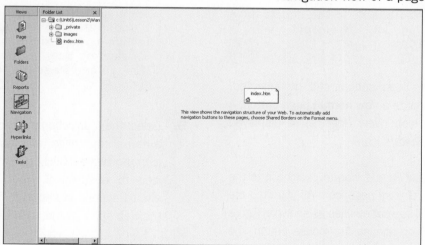

Speech Recognition

If your computer has speech recognition capability, enable the Command mode and say the command to switch to Navigation view.

2. Click the **Create a new normal page** button on the Standard toolbar. A New Page 1 icon is displayed below the *index.htm* icon on your screen.

3. Click the **New Page 1** icon. The background color of the icon changes (usually from yellow to blue) to indicate it is selected. Then click inside the text box containing the icon label to select the text. Key **Guitars** and press **Enter**.

Hot Tip

If you accidentally double-click a page icon, your screen will switch to Page view. If this happens, your page will be saved as *new_page_1.htm*. Click the **Navigation** button on the Views bar to return to Navigation view. Then, you must rename the Web page. If it isn't already displayed, open the **View** menu and choose **Folders** to display the Folder List. Then, right click the *new_page-1.htm* filename. Choose **Rename** in the shortcut menu and key the correct name for the Web page.

4. The *Guitars* icon should still be selected. Click the **Create a new normal page** button. A new page icon (*New Page 1*) is displayed below the *Guitars* icon.

5. Drag the *New Page 1* icon to position it to the right of the *Guitars* page icon. As you drag the icon, you will see dotted lines as shown in Figure 2-4. When you release the mouse button, the

two page icons should be at the same level in the navigation structure.

FIGURE 2-4
Repositioning a page icon in the navigation structure

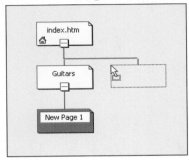

6. Make sure *New Page 1* is selected. Click in the text box, key **Instruction**, and press **Enter**.

7. Make sure the *Instruction* page icon is selected. Click the **Create a new normal page** button. Label the new page icon **Lessons Online**.

8. Select the *Instruction* page icon again, create a new normal page, and label the new page icon **Books**.

Hot Tip

You can also add a new page under an existing page by right-clicking the existing page and selecting **New** in the shortcut menu and **Page** in the submenu.

9. Select the *Instruction* page icon again, create a new normal page, and label the new page icon **Software**. Click outside the *Software* icon to deselect it. Your Navigation view should appear as shown in Figure 2-5. Leave the web open for the next Step-by-Step.

FIGURE 2-5
Web navigation structure displayed in Navigation view

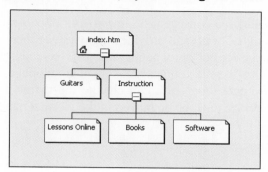

Add Content to and Save Web Pages

To add new content or to edit existing content on a Web page, you need to display the page in Page view. If the text you are keying extends beyond the right margin, FrontPage will automatically wrap the text to the next line. This feature is called ***word wrap***. Press Enter only to start a new paragraph. The width of the browser window will determine where the text will wrap when it is viewed in a browser.

To edit text on a Web page, select the text just as you would in other Office applications. You can move, copy, or delete the text. You can also format the selected text or insert graphics next to the text.

After completing the edits, you can save the changes by clicking the Save button or by opening the Format menu and choosing Save. However, if your web has multiple pages, only the changes for the current Web page will be saved. If you fail to save the changes on one or more Web pages before your exit the application, FrontPage will prompt you to save the changes to those pages.

Hot Tip

To check your spelling, open the **Tools** menu and choose **Spelling** or press the shortcut key **F7**.

STEP-BY-STEP ▷ 2.3

1. Double-click **index.htm** in the Folder List. The display changes to Page view and the home page appears in the pane on the right with the insertion point blinking. Key the following: **Warner Guitars is your factory-direct source for top-quality guitars and guitar instruction.**

2. Click the **Save** button on the Standard toolbar. The changes to the home page are saved. Leave the web open for the next Step-by-Step.

Add a Theme

A *theme* is a way to maintain a consistent design in your document with elements such as fonts, graphics, colors, and backgrounds. FrontPage provides many preset themes that will give your pages a professional look. A theme can be applied to all pages or to just a selected page. If desired, you can apply different themes to each page in a web. If you apply the theme to all pages in the web, then the theme is applied to new pages as you create them. You can change the theme at any time, and in any view. However, to apply a theme, the page must be displayed in the Normal pane.

STEP-BY-STEP ▷ 2.4

1. Open the **Format** menu and choose **Theme** to open the Themes dialog box.

2. Turn on the options **All pages**.

Speech Recognition

If your computer has speech recognition capability, enable the Command mode and say the commands to open the Themes dialog box and select the options described.

3. Select **Blends** in the list box at the left. The sample of the selected theme is displayed at the right.

4. Below the list of themes are four options. If necessary, turn on the options for **Vivid colors**, **Active graphics**, and **Background picture**. The options are turned on when there is a checkmark in the box next to the option. As you turn on each option, the sample in the dialog box is updated.

5. When your screen matches Figure 2-6, click **OK**. If you are prompted about permanently replacing existing formatting information, click **Yes**. The theme is applied to all the pages in the web.

FIGURE 2-6
Themes dialog box

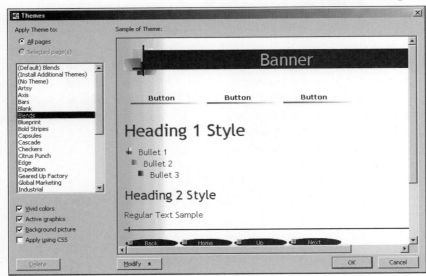

Computer Concepts

The active graphics option pro-vides animated page elements. For example, when you move the mouse pointer over a bullet, the bullet graphic will change colors.

6. Notice that the current page is now formatted with the background color gradient and the font style has changed to the font style spec-ified in the theme.

7. Save the changes and leave the web open for the next Step-by-Step. Because you applied the theme to all pages, the theme design is saved for all pages when you save the changes to the current page.

 Did You Know?

You can remove a theme or apply a different theme at any time.

Add a Page Banner

You can quickly add a title to a page by inserting a page banner. If you have applied a theme, the page banner is formatted based on the style and graphics of the theme. The banner shows the same title that you assigned to the page in Navigation view. If desired, you can edit the banner text – at any time after you add it to a page. If you change the page banner text, the page label in the navigation structure will also change.

STEP-BY-STEP 2.5

1. Position the insertion point at the beginning of the text on the *index.htm* page. Press **Enter** and then reposition the insertion point to the new blank line above the paragraph.

2. Open the **Insert** menu and choose **Page Banner**. The dialog box shown in Figure 2-7 is displayed. Notice that the Picture option is already selected. This means the banner text will be presented in a graphic consistent with the theme you have chosen.

3. The text box under *Page banner* shows *index.htm*. Select the text in the text box, then key **Warner Guitars**. Click **OK**. A banner containing the new text is positioned at the insertion point.

FIGURE 2-7
Page Banner Properties dialog box

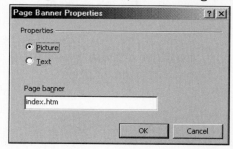

4. Change to Navigation view. Notice that the page in the navigation structure is updated and contains the label *Warner Guitars*. However, the filename *index.htm* in the Folder List remains unchanged.

5. Click the **Page** button in the Views bar to switch back to Page view. Click below the paragraph of text and key the following:

At Warner Guitars, your personal enjoyment of studying and playing the guitar is our priority.

Speech Recognition

If your computer has speech recognition capability, enable the Dictation mode and dictate the Web page content.

6. If necessary, display the Folder List and then double-click **instruction.htm** in the Folder List to open the *Instruction* page.

7. Open the **Insert** menu and choose **Page Banner**. Do not change the text in the text box because you want to use this text in the banner. Click **OK**. The banner text (*Instruction*) is the same as the title of the page in the navigation structure.

8. Notice that there are now two page tabs displayed at the top of the page as displayed in Figure 2-8. Although you have created six pages in your web, only two of the pages are open. You can quickly access the open pages by clicking one of these tabs.

Did You Know?

The Undo and Redo features are available in FrontPage and they work the same as in other applications. When necessary, click the **Undo** or **Redo** button on the Standard toolbar, or open the **Edit** menu and choose **Undo** or **Redo**. FrontPage also offers another way to undo all editing since you last opened or saved your web. Open the **View** menu and choose **Refresh**, or press **F5**. However, proceed with caution because you cannot restore the web after you execute the Refresh command.

9. Save the changes to the current page.

10. Notice that the *Index.htm* tab displays an asterisk. This asterisk indicates that there are changes on the page that have not been saved. Click the **Index.htm** tab to display that page, then save the changes to that page. The asterisk will disappear. Leave the web open for the next Step-by-Step.

FIGURE 2-8
Page tabs displayed in Page view

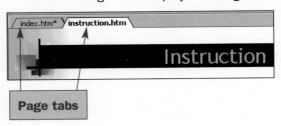

Insert Text from Another Application

If the information you want to incorporate into your Web page already exists in a text-based format, you do not need to recreate it in FrontPage. You can insert the existing file in your Web page. FrontPage will convert the file to HTML format. However, you may lose some formatting, such as bullets and numbering, when FrontPage does the conversion.

STEP-BY-STEP ▷ 2.6

1. The insertion point should be positioned after the banner on the *instruction.htm* page. Press **Enter**.

2. Open the **Insert** menu and choose **File**. The Select File dialog box is displayed.

3. Click the down arrow in the *Look in:* box and locate the folder for the data files. Click the down arrow in the *Files of type:* box and select either **All files** or **Word** in order to see the ".doc" files contained within this folder. Select **Step2-6a** and click **Open**. The contents of the file are inserted in the page. If you get a message about installing a converter to display the file correctly, click **Yes** and proceed through the installation process.

4. Select the last three lines and click the **Bullets** button on the Formatting toolbar. Bullets for the *Blends* theme are applied to the three lines of text.

5. Save the changes to the current page.

6. Double-click **lessons_online.htm** in the Folder List to display the *Lessons Online* page.

7. Open the **Insert** menu and choose **Page Banner** and click **OK**.

8. Press **Enter**, then insert the file **Step2-6b** from the data files. If prompted to install a converter to display the file correctly, click **No**.

9. Save the changes to the current page and leave the web open for the next Step-by-Step.

Did You Know?

You can create custom bullets to use in your Web pages. You must first create the bullet graphics and save them in a GIF or JPEG format. Then, to apply the bullet format, open the **Format** menu, choose **Bullets and Numbering**, and select the **Picture Bullets** tab. Select the option **Specify picture** and then locate the file containing your bullet graphic.

Insert a Link Bar and Other Hyperlinks

When visitors open your home page, you want them to be able to access information throughout your web easily. You can create a *hyperlink* to help visitors move around in your web. The hyperlink takes the user to a new destination called a target. The target of the hyperlink can be a different location on the same Web page or to a location on another Web page. You can display multiple hyperlinks for the main pages of your web in a link bar. A *link bar* is a collection of buttons that make it easy to navigate the main pages of a Web site. Link bars are simply hyperlinks to pages that are part of the same web structure. You can show the link bar on each page so visitors can always go to the main pages quickly and easily. If you have applied a theme to your pages, the link bar is formatted based on the style and graphics of the theme.

The easiest way to add a link bar is to have FrontPage set it up according to the web navigation structure you created earlier. This means the hyperlinks in the link bar are based on your navigation structure. The hyperlinks are labeled using titles you gave the pages in your navigation structure. FrontPage will automatically add or delete hyperlinks to the link bar as you add or delete pages to the web.

When you create a link bar based on the navigation structure, you need to identify the level for which you want your hyperlinks to display. For example, if you want links for parent-level pages, hyperlinks will be included for all pages in the level directly above the current page. If you choose to format links for child-level pages, hyperlinks are created for all pages directly below the current page.

S TEP-BY-STEP ▷ 2.7

1. Click the **index.htm** page tab to display the home page. Position the insertion point below the last paragraph of text.

2. Open the **Insert** menu and choose **Navigation**. The Insert Web Component dialog box is displayed.

3. If necessary, select **Link Bars** under *Component type:*. Under *Choose a bar type:*, select **Bar based on navigation structure**. When your dialog box looks like Figure 2-9, click **Next**.

FIGURE 2-9
Insert Web Component dialog box

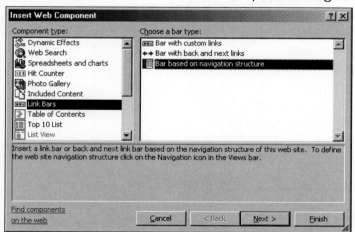

4. Under *Choose a bar style:*, make sure **Use Page's Theme** is selected and then click **Next**. Under *Choose an orientation*, make sure the first option (*horizontal*) is selected. Click **Finish**.

5. The Link Bar Properties dialog box shown in Figure 2-10 is displayed. This dialog box enables you to select the parts of the navigation structure that you want to appear on the link bar. No changes are necessary since the link bar should contain links to the child level pages. Click OK. A link bar with two buttons is inserted at the position of the insertion point.

FIGURE 2-10
Link Bar Properties dialog box

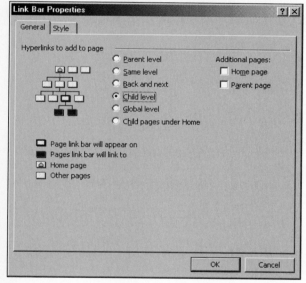

Hot Tip

The Link Bar Properties dialog box provides a visual image for each level option. Select an new option in the Link Bar Properties dialog box, and the illustration under *Hyperlinks to add to page* will change to reflect the new level selected. As noted in the legend of the dialog box, the page containing the link bar is white with a blue border, and the target pages are displayed in blue.

8. Click the **Navigation** button in the Views bar. Click the home page icon (which is labeled Warner Guitars) to select it, then click the **Create a new normal page** button and label the new page icon **Instructors**.

9. Click the **Page** button on the Views bar and then, if necessary, click the **index.htm** page tab to display the home page. Notice that the link bar on the home page has been updated and now includes a third button for *Instructors*.

10. Click the **instruction.htm** page tab to display the *Instruction* page. Position the insertion point below the banner and in front of the first line of text. Press **Enter**, then move the insertion point into the new blank line.

6. Click the **Center** button on the Formatting toolbar to center the navigation bar on the page.

7. Save the changes to the current page.

11. Insert a link bar based on the navigation structure. Use the page's theme and choose the **horizontal** orientation. Make sure the **Child level** and **Home page** options are selected in the Link Bar Properties dialog box. Center the link bar. Notice that this link bar is different because these links connect you to different targets.

455

12. Select the first bulleted item **Lessons Online**. Click the **Insert Hyperlink** button on the Standard toolbar. The Insert Hyperlink dialog box shown in Figure 2-11 is displayed.

13. Make sure the options **Existing File or Web Page** and **Current Folder** are selected. Select the filename **lessons_online.htm (open)**. Click **OK**. Click outside the selected text to deselect the text. The font color of the text changes and the text is underlined to indicate the text is formatted as a hyperlink.

14. Select the second bulleted item and create a hyperlink to the filename **books.htm**.

15. Select the third bulleted item and create a hyperlink to the file **software.htm**. Save the changes to the current page and leave the web open for the next Step-by-Step.

FIGURE 2-11
Insert Hyperlink dialog box

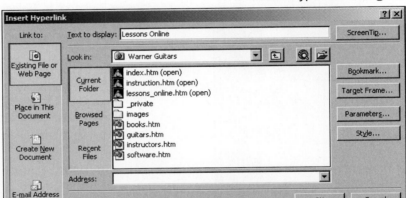

Insert and Format Graphics

Banners and link bars are two examples of graphical elements that help liven up the appearance of your page. You can also add other graphics such as clip art, pictures, and video to enhance the appearance and effectiveness of your pages.

Add Pictures and Clip Art

You can add pictures or clip art from a file, scanner, digital camera, video camera, or the Internet. When you insert a graphic, it is positioned at the place where the insertion point is located. If you need to, you can resize the graphic. You can also align the graphic within the line of text (left, center, or right).

The graphics you add to the Web pages will be saved in the images folder. FrontPage created this folder when it first created your web.

S TEP-BY-STEP ▷ 2.8

1. Display the **index.htm** page.

2. Position the insertion point after the banner and in front of the first line of text. Open the **Insert** menu and choose **Picture**. Select **Clip Art** in the submenu. The Insert Clip Art task pane similar to the one shown in Figure 2-12 is displayed.

FIGURE 2-12
Insert Clip Art task pane

3. Select the text (if any exists) in the *Search text:* box, then key **guitar**. Click **Search**. Images matching the keyword *guitar* are displayed under *Results*.

4. Select an appropriate image. The picture is inserted in the document at the place where the insertion point is located. Leave the Insert Clip Art task pane open.

Hot Tip

If the results for your search are minimal, make sure the *All collections* option is selected in the *Search in* box under *Other Search Options*. Click the down arrow in the *Results should be:* box and make sure Clip Art is selected. Remove checkmarks from all other options. If you still cannot locate an appropriate clip art image, try searching for clips online. Also, additional clip art images are available on the Microsoft Office XP Media Content disk.

5. Click the picture to select it, then click the **Align Right** button on the Formatting toolbar to position the picture at the right side of the page.

Hot Tip

If you need to resixe the picture, click to select it. Eight sizing handles will display around the boundaries of the picture. To make the image smaller, drag one of the corner handles toward the center; to make the image bigger, drag a corner handle outward.

6. Click the **Save** button on the Standard toolbar. The Save Embedded Files dialog box, similar to the one shown in Figure 2-13, is displayed.

7. Click the **Change Folder** button in the dialog box. The Change Folder dialog box, similar to the one shown in Figure 2-14, is displayed.

8. Double-click the **images** folder, then click **OK**. You'll see *images/* in the Folder column in the Save Embedded Files dialog box. Click **OK** to close the dialog box.

9. Display the *Instruction* page. Position the insertion point in front of the first line of text and insert an appropriate clip art image. Resize the image as needed, but leave it aligned at the left.

10. Click the **Save** button. When the Save Embedded Files dialog box is displayed, click **OK**. There is no need to change the folder since the **images** folder is already selected. Leave the web open for the next Step-by-Step.

Computer Concepts

You can specify the format of the graphic image by clicking the Picture Options button in the Save Embedded Files dialog box. GIF and JPEG are two common graphics formats used on the Internet. The GIF (Graphics Interchange Format) format is best for storing line art and computer-generated drawings. The images should contain no more than 256 colors. The JPEG (Joint Photographic Experts Group) format is best for photos and images that contain more than 256 colors.

FIGURE 2-13
Save Embedded Files dialog box

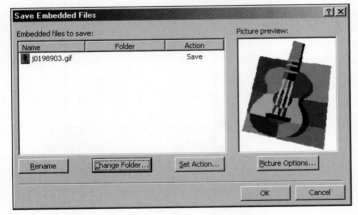

FIGURE 2-14
Change Folder dialog box

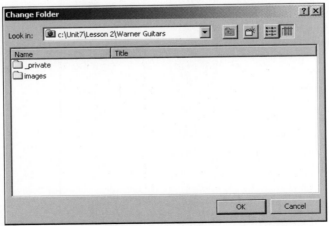

Add a Movie Clip

You can also insert movie clips in your pages. When you insert a movie clip, it is inserted at the location of the insertion point. The animation usually begins when the page is first opened in a browser.

STEP-BY-STEP ▷ 2.9

1. Display the **lessons_online.htm** page and position the insertion point after the banner and before the first paragraph of text. Press **Enter** and then move the insertion point to the new blank paragraph.

2. Make sure the Insert Clip Art task pane is displayed. Select a movie clip from the Clip Art Gallery:

   a. Click the **Modify** button at the bottom of the task pane to show the *Search For* options.

   b. In the *Search text:* box, key **music**.

   c. If necessary, select the **All collections** option in the *Search in:* box.

   d. Click the down arrow in the *Results should be:* box. If necessary, click the plus sign next to *All media types* to display the submenu with four options. Select the **Movies** option, and deselect all other options. Your task pane should match Figure 2-15.

3. Click **Search** in the task pane. The *Results* list is displayed. Point to one of the images (but do not select it) and then click the down arrow. Choose **Preview/Properties** in the shortcut menu. A dialog box will open and display the movie clip as it will appear on the Web page. Click **Close** in the dialog box and then preview another movie clip from the *Results* list.

4. When you've found an appropriate clip, select the image in the task pane. The clip is inserted at the place where the insertion point is located. Note that the movie clip sequence will not play until you preview the Web page.

5. Click the **Save** button. When the Save Embedded Files dialog box is displayed, click **OK**. Close the Clip Art task pane. Leave the web open for the next Step-by-Step.

FIGURE 2-15
Insert Clip Art task pane with search options selected for movie clips

Use Help to Learn about Creating a Marquee

Another animated feature you can add to a Web page is a marquee. A *marquee* is a region on a Web page that displays a horizontally scrolling text message. You can use a marquee to draw attention to an area of the page or to emphasize important information. Use the Help screens to learn how to create and format a marquee.

S TEP-BY-STEP ▷ 2.10

1. If the Office Assistant is displayed, right-click the Office Assistant and choose **Options** in the shortcut menu. In the Options tab, turn off the option **Use the Office Assistant** and then click **OK**.

2. Open the **Help** menu and choose **Microsoft FrontPage Help**.

3. If necessary, click the **Index** tab. In the *Type keywords:* box, key **marquee**. A semi-colon will be automatically inserted at the end of the text. Click **Search**. A list of topics will display under *3. Choose a topic.* See Figure 2-16.

4. Information related to the first topic **Create a marquee** is displayed in the pane on the right. Read the information. Be sure to click the link **Tips** to display information about previewing and formatting the marquee.

▪ Computer Concepts

Leave the Help screen open so you can quickly return to the Help screens to refresh your memory. To return to the Help screens, click the Microsoft Help button in the task bar.

5. Click the **Microsoft FrontPage** button in the task bar to switch to your web. If necessary, display the lessons_online.htm page. Position the insertion point in front of the movie clip and press **Enter**. Then move the insertion point to the new blank paragraph.

6. Key **Your first lesson is free!** as the marquee at the top of the page. (Hint: Click the **Microsoft FrontPage Help** button in the task bar if you need to refer back to the Help information.)

FIGURE 2-16
Index tab in Help dialog box

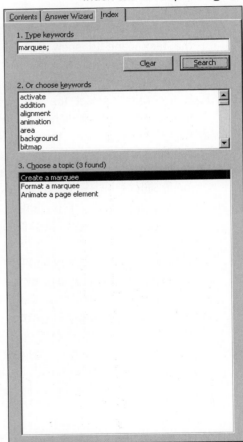

7. Click the **Microsoft FrontPage Help** button in the task bar to return to the Help screens. Click the link **Format a marquee** in the pane on the left. Then click **Show All** at the top of the pane to display all the information related to the topic. Review the information about formatting behavior and attributes and formatting font properties.

8. Switch back to the Web page and format the marquee properties, changing the background color that displays behind the text to a color that fits in with the theme. You will get to preview the revised marquee in Step-by-Step 2.11.

9. Switch back to Help and close the Help screens.

10. Save the changes to the current page and leave the web open for the next Step-by-Step.

Computer Concepts

Carefully consider the use of graphics in your Web site. When you add pictures, videos, and movie clips, the size of your site increases quickly. The file size will impact how much time it will take visitors to download pages from your site. Furthermore, your ISP (Internet Service Provider) may limit the file size of the Web site that you publish.

View the Graphic Files and Hyperlinks

Folders view enables you to quickly view the list of files contained within a folder. This view also displays information about each of the folders such as the file size, the type of file, the date the file was modified, who modified it, and any additional comments that a person may have made.

FrontPage also automatically tracks and repairs the internal hyperlinks in your web whenever you move, rename, or delete a file. Hyperlinks view provides a graphical representation of the hyperlinks in your web. In Hyperlinks view, each page is represented with an icon. The index.htm page is displayed with a different icon, indicating that it is the home page.

Computer Concepts

You can delete the current web in Folders view by right-clicking the top-level folder and choosing **Delete** in the shortcut menu. FrontPage will prompt you to confirm the deletion. If you choose to delete a web, the deletion is permanent, and you won't be able to restore the deleted files or folders.

1. Click the **Folders** button in the Views bar. A list of all the web folders is displayed as shown in Figure 2-17.

2. Click the **images** folder in the Folder List. The display in the right panel changes to display the files stored in the images folder (the two clip art images and the one movie file).

3. Click the folder at the top of the Folder List to view the .htm files again. Then click the **instruction.htm** filename in the right panel.

4. Click the **Hyperlinks** button in the Views bar. The hyperlinks for that page are displayed in the right panel as shown in Figure 2-18. A plus (+) symbol on the page icon indicates that those pages also contain hyperlinks.

5. Select other pages in the Folder List to view the hyperlinks.

6. Switch to Page view. Leave the web open for the next Step-by-Step.

FIGURE 2-17
Folders view of web

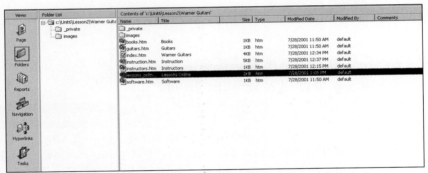

FIGURE 2-18
Hyperlinks view of Instruction page

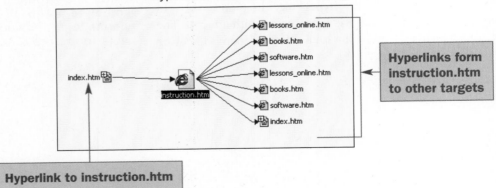

Hyperlinks form instruction.htm to other targets

Hyperlink to instruction.htm

View and Print the Web Site

Before you publish your Web site, you will want to view the pages as they will appear in a Web browser. As you view the pages, you can test the link bar and any other hyperlinks you created. If you do plan to publish to the Web, you need to be aware of what will and will not work with different browsers. For example, the marquee you created may not be supported in all browsers. If the feature is not supported it can cause text and graphics to be misplaced, and visitors to your site may be upset if the Web page is dysfunctional.

If desired, you can print each of the pages in the Web site. To print, you must open each page in Page view. You can only print one page at a time. The hyperlinks and pictures will print just as they look on the screen in Page view.

Once you have viewed your pages and tested your hyperlinks, your web can now be published. You can publish a web to a Web server, to an FTP server, or to a location on your local computer. However, if you publish to a location on your local computer, your Web site will not have the full FrontPage functionality unless your computer is a server that has the required server extensions. Because you need to specify the publishing location and set publishing options, publishing your Web site is beyond the scope of this lesson. However, if you'd like to learn about publishing your web, search for the keyword *publish* in Microsoft FrontPage Help.

S TEP-BY-STEP ▷ 2.12

1. Display *index.htm* in Page view. If you have Internet Explorer installed on your computer, click the **Preview** tab at the bottom of the screen. If you do not have Internet Explorer on your computer, click the **Preview in Browser** button on the Standard toolbar. If you are prompted to save the changes, click **Yes**, then click **OK**.

2. Click the **Instruction** link on the link bar to move to the *Instruction* page. Then click the **Home** link to return to the home page.

3. Click the **Instruction** link on the link bar on the home page to return to the *Instruction* page. Then click the **Lessons Online** link on the link bar to preview the marquee animation and play the movie clip.

4. Click the **Normal** button at the bottom of the page to exit the preview or close your browser. The home page will display. If desired, click the **Preview** button again to test the other hyperlinks.

5. If you are permitted to print, open the **index.htm** file, then click the **Print** button on the Standard toolbar to print the current page.

6. Close all the open pages.

COMPUTER ETHICS

The Internet has opened up a new arena for rules of conduct. A basic understanding of computer ethics will help users make informed and moral decisions in their everyday access to Web sites. For example, users should know how to protect themselves from harassment while they are online. They must also know how to protect their data (such as personal and financial information) so it is not misused. Another concern is copyright issues. When accessing information on the Internet, users must respect the work of others and not use another's work without prior permission.

Summary

In this lesson, you learned:

■ Similar to other Office applications, FrontPage displays a menu bar, a Standard toolbar, a Formatting toolbar, a task pane, the taskbar, and the status bar when you are in Page view. However, unlike other Office applications, the status bar displays information and messages. The Views bar and the Folder List are also unique to FrontPage.

■ FrontPage provides several wizards and templates to help you create professional-looking Web pages.

■ To create a Web site, you begin with a single page called the home page. FrontPage saves the page in HTML format so it can be viewed on the Internet.

■ When you display the Web page in Navigation view, you can see the navigation structure of your web. You can add pages in this view, and you can also edit the navigation structure in this view.

■ To add new content or to edit existing content on a Web page, you need to display the page in Page view. To edit text on a Web page, select the text just as you would in other Office applications.

■ FrontPage provides a variety of themes that you can apply to your Web pages for a consistent and professional-looking design.

■ If you have created a navigation structure, you can automatically create a page banner for each page of the web. The page banner is formatted with the theme elements and contains the same text as the label for the page in the navigation structure.

■ You can use the standard copy and paste or insert methods to insert text from other applications.

■ A link bar provides hyperlinks so viewers of the page can move to new locations in the Web site quickly and easily. The easiest way to add a link bar is to base it on your navigation structure.

■ You can add a variety of graphics to Web pages including clip art, photos, scanned images, and movie clips.

■ A marquee is a region on a Web page that displays a horizontally scrolling text message. You can use a marquee to draw attention to an area of the page or to emphasize important information.

■ You can use the Preview and Print features to view your pages as they will display on the World Wide Web.

VOCABULARY REVIEW

Define the following terms:

HTML	Link bar	Web site
Hyperlink	Marquee	Word wrap
Home page	Theme	

TRUE/FALSE

Circle T if the statement is true or F if the statement is false.

T   F   1.   In FrontPage, a web can be one page or a number of pages.

T   F   2.   FrontPage saves the home page with the filename *default.htm*.

T   F   3.   If you want, you can apply a different FrontPage theme to each page in a web.

T   F   4.   Hyperlinks in a link bar are based on the files you see in Folders view.

T   F   5.   A page banner must be identical to the filename for that page.

FILL IN THE BLANK

Complete the following sentences by writing the correct word or words in the blanks provided.

1.   _____ code is a system for marking text so that it can be published on the World Wide Web.

2.   When you display a web in _____ view, you can see the navigation structure of the web as you add new pages to it.

3.   To edit the content on a Web page, you must display the page in _____ view.

4.   You should save all pictures in the _____ folder in your web.

5.   Before you publish a Web site, you should view the web in a(n) _____.

PROJECT 2-1

Your family's farm operates a small but thriving business selling birdseed in the fall and winter. The family would like to expand operations. You suggest a Web site as a means of letting people know about the business and perhaps one day generating online orders.

1.   If necessary, launch FrontPage. Use the One Page Web template to create a new web named **For the Birds** followed by your initials.

2.   Display the **index.htm** page and insert the file **Project2-1a** from the data files on the index page. If prompted to install a converter, click **No**.

3. Switch to Navigation view and add a new page below the home page. Name the new page **Seed Products**.

4. Select the home page icon (*index.htm*) and add a second new page. Name the new page **Feeding Tips**.

5. Add content to the new pages as follows:
   A. Display the *seed_products.htm* page in Page view and insert the file **Project2-1b** from the data files. If prompted to install a converter, click No.
   B. Display the *feeding_tips.htm* page in Page view and insert the file **Project2-1c** from the data files. If prompted to install a converter, click No.

6. Save the changes in each page and leave the web open for the next Project.

PROJECT 2-2

1. Display the **index.htm** page in Page view. Apply the **Nature** theme (or another appropriate theme of your choice) to all pages. If necessary, turn on the options for **Vivid colors**, **Active graphics**, and **Background picture**. When prompted to permanently replace formatting, click **Yes**.

2. Position the insertion point at the left of the first word on the page and press **Enter** to insert a blank line. In the blank line, insert a page banner with the text **For the Birds**.

3. Press **Enter** to move to a new line below the banner and insert a link bar based on the navigation structure. Format the link bar using the page's theme and the vertical orientation. Include links to child-level pages.

4. Insert similar page banners and link bars on the other two pages. Use the page filenames for the banner text. The link bars should have links to same level pages and the home page.

5. Display the *seed_products.htm* page in Page view and apply bullet formatting to the four types of seeds listed.

6. Switch to Navigation view and add a new page below the **Seed Products** page icon. Move the new page to the left of the Seed Products page and change its name to **About Us**. Open the new page in Page view and key the following paragraph:

   For the Birds is a family-owned operation dedicated to feeding our feathered friends. We have been creating special birdseed mixes for over five years from our farm in rural Indiana. We hope you share our love for birds and our determination to protect vanishing bird habitats throughout the country.

7. Add a page banner and a link bar with the same level and home page links to this new page.

8. Display the *index.htm* page in Page view and notice that the link bar has changed to show a link to the new page you added. In the last full paragraph on this page, select the words **Seed Products** and create a link to the *seed_products.htm* page.

9. Insert a clip art picture somewhere on this page that relates to birds. (*Hint:* Check the options for the media file types before you begin your search, and make sure Clip Art is selected.) Resize the image if needed, then save the clip art graphic in the **images** folder.

10. Preview the web in your browser. Test all the hyperlinks to move from page to page in the web.

11. If you have permission to print, print the **index.htm** page. Close the open pages and exit FrontPage.

WEB PROJECT

Everyone in your family has always said your mother's fudge could make you all rich, if you could only find a way to sell it to the public. Could your family really make money this way? Search the Web to find out what kinds of companies or organizations sell fudge online. Determine how many flavors you would have to convince your mother to make to give customers a good choice and how much you could charge for each pound. Then create a FrontPage web with at least two pages that you could use to publish information about Mom's Fudge on the Web.

TEAMWORK PROJECT

In this lesson, you have learned the basics of using FrontPage. FrontPage offers many more features to make it easy to construct a very sophisticated Web site. To learn more about some of these features, study them in small groups and then present the information gathered to the class. Follow these steps:

1. Below is a list of features that can add visual interest and usefulness to a FrontPage web. These features were beyond the scope of this lesson, but you can learn how to use them on your own using the Help screens.
   Adding a photo gallery
   Inserting a video clip
   Separating content with horizontal lines
   Adding a table
   Applying borders and shading
   Adding the date and time
   Formatting symbols
   Formatting backgrounds
   Checking spelling
   Creating dynamic HTML effects

2. Divide into teams of two or three students. Each team will explore one feature by reading the Help information available on it and then explore using the feature in FrontPage to find out exactly how it works.

3. Each team should then demonstrate its feature to the rest of the class. Be ready to answer questions from your classmates!

CRITICAL THINKING

You might have found that the clip art graphic you inserted on pages in this lesson had a background that didn't look all that great against the theme background you applied. Is there a way to get rid of that white background? If so, how?

Use the Help system in FrontPage to find out about making a color "transparent." Create a Web page to describe the process. Insert a graphic on the page and make the background (or another color) transparent as a demonstration of what you have learned.

UNIT
REVIEW

Publisher and FrontPage

COMMAND SUMMARY—PUBLISHER

FEATURE	MENU COMMAND	KEYSTROKES	TOOLBAR BUTTON	LESSON
Automatic copyfitting	Format, AutoFit Text			1
Center text/objects			≡	1
Clip art, insert	Insert, Picture, Clip Art		🖻	1
Help, get	Help, Microsoft Publisher Help	F1	? / Type a question for help	1
New publication, start	File, New	Ctrl + N	🗋	1
Page, display			1 2	1
Picture, move			⊹	1
Picture frame, insert			🖾	1
Print publication	File, Print	Ctrl + P	🖨	1
Publication Gallery, display			🗗	1
Save new publication	File, Save As		💾	1
Save publication	File, Save	Ctrl + S	💾	1
Task pane, show	View, Task Pane			1
Text frame, insert	Insert, Text Box		🗛	1
Toolbar, display buttons			»	1
Zoom	View, Zoom		100% ▾	1
Zoom, in	View, Zoom	F9	🔍	1
Zoom, out	View, Zoom	F9	🔍	1

COMMAND SUMMARY—FRONTPAGE

FEATURE	MENU COMMAND	KEYSTROKES	TOOLBAR BUTTON	LESSON
Align right	Format, Paragraph	Ctrl + R		2
Align center	Format, Paragraph	Ctrl + E		2
Bullets	Format, Bullets and Numbering			2
Clip art, insert	Insert, Picture, Clip Art			2
Folder List, display	View, Folder List			2
Folders view	View, Folders			2
Help, get	Help, Microsoft FrontPage Help	F1	Type a question for help	2
Hyperlink, insert	Insert, Hyperlink	Ctrl + K		2
Hyperlinks view	View, Hyperlinks			2
Link bar, insert	Insert, Navigation			2
Navigation view	View, Navigation			2
New page, insert	File, New, Page or Web			2
New Web, create	File, New, Page or Web			2
Normal view			Normal	2
Page banner, insert	Insert, Page Banner			2
Page view	View, Page			2
Preview page			Preview	2
Preview Web	File, Preview in Browser			2
Print page	File, Print	Ctrl + P		2
Save new page or Web	File, Save As			1
Save page or Web	File, Save	Ctrl + S		1
Task pane, show	View, Task Pane			2
Theme, apply	Format, Theme			2

TRUE/FALSE

Circle T if the statement is true or F if the statement is false.

T F 1. In Publisher, you can create only one personal information set.

T F 2. Before you create a publication in Publisher, it is a good idea to mock up your publication to get an idea of where text will appear.

T F 3. You can easily change the color scheme used for a Publisher publication.

T F 4. You must hide the layout guides in a Publisher publication if you don't want them to print.

T F 5. To delete a picture frame in Publisher, you must delete the picture inside the frame before you can delete the picture frame.

T F 6. When you insert a file from another Office application into a web, you must first convert the file to HTML format.

T F 7. If you apply a theme to all pages in a web, the theme is applied to new pages as you create them.

T F 8. Page banners can consist of either text or a picture.

T F 9. When you add a link bar to a Web page, you can base the hyperlinks on your navigation structure.

T F 10. Hyperlinks view shows you a summary of information about your web.

MATCHING

Match the correct term in Column 1 to its description in Column 2.

Column 1

Column 2

____ 1. link bar

____ 2. HTML

____ 3. mock-up

____ 4. automatic copyfitting

____ 5. layout guides

____ 6. scratch area

____ 7. web

____ 8. picture frame

____ 9. Navigation view

____ 10. sizing handles

A. A model, usually full-scale, used for planning a design and layout

B. A temporary storage area in Publisher that can hold graphics or text

C. A placeholder designed to hold a graphic

D. Small squares surrounding an object that indicates it is selected

E. View that allows you to see a summary of elements contained in the Web site

F. Feature that resizes text to fit inside a text frame

G. Allows you to see and edit the structure of a Web site's pages

H. A display of hyperlinks that allow you to jump from page to page in a Web site

I. A system for marking text that allows it to be read on the World Wide Web

J. A group of connected pages that can be viewed on the Internet

K. Pink and blue lines that help you align objects and maintain a consistent look

CROSS-CURRICULAR PROJECTS

MATH

Use the Internet or other reference to track the performance of a specific stock over the past month. Record the opening price at the beginning of the month and the closing price at the end of the month. Calculate how much you would have gained (or lost) if you owned 100 shares of the stock. Use Publisher to create an informational document giving the name of the stock, some information about it, and its financial performance over the last month.

SOCIAL STUDIES

Do some research in your community to determine what important issues might be present on the ballot for the next regularly scheduled election. Choose one issue or candidate and create a FrontPage Web site that explores the issue or gives information about the candidate. Take a poll in your class and in your neighborhood to find out possible voter reactions for or against the issue or candidate and create new pages in the web to summarize the results of your polls.

SCIENCE

Every year, weather disasters strike many regions of our country. Choose a specific weather disaster from the previous year that you want to study. First, find out what causes this particular type of weather (for example, find out how a hurricane forms and moves across the ocean). Then research your specific disaster to discover if lives were lost and what kind of property damage occurred. Use Publisher to create and illustrate a publication about your chosen weather disaster.

LANGUAGE ARTS

Create a web called **Language Watch** devoted to finding language lapses in your local media or from Web sites you frequently visit. Devote one page to spelling and one to grammar. You can add other pages if desired, such as misleading headlines, inappropriate use of slang, overuse of clichés, and so on. Monitor the media for a week or so to see if you can add any items to your web. For each item you add, explain what rule of grammar or spelling (or common sense) has been broken and provide a suggestion for correcting the error.

PROJECTS

PROJECT 1

1. If necessary, launch Publisher. Start a new publication from a calendar design. Select the **Art Right Calendar** template.

2. Keep the landscape orientation and monthly options as suggested. Click the **Change date range** button in the Calendar Options pane and change the start and end calendar dates to **November** of the current year. Save the publication as **Petersen** followed by your initials.

3. Replace the company name with **Petersen's Books and Music**.

4. Zoom in so you can easily read the text in the text boxes at the top of the calendar. Replace the sample tag line text in the top right corner with **Inspiration for eyes and ears**.

5. Insert the following address in the top left corner of the calendar:
    Petersen's Books and Music
    9002 Foster Avenue
    Norwood, OH 45223

6. Insert the phone number **513-555-2665** and e-mail address **petersen@jumpoff.net**. If any other information is displayed, such as a fax number, delete that information. Change the font size of the address, phone number, and e-mail information to 11 point.

7. Delete the sample picture and insert a graphic related to books or music. Resize and reposition the graphic as needed to fill the space. Delete the frame that contains the sample caption.

8. Select the logo at the bottom of the calendar. Use the Wizard to create a new logo for Petersen's using one of the Logo Designs and entering the company name. Depending on the logo chosen, you may have to resize it in order for the company name to be visible.

9. Petersen's hosts a Book Club meeting every Wednesday night. Create new text frames at the bottom of each Wednesday in the calendar and key **Book Club** in each frame. Center the words in each frame. (*Hint:* To make it easy to see the text and align the frames, use the Zoom option to enlarge the view.)

10. Save your changes. When prompted to save the new logo to the Primary Business personal information set, click **No**. Close the publication.

PROJECT 2

Recently, a fast-food franchise announced plans to purchase Odeon Cinema, a run-down movie theater in your town, and replace it with a brand-new fast-food restaurant. You and several other dedicated moviegoers wish to fight this purchase and restore the theater. You decide a Web site on local intranets and the Web might help you raise awareness and funds.

1. Start FrontPage and create a new one-page web with the name **Save the Odeon**.

2. Display the **index.htm** page in Page view and key the following text:
Moviegoers Unite!
We have recently learned that the Burger Busters chain of fast-food restaurants has made an offer to purchase the Odeon Cinema, our town's only independent first-run movie theater. Attendance at the Odeon has been declining in recent years, and the old building is starting to look a little shabby. A group of dedicated moviegoers has formed the Odeon Restoration Committee to explore options for purchase and restoration of the historic property.

3. Add a new page in Navigation view and change the name to **About the Odeon**. Open the page in Page view and insert the file **Project2a** from the data files. If prompted to install a converter, click **No**.

4. Add a page to the navigation structure below the *About the Odeon* page and name the new page **Pictures**. Add the following text to the new page:
We are currently collecting pictures of the Odeon in its heyday. If you have any pictures of the theater from the early days of its operation, please contact the Odeon Restoration Committee. This page will display the best pictures we can find.

5. Add two more pages to the navigation structure at the same level as the *About the Odeon* page. Name the first page **Pros and Cons**. Name the second page **Join the ORC**.

6. Display the **pros_and_cons.htm** page in Page view and insert the file **Project2b** from the data files. If prompted to install a converter, click **No**.

7. Display the **join_the_orc.htm** page in Page view and insert the following text:
   If you would like to join the effort to save the Odeon, contact the Odeon Restoration Committee using the e-mail address below, or call 513-555-6901. We hope to see you at our next public meeting!
   Contact us:

8. Position the insertion point after the text *Contact us:*. Insert a space and key **ORC@nexus.net**. Press the spacebar once to format the e-mail address as a hyperlink.

9. Save the changes and leave the web open for the next Project.

PROJECT 3

1. Display the **index.htm** page. Apply the **Romanesque** theme to all pages. (If you do not have this theme installed, apply another appropriate theme.) When prompted to permanently replace existing formatting information, click **Yes**.

2. Select the heading on the *index.htm* page and change its size to 14 point and its style to bold. (*Hint:* Use the **Bold** button to change the style. Click the **Font Size** list box and choose **4 (14 pt)** to change the size.)

3. Insert a new paragraph above the heading on the *index.htm* page. Position the insertion point in the new paragraph and then insert a page banner. Change the page banner text to **Save the Odeon**.

4. Insert a new paragraph below the page banner. Position the insertion point in the new paragraph and then insert a link bar based on the navigation structure. Use the page's theme and the horizontal orientation. Create hyperlinks to Child-level pages. Center the link bar.

5. Insert page banners on all other pages using the page filename for the banner text. On three of the pages (*about_the_odeon.htm, join_the_orc.htm*, and *pros_and_cons.htm*), use the navigation structure to insert centered link bars, with links to Same level pages and the Home page. On the *pictures.htm* page, insert a centered link bar with links to the Same level pages (even though there currently are no others), the Home page, and the Parent page.

6. Display the *about_the_odeon.htm* page and format the word *pictures* in the last sentence of text as a hyperlink to the *pictures.htm* page.

7. Display the *pros_and_cons.htm* page. Format the three paragraphs that appear below the first paragraph with bullets. Then format the three paragraphs below the *By contrast...* paragraph with bullets.

8. Display the *index.htm* page in Page view and insert a clip art graphic or movie clip relating to movies below the *Moviegoers Unite!* heading. Center the graphic and resize if needed.

9. Save the changes to all the pages and save the embedded file in the images folder.

10. Preview the web in the browser and test all the hyperlinks. Make any necessary corrections.

11. Save any changes and then close the web.

SIMULATION

Your rail-trails organization has asked you to create informational materials for two local events: a 10K run along one trail that benefits the rail-trails organization and the annual Tour-for-a-Cure ride that benefits diabetes research. You decide to create a publication and a Web site to get the word out for these events.

JOB 1

1. If necessary, launch Publisher. Edit the personal information for the **Other Organization** set using the following information. Delete all information for the name, tag line, and job title boxes.
   Address: **6712 Chestnut Avenue**
                              Blue Ash, OH 45239
   Phone: **513-555-0034**
   E-mail: **lmrt@earthlink.net**
   Organization name: **Little Miami Rail-Trails**

2. Start a new publication from a flyer design. Choose the Fund-raiser category and select the **Fun Run Flyer** template.

3. Save the publication as **10K Run** followed by your initials.

4. Apply the **Tropics** color scheme. Select the text *name of charity* that follows *Proceeds will benefit* and change it to **Little Miami Rail-Trails**. Select the race date and change it to **April 28**. Change the time to **8 a.m.** Runners must pre-register by **April 25**.

5. In the Entry fee text box, delete the line of text for senior citizen runners. Then, change the entry fees to the following:
   Pre-registration: **$15.00**
   Race-day registration: **$20.00**

6. Insert the following description of the course in the proper location:
   The Little Miami Rail-Trails Run takes place on the Miami Extension Trail. The trail is mostly flat with several rolling hills. Water is supplied at the turnaround and the end of the course.

7. The contact person is **Gerry Schindholm** and her number is **513-555-0034**.

8. There are no prizes, so delete the *Prizes* graphic. All participants will receive a T-shirt, so delete the information in the text frame about prizes and leave the T-shirt information. Then format the text box for best fit.

9. Below the *Sponsored by* heading, edit the first sample logo to create a logo for the rail-trails organization using its initials, **LMRT**. Insert **Little Miami Rail-Trails** in the text frame below the logo.

10. Delete the remaining two sample logos, but do not remove the text boxes below those logos. In the remaining Organization Name text frames, insert the names of the two other sponsors for the race: **Walker Electronics** and **Blue Ash Sports Plus**.

11. Replace the text in the *Waiver* text frame with the following:
   Waiver: I hereby waive all claims against Little Miami Rail-Trails, sponsors, or any personnel for any injury I might suffer in this event.

12. If desired, replace the picture with another appropriate image.

13. Save your changes and close the publication.

JOB 2

1. If necessary, launch FrontPage and create a new one-page web named **Tour**.

2. Display the *index.htm* page in Page view and insert the following text:
   On one special day, June 9, more than 50,000 riders in some 30 states across the country will ride as part of the biggest diabetes cycling fundraising event of the year.
   Teams from across the country will compete in the Tour-for-a-Cure to raise pledges for the American Diabetes Association, America's leading advocate for diabetes research and awareness. Pledges pay for activities to prevent and cure diabetes.

3. Apply an appropriate theme to all pages of the web. When prompted to permanently change the formatting, click **Yes**.

4. Add a new page in Navigation view and name it **Diabetes Research**. Display the page in Page view and insert the file **Job2a** from the data files. When prompted to install the converter, click **No**.

5. Format all the percent paragraphs with bullets.

6. Position the insertion point after the colon in the last line of text, insert a space and key **www.diabetes.org**. Press the **Spacebar** to format the URL as a hyperlink.

7. Add a new page in Navigation view at the same level as the *Diabetes Research* page and name it **Course**. Display the page in Page view and insert the file **Job2b** from the data files. When prompted to install a converter click **No**.

8. Add a new page in Navigation view at the same level as the *Diabetes Research* page and name it **Teams**. Display the page in Page view and insert the file **Job2c** from the data files. When prompted to install a converter, click **No**.

9. Add a new page in Navigation view at the same level as the *Diabetes Research* page and name it **Pledges**. Display the page in Page view and insert the file **Job2d** from the data files. When prompted to install a converter, click **No**.

10. Add a page banner to the home page with the text **Tour-for-a-Cure**. Add a link bar (either horizontal or vertical orientation) to the home page based on the navigational structure with links to all the Child-level pages. If the link bar is formatted for horizontal orientation, center it.

11. Add a page banner to each of the other pages in the web using the page filename in the banner. Then add a link bar (either horizontal or vertical orientation) to each of the other pages. Base the links on the navigation structure to each page with links to the home page and same level pages. If the link bar is formatted for horizontal orientation, center it.

12. Illustrate the pages as desired with clip art graphics. Resize the graphics as needed and position them on the page. Save the embedded files in the images folder.

13. Save any open pages and then preview the web in the browser. Close the web.

PORTFOLIO CHECKLIST ▽

Include the following files from this unit in your portfolio.

___	Clean-Up	___	Warner Guitars
___	Holidays	___	For the Birds
___	Run	___	Save the Odeon
___	Petersen	___	Tour

INTEGRATED PROJECTS

The integrated projects in this section will help you learn how to use more than one Office application in a document. These projects represent only a few of the ways Office applications can be used together. After you complete these projects, you should be able to think of many more ways to use Office applications together.

When you paste data from one application to another, the Paste Options button will display in the lower-right corner of the pasted text or object. When you point to the Paste Options button, a down arrow will display. Click the down arrow to specify how you want to format the data.

Note

The statistics used in these worksheets are fictitious.

PROJECT 1

In this project, you will insert an Excel worksheet chart into a Word document. After you insert the chart, you will format it to make it look more attractive in the document.

1. Launch Word and open **Project1a** from the data files. Save the document as **Snow Fun** followed by your initials.

2. Format the first line of the title 18-point bold Comic Sans MS (or another font of your choice if this font is not available). Format the second line of the title in 16-point Comic Sans MS.

3. Position the insertion point at the end of the second-to-last paragraph in the document (ending with ...*to get around.*).

4. Press **Enter** twice and key the paragraph below:
   Snowmobile sales during the 1990s reveal the increasing popularity of this pastime, not merely in the United States but in other countries as well. The chart below shows snowmobiles sold between 1993 and 2000 in the United States, Canada, and around the world.

5. Press **Enter** after completing the paragraph, and then move the insertion point down into the next blank line above the last paragraph.

6. Launch Excel and open **Project1b** from the data files. Save the worksheet as **Unit Sales** followed by your initials.

7. Format the cell range B5:I8 using the **Number** format with the **1000s separator** and **0 decimals**.

8. Create a chart from the data in the worksheet by following these steps:
   A. Select the cell range A5:I7 and click the **Chart Wizard** button. In the Step 1 of 4 dialog box, select the first **Column** chart in the second row (Clustered column with a 3-D visual effect).
   B. In the Step 2 of 4 dialog box, click the **Series** tab. At the bottom of the dialog box, click the **Collapse Dialog** button for the *Category (X) axis labels* text box. In the worksheet, select cell range B4:I4. Click the **Expand Dialog** button to return to the Chart Wizard. The year labels are now in place for the X axis.

C. In the Step 3 of 4 dialog box, key the chart title **Unit Sales**. Click the **Legend** tab and select the **Bottom** option for placement.

D. In the Step 4 of 4 dialog box, accept the default choice to display the chart as an object in Sheet1 and finish the chart.

9. Reposition the chart so the top left corner is at the top of cell A10. Then resize the chart so the lower-right corner is at the bottom of cell H25.

10. Click the outside border of the chart if necessary to select it. Click the **Copy** button on the Standard toolbar.

11. Switch to the Word document. Your insertion point should be in the blank line just above the last paragraph.

12. Click the **Paste** button on the Standard toolbar to paste the chart you copied from Excel. The Paste Options button displays at the lower-right corner of the chart.

13. Point to the Paste Options button and then click the down arrow to display a shortcut menu. Select **Excel Chart (entire workbook)**. This option enables you to edit the chart in Word, using the same tools you would use to edit the chart in Excel.

14. Double-click anywhere on the chart to select it. A hatched border will display around the chart when it is properly selected. Notice that the toolbars and menu bar show Excel tools and commands.

15. Change the chart format as follows:
    A. Click the chart title to select it. Change the font size to 14 point.
    B. Double-click any one of the numbers on the vertical axis. In the Format Axis dialog box, change the font of the axis labels to 10-point bold.
    C. Double-click any one of the dates on the horizontal axis. In the Format Axis dialog box, change the font of the axis labels to 10-point bold.
    D. Double-click the legend to select it. Change the legend text to 10-point bold.

Computer Concepts

There are three different ways to incorporate an Excel spreadsheet in a Word document. You can insert the entire Excel workbook, which allows you to double-click the pasted chart and edit it using the same tools you would use to edit the chart in Excel. You can insert a picture of the chart, which makes the overall Word file size smaller, but won't allow you to make changes to the chart. Or, you can create a link to the Excel Chart; the chart in the Word document will then be updated if you go back to Excel and make any changes to the data in the chart.

16. Click anywhere outside the chart to deselect it. If necessary, press **Enter** to insert a blank line between the chart and the paragraph before it, and also between the chart and the paragraph after it.

17. Save your changes to the Word document and close Word. Save your changes to the Excel worksheet and close Excel.

PROJECT 2

In this project, you will link Excel worksheet data to a PowerPoint slide. When you link data, you create a connection between the original document (the source document) and the document into which you insert the data (the destination document). After you insert the data, you will format and update the data in Excel, and then see how the data changes on your PowerPoint slide.

1. Launch PowerPoint. Open **Project2a** file from the data files. Save the presentation as **Good Cents** followed by your initials.

2. Apply the **Mountain** (or some other appropriate) design template to the presentation.

3. Add a new **Title and Text** slide at the end of the presentation and key the title **Economic Statistics**.

4. Insert the following bulleted items on the slide:
   Average retail price of new snowmobile in 2000: $8,780
   Total annual expenditures by U.S. snowmobilers: over $6 billion
   Snowmobile sales increased throughout the 1990s

5. Add a new slide with the **Title Only** layout. Key the title **Sales in the 1990s**.

6. Click anywhere outside the title placeholder to deselect the placeholder.

7. Launch Excel. Open **Project2b** from the data files. Save the worksheet as **Dollar Sales** followed by your initials.

8. Select the cell range A4:F9 and click the **Copy** button on the Standard toolbar.

9. Switch back to PowerPoint. With slide number 7 displayed in Normal view, open the **Edit** menu and choose **Paste Special**. The Paste Special dialog box opens.

10. Click the **Paste link** option. By default, PowerPoint assumes you want to paste the data as a Microsoft Excel Worksheet Object. Click **OK**.

> **Computer Concepts**
>
> To link data from a worksheet to any Office XP document, you must use the Paste Special command in the document where you will insert the data. This command opens the Paste Special dialog box, where you can choose to paste or paste link the data, and specify the format of the data you are inserting.

11. The linked worksheet object appears on the slide with sizing handles around it. Drag the sizing handles to resize the worksheet object so that it is about half an inch from the sides of the slide. Then reposition the object so it is centered horizontally on the slide.

12. Right-click the worksheet object and select **Format Object** in the shortcut menu. If necessary, select the **Colors and Lines** tab in the Format Object dialog box. Under *Fill*, click the down arrow in the **Color** box. Select one of the light colors displayed in the first row. These colors are all used in the color scheme for the slide design. Click **OK**. The background color of the worksheet object changes.

13. Save the changes to the presentation and deselect the worksheet object by clicking anywhere on the slide.

14. Switch to the **Dollar Sales** worksheet by selecting it from the task bar (or double-clicking the worksheet in the PowerPoint slide) and make the following changes to it:
    A. In cell F5, insert the value **343.3**. In cell F6, insert the value **854.7**.
    B. Calculate the total sales for each year. (If you use AutoSum, be sure not to include the dates in row 4.)

15. Save your changes and close the worksheet. Close Excel.

16. Switch to the presentation. Right-click the Microsoft Excel object on slide number 7 and choose **Update Link** in the shortcut menu. The Excel data is updated.

17. If desired, preview the slide show. Save your changes and close the presentation. Close PowerPoint.

Computer Concepts

If you want to change or update linked data, you need to go back to the original application. In this case, you will return to the Excel worksheet to make your changes, which you can then transfer to the slide when you switch back to PowerPoint.

Computer Concepts

If you close your presentation and reopen it later after the Excel data has been updated, PowerPoint will detect that the linked object has been updated. PowerPoint will then prompt you to update the link before opening the presentation.

PROJECT 3

In this project, you will integrate Word and PowerPoint. PowerPoint slides can function as illustrations in Word documents. When you paste a slide into a Word document, you can resize and position the slide just as you would any other picture.

1. Launch Word and open **Project3a** from the data files. Save the document as **Safety First** followed by your initials.

2. Launch PowerPoint and open **Project3b** from the data files. Save the document as **Riding Safely** followed by your initials.

3. Apply the **Stream** design template to the presentation. Open the Color Scheme task pane and select a color scheme of your choice.

4. Switch to Slide Sorter view and select slide number **2**. Click the **Copy** button on the Standard toolbar to copy the entire slide.

5. Switch to the Word document and click at the end of the second paragraph that ends …*collide with another object*. Click the **Paste** button on the Standard toolbar. The slide is inserted as a graphic object in the Word document.

6. Click the slide content to select the object. Hold down the **Shift** key and drag the lower right sizing handle upward and inward until the slide is about 3.5 inches wide. (*Hint*: If necessary, display the ruler and check the slide width on the ruler above the slide.)

7. With the slide still selected, open the **Format** menu and choose **Object**. Click the **Layout** tab. Select the **Square** text wrapping option and then click the **Right** horizontal alignment option.

8. If necessary, adjust the position of the slide object so that the entire third paragraph appears to the left of the slide (with no single lines of text above or below the slide object).

9. Preview the document. If the font color for the document title does not complement the color scheme you chose for the presentation slide, change the font color for the title. Save your changes and close the document. Close Word.

10. Save your changes to the PowerPoint presentation and close it. Close PowerPoint.

PROJECT 4

In this project, you will integrate Access and Publisher. When you display an Access table or the results of an Access query, you can copy the data in the same way you would copy worksheet data. You can paste the copied data in any Office application and then work with it the same way you would work with a table or worksheet.

1. Launch Access and open **Project4a** from the data files. This database stores information for a snowmobile outfitting company named *Rider*.

2. Click the **Queries** button in the Object bar to list the queries for this database.

3. Double-click the **Sale Price** query to run the query. This query displays items from the database that have a special sale price at this time of year.

4. Select all rows of data in the query results. Click the **Copy** button on the Standard toolbar.

5. Launch Publisher and open the **Project4b** publication from the data files. (If you see a message regarding opening the file with a different printer selected, select **Yes**.) Save the publication as **Preseason Sale** followed by your initials. This publication is a sale flyer for the Rider company.

6. Click the **Paste** button on the Standard toolbar to paste the data from the database. The table is inserted in a tall and narrow format.

7. Drag the side sizing handles to resize the pasted object and expand the width of the table to the blue guidelines on each side of the publication. Then reposition the table and resize it so that it fills the bottom area of the publication.

8. With the object still selected, drag the pointer over all the text in the object and change the point size to 11.

9. Edit the first column heading to read **Category**. (*Hint*: Zooming in will make it easier to read the contents in the object.) Then select the gray-shaded column headings. Click the **Fill Color** button on the Formatting toolbar and choose a color that compliments the color scheme in the publication.

10. The company is already out of stock on the second *Bibs* entry in this column. Position the insertion point in the second row containing information about the SuperSport Bibs, open the **Table** menu, choose **Delete**, and then select **Rows** in the submenu.

11. Replace the picture on the sale flyer with one that relates to snowmobiles, snow, or winter sports.

12. Save your changes and close the flyer and Publisher. Close the Access query results, the database, and Access.

PROJECT 5

In this project, you will link data from Excel to a Word document. After you have inserted the linked data, you will change it in Excel and then return to the Word document to see the updates.

1. Launch Word and open **Project5a** from the data files. Save the document as **Sales Memo** followed by your initials.

2. Choose an appropriate winter outdoors clip art picture to jazz up the letterhead at the top of the memo. Resize the picture as needed. You can choose where to position the picture and wrap text around it if desired.

3. Launch Excel and open **Project5b** from the data files. Save the document as **Online Sales** followed by your initials.

4. Select cell range A4:G30. Click the **Copy** button on the Standard toolbar.

5. Switch to the Word document and position the insertion point in the last blank line in the document.

6. Click the **Paste** button. The worksheet data appears in a table in the Word document. Point to the **Paste Options** button at the lower-right corner, and then click the down arrow. Select **Keep Source Formatting and Link to Excel**.

7. Select the table. (*Hint*: With the insertion point in the table, open the **Table** menu, choose **Select**, and then select **Table** in the submenu.) AutoFit the column widths for the contents and distribute the rows evenly.

8. Click anywhere outside the table to deselect it. If the table wraps to a second page, adjust the top and bottom margins to fit the entire document on one page.

9. You decide the data would be more meaningful if grouped by category so you can see what types of items are selling well at this time of year. Return to the Excel worksheet. Deselect the current selection by double-clicking in an empty cell outside of the selection area, then click anywhere in the column of data under the **Category** heading. Sort the sales data by Category.

10. Create a formula in cell G5 that multiplies the quantity sold times the price. Format the resulting value for currency with two decimal places, and then fill the formula down for the other cells through row 27. AutoFormat the column width to display the results.

11. Use AutoSum to total the items sold and the total sales.

12. Save your changes and close the worksheet. Close Excel.

13. Return to the Word document and notice that all the changes you made in Excel have automatically been updated in the table in Word.

14. Center the table by clicking it once to select it. Then open the **Table** menu and choose **Table Properties**. If necessary, select the **Table** tab and select **Center** alignment. Click **OK**.

15. Save your changes. Close the document and then close Word.

APPENDIX A

WORKING WITH WINDOWS 2000

Windows 2000 provides a visual environment for you to run your personal computer. In this graphical environment, familiar pictures are used to represent applications, files, and tasks. To execute a command or open a file, you simply click one of the pictures.

Windows 2000 offers a variety of features that enable you to manage your applications and files easily and efficiently. This introduction presents some basic features of the Windows 2000 program.

The Windows 2000 Desktop

When you start Windows 2000 you see what's called the desktop. (See Figure A-1.) The desktop is designed to be your workplace. From this workplace, you can perform a variety of tasks, including finding and opening your files, dialing your phone, viewing a clock, using the calculator, and even placing deleted files in the recycling bin. These tools are within easy reach as you work with other applications. Windows 2000 allows you to work on more than one task at a time. For example, you can be working on a spreadsheet at the same time you are working on a word processing document.

FIGURE A-1
Windows 2000 Desktop

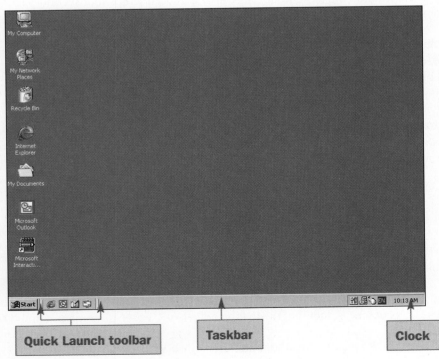

486

Identifying the Parts of the Windows 2000 Desktop

The items displayed on the desktop vary depending on your computer setup. When you begin Windows 2000, your screen may look very different from Figure A-1; however, you should see the five icons described below somewhere on your screen.

My Computer

Use My Computer to see the contents of your computer. The contents of your floppy disk, hard disk, CD-ROM drive, and mapped network drives will display.

If your computer is connected to a network, use My Network Places to locate shared resources on the network to which your computer is connected.

The Recycle Bin is a temporary storage (waste basket) for deleted files. If you open the Recycle bin, you will see the items that have been deleted. The items are not permanently deleted until you empty the recycle bin.

Use Internet Explorer to launch the Internet Explorer Browser.

Use My Documents to open the My Documents folder on your computer. This folder is the default storage location for the files you create in your Office applications.

The taskbar is usually visible when Windows is running. The taskbar is the strip displayed at the bottom of the screen in Figure A-1. It can, however, run from left to right along the top of the screen; or, alternately, it can be placed so that it runs from top to bottom along either side of the screen. You can quickly launch some applications by clicking the icons in the Quick Launch toolbar at the left side of the taskbar.

On the right side of the taskbar are icons that enable you to quickly access your anti-virus program, adjust volume controls, and so forth. You can also double-click the clock to display a calendar or reset the time.

Using the Mouse to Move Around the Desktop

Somewhere on your screen you should see a mouse pointer. Generally, this mouse pointer is shaped like an arrowhead. To move the mouse pointer, simply slide the mouse around on the surface of your desk. If you run out of desk space on which to move the mouse, pick up the mouse and put it down where you have sufficient space to move it. Lifting the mouse does not move the mouse pointer on the screen.

Computer Concepts

If you have upgraded from Internet Explorer 4.0 or Windows 98, the desktop Channel bar is available. The Channel bar enables you to quickly open Web channels from your desktop without first opening the browser.

Hot Tip

If the taskbar is not visible, the Auto hide option may be turned on. This means that the taskbar is hidden when not in use. To make the taskbar appear, you simply move your mouse to the edge of the screen where the taskbar is located and it will automatically appear. To turn off the Auto hide option, click the **Start** button, choose **Settings**, and then select **Taskbar & Start Menu Properties** in the submenu. Turn off the Auto hide option. The option is turned off when there is no checkmark in the box. You can also access the properties of the task bar by right-clicking on an empty area of the task bar and choosing Properties from the menu.

Some terms with which you should become familiar are:

- ■ Point—Position the tip of the mouse pointer on an item. Do not push any mouse buttons when you are instructed only to point. Because you always need to point to something before you take any other mouse action, such as clicking, you may not always be instructed to point first.

- ■ Click—Press and release the mouse button quickly. Do not move the mouse as you click. Clicking instructs the computer to perform an action such as select an item or execute a command. Clicking generally refers to the left mouse button unless you are instructed otherwise.

- ■ Double-click—Press and release the mouse button twice in rapid succession. Hold the mouse firmly as you double-click so the mouse does not move. Double-clicking is often used to tell your computer to open a folder or file or to select an item and carry out a command at the same time. For example, double-clicking a filename in the Open dialog box automatically selects and carries out the command to open the file without having to click OK.

Computer Concepts

The instructions in this text describe the double-click method for opening folders and files. Your computer manufacturer or your lab administrator may have set the options in your computer so that you need only single-click to open a file or folder. This is referred to as the Web style. To change this setting, click the **Start** button, choose **Settings**, select **Control Panel** in the submenu, and then select **Folder Options** in the Control Panel dialog box. Then make your selection in the Folder Options dialog box.

- ■ Right-click—Click the right mouse button. Right-clicking is used to display a shortcut menu.

- ■ Triple-click—Press and release the mouse button three times in rapid succession. Do not move the mouse as you triple-click. Triple-clicking is used to select whole sections or paragraphs of text in applications such as Microsoft Word.

- ■ Drag—Hold down the mouse button as you slide the mouse. Dragging is used to select (highlight) blocks of text or objects and to reposition items. When you release the mouse button, the action (such as selecting) is completed.

Choosing Options in the Start Menu

The Start button is located in one of two places: at the far left corner of the taskbar when at the top or bottom of the screen; or at the top of the taskbar when the taskbar is located on either side of the screen. The Start menu includes everything you need to begin using Windows 2000. To open the Start menu, simply click the Start button. The Start menu (or one similar to it) shown in Figure A-2 is displayed.

FIGURE A-2
Start Menu

The following list provides an explanation of each command in the Start menu. Depending on your computer setup, all the commands may not display, or you may see additional commands not described here.

■ Windows Update—If you are connected to the Internet when you click Windows Update, a Microsoft Web page is displayed where you can choose from options to update your system.

■ New Office Document—When you click New Office Document, a dialog box displays and you can choose from several templates and wizards to create a new document.

■ Open Office Document—When you click Open Office Document, the Open Office Document dialog box displays and you can locate an exsiting document to open.

■ Programs—When you click Programs, a list of all available programs (applications) is displayed. Using Windows allows you to multi-task; that is, to run more than one application at a time.

■ Documents—When you click Documents, a list of the most previously opened documents is displayed. This provides a shortcut to opening a file you worked with recently. It can also be a shortcut to open an application. When you click a document name to open it, the document and the application in which it was created are both opened.

■ Settings—When you click Settings, a list of system components is displayed. You can view and change the settings for the control panel, printers, and taskbar.

■ Search—When you click Search, you can search for a file, a folder, a shared computer, or a mail message.

■ Help—When you click Help, the Help dialog box is opened and you can search for answers to questions.

■ Run—When you click Run, you can key a MS-DOS command to start an application or open a folder. To use the Run command, you must know the name and path of the application you want to start.

■ Shut Down—When you click Shut Down, you can log off, stand by, or restart the computer.

Working with Windows

A window is an on-screen area in which you view application folders, files, or icons. If you have spent any time viewing pages on the Web, you will see some familiar elements in the windows that display in Microsoft Windows 2000, such as the Back and Forward buttons. Figure A-3 identifies some of the most common window elements, and each of those elements is described in detail below.

FIGURE A-3
Common window parts

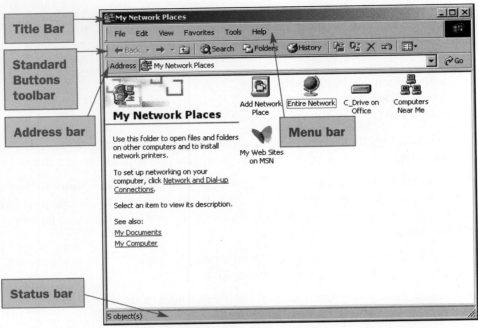

- The title bar at the top of the window displays the name of the application or document.

- The menu bar lists available menus for executing commands.

- The Standard Buttons toolbar contains buttons and other elements that help you access various functions and commands easily and quickly.

- The Address Bar identifies the current window that is active. The Address Bar also makes it convenient for you to enter URLs without opening your browser.

- The Status bar provides information about the objects in the window. For example, in Figure A-3, the Status bar indicates that there are five objects in My Network Places. When you select an object in the window, the object is described on the status bar.

  You can choose to display or hide the Status bar. Open the Tools menu, click Options, select the View tab, and check or clear the Status bar option under Show.

  As you work, you can have multiple windows displayed on your screen at the same time. All of the open windows display as buttons on the taskbar. The active window button looks indented. You can alternate between the windows by clicking the button on the taskbar. The application opens to its previous size and position.

Maximizing and Minimizing Windows

Windows can be maximized (enlarged) to fill the desktop. To maximize a window, click the Maximize button at the right side of the title bar.

To restore the window to its former size and location, click the Restore button at the right side of the title bar. Note that the Restore button is only visible after you have maximized the window.

When you no longer need to work with a window, you can conserve screen space by minimizing it to its smallest possible size. You can do this by clicking the Minimize button at the right side of the title bar. You can then restore the minimized window to its former size by clicking the Restore button. If the Word window or another Word document is showing, open the Window menu and then choose the name of the document you want to restore in that menu. If all the application documents are minimized, click the name of the document you want to restore on the taskbar, or hold down ALT and press TAB until you see the document you want. Pressing ALT and TAB to find the document you want is called toggling.

If you want to view your desktop without closing or minimizing all your windows, click the Show Desktop button in the Quick Launch toolbar on the task bar.

Moving and Sizing Windows

You may occasionally want to reposition (move) a window to see another area of the screen more clearly. To move a window on the desktop, drag the window's title bar.

You can resize a window by dragging one of the window borders. First, point to the border. When you see a two-headed sizing arrow, drag the border up, down, left or right until the window is displayed in the desired size. If you drag a corner of the window, the window will be resized proportionately.

To view two windows at the same time, right-click the mouse on an empty area of the taskbar. Then choose one of the options that displays in the shortcut menu. The Cascade Windows option arranges all the open windows so that they are stacked, but you can see at least a portion of each window and you can reposition the windows as desired. Tile Windows Horizontally arranges the windows so that all open programs are displayed, one at the top and one at the bottom of the screen. Tile Windows Vertically arranges the windows so that two programs are displayed side by side. If you choose the Minimize All Windows option, all the windows are minimized and the desktop will display.

Starting and Closing an Application

You have several options for starting an application. You can click a shortcut icon on the desktop, use the Start menu, or open a document from the desktop, which will automatically start the application in which the document was created.

Figure A-4 shows a desktop that contains several shortcut icons. To start an application, all you need to do is double-click the shortcut icon.

Desktop with several shortcut icons

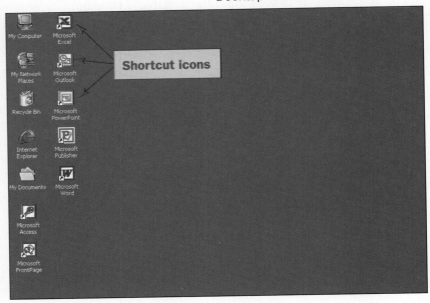

If there is no shortcut icon on the desktop, you can use the Start button. Click the Start button and point to Programs. This opens a popup box that displays the names of the applications on your computer. Point to the folder containing the application, then click the application name.

If you want to open a specific document, you can locate the document and then open the document and the application at the same time. First, double-click the My Computer icon on the desktop, then double-click the drive icon and folder icon where the document is stored. For example, double-click Local Disk (C:) and then double-click the folder Documents and Settings. Then double-click the folder containing your name, and double-click the folder My Documents. The last step is to double-click the filename for the document you want to open. The document will open in the application in which it was created.

Every time you start an application or open a window, a button representing that window appears on the taskbar as shown in Figure A-5.

FIGURE A-5

Taskbar with open applications and windows

To close an application, click the Close button in the upper-right corner of the window title bar. If you see two Close buttons as shown in Figure A-6, the top Close button is for the application window and the other Close button is for the document window. When you close an application window, the document is also closed and the document button and/or application button is removed from the taskbar.

Another way to close an application is to open the File menu and choose Exit. You can also click on the program control button shown in Figure A-6 and choose Close. Or, simply double-click the program control button.

Program control button

Application Close box

Document Close box

Working with Menus

Every window displays a menu bar with several menus. Each menu provides a list of commands. When you click the menu name, the menu opens and the list of commands is displayed, such as shown in Figure A-7.

Not all menu options are available to you all the time. Commands in dark print are currently available; dimmed commands are not available.

As you move the pointer down the list of options, the highlight also moves. To execute the command, click the desired option.

As you look at the available commands, you may notice several visual elements. These elements are described below.

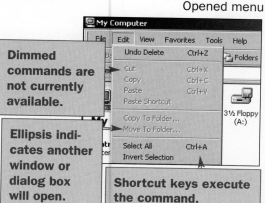

Dimmed commands are not currently available.

Ellipsis indicates another window or dialog box will open.

Shortcut keys execute the command.

- Ellipsis—An ellipsis is the series of three periods. When you choose a command followed by an ellipsis, a second window or dialog box will be displayed. You will learn about dialog boxes later.

- Shortcut Keys—Shortcut key combinations are displayed at the right of some menu commands. A series of keystrokes you can use to execute the command on your keyboard without having to use the menu bar. These shortcut keys work similar to selection letters. However, it is not necessary to display the menu before you press the shortcut keys.

- Right-pointing Arrow (not shown in Figure A-7)—A right-pointing arrow indicates that another menu will appear when you point to the command. If you click the command, the second menu will display immediately. If you rest the pointer on the command, the second menu will open automatically after a short period of time.

Using Scroll Bars

Scroll bars enable you to move rapidly through a list, the contents of a window or screen, or any other set of information that does not fit in the display area. The scroll bar is a shaded rectangular box that contains scroll arrows and a scroll box. The arrows can move left and right or up and down. The location of the scroll bar on the screen varies, and it can be displayed in either a horizontal or vertical position. Both horizontal and vertical scroll bars are illustrated in Figure A-8.

Scroll box

Compact Disc (E:)

Control Panel

Scroll bar arrows

To scroll in small increments, you can click the scroll bar arrows. To scroll in larger increments, you can drag the scroll box. If you are working with a large document or if the scroll bar is for a long list, you can also scroll in large increments by clicking above or below (or to the left or right) of the scroll box.

Although scrolling changes the view on the screen, it does not reposition the insertion point. After scrolling to the desired location, you must click to move the insertion point.

Using Help

If you have questions about Windows, you can use the Microsoft Help feature. Click the Start button and choose Help. Then select one of the four tabs illustrated in Figure A-9. A description of each tab is given below.

FIGURE A-9
Windows 2000 help window

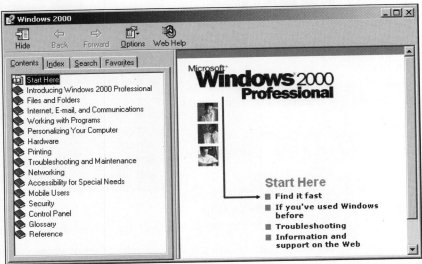

■ The Contents tab displays a table of contents with general topics displayed by category. When you click a topic, a list of subtopics is displayed.

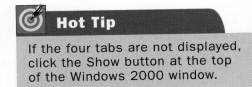

■ The Index tab lets you enter a key word or scroll through a list to locate a topic. Topics are displayed as links to information about the topic.

■ The Search tab displays a task pane so you can enter search text. Only topics related to your search text are displayed in the results.

■ You can maintain a list of Help topics for quick future reference by clicking the Favorites tab and then clicking Add. This feature is only available in the main Windows Help file. You cannot maintain a list of favorites using the Help feature in the Office applications.

Help topics are displayed as links. When you point to the links, they are represented by colored, underlined text. When you click a link, information about the topic displays. To return to windows previously viewed, click the Back Button or the Forward Button on the Standard Buttons toolbar.

Organizing Your Files

Effective file management is essential so that you can quickly retrieve files and save new or edited files. Windows 2000 offers many features that will enable you to organize and maintain your files.

Viewing Files and Information About Files

Efficient organization begins with knowing how to view the files you've saved. When you double-click My Computer on the desktop, a window will display the contents of your computer. The contents may be identified in a list of drive names which may also contain some details about the drives. Or, the contents may be illustrated with the default setting of large icons, as shown in Figure A-10. You can change how the contents of your computer display by opening the View menu and choosing a different display option.

FIGURE A-10
My Computer Contents

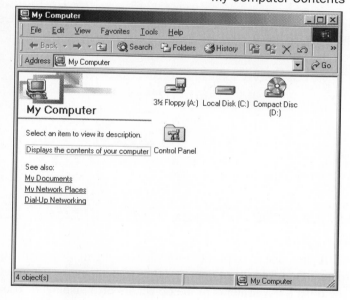

To see the files and folders stored on each drive, double-click the drive icon. Folders are displayed with a yellow folder icon at the left. Files are displayed with an icon that identifies the application in which the file was created. If you select the folder or file, you can display details about the item. Details include the file size, the type of file, and the last date the file was modified.

To change the view, do one of the following:

- Click the down arrow on the Views button and then select List to arrange the list in alphabetical order.

- Click the down arrow on the Views button and then select Details from the View menu to view information about the file size, the type of file, and the date the file was modified.

Using Windows Explorer

Windows Explorer enables you to view everything on your computer in one screen. You can organize and manage files in Windows Explorer just as you can in My Computer.

To display Windows Explorer, click the Start button, choose Accessories, and then select Windows Explorer. A shortcut for starting Windows Explorer is to right-click on the Start button and choose Explore in the shortcut menu.

The drives, folders, and files are displayed in a hierarchical or "tree" view in the pane on the left. To change the way objects are displayed, open the View menu and select a different view option. (Alternatively, you can click the down arrow on the View button and choose a view option from the list.) When you click any of these objects in the left pane, a more detailed view of the object is provided in the pane on the right as shown in Figure A-11. For example, if you click on a drive in the left pane, the folders stored on that drive are displayed in the pane on the right.

FIGURE A-11

Windows Explorer View of the 3 ½ Floppy (A:) drive displayed in List view

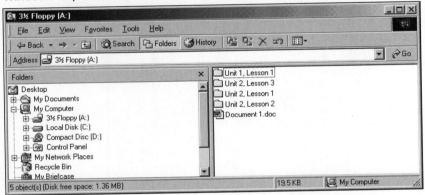

The objects in the left pane that have plus (+) signs next to them are expandable. For example, a drive can contain several folders, and a folder can contain other folders and/or documents. When you click the plus sign to the left of the object, the contents of the object are also displayed. You can continue to expand objects in the left pane in this manner until you find the folder you're looking for. Then, you can select that folder to display its contents in the right pane. When you click a plus sign, it automatically changes to a minus (-) sign. To hide the contents of the object, simply click the minus sign. The objects for that folder will collapse and will no longer be visible – which can make it easier to sort through your folders.

Creating and Naming Folders

Folders enable you to organize and manage your files. You can create new folders and subfolders within a folder. You can also easily name, rename, move, copy, and delete folders.

To create a new folder, double-click My Computer or open Windows Explorer. Select the disk and/or folder where you want the new folder stored. Open the File menu, choose New, then select Folder in the submenu. A new folder icon is displayed with the words New Folder. The new folder is already selected. Key the folder name and press Enter.

To rename a folder, click the folder to select it. Then open the File menu and choose Rename. Key the new name and press Enter. You can also rename a folder (or file) by right-clicking on the folder. Then choose Rename in the shortcut menu, key the new name, and press Enter.

Copying and Moving Folders and Files

You may decide to create a new folder to organize files that have already been saved. Or you may want to copy a folder from your hard disk to a floppy disk. You can even move a subfolder to a different parent folder. Both My Computer and Windows Explorer make it easy to copy and move folders.

The procedures for managing files are similar to the way you manage folders. You must first click the file to select it. To select multiple filenames, do the following:

■ To select two or more adjacent folders or files, click the first folder or file in the series, hold down Shift, then click the last folder or file in the series. The number of selected objects is displayed in the Status bar.

■ To select two or more adjacent folders or files, hold down Ctrl and then click each of the folders or files. The number of selected objects is displayed in the Status bar.

After you have selected the file(s) or folder(s) in My Computer or Windows Explorer, you may do one of the following:

■ To copy a folder or file, click the Copy To button on the Standard Buttons toolbar, and then select the destination.

■ To copy a folder or file to a location on a different disk, drag it on top of the destination disk icon.

■ To copy a folder or file to a new location on the same disk, hold down Ctrl as you drag the folder to the new location.

■ To move a folder or file, click the Move To button on the Standard Buttons toolbar, and then select the destination.

■ To move a folder or file to a new location on the same disk, drag it to the new location.

■ To move a folder or file to a new location on a different disk, hold down the Shift key as you drag the folder on top of the destination disk icon.

■ To move or copy a folder or file to a new location (whether on a different disk, on the same disk, in a different folder, or the same folder), right-click and drag the file or folder to the new location. When you release the mouse button a menu opens from which you can choose to Move the item or Copy it (or Cancel the entire action if you have made a mistake).

Removing and Restoring Folders and Files

Deleting folders and files frees up disk space. When you delete a folder, you also delete all the files stored in the folder. Folders and files deleted from a hard disk are transferred to the Recycle Bin. The deleted objects remain in the Recycle Bin until you empty it. However, folders and files deleted from a floppy disk or a network drive are not transferred to the Recycle Bin. Instead, they are permanently removed from the floppy disk or network drive.

There are five ways to delete a folder or file:

- Select the folder or file and press the Delete button in the Standard Buttons toolbar.

- Select the folder or file, open the File menu, and choose Delete.

- Select the folder or file, and press the Delete key on the keyboard.

- Drag the folder to the Recycle Bin.

- Right-click on the folder or file and choose Delete from the shortcut menu.

Regardless of the method you use, Windows will prompt you to confirm that you want to continue with the deletion.

If the Recycle Bin has not been emptied, you can recover a folder or file you've deleted. Double-click the Recycle bin icon and open the File menu. If necessary, select the folder or file and choose Restore. The document is removed from the Recycle Bin and returns it to the location you deleted it from.

To empty the Recycle Bin, double-click the Recycle Bin icon and then choose Empty Recycle Bin from the File menu. Click Yes when Windows prompts you to confirm that you want to delete all the objects.

When the Recycle Bin gets too full, objects will automatically be deleted. You can change the capacity of the Recycle Bin by right-clicking the Recycle Bin icon and choosing Properties in the shortcut menu.

Working with Dialog Boxes

A dialog box asks for information necessary to complete a command. When you move around in a dialog box, your position is indicated by a highlight, a dotted rectangle, or a blinking vertical line known as the insertion point. You can change as many options as desired before you close a dialog box. Figure A-12 and Figure A-13 illustrate the variety of formats used to present dialog box options. A description of dialog box formats is provided below.

FIGURE A-12
Dialog box options

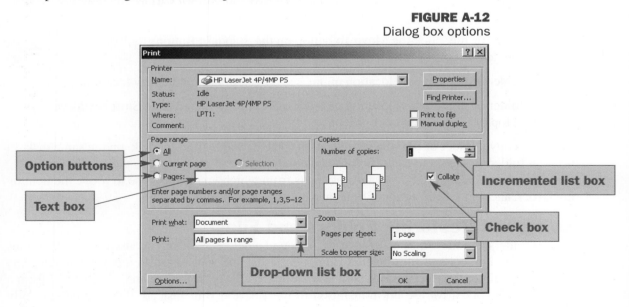

FIGURE A-13

Dialog box options with open list box and folder tabs

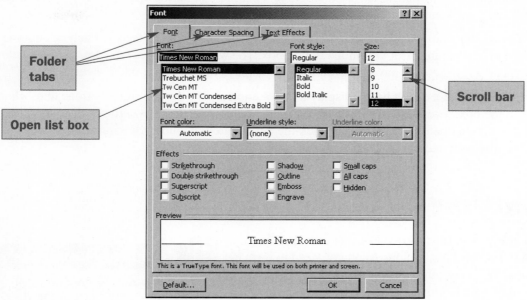

- Option Buttons—Option buttons are arranged in groups. The selected option button contains a dark circle. Click the button to select an option. Only one option button in a group can be selected.

- Check boxes—Check boxes are toggle items that can be turned on and off. A checkmark indicates that the option is turned on (selected). You can select more than one check box option at a time. To turn a check box on or off, click the check box.

- Drop-Down List Boxes—A drop-down list box shows only a single item (the current selection) from a list. Click the arrow next to the list box to open it and display more items; then click the desired item to select it. The list box automatically closes when you do this. If the arrow is detached from the box (shown in the Font: box in Figure A-13), you have a choice of keying an entry or opening the list box and clicking an item in the list. Some list boxes have scroll bars that enable you to scroll through the list when there are many options to choose from.

- Incremented List Boxes—Incremented list boxes allow you to click increment arrows to gradually increase or decrease the measurement shown in the text box next to the arrows. Click the up or down increment arrows until the desired measurement is displayed, or click in the text box and key a measurement.

- Text Boxes—Text boxes are boxes into which you enter text. When you point to a text box, the arrow pointer changes to an I-beam. Once you click in the text box, the highlight becomes the insertion point. In empty text boxes, you simply click and key the desired text. In text boxes that contain text, you click in the box to select the current entry, and then key the new entry. The current entry is replaced with the new entry.

- Command Buttons—Choosing a command button carries out the command listed on the button. If the command button has no ellipsis mark, the command is immediately executed. For example, OK means to accept all the existing entries in a dialog box and close it. Cancel means to exit the dialog box without making any changes. Cancel becomes Close in some dialog boxes when an immediate change takes place in the document with the dialog box remaining open. A command button with an ellipsis opens a related dialog box. A command button with an arrow opens a submenu. Click a command button to select it.

- Sheet Tabs—Sheet tabs are used in dialog boxes with more than one category. Each category is displayed on a separate sheet within the dialog box. To switch categories (sheets), simply click the tab. The selected sheet will have the bold tab and displays on top of the other sheets.

- Open List Boxes—Open list boxes display a list of choices. If there are more options than what will fit in the box, a vertical scroll bar is displayed so you can scroll down to see the other choices. To select from an open list box, simply click the desired item. Double-clicking an item will generally select the item and close the dialog box at the same time.

Formatting a Floppy Disk

You can purchase floppy disks that are already formatted, but there may be occasions when you need to format a floppy disk. You may purchase disks that are not formatted, or you may want to erase existing data on a disk. To format a floppy disk, you prepare the disk for use on a specific type of drive. A full format will erase all existing data stored on the disk.

Computer Concepts

If at any point you accidentally open the wrong dialog box or decide not to change any settings, click Cancel to exit the dialog box. If you should need to see something in a document that is hidden by the dialog box, drag the title bar for the dialog box to move it out of the way.

S TEP-BY-STEP ▷ A-1

1. Insert a floppy disk into the appropriate disk drive.

2. Double-click **My Computer** or open **Windows Explorer**.

3. Right-click the drive where the floppy disk is located and choose **Format** in the shortcut menu. The Format dialog box shown in Figure A-14 is displayed.

4. If necessary, change the Capacity setting.

FIGURE A-14
Format dialog box

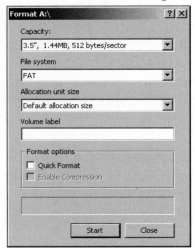

Computer Concepts

The capacity of most high-density 3.5" disks is 1.44 MB. Select 3.5", 720 KB if you are formatting a double-density disk.

5. Choose a format option:

    a. Quick Format formats the disk and removes all files from the floppy disk, but it does not scan the disk for errors. Use this option if the disk has been previously formatted and you do not believe the disk is damaged.

    b. Enable Compression formats the disk so that folders and files on it are compressed. This option is only available on NTFS drives.

6. You can give the disk a label by keying a label in the Volume label text box. If the disk already has a label, the Label text box will display in the Volume label text box. If desired, replace the existing label by keying a new label.

7. Click the **Start** button in the dialog box.

8. Click the **Close** button when the format is complete.

Copying a Disk

It is always a good idea to have a backup copy of the files you create. If your files are stored on a floppy disk, you can copy the entire contents of the disk. The disk you copy from is called the source disk. The disk you copy to is called the destination disk.

Computer Concepts

Be sure the destination disk does not store any valuable data, because Windows will automatically delete any existing data on the destination disk.

STEP-BY-STEP A-2

1. Insert a floppy disk into the appropriate disk drive.

2. Double-click **My Computer** or open **Windows Explorer**.

3. Right-click the drive where the floppy disk is located and choose **Copy Disk** in the shortcut menu. The Copy Disk dialog box shown in Figure A-15 is displayed.

FIGURE A-15
Copy Disk dialog box

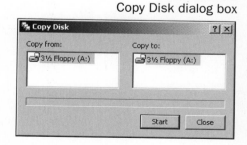

4. Click the **Start** button in the dialog box.

| Start |

6. Click the **Close** button when the format is complete.

| Close |

5. Follow the screen prompts.

Shutting Down Your Computer

To avoid damaging files, always use the Shut Down command to shut down Windows 2000 and turn off your computer. Click the Start button and choose Shut Down. When the prompt is displayed asking what you want to do, select Shut Down. ALT + F4 is a keyboard shortcut to choosing Shut Down in the Start menu to close Windows. You must press ALT + F4 for each open application and folder until you reach the Shut Down Windows dialog box.

APPENDIX B

WORKING WITH NEW FEATURES IN OFFICE XP APPLICATIONS

The Microsoft Office XP suite provides a variety of applications including Microsoft Access, Microsoft Excel, Microsoft FrontPage, Microsoft Outlook, Microsoft PowerPoint, Microsoft Publisher, and Microsoft Word. The applications available in your suite depend upon the edition of Office XP installed on your computer.

If you've worked with earlier versions of Office, you'll notice there are several new features in the Office XP applications. The applications share common features, which makes it easier for you to learn all the applications.

Using Menus and Toolbars

When you first start an Office application, the menus and toolbars display only basic commands and buttons. As you work with the application, Office personalizes the menus and toolbars by displaying the commands and buttons that you use most frequently. Commands are added to menus, and buttons are added to toolbars when you choose them. Likewise, commands and buttons are dropped when they haven't been used recently.

To expand a short menu to view all the commands, click the double arrows at the bottom of the menu. Alternatively, you can wait a few seconds after displaying a menu, and the display will change to show the full set of commands. If you always want the application to display the full set of commands for each menu, open the Tools menu and choose Customize. Then click on the Options tab and put a check mark next to Always show full menus.

To make more screen space available for your work, toolbars often share space in a single row. To expand a short toolbar to view all the buttons, click the Toolbar Options button at the right side of the toolbar. When you turn a button on in this list, the button will be displayed on the toolbar until you close the application or until other buttons are added to the toolbar. If necessary, use the move handle on the toolbar to drag the toolbar to its own row so there is room for all buttons to display.

Opening and Closing Documents

When the Open and Save dialog boxes are displayed, you can quickly access all files at one time from every Office application. You can use the Places Bar to go to the folders and locations you use the most. The Places Bar is illustrated in Figure B-1.

Places Bar in the Open dialog box

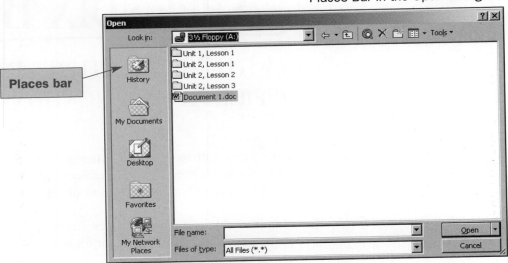

When you use the Places Bar, you can:

- Click the History button to display the last 20 to 50 documents and folders with which you have worked.

- Click the Back button to return to previously opened files and folders.

Each open document or application has a button displayed in the taskbar. The button shows a title with the document or application name. You can click the button in the taskbar to quickly switch from one document or application to another. If you have several documents or applications open at the same time, the buttons will not display the full title. However, when you rest the mouse pointer over the button, the name of the document or application will display in a ScreenTip as shown in Figure B-2.

FIGURE B-2
Document name displays when pointer rests over document button in the taskbar

You can quickly display the Windows desktop while you have applications open by clicking the Show Desktop button in the taskbar. To return to the application, click the application button (or a document button) in the taskbar.

Working with Task Panes

The new task panes are a Web-style command area that eliminate the need for you to open a dialog box. The task pane displays either at the right or left side of the window, but you can move it as needed anywhere on the screen. Most Office applications provide task panes for New Document, Clipboard, and Search. Outlook is the most notable exception in that the only task pane it displays is the Clipboard task pane.

A New Document task pane from Microsoft Word is shown in Figure B-3. The New Document task pane will appear slightly differently, depending upon the application being used, but it always provides several options for opening an exisiting document or creating a new document. The New Document task pane automatically displays when you launch an application unless you deselect the Show at startup option at the bottom of the task pane.

FIGURE B-3
New Document task pane

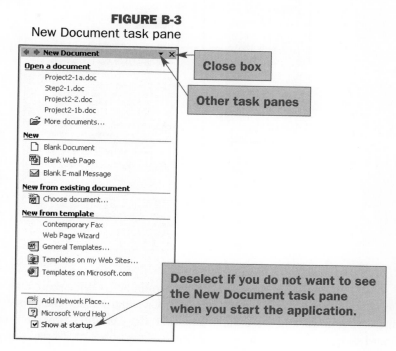

To manually display the task panes in most Office XP applications, open the View menu and choose Task Pane. To display the task panes in Microsoft Outlook and Microsoft Access, you must open the View menu, choose Toolbars, and then choose Task Pane from the submenu. Once you have a task pane open, you can switch to other task panes by clicking on the Other Task Panes arrow button on the task pane title bar and then selecting a task pane from the list of those available. Remember that the available task panes will vary with the application being used. To remove the task pane, click the Close box in the task pane title bar.

Collecting and Pasting with the Office Clipboard

The Office Clipboard enables you to collect objects from all of your applications, including your Web browser, and then paste them when you need them. The new Clipboard stores up to 24 objects. You can select one or more of the objects in the Clipboard task pane, and then paste them into an open document. The Clipboard task pane illustrated in Figure B-4 shows objects from several different applications. Notice that objects are identified by an icon for the application in which they are created. Also notice that some of the contents (such as text and pictures) are displayed to help you identify the item.

Office Clipboard task pane with objects from different applications

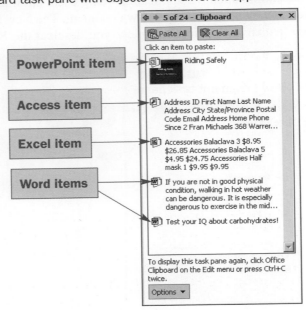

When you use the Cut and Copy commands, Office stores the selected text in the Clipboard. When you cut or copy more than one item, the Clipboard task pane appears automatically. You can use the Cut and Copy buttons on the Standard toolbar, the Cut and Copy commands from the Edit menu, or the keyboard shortcuts to add additional items to the Clipboard. To paste any one of the items, simply place your insertion point at the desired location of the item and then click the item. The contents of that clipped item are inserted at the location of the insertion point. To paste all of the items at once (in the order in which they were copied or cut), click the Paste All button. Pasting the contents of the Clipboard does not delete the contents from the Clipboard. However, when you turn off the computer, the Clipboard contents are erased.

To manually display the Clipboard task pane, open the View menu and choose Task Pane (or choose Toolbars and then Task Pane from the submenu). Then select Clipboard from the Other Task Panes drop down list in the task pane title bar. You can also open the Clipboard task pane by making sure that you do not have anything selected and then clicling Ctrl+C twice. Additionally, if the Clipboard task pane is open in one Office application, or if the Clipboard contains items, an icon will appear in the system tray on your taskbar. Double-clicking this Clipboard icon while in any other Office application will open the Clipboard task pane in that application as well.

At any time, you can choose to remove items from the Clipboard. To remove a single item, point to the item in the task pane, click the down arrow, and select Delete in the shortcut menu. To remove all items, click the Clear All button. If you copy 25 items to the clipboard, the first item you copied to the clipboard is automatically removed. The remaining items in the Clipboard are then renumbered and the newest item you copied to the clipboard becomes item 24.

When you close the Clipboard task pane three times in a row without using it, it will no longer automatically display during this session of the Office applications. If you do not want the Clipboard to appear automatically, you can click the Options button at the bottom of the task pane and remove the checkmark from (turn off) the Show office Clipboard Automatically option.

Using the Speech and Handwriting Interfaces

Now you can dictate text and issue basic commands by speaking to your computer. The speech interface is explained in detail in Appendices D-G.

Office XP also includes a handwriting interface that enables you to enter text using an electronic tablet and pen (or even an ordinary mouse). For example, you can insert your signature at the end of a letter you have created in Word. Alternatively, Office will convert your handwritten characters to regular text.

Getting Help

The Ask a Question box is a new alternative to using the Office Assistant. The Ask a Question box displays at the right side of the menu bar in all applications as shown in Figure B-5. Simply click in the box, key your question, and press Enter. To repeat a question, click the down arrow in the box and select the question.

You can also click the Office Assistant to ask a question in the same way that was available in previous Office applications.

Although it is not as convenient as using the Ask a Question box and the Office Assistant, you will find more options in the Help window. To open the Help window, the Office Assistant must be turned off. To turn off the Office Assistant, open the Help menu, and choose Hide the Office Assistant. You can then display the Help window by opening the Help menu and choosing Help (i.e., Microsoft Word Help) or by pressing the F1 key. You can also access the Help window from the New Document task pane.

Additionally, you can find answers for frequently asked questions for all Office products at the Microsoft Office Assistance Center Web site. You'll also find other information such as important product updates, online services, and clip art. To go to the Microsoft Web sites, open the Help menu and choose Office on the Web.

FIGURE B-5
Ask a Question box

Type a question for help

APPENDIX C

DEVELOPING KEYBOARDING SKILLS

Correct Posture and Technique

Good posture is very important in developing good keyboarding skills. Your keyboarding accuracy and speed are both affected by your posture. Review the following checklist to ensure that you are sitting correctly at the keyboard.

✔ Center your body in front of the G and H keys on the keyboard, 6 to 8 inches from the front frame of the keyboard.

✔ Sit up straight.

✔ Keep your feet flat on the floor.

✔ Keep your wrists low and not arched.

✔ Keep your elbows relaxed and at your sides.

✔ Make sure your fingers are curved and resting lightly over the home row keys.

✔ Make sure your thumbs are above the center of the spacebar.

Touch keyboarding means that you can enter text and data without looking at the keyboard. In touch keyboarding, each finger is anchored over a home row key. The home row keys are displayed in Figure C-1.

Hot Tip

Do not use both thumbs. Instead, choose which thumb you will use and always use that thumb. Generally, if your right hand is your dominant hand, you will use your right thumb.

FIGURE C-1

Each finger is used to strike a limited number of keys. The colors in Figure C-1 identify which finger reaches to each key. After reaching for a key not on the home row, the finger is repositioned over the correct home row key. Review the following checklist to ensure that you are using the correct keying technique:

✔ Review Figure C-1 for key positions.

✔ Strike the keys with the tips of your fingers.

✔ Use quick, sharp, tapping strokes.

✔ Keep your eyes focused on the copy in the text.

✔ Resist looking up.

✔ Maintain an even pace.

Skill Builders

The keyboarding drills in this section provide practice for developing both speed and accuracy in your touch keyboarding skill. A brief review of the keyboard as well as a discussion for correct technique is provided. Your objective in developing keyboarding skills should be to use correct technique and improve your accuracy. Accuracy and correct technique are more important than speed. Your speed will improve in time when you keyboard correctly and accurately.

To achieve the best results, you should practice these drills for several consecutive days. For example, devote a block of time each day for a week or two in which you concentrate on skill building.

Use the following guidelines to calculate your keyboarding speed:

■ Each letter or space is referred to as a character.

■ Five characters equals one word. Each line has 60 strokes, or 12 words.

■ For each complete line keyed, count 12 words.

■ For each partially keyed line, use the scale under the drill lines to determine the number of words.

Skill Builder 1—Home Row Drills

These drills focus on words composed of keys from the home row. You can use these drills to concentrate your skill development on learning and practicing new keys and reaches. You will find these drills helpful in developing correct technique and improving your accuracy.

```
 1  ff jj dd kk ss ll aa ;; a aa aaa l ll lll; al all; alas; all
 2  j jj jjj jas jad jag f ff fff fad fad; k kk kkk d dd ddd dad
 3  s ss sss ask lass flask sass sad g gg ggg; lag sags gas gags
 4  hh hhh gash sash dash had slash half shall salad flags halls
 5  ash dad lad had sad fall a glad flag glass sash lass gas has
 6  shall ask hall; fad a flask ad as gag; ads asked for the fad
 7  salad gala a half dash sash hall jag sag ads a slash ash gag
 8  he had dad falls she flasks glass ads sad lass has lads gala
 9  hall gash gag ad half flash had half dad shall she ask flags
10  dads; glass had falls has flask lad; salad ad had; lads; sag
```

| 1 | 2 | 3 | 4 | 5 | 6 | 7 | 8 | 9 | 10 | 11 | 12 |

 Hot Tip

Keep the tips of your fingers anchored over the home row keys. Strike the keys with quick, sharp, tapping strokes.

Skill Builder 2—Third Row Drills

These drills focus on words composed of keys from the third row (the row above the home row). You can use these drills to concentrate your skill development on learning and practicing new keys and reaches. You will find these drills helpful in developing correct technique and improving your accuracy.

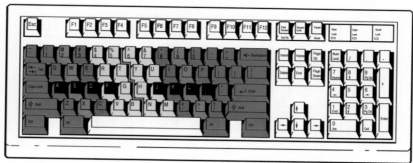

```
 1  saw wrist shift do write shoulder yellow fire sport foggy it
 2  hook quote at tray quart weird spot short load try fade gift
 3  real dog rug type hole this poor wet fight far jury flake of
 4  pot hires query pup sweet if pulley tales she grades put yet
 5  straight draw ladies resort diary proud golf tee party heart
 6  low tire toe shoot sport wrote jogger leak graduate quit sod
 7  does sod gross least sword fake tale frost diesel federal go
 8  wait theory shutter tooth they reader priest greed story pie
 9  dark hottest upward sputter squeak thought hay thread or why
10  pit press frog false pewter hug soup tries paw sake hide way
```

| 1 | 2 | 3 | 4 | 5 | 6 | 7 | 8 | 9 | 10 | 11 | 12 |

 Hot Tip

Take your time and focus on using proper technique. Proper technique includes good posture and correct key reaches.

Skill Builder 3—First Row Drills

These drills focus on words composed of keys from the first row (the row below the home row). You can use these drills to concentrate your skill development on learning and practicing new keys and reaches. You will find these drills helpful in developing correct technique and improving your accuracy.

 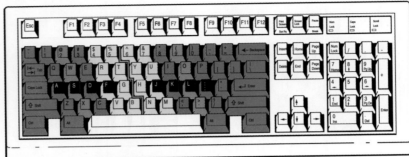 

1 low tire toe shot tell sports wrote jogger graduate quit sod

2 band dazzle jam quick box badge mom keen thick clown book in

3 ax pick song dock boom more ink hand lock mini bum mail than

4 cabbage mood teens lace milk zigzag bee masks fizz him bring

5 than name mall zinc junk buck cave active man winter own zoo

6 move cabin ox zebra drain valve basin velvet noon baby niece

7 basic gang club comb mine swan white king deck town six bend

8 vivid stand balloon flock bear month sax club click tone her

9 exit zinc nod rink mix more mum cook kick cast mad think mud

10 games bang vice cable vein build bulk max king sunk jack mad

| 1 | 2 | 3 | 4 | 5 | 6 | 7 | 8 | 9 | 10 | 11 | 12 |

 Hot Tip

Be sure to reposition your fingers on the home row keys after making key reaches.

Skill Builder 4—Capitalization and Punctuation

These drills focus on using the shift key and the punctuation keys. These drills will help you improve your technique.

1 Sue went to France, Jo went to Germany, and I went to Italy.

2 Have you read John Grisham's book? I heard it's interesting.

3 Dr. Norman Strickler said, "My research supports my theory."

4 When does the show start? I don't want to be late. Let's go!

5 We had two representatives: Jeffrey Stone and Melise Frecka.

6 Kelly is self-employed. She works on a month-to-month basis.

7 The fall session begins today and ends Thursday, December 6.

8 Alaina said, "I am sorry I am late." He said, "That's okay."

9 These three players won a gold medal: Alger, Amy, and Chris.

10 Where did you find the data? What search engine did you use?

| 1 | 2 | 3 | 4 | 5 | 6 | 7 | 8 | 9 | 10 | 11 | 12 |

Hot Tip

Use both hands to create a capital letter. For example, when you are capitalizing a right-hand key, press the left Shift key and hold it down as you strike the key with your right hand. Release both keys at the same time.

Skill Builder 5—Paragraphs

These drills focus on the alphabet keys in all three rows. The paragraphs of text contain many high frequency words. Punctuation and capital letters are also emphasized. Use these drills to improve your speed.

 Hot Tip

Use Tab to indent the first line of each paragraph. Use your left pinky finger to strike the Tab key.

The world's most popular sport is soccer. The game of soccer as we know it today was developed in Britain. The word soccer comes from assoc., the abbreviation for association. Millions of people play soccer. It is the national sport of many nations including most European and Latin-American countries. In Britain and many other countries, soccer is called football or association football. The World Cup is soccer's most famous international competition. It is held every four years.

| 1 | 2 | 3 | 4 | 5 | 6 | 7 | 8 | 9 | 10 | 11 | 12 |

 Hot Tip

Allow the word wrap feature to control the line endings. Your line endings may not match those shown here. Press Enter only at the end of the paragraph.

Skill Builder 5—Paragraphs (continued)

In most countries there are more bicycles than automobiles. Bicycle riding has become increasingly popular in the United States. People use bicycles for transportation, recreation, and exercise. Mountain bikes are designed for riding on rough terrain such as dirt tracks and forest paths. They have sturdy frames, flat handlebars, and wide, knobby tires. On the other hand, road bikes are designed for riding on pavement. They have thin tires and curved handlebars. Both types of bikes have gear systems that make pedaling easier at certain times. Low gears make it easy to pedal up hills or against the wind. High gears give the rider maximum speed on level or downhill surfaces.

| 1 | 2 | 3 | 4 | 5 | 6 | 7 | 8 | 9 | 10 | 11 | 12 |

Hot Tip

Keep your eyes on the copy. Resist the temptation to look at the keyboard.

Skill Builder 5—Paragraphs (continued)

Liquids and solvents can leak into the soil and contaminate soil and water. Numerous industries are faced with the challenge of cleaning up the soil and water. Cleanup costs are enormous; industries spend millions of dollars each year to clean up hazardous wastes.

During the last decade, scientists have been exploring innovative alternatives to save both time and money and to improve safety. Overall there are more than one hundred new technologies in various stages of development. The new technologies focus on treating the pollution on-site. Supporters contend that these new technologies will yield a more complete cleanup at a fraction of the cost.

| 1 | 2 | 3 | 4 | 5 | 6 | 7 | 8 | 9 | 10 | 11 | 12 |

Skill Builder 5—Paragraphs (continued)

Did you know that not all bacteria are bad? Some bacteria can cause disease, but others can cure. For example, we use bacteria to make cheese and yogurt. The bacteria used to make yogurt is good bacteria. The good bacteria produce natural antibiotics that fight the bad bacteria in our bodies. The good bacteria can promote good health and strengthen your immunity. In most cases yogurt contains more protein than milk. Yogurt is also low in fat and rich in vitamins.

When you make yogurt you must heat milk to boiling to kill the bad bacteria in the milk. Then you let the milk cool before adding the good bacteria so the good bacteria will not be killed. You must keep the mixture at a constant, warm temperature so the bacteria can grow and multiply. The good bacteria feeds on the sugar lactose in the milk and turns into lactic acid. The lactic acid makes the milk turn into curds. The clear liquid that remains is called whey. You should eat the whey because it is loaded with vitamins and potassium.

| 1 | 2 | 3 | 4 | 5 | 6 | 7 | 8 | 9 | 10 | 11 | 12 |

Hot Tip

Try to key at a steady pace. When you are working on developing speed, do not stop to correct errors.

Skill Builder 5—Paragraphs (continued)

The mermaid is a mythical creature of legend. There are many stories about mermaids. According to popular belief, mermaids are half human and half fish. They have the head and body of a woman. Their lower half is a long, scaly fish tail.

According to legend, mermaids sat on rocks and combed their long golden hair as they sang. Sailors passing by heard the singing. The sailors tried to follow the mermaids and wrecked their ships on the rocks.

Some stories say the mermaids had a magic cap. When they put the magic cap on a mortal, the mortal could live in the sea. There are also mermen who are said to have captured mortal maidens. The mermen and mermaids are often found in poetry and art.

| 1 | 2 | 3 | 4 | 5 | 6 | 7 | 8 | 9 | 10 | 11 | 12 |

Hot Tip

If you do not have access to a timer, ask your instructor or friend to time you for 2, 3, or 5 minute periods.

GLOSSARY

A

Absolute cell reference A cell reference that does not change when the formula is copied or moved to a new location.

Active cell In Excel, a selected cell.

Animation Special visuals or sound effects added to text or an object on a PowerPoint slide.

Animation schemes Predesigned sets of visual effects added to text on PowerPoint slides.

Antonym A word that has a meaning opposite another word.

Argument A value, cell reference, range, or text that acts as an operand in a function formula.

Ascending order Sorts alphabetically from A to Z and numerically from the lowest to the highest number.

AutoComplete Word suggests the spelling of frequently used words.

AutoCorrect Word automatically corrects errors as you enter text.

Automatic copyfitting A Publisher feature that automatically resizes text to fit inside a text frame.

B

Banner A full-width headline that spans across multiple newsletter-style columns, such as the title for a newsletter or report.

C

Cell The intersection of a single row and a single column.

Cell comment A message that helps explain the information contained in the cell.

Cell reference Identifies the column letter and row number (for example, A1 or B4).

Chart A graphical representation of worksheet or table data.

Client A computer that uses the services of another program. The client program is used to contact and obtain data or request a service from the server.

Clip art Prepared pictures and other artwork you can insert into a document.

Clip Organizer A wide variety of pictures, photographs, sounds, and video clips that you can insert in your document.

Clipboard A temporary storage area for text and/or graphics that are to be cut or copied and then pasted to another location.

Conditional formats Apply various formats to cell contents when certain conditions are met.

Contacts Persons with whom you communicate.

Count function An Excel math function that counts the number of cells that contain numbers.

Crop To trim a graphic.

D

Database A collection of related information organized for rapid search and retrieval.

Datasheet view A view in Access that displays the table data in columns and rows.

Default A setting that is automatically used unless another option is chosen.

Dependent cells Worksheet formulas that reference a particular cell.

Descending order Sorts alphabetically from Z to A and numerically from the highest to the lowest number.

Design view A view in Access that displays the field names and what kind of values you can enter in each field. Use this view to define or modify the field formats.

Desktop publishing The process of using a computer to combine text and graphics to create an attractive document.

Drag-and-drop Drag the mouse to move or copy selected text to a new location.

Drawing canvas An area upon which you can draw, arrange, and resize multiple shapes.

Drawing objects Artwork that you create using drawing tools.

E

Embedded chart A chart created on the same worksheet as the data.

Emphasis effect Controls the animation effects after the text or object appears on a PowerPoint slide.

Entrance effect Controls how the text or object animates as it appears on a PowerPoint slide.

Entry Data entered into a cell.

Event A scheduled item in the Outlook calendar that lasts 24 hours or longer.

Exit effect Controls the animation effects at the end of the animation sequence on a PowerPoint slide.

F

Field A single piece of information in a database. In Word, a special instruction that automatically inserts variable data. In Outlook, each piece of information in an Outlook form.

Field name A label to identify a field in a database.

Field properties Specifications that allow you to customize an Access field beyond choosing a data type.

Field selector A small box or bar that you click to select a column in a table in Datasheet view.

Fill handle A small square in the bottom right corner of an active cell in a worksheet.

Filling A method of copying data in a worksheet.

First-Line indent Only the first line of the paragraph is indented.

Folder In Outlook, stores information and enables you to organize and store many kinds of personal and business information.

Font The general shape and style of a set of characters.

Footer Text and/or graphics appearing at the bottom of each page of a document.

Form In Outlook, a set of controls in which you enter a piece of information to be stored in an item.

Formula Equation used to calculate values in a spreadsheet cell.

Frame A tool that makes it easy to position objects in a document.

Frames page A Web page divided into separate panes called frames in which files and graphics can be organized.

Function A predefined formula that performs calculations.

Function formula A special formula that names a function instead of using operators to calculate a result.

G

Graphics Items other than text, including photos, clip art, and drawing objects.

Gridlines Nonprinting lines that display on the screen to show the boundary lines of a table.

H

Hanging indent In a paragraph, all lines but the first "hang" (are indented) to the right of the first line.

Hard column break A manual column break.

Hard page break A manual page break.

Header Text and/or graphics appearing at the top of each page in a document.

Header row Labels at the top of columns in a worksheet.

Home page An entry page for a set of Web pages and other files in a Web site.

HTML An acronym for HyperText Markup Language; a system for marking text so that it can be published on the World Wide Web.

Hyperlink A link that allows users to jump from one Web page or document to another location (called a target) within the same Web page or document or to another Web page or document. See *link*.

Hypertext transfer protocol (HTTP) The protocol used to transmit and receive all data over the World Wide Web.

I

I-beam When positioned on text, the mouse pointer becomes an I-shaped pointer.

Insert mode In this default mode, new text is inserted between existing characters.

Internet A global network connecting millions of computers, making it possible to exchange information.

Internet Service Provider (ISP) Also called ISP or access providers, they are the remote computer system through which you connect to the Internet.

Item A particular piece of information stored in an Outlook folder.

L

Landscape orientation The document content is formatted with the long edge of the page at the top.

Layout guides Automatically formatted pink and blue lines on all pages of a Publisher document that help you align objects and maintain a consistent look.

Link Connection in a document that allows you to jump to another section of the same document, to another document on the World Wide Web, to a Help Screen, or to a Web site.

Link bar A collection of buttons (either graphic or text) formatted as hyperlinks to pages that are part of the same Web structure.

Logical functions Used to display text or values when certain conditions exist.

M

Marquee A region on a Web page that displays a horizontally scrolling text message. In Excel, an animated, dotted-line border surrounding cells when you cut or copy cell contents.

Mathematical functions Perform calculations that you could do using a scientific calculator.

Merge In Excel, combine multiple cells into a single cell.

Merging cells Converting two or more cells into a single cell.

Mixed cell reference A cell reference that contains both relative and absolute cell references.

Mock-up A model, usually full-scale, used for planning a design and layout.

N

Normal view In Word, the display of a document in a simple layout. In PowerPoint, a view of a presentation that shows the outline pane, the slide pane, and the notes pane.

Normal view Operand A number or cell reference in a spreadsheet formula.

O

Operator A symbol that tells Excel what mathematical operation to perform in a worksheet formula.

Order of evaluation The sequence used to calculate the value of a complex formula.

Orientation Determines whether your document will be printed lengthwise or crosswise on the sheet of paper. The default page orientation in all Office applications is portrait (taller than wide), but you can change it to landscape (wider than tall).

Overtype mode In this mode, new text replaces existing characters.

P

Path Identifies the disk and any folders relative to the location of the document.

Placeholders Provide placement guides for adding text, pictures, tables, or charts.

Points A unit of measure for fonts. One inch equals approximately 72 points.

Portrait orientation The document content is formatted with the short edge of the page at the top.

Precedent cells Worksheet cells that provide data to a formula.

Primary key Uniquely identifies each record in an Access table.

Print Layout view The display of a document where the display shows the document as it will look when it is printed.

Q

Query Enables you to locate multiple records matching a specified criteria in a single action.

R

Range A selected group of cells.

Record A group of fields in a database.

Record selector A small box or bar that you click to select a row in a table in Datasheet view.

Relative cell reference A cell reference that is adjusted when the formula is copied or moved to a new location.

Report A database object that allows you to organize, summarize, and print all or a portion of the data in a database.

S

Scratch area A temporary storage area around a Publisher document where you can hold objects until you are ready to use them in your document.

Scroll Move through the pages of a document on the screen without repositioning the insertion point.

Select Identify text for editing or formatting.

Select text Identify text or blocks of text for editing or formatting.

Server A computer that handles requests for data, e-mail, file transfers, and other network services from other computers (clients).

Sizing handles Small squares or circles surrounding a graphic or object, indicating that it is selected.

Slide design Specifies a color scheme, text format, backgrounds, bullet styles, and graphics for all the slides in a PowerPoint presentation.

Slide Show view Allows you to view a PowerPoint slide in full view.

Slide Sorter view Displays PowerPoint slides as thumbnails.

Smart objects Preformatted design elements in Publisher that you can customize.

Soft page break Page breaks that Word automatically formats as needed when text reaches the bottom margin.

Sound effect A recorded sound that can be added to animated text or objects on a PowerPoint slide.

Splitting cells Converting a single cell into two or more cells.

Spreadsheet A grid of rows and columns containing numbers, text, and formats.

Statistical functions Describe large quantities of data.

Synonym A word with the same meaning or nearly the same meaning.

T

Template A file that contains formatting and text that you can customize to create a new document similar to, but slightly different from, the original.

Text boxes Boxes that contain text and can be resized and positioned like other drawing objects.

Theme A consistent design with elements such as fonts, graphics, colors, and backgrounds.

Thumbnails Miniature pictures of clip art and photos.

Toggle Turn an option on and off using the same procedure.

Transitions Determine the changes in the display that occur as you move from one PowerPoint slide to another in Slide Show view.

Trigger Starts the animation on a PowerPoint slide.

Trigonometric functions Perform calculations that you could do using a scientific calculator.

U

Uniform Resource Locator (URL) An address for a resource or site on the World Wide Web. Web browsers use this address for locating files and other remote services.

W

Web browser An interface to the World Wide Web that interprets hypertext links and lets you view sites and navigate from one Internet node to another.

Web site A home page and any additional Web pages that can be accessed from the home page, and the images and other types of files that are displayed on the Web pages.

Wizard Similar to a template, a wizard asks you questions and formats a document according to your preferences.

Word wrap Text automatically moves to the next line when it reaches the right margin.

Workbook A collection of related worksheets.

Worksheet A grid of rows and columns containing numbers, text, and formulas.

World Wide Web (WWW) A collection of resources and interlinked documents that work together using a specific Internet protocol.

INDEX

Publication
    changing color scheme, 428
    creating from scratch, 437-438
    printing, 435-436
Publication design, planning, 420-422
Publication template, selecting, 422-424
Publisher
    command summary, 470
    identifying screen parts, 426-427
Punctuation skills, drills for, 513

Q

Queries, 331
    creating, 370-372

R

Range, 235
Records, 333
    adding and deleting in Datasheet view, 349
    editing in Datasheet view, 347-348
    entering in Datasheet view, 336-337
Record selector, 349
Recycle Bin, 497-498
Redo command, 40, 192-193, 239-240, 452
Relative cell references, 275
Reminder, for task, 408
Repeat command, 40
Replace command
    Access, 366-368
    Find and, 81-83
Report, creating in Access, 372-376
Rows
    freezing, 256
    hiding and unhiding, 254-255
    inserting and deleting
        in Excel, 246-248
        in Word, 96-98
Rulers, 427
Run command, 489

S

Sans serif typefaces, 191
Saving document, 7-8
Scratch area, 426-427

Screen
    Access, 328-331
    Excel, 228-229
    FrontPage, 445-446
    Outlook, 396-399
    PowerPoint, 170-171
    Publisher, 426-427
    Windows 2000 desktop, 487
    Word, 25
ScreenTips, 10, 178
Scroll bars, 493-494
Scrolling, 28
    in datasheet or form, 364-366
Search command, 489
Search tab, Help, 494
Selecting text, 41-42
Serif typefaces, 191
Server, 13
Settings command, 489
Shading, formatting, 119-120
    for table, 105
Sheet tabs, 500
Shortcut keys, 493
Shortcuts, Outlook, 396-397
Shrink Text on Overflow option, 429
Shut Down command, 489, 502
Sizing handles, 116, 193, 303, 428, 457
Slide design, 173
Slide Finder, 187-189
Slide layout, 175
Slides
    adding, 175-176
    adding text to, 176-177
    deleting, copying, and rear-ranging, 177-178
    editing text, 176-177
    selecting multiple, 178
Slide Show view, 170
Slide Sorter view, 170
Slide transitions, formatting, 210-211
Smart objects, 434
Soft page breaks, 63
Sorting information. See Data, sorting
Sound clip, adding, 213-214
Sound effects, 207-208
Source disk, 501
Spam, 416
Speech interfaces, 507
Speech recognition feature, 12

Spell checking, 70-76, 195
    correcting errors automatically, 76
    turning off wavy lines, 75
Splitting cells, 98
Spreadsheet. See Worksheet(s)
Standard Buttons toolbar, 490
Start menu, 488-489
Statistical functions, 283-284
Status bar, 490
Subfolders, 496
SUM function, 285
Synonym, using Thesaurus to find, 77

T

Tables
    Access, 331, 333-337
    centering, 99
    converting text to, 105-106
    creating, 91-96
        with wizard, 333-335
    editing text, 99-100
    formatting borders and shading, 105
    inserting text, 93
    modifying, 337
    removing borders, 95-96
    See also Cell(s), Column(s), Rows
Tabs, formatting, 60-61
Target frame, 144
Taskbar, hiding and unhiding, 487
Task panes, 504-505
Tasks, 397
    completing and deleting, 409
    organizing and managing, 407-409
Template
    design, 173-174
        opening from application CD, 187
    publication, 422-424
    for Web pages, 133-136, 446-447
    See also Wizard
Text
    adding and editing, 176-177
    aligning, 235-236
        in table cells, 103-104
    changing appearance of, 191-192
    converting to table, 105-106